P9-CBX-436

Nelson's Annual

Preacher's Sourcebook

2006 EDITION

Nelson's Annual Preacher's Sourcebook

2006 EDITION

ROBERT J. MORGAN, EDITOR

THOMAS NELSON PUBLISHERS
Nashville

© 2005 by Robert J. Morgan

Published in Nashville, Tennessee, by Thomas Nelson, Inc.

Published in association with the literary agency of Alive Communications, 7680 Goddard Street, Suite 200, Colorado Springs, CO 80920.

All rights reserved. Written permission must be secured from the publisher to use or reproduce any part of this book except for brief quotations in critical reviews or articles.

Unless otherwise indicated, scripture quotations are from the *New King James Version of the Bible*, © 1979, 1980, 1982, 1990, Thomas Nelson, Inc., Publishers.

Verses marked "NIV" are taken from the *Holy Bible: New International Version*, copyright © 1973, 1978, 1984 by the International Bible Society. Used by permission of Zondervan Publishing House. All rights reserved.

Typesetting by BookSetters, White House, Tennessee

Morgan, Robert J. (ed.)
    Nelson's annual preacher's sourcebook, 2006 edition.

ISBN 1-4185-0132-8

Printed in the United States of America

1 2 3 4 5 6 7—10 09 08 07 06 05

Contents

Special Occasion Sermons

Classics for the Pastor's Library

Conversations in the Pastor's Study

Introduction and Acknowledgements

Busy?

Yes, I know. That's why we're here with another edition of *The Preacher's Sourcebook*. Not many of us can hire a personal research assistant. Few of us can sit in the studies of great preachers and pick their brains. We seldom have the opportunity to meet genuine Christian heroes. And when was the last time a respected voice teacher sat down with you and reviewed techniques of public speaking?

So we've brought it all together for you between two covers. Here are sermon outlines for every week of the year, along with children's sermons, quotes, illustrations, prayers, interviews, profiles, wedding and funeral suggestions, and a handful of messages for special occasions.

If this book is helpful to you or if you have suggestions for future volumes, please contact me through www.robertjmorgan.com.

I want to take a moment to thank my editor, Michael Stephens. This is our first volume together! I'm also thankful to Wayne Kinde of Thomas Nelson who has given this book his wholehearted support. And I appreciate so much the great efforts of Carla Nelson and Bethany Neff in getting this book into the public arena.

Thanks, Katrina, for your never-ending encouragement!

Joshua Rowe, my assistant, deserves most of the credit for the Sourcebook.

And thanks, Sherry Anderson, for your effective ministry at my side for many years now. This volume goes out dedicated to you in grateful appreciation for your loyal partnership in the Lord's work.

Editor's Preface

"Thoreauly" Equipped for Every Good Work

Somewhere, someone is sitting down, glancing at this page, and reading these words in a state of utter exhaustion. Perhaps you're a pastor or you work on a church staff. Perhaps you're a deacon, a trustee, or a children's worker. Perhaps you're a parent, a caregiver, or a community volunteer.

To that person, I'd like to share a word of personal testimony.

As I write this, I'm recovering from a prolonged period of habitual fatigue. It began five years ago when several things converged together in my life. My wife's multiple sclerosis worsened, requiring all kinds of adjustments in our schedule and lifestyle. My daughter's waywardness took a sharp left turn, causing us days and nights of anxiety. We opened a new wing of our church, leading to accelerated growth and heavier demands. My writing ministry took off full force, doubling my work load and presenting me with new sets of deadlines every month. During this time, I also passed the half-century mark and tried to ignore the silent grumblings of an aging body. In the middle of it all, my dear mother passed away. The responsibility for her mountain home and acreage fell on my shoulders, and my sister and I opened it as a bed and breakfast.

Being a workaholic, I pressed right on, working seven days a week and putting in ten to fifteen hour days. It all caught up to me when I had three book deadlines falling due the same day! To make matters worse, we were at that very moment launching a major campaign at church while coping with the resignations of two staff members.

Realizing I was spent, I took some time off—a week in the mountains followed by time with a friend bumming around France. I took two books with me—the Bible and Henry David Thoreau's *Walden*. Perhaps on another occasion, I'll tell how the Bible spoke to me. For now, I want to quote Thoreau a little. See if any of this applies to you.

> *Many are concerned about the monuments of the West and the East—to know who built them. For my part, I should like to know*

who in those days did not build them—who were above such tri-
fling.
    Worst of all (is) when you are a slave-driver of yourself.
    He has no time to be anything but a machine.
    A man is rich in proportion to the number of things which he
can afford to let alone.
    Our life is frittered away by detail. An honest man has hardly
need to count more than his ten fingers, or in extreme cases he
may add his ten toes, and lump the rest. Simplicity, simplicity,
simplicity! I say, let your affairs be as two or three, and not a hun-
dred. . . . Keep your accounts on your thumb-nail.
    Simplify, simplify.

As I read those words, I thought about the way my dad used to clean out the springs behind our house in the hills. Those springs supplied our water. When they were well-tended, our water was pure and plentiful. But after he passed away, the springs were neglected and our water supply gradually became muddy and meager.

The Bible says, "All my springs are in You" (Ps. 87.7). If we're going to have living water flowing from our inmost being, we've got to tend the springs. So I made some . . . well, not resolutions as much as realignments. Here's how I recorded it in my journal:

Realignments:

Seeing that: (1) I've faced five years of difficult problems and demanding responsibilities; and that (2) my reserves are drained and my gauges are low; and that (3) I want my remaining years to be more productive for the Lord than all previous ones . . .

Therefore I want to make some midlife realignments:

1. To reclaim my mornings for study. It's necessary to recover much more time during my weekday mornings (Monday-Friday) for pure study—to the ministry of the Word and of prayer. This means keeping a "closed door," allowing few distractions (especially phone and e-mail), and being available to just an open Bible and notepad, as it were.

2. To leave my office door open in the afternoons, signaling my availability to the needs of others.

3. To allocate time each day for exercise.

4. To take an extra weeknight (Monday, Tuesday, or Thursday) to be at home with Katrina.

5. To take Saturdays off (more or less).

6. And to reduce all other work as necessary to meet these realignments.

This has meant some changes in numerous areas. At church, we've adjusted my role so as to turn over the daily administration of the church to someone else. I now devote my time to teaching and preaching, to vision casting, to mentoring a handful of college guys, and to making critical pastoral and evangelistic prospects. And I do little else. In the writing side of my ministry, I'm determined to be more cautious on taking on assignments. In my personal life, I'm doing less—but enjoying it more.

Remember Paul's advice to the church leaders of Ephesus? He said, "Therefore take heed to yourselves and to all the flock, among which the Holy Spirit has made you overseers" (Acts 20:28). We must take care of ourselves or we'll be in no condition to take care of our flocks.

Perhaps you need to make some realignments, too. I'm sure they'll be different from mine, but I wanted to share my testimony to prompt you to consider taking a little time away—maybe in a tent by the lake or at a nearby state park or resort. If nothing else, go sit Elijah-like under the nearest juniper tree. Take your Bible and a good book. Rest. Think. Ponder. Pray. Make some realignments if you need to. Cut out some things. Say no to something. Too many of us in the ministry are collapsing from exhaustion. We're burning out faster than replacements are arriving. We need the wisdom of God to regulate our lives at a sane and sanctified pace.

> We need to tend the springs . . .
> to take heed to ourselves . . .
> and to simplify, simplify!

Create a Sermon Series!

If you would like to publicize and preach a series of messages, you can assemble your own by mixing and matching various sermons and sermon outlines in this *Sourcebook*. Here are some suggestions:

Soon and Very Soon

- This May Be the Year (January 1)
- The Majesty of the Unveiled Christ (September 10)
- The Mastery of the Unveiled Christ (September 10)
- The Ministry of the Unveiled Christ (September 10)
- When Millions Disappear (October 29)
- The Marks of the Day (November 12)
- Practical Applications for the Lord's Coming (November 26)

Becoming a Mighty Church

- Shepherds and Servants (January 8)
- Kingdom Workers: Parts 1-4 (June 4, July 16, August 13, September 3)
- Body Life (June 25)
- The Marks of a Mighty Church (June 25)
- Church (September 3)
- Dealing with Open Sin in the Church (November 5)
- Multiply the Membership (November 19)

Disobedience and Discipline

- The Discipline of Destruction (January 15)
- The Discipline of Disappointment (May 7)
- The Discipline of Disqualification (July 9)
- Living with Leanness (August 27)
- The State of Barrenness (September 3)
- Broken Commitments (November 5)

Family Matters

- Be a Man (March 5)
- God's Word to Parents (May 14)
- The Challenge of Children (May 14)
- Training Our Children in the Way They Should Go (June 18)
- Three Important Words for Dads (June 18)
- Winning Our Spouses to Christ (July 9)
- The Virtue of Marriage (August 20)

Contributors

Dr. Timothy K. Beougher
Billy Graham Professor of Evangelism and Associate Dean of the Billy Graham School of Missions, Evangelism and Church Growth, The Southern Baptist Theological Seminary, Louisville, Kentucky

Dr. Stuart Briscoe
Minister at Large, Elmbrook Church, Brookfield, Wisconsin

Rev. Dan Chun
Senior Pastor, First Presbyterian Church of Honolulu, Co-Founder and Chairman of the Board of Hawaiian Island Ministries

Dr. Ed Dobson
Pastor, Calvary Church in Grand Rapids, Michigan, and Moody Bible Institute's 1993 Pastor of the Year

Rev. Billy Friel
Pastor, First Baptist Church, Mt. Juliet, Tennessee

Remember (January 1)
Be a Man (March 5)
Kept by God (March 19)
Thankful for Affliction (April 30)
Winning Our Spouses to Christ (July 9)

Rev. Peter Grainger
Pastor, Charlotte Baptist Chapel, Edinburgh, Scotland

Defrauding God (January 22)
The Challenge of Children (May 14)
The Problem of Anger (July 2)
Broken Commitments (November 5)

Pastor J. David Hoke
Senior pastor of New Horizons Community Church, Voorhees, NJ since 1987 and Team Chaplain for the Philadelphia Eagles of the NFL since 1993.

The Poor in Spirit (February 12)
Dealing with Satan's Strategy: Part 1 (March 12)
Dealing with Satan's Strategy: Part 2 (March 12)
Faithfulness (May 7)
Body Life (June 25)
Peace (July 16)
The How and Why of Giving (August 20)
Church (September 3)
Developing a Heart for Ministry (September 24)
Developing a Heart for Others (October 15)
Developing a Heart for God (November 12)
Preparation for Ministry (Baptism Sermon)
Thinking Biblically about Abortion (Sanctity of Human Life Sermon)
For Granted or for Gratitude (Thanksgiving Sermon)
The Marriage Covenant (Wedding Sermon)

Rev. Mark Hollis
Former minister of 15 years and current freelance writer in Nashville, Tennessee. Master of Arts in Pastoral Counseling.

When God Calls Your Name (May 14)
Encouraging Words (May 28)
When God Turns Scoundrels into Saints (June 11)
Remain in Me (July 9)
Heaven-Inspired Living in a Hell-Bent World (August 20)
Tragedy to Triumph (October 8)

Dr. David Jackman
Director, Cornhill Training Course, London, England

Christ: The Eternal Reality (June 11)
Sacrifice: The Authentic Demonstration (July 2)
Unity: The Essential Requirement (November 19)

Dr. David Jeremiah
Senior Pastor of Shadow Mountain Community Church, El Cajon, California, and chancellor of Christian Heritage College

Four Men Who Found Christ (April 8)
Easter: How Do We Know and Why Does it Matter (April 16)
Worshipping God by Name (August 13)
Courage When Fear Dominates (October 15)
Facing the Giant of Loneliness (December 3)

Rev. Todd M. Kinde
Pastor of Grace Bible Church, Grandville, Michigan. Former pastor of North View Alliance Church, Grand Rapids Michigan.

Shepherds and Servants (January 8)
Overcoming Impatience (January 29)
Covenant Renewal (February 26)
Overcoming Ambiguity (March 26)
A Farewell Challenge (April 2)

A Root out of Dry Ground (December 17)

George W. Noble

Author of 750 Bible and Gospel Studies, *published in 1909.*

The Trinity in Action (July 30)

Dr. Stephen Olford

Evangelist, Founder of the Stephen Olford Center for Biblical Preaching, Memphis, Tennessee

The State of Barrenness (September 3)

Rev. Kevin Riggs

Former Pastor, Franklin Community Church, Franklin, Tennesse

The Blessings of Living in a Non-Christian World (September 17)
Taking Advantage of Living in a Non-Christian World (October 29)
House Rules (November 19)
Reasons to Live a Holy Life (December 17)

Joshua D. Rowe

Assistant Editor to Robert J. Morgan and Graduate of Columbia International University, degrees in Bible and Biblical Languages

Don't Despair (January 29)
Teaching, Testing, and the Transfiguration (August 6)
Responding to Revelation (October 22)

William Graham Scroggie (1877–1959)

Scottish minister and writer

Conditions of Revival (February 19)
Is the Bible the Word of God (June 18)

Rev. Richard Sharpe Jr.

Director of Small Church Ministries and President of Christian Home Crusade

A.B. Simpson (1843–1919)
Canadian-American Minister and Keswick Theologian

Rev. Charles Haddon Spurgeon (1834–1892)
Pastor, Metropolitan Tabernacle, London

R. A. Torrey (1856–1928)
American evangelist, pastor, educator, and writer

Thomas Watson (1620–1686)
English minister and teacher

Dr. Melvin Worthington
Executive Secretary, National Association of Free Will Baptists

The Seriousness of Shifting Standards (February 12)
The Father's Friend (February 26)
The Deadly Defect (March 5)
Honoring Our Parents (March 19)
The Temptation in Worship (April 23)
Accent the Ascension (August 6)
The Virtue of Marriage (August 20)
Living with Leanness (August 27)
Generosity in Giving (September 17)
Guidelines for Giving (October 8)
In His Image (October 22)
Obedient Offspring (November 5)
Multiply the Membership (November 19)
No Other Name (December 3)
It's Incredible (December 17)

All other outlines are from the pulpit ministry of the general editor, Rev. Robert J. Morgan, of The Donelson Fellowship in Nashville, Tennessee. Special appreciation goes to Mitchell Cooper for his invaluable assistance.

2006 Calendar

January 1	New Year's Day
January 6	Epiphany
January 8	
January 15	**Sanctity of Human Life Sunday**
January 16	Martin Luther King, Jr. Day
January 22	
January 26	Australia Day
January 29	
February 1–28	Black History Month
February 1	National Freedom Day
February 2	Groundhog Day
February 5	**Super Bowl Sunday**
February 12	**Lincoln's Birthday**
February 14	Valentine's Day
February 19	
February 20	President's Day
February 22	Washington's Birthday
February 26	
March 1	Ash Wednesday
March 5	**First Sunday of Lent**
March 12	**Second Sunday of Lent**
March 14	Purim
March 17	St. Patrick's Day
March 19	**Third Sunday of Lent**
March 20	Spring Begins
March 26	**Fourth Sunday of Lent**
April 2	**Fifth Sunday of Lent; Daylight Savings Time Begins**
April 9	**Palm Sunday**
April 13	Holy Thursday; Jefferson's Birthday; Passover

(all **boldface** dates are Sundays)

April 14	Good Friday
April 16	**Easter Sunday**
April 22	Earth Day
April 23	
April 25	Holocaust Remembrance Day
April 26	Administrative Professionals Day
April 30	
May 4	National Day of Prayer
May 7	
May 14	**Mother's Day**
May 20	Armed Forces Day
May 21	
May 25	Ascension Day
May 28	
May 29	Memorial Day
June 4	**Pentecost**
June 11	**Trinity Sunday**
June 14	Flag Day
June 18	**Father's Day**
June 21	Summer Begins
June 25	
July 1	Canada Day
July 2	
July 4	Independence Day
July 9	
July 16	
July 23	**Parent's Day**
July 30	
August 6	**Transfiguration Day; Friendship Day**
August 13	
August 20	

August 27	
September 3	
September 4	Labor Day
September 10	**Grandparent's Day**
September 17	
September 22	Native American Day
September 23	Autumn Begins; Rosh Hashanah Begins
September 24	
October 1-31	Pastor Appreciation Month
October 1	
October 2	Yom Kippur Begins
October 8	**Clergy Appreciation Day**
October 9	Columbus Day
October 15	
October 16	Bosses' Day
October 22	**Mother-in-Law Day**
October 29	**Reformation Sunday; Daylight Savings Time Ends**
October 31	Halloween
November 1	All Saints' Day
November 5	
November 11	Veterans' Day
November 12	**International Day of Prayer for the Persecuted Church**
November 19	
November 23	Thanksgiving Day
November 26	
December 3	**First Sunday of Advent**
December 7	Pearl Harbor Remembrance Day
December 10	**Second Sunday of Advent**
December 16	Hanukkah Begins
December 17	**Third Sunday of Advent**
December 21	Winter Begins

(all **boldface** dates are Sundays)

December 24	Fourth Sunday of Advent; Christmas Eve
December 25	Christmas Day
December 26	Kwanzaa Begins
December 31	New Year's Eve

SERMONS AND
WORSHIP SUGGESTIONS
FOR 52 WEEKS

JANUARY 1, 2006

SUGGESTED SERMON

This May Be The Year!

Date preached:

Scripture: 1 Peter 4:7–11, especially verse 11:
But the end of all things is at hand; therefore . . .

Introduction: This may be the year! Peter expected Jesus to return in his own day, and if the return of Christ seemed imminent to Peter, how much more to us! Peter longed for the Lord's return; and if we're alert, we'll wake up every morning saying, "Maybe this is the year Christ will return. What if it were today?" What, then, are the implications? How should we live? If we knew for certain that we were the last generation of Christians on earth, would it make a difference in our lives? Peter wrote: "The end of all things is at hand . . ." And he went on to specify four activities that should mark our lives this New Year.

1. **Be Serious and Watchful in Prayer (v. 7).** "The end of all things is at hand; therefore be serious and watchful in your prayers." The Greek word for "serious" means "sane, sensible". The word "watchful" was used for staying sober as opposed to being drunk. Together, these two terms indicate that we need to keep our wits about us, to be alert, clear-headed, and self-controlled. I get the idea here that God puts more value on our prayers than we do. He considers prayer a serious activity that can influence world events. The prophet Daniel was aware of current events and it influenced the way he prayed (see Dan. 9). Are you a person who watches quite a bit of television? Try offering one of your programs as a sacrifice. Tell the Lord, "I'm giving up this show to devote that hour or half-hour each week to praying over national and world events." Have you ever used a newspaper as a prayer guide? Have you ever prayed through a copy of *Time Magazine?* Pray for current events and world leaders. Become a world prayer warrior this year.

2. **Have Fervent Love for One Another (v. 8).** "The end of all things is near, therefore . . . have fervent love for one another." The Greek word for "fervent" conveys the idea of strenuous effort, like a horse on a full stretch barreling toward the finish line. This kind of love covers a multitude of sins.

This kind of love enables us to minimize the faults of others and to maximize their strengths. It can transform our relationships this year.

3. **Be Hospitable to One Another (v. 9).** "The end of all things is near, therefore . . . be hospitable to one another." When Jesus left Nazareth, He spent three years sleeping in homes other than his own. He didn't own a house, and there were few hotels in those days. For about a thousand nights in a row, Jesus either slept under the stars or borrowed a bed in someone's house. When was the last time your home was open to Jesus? for His purposes? I know that sometimes we can't bring people into our homes. But if you can't bring your neighbor into your kitchen, take your kitchen to your neighbors. Bake a pan of brownies for them and invite them to church.

4. **Minister to One Another (vv. 10–11).** "The end of all things is near, therefore . . ." we should minister to one another using our spiritual gifts. Two basic types of gifts are mentioned here: speaking gifts and serving gifts. Some have speaking gifts: "If anyone speaks, let him speak as the oracles of God." Whenever you tell someone about Christ, it is Christ Himself using your mouth to speak His message. When God gives you an opportunity to teach, preach, witness, evangelize, or encourage someone, it's as though Jesus Himself were personally speaking to those people. The other kind of gift is the serving gifts. We're to serve in the strength He provides. How? First, we serve Him with the strength of body He provides. Second, we serve Him with the strength of attitude He provides (see Phil. 4:13 where Paul writes about his ability to serve with an attitude of contentment). Third, we're to serve with the strength of effectiveness He provides.

Conclusion: In the light of Christ's return, let's devote this year to prayer, love, hospitality, and ministry. The result? It's all for His glory! The paragraph ends at 1 Peter 4:11: ". . . that in all things God may be glorified through Jesus Christ, to whom belong the glory and the dominion forever and ever. Amen."

STATS, STORIES AND MORE

King Edward VII of England was well known for his drinking, immorality, and debauchery. He became the King of England in 1901 and reigned for nine years before dying in 1910. In 1910 a Christian named Joe Evans, known as a man of prayer, was on holiday in New York in the Adirondacks. One morning he arose with a strange burden to pray for King Edward. The burden increased through the day, and by the end of the day Joe was praying with great agony of soul for the King's conversion. Finally a sense of peace and release came, and he grew convinced that God had heard his prayer. The following day came the sudden news, "King Edward is dead."

Years passed, and Joe Evans was one day sharing dinner with Dr. J. Gregory Mantle of England, who was one of the most influential and prominent evangelical ministers in England in the early 1900's. During their conversation, Dr. Mantle said, "Joe, did you know that Edward VII was saved on his deathbed?" The king was in France when he was taken ill. He was brought to England and there was hope that he might recover. However, there came a turn for the worse. At that time His Majesty called one of his lords-in-waiting and ordered him to go to Paternoster Row and secure for him a copy of a tract that his mother, Queen Victoria, had given to him when he was a lad. It was entitled *The Sinner's Friend*. After much searching, the lord-in-waiting found the tract, brought it to His Majesty, and upon reading it, King Edward VII earnestly repented and received the Lord Jesus as his Savior. (This story was told by Dr. V. Raymond Edman and is recounted in his autobiography, *Out of My Life*).

APPROPRIATE HYMNS AND SONGS

Days of Elijah, Robin Mark, 1997 Daybreak Music, Ltd.

Soon and Very Soon, Andrae Crouch, 1971 Bud John Songs, Inc./Crouch Music Company

My Faith Looks Up to Thee, Ray Palmer/Lowell Mason, 1997 by Integrity's Hosanna! Music and Word Music

Love is the More Excellent Way, Babbie Mason / Turner Lawton, 1996 Word Music, Inc./May Sun Music

Make Us One, Carol Cymbala, 1991 Word, Inc./Carol Joy Music

The first day of the New Year marks the death in 379 of Basil the Great, Archbishop of Cappadocia. A lawyer and professor of rhetoric, Basil gave up his profession and inheritance to found a monastery and work with the poor. He founded a hospital, perhaps the first in Christian history, especially for the care of lepers. ❀ January 1, 1431 is the birthday of Rodrigo Borgia who later became Pope Alexander VI, one of the most corrupt men ever to serve in the church. ❀ On January 1, 1519, Ulrich Zwingli, on this 36th birthday, began his expositional ministry in Zurich, announcing he would break a thousand years of tradition by abandoning the weekly-prescribed readings as a basis for his sermons. Instead, he would teach verse-by-verse through the New Testament, beginning immediately. He proceeded to preach that day from Matthew 1 on the genealogy of Christ. ❀ January 1, 1865 is the birthday of James Rowe, author of the hymn "Love Lifted Me." ❀ Frances Ridley Havergal wrote her great New Year's Hymn, "Another Year is Dawning," for use by friends on this day in 1874. ❀ Pastor and devotional writer, F. W. Boreham, was born on this day in 1888. ❀ Chinese preacher, Watchman Nee, preached one of his last sermons before being arrested by the Communists on this day in 1951, saying, "The only guarantee you can count on for tomorrow is that you will be persecuted for living a godly life in Christ Jesus."

Quotes for the Pastor's Wall

❝ Simplicity, Simplicity, Simplicity! **❞**

—Henry David Thoreau

WORSHIP HELPS

Call to Worship:
Psalm 117
"Oh, Praise the LORD, all you Gentiles! Laud Him, all you peoples! For His merciful kindness is great toward us, and the truth of the LORD endures forever. Praise the Lord!"

Pastoral Prayer:
Lord, another year is dawning, and we ask that it be another year of progress, another year of praise, another year of singing your praises all the days. We don't know what this year may yield, but we know that goodness and mercy follow us all our days; so we trust you, face forward, and march into 2006 with joy, cheer, faith, optimism, and a determination to serve You more faithfully than ever before. Put a hedge around us, around our families, and around all that we have. Bless our church, and give us a greater range of ministry along with more souls for the kingdom, higher goals for our congregation, and deeper commitment to our Savior. We are Yours, O Lord, and we dedicate to You this New Year in the name of Jesus Christ our Lord.

Suggested Scripture Readings:
Proverbs 3:1–10
Matthew 24:1–13
1 Thessalonians 4:13–18
2 Corinthians 5:12–17

Kids Talk

Tell the children you have three newspapers. Say: "Here is yesterday's newspaper," and show it to them; then say, "Here is today's paper," and show it to them, pointing out some of the headlines. Then hold up a blank piece of newsprint or a large sheet of paper as a facsimile. Ask the children why it is blank. Explain that no one can tell the future, and no one knows what will happen tomorrow. But God knows, and we can trust Him every day of the New Year.

Additional Sermons and Lesson Ideas

I Surrender All

Date preached:

By Dr. Timothy Beougher

SCRIPTURE: Ephesians 5:15–16; Joshua 3:5

INTRODUCTION: Scripture commands us to be consecrated, an idea foreign to many of us. Let's look to God's Word for guidance on this subject:

1. The "Why" of Consecration
   A. Our Battle is Spiritual (Eph. 6:10–12).
   B. We Must Fight with Spiritual Weapons (2 Cor. 10:3–5)
   C. God Works through Clean Vessels (Josh. 7:11–13; 2 Tim. 2:20–22).
2. The "How" of Consecration
   A. Dedicate Yourself Wholly to God (Rom. 12:1).
   B. Reject the Pathway of Sin (Rom. 12:1).
   C. Allow God's Word to Transform Your Mind (Rom. 12:2).

CONCLUSION: A consecrated life is one that can sing to the Lord unreservedly, "I surrender all."

Remember!

Date preached:

By Rev. Billie Friel

SCRIPTURE: 1 Corinthians 11:23–26

INTRODUCTION: A cartoon portrayed a woman handing some glasses to a man behind the counter and saying, "I'm returning the glasses I bought for my husband. He's still not seeing things my way." How important that we see the meaning of the Lord's Supper from God's perspective.

1. A Vicious Death. Mel Gibson's "The Passion," raised our awareness of Jesus' sufferings from the flogging and on the cross. These scriptures describe the vicious effects of crucifixion: Psalm 22:14–17; Isaiah 53:5; Revelation 5:6.
2. A Vicarious Death. Death comes because of sin (Rom. 6:23; Ex. 18:20), but Jesus never sinned (Heb. 4:15). Christ died for us (Rom. 5:8), in our stead. God "laid on Him the iniquity of us all" (Is. 53:6).
3. A Voluntary Death. Jesus came because God loved the world (John 3:16). No one took Jesus' life, for He voluntarily died (Phil. 2:8) because sin could not be conquered any other way (Eph. 1:7).
4. A Victorious Death. Only through Jesus' blood are we justified, saved from the Father's wrath, and reconciled to God (Rom. 5:9–10; Is. 53:10–11). Sin's penalty has been met, for Jesus paid it all!

CONCLUSION: The next time you partake of the Lord's Supper, remember! Remember the vicious, vicarious, voluntary, and victorious death of Jesus Christ in your place.

JANUARY 8, 2006

SUGGESTED SERMON

Shepherds and Servants

Date preached:

By Rev. Todd M. Kinde

Scripture: Acts 6:1–7, especially verses 3, 4:
Therefore, brethren, seek out from among you seven men of good reputation, full of the Holy Spirit and wisdom, whom we may appoint over this business; but we will give ourselves continually to prayer and to the ministry of the word.

Introduction: When you think of leadership what images come to your mind? Do you envision the uniformed field marshal or the suited business executive? Perhaps you think of a charismatic personality type or a visionary. Jesus' leadership and ministry were characterized by being powerful in word and deed (Luke 24:19); and those two terms—word and deed—should characterize church ministry as well (Colossians 3:15–17; 2 Thessalonians 2:16–17). Jesus has established two offices of leadership within the church to fulfill this ministry: shepherds and servants.

I. **Shepherds Should be Powerful in the Word, Proclaiming Truth.** The shepherd is a wonderful image of leadership. The shepherd was used as an image of kings in the ancient world. David became the consummate Shepherd King for Israel who led with integrity of heart and skillful hands (Ps. 78:70–72). You who are elders/leaders in the church should be characterized by these actions:

A. **Proclaim.** The task of proclaiming is not limited to what we might call the pulpit ministry, nor is proclaiming limited to leadership. Stephen, who was probably a deacon, was a dynamic preacher. One trait of a church elder is the ability to teach (1 Tim. 3:2; 2 Tim. 2:2, 24). Not every teacher is an elder but every elder is a teacher. The preaching and teaching tasks of the shepherd fulfill Jesus' command to Peter, "Feed my sheep" (John 21:17).

B. **Pray.** Preaching is never to be disconnected from praying. Martin Luther stated, "He who has prayed well has studied well." As we read earlier in Acts 6:4, the apostles were devoted to prayer and to the ministry of the Word. This has been the dual focus and connection for the leaders of

God's people from ancient times (1 Samuel 12:23), and continues to be important in the New Testament church (James 5:14–16).

C. **Protect.** Paul counsels the elders to watch over the flock and to be on guard (Acts 20:28–31). We see quite clearly that the elders as shepherds of the local church are to protect the sheep from anything that would undermine the truth of our faith, including false teachers and false doctrine.

D. **Prepare.** These tasks are not an end in themselves. Proclaiming, praying, and protecting are to prepare the sheep for mission (Eph. 4:11–13). The Greek word for "pastor" in Ephesians 4:11 is also the word "shepherd." The task of the elder is to prepare God's people for service so that the body of Christ may be built, unified, and full.

2. **Servants Should Be Powerful in Deed Displaying Mercy.** The early church as recorded in Acts 6 had its growing pains, and some people were being overlooked. The apostles could not fulfill the work alone. They needed assistants who could manage the service aspect of the local church life together. They needed servants who were powerful in deed. As deacons, the following actions should characterize your ministry.

A. **Direct.** The deacon assists the elder in directing the ongoing and daily needs of congregational life. Deacons manage the various programs within a fellowship. In Acts 6 the food pantry was not operating effectively, so individuals who were full of wisdom and the Holy Spirit were needed to direct it. The elders are the spiritual directors, while the deacons are the program directors. We must give ourselves some room for flexibility. There is interchange between the shepherds, the servants, and the sheep as we seek to fulfill God's purpose for us.

B. **Distribute.** Deacons are also charged with the task of distributing benevolence and care among the needy in the fellowship. James instructed us that true religion cares for the widow and the orphan (James 1:27). These tasks are not an end in themselves, but acts of mercy and management are a display of God's grace and love to those watching us (John 13:34–35).

Conclusion: As the ministry of Christ was characterized by being powerful in word and deed, so too should our church be. Christ has given His church two offices to lead and care for her in the formation of community and in the accomplishment of mission: shepherds and servants, also called elders and deacons. Is the Lord calling you to one of these types of leadership in our church?

STATS, STORIES AND MORE

Great quotes about leadership:

"I have never accepted what many people have kindly said, namely that I inspired the Nation. It was the nation and the race dwelling around the globe that had the lion heart. I had the luck to be called upon to give the roar."—Winston Churchill in a speech in November, 1954.

"A leader takes people where they want to go. A great leader takes people where they don't necessarily want to go, but ought to be."—Rosalynn Carter

"A leader is one who knows the way, goes the way and shows the way."—John Maxwell

"An army of sheep led by a lion would defeat an army of lions led by a sheep."—Arab Proverb

Servanthood, not Fame

Walt Disney was once asked, "How does it feel to be a celebrity?" This was his answer: "It feels fine when it helps to get a good seat for a football game. But it never helped me to make a good film, or a good shot in a polo game, or command the obedience of my daughter. It doesn't even seem to keep fleas off our dogs—and if being a celebrity won't give one an advantage over a couple of fleas, then I guess there can't be much in being a celebrity after all."

"Don't confuse fame with success. Madonna is one; Helen Keller is the other."
– Erma Bombeck.[1]

APPROPRIATE HYMNS AND SONGS

Be Bold Be Strong, Morris Chapman, 1984 Word Music, Inc.

Lift High the Cross, George William Kitchin / Michael Robert Newbolt / Sydney Hugo Nicholson, 1974, 1992 Hope Publishing Company

Freely Freely, Carol Owens, 1972 Bud John Songs, Inc.

Sweet Hour of Prayer, William W. Walford / William B. Bradbury, Public Domain

What a Friend We Have in Jesus, Joseph M. Scriven / Charles C. Converse, Public Domain

FOR THE BULLETIN

Today is the birthday (1583) of Dutch theologian Simon Episcopius, student of Jacob Arminius and who, following the death of Arminius, became the leader and systematizer of Arminian doctrine. ❋ Today marks the death in 1642 of Galileo Galilei, Italian astronomer and mathematician, whose theories about the solar system incurred the wrath of the European Church. ❋ Elizabeth Hooton from Nottingham, England, became the Quaker's first woman preacher. Her beliefs landed her in jail, and she was sent to a grim succession of English prisons before being released at age sixty. She booked passage to Boston, but when authorities there wouldn't admit her, she sailed to Virginia and started for New England by foot. Her grandmotherly age didn't keep her from the whipping post at Cambridge, Watertown, and Dedham. She remained undaunted, and when nearly seventy, she said, "The love I bear to the souls of men makes me willing to undergo whatsoever can be inflicted to me." In 1671 she boarded ship for the West Indies to do missionary work. The ship reached the islands the first week of 1672, but Elizabeth Hooton, the Quaker's first convert and first woman preacher, had fallen ill. She died on January 8 and was buried in the Jamaican sands. ❋ Today is the birthday of: hymnist Lowell Mason (1782), missionary martyr Eleanor Chestnut (1868), and Methodist preacher Clovis Chappell (1881). ❋ Jim Elliot and four other American Plymouth Brethren missionaries were martyred by the Auca Indians in Ecuador, on this day in 1956.

WORSHIP HELPS

Call to Worship

God is in His temple, the almighty Father! Round His footstool let us gather;

Him with adoration, serve the Lord most holy, who hath mercy on the lowly.

Let us raise hymns of praise for His great salvation; God is in His temple!

(William T. Matson, 1833–1899)

Suggested Scripture Reading:

Exodus 18:9–24

Psalm 95:1–7; 133

Acts 6:1–7

Pastoral Prayer:

Almighty Father, you have blessed us with a church full of potential, promise, and people of faith. You have given us leaders, both in the pulpit and in the pew, who love Your Name and lift praises to You. We confess, Lord, our unworthiness, and we call on You for wisdom. Give us wisdom to guide the affairs of the body of Christ. Give us wisdom to meet the needs of our community. Give us souls for our labors. Give us strength for our duties. Give us ideas and methods and means for doing Your work. Oh Lord, at the beginning of this new year, give us a new burst of energy that will enflame our ministries both here and around the world. We pray in Jesus' Name, Amen.

Kids Talk

Ask the children if they know the name of the President of the United States. Ask if they know the Vice President, the governor of your state, then the mayor of your city or town. Remind them that 1 Timothy 2:1–2 tells us to pray for those in authority over us. Lead the children in prayer for our leaders.

Additional Sermons and Lesson Ideas

Bringing God Pleasure

Date preached:

SCRIPTURE: Philippians 2:12–13

INTRODUCTION: Abraham Maslow found a relationship between longevity and a person's sense of purpose. Those with a strong sense of mission and purpose will most likely live longer. We're made to worship God, to bring Him pleasure. God wants to work in us both to will and to do His good pleasure. That means we must:

1. Experience His Pardon. Ephesians 1:3–9 states that God provided our salvation according to His good pleasure.
2. Sing His Praises. Psalm 149 says that the Lord takes pleasure in His people and loves to hear us sing in the assembly of the saints.
3. Obey His Precepts. According to 1 Chronicles 29:17, God finds pleasure in uprightness. See also Psalm 5:4 and 147:11.
4. Practice His Presence. Zephaniah 3:17 indicates that we as His people live in His presence, always on holy ground. Everything we do is sacred. Everything we do should be designed for His glory. See Colossians 3:23.

CONCLUSION: Deuteronomy 6:5 says, "You shall love the LORD your God with all your heart, with all your soul, and with all your strength." This is a person's greatest purpose in life.

Asking Amiss

Date preached:

By Dr. Melvin Worthington

SCRIPTURE: James 4:1–3

INTRODUCTION: Prayer is one of the wonderful privileges of being a Christian. James reminds us that in spite of the precepts, promises, and purpose of prayer, it is possible to "ask amiss" (James 4:3).

1. The Power of Lust: Its Desire (v. 1). Lusting after worldly things produces shameful acts such as wars and fightings even among members of the church.
2. The Poverty of Lust: Its Disappointment (v. 2). Lust after things does not satisfy. In spite of all the striving, lust is a substitute for the gifts God desires us to have.
3. The Prayer of Lust: Its Design (v. 3). We ask but do not receive. The wrong attitude, affections, appetites, and ambitions will spoil one's prayer life.

CONCLUSION: Prayer must be uttered with the right motive. It must be made with a good spirit and good intentions. Effective and efficient prayer is according to God's Word, will, way, and wisdom. We must be on guard lest we ask amiss.

Charles Fuller

If the stress and strain of life is getting you down, you might want to read a biography of radio evangelist Charles Fuller.

Fuller (1887–1968) was a Los Angeles native who graduated from Biola University and became the pastor of Calvary Church in Los Angeles. In the late 1920s and early 1930s, Fuller began buying and selling orange groves, and the enterprise was successful, especially when oil was found on one of the plots. But when the Great Depression struck, some of Fuller's financial deals went awry and he was unable to meet some personal financial obligations. Charles, a noted pastor, faced the humiliation of having his home auctioned out from under him to pay his mounting debts. His wife recorded in her journal, "No money to meet bills. . . . It is almost more than Charles can bear. He is *so* depressed, *so* burdened that he says he can stand no more."

But things grew worse. The couple's son fell ill to prolonged attacks of bronchitis and pneumonia. On January 8, 1932, as Charles was at the lawyer's office trying to stave off disaster, his wife called to say that Dannie, age six, had grown so weak a pulse beat was no longer discernable.

Dannie pulled through, but the stress of their multiple problems so exhausted Charles that when he stood in the pulpit of Calvary Church each Sunday he wondered if he could last through the sermon. When it became clear that Calvary Church wanted a new pastor, Charles felt he should resign. The morning after his final sermon, the nation's economic depression deepened. President Roosevelt closed all the banks.

Five days later, Long Beach suffered a severe earthquake, which killed 115 people and caused millions of dollars of damage. About the same time, one of Charles Fuller's business partners declared bankruptcy, and Charles incurred additional debt.

One morning in August 1933, Mrs. Fuller could bear the strain no longer. When Charles left home to go into Los Angeles and plot his next moves to remain solvent, she went into her study and in desperation started reading a sermon Charles Spurgeon had preached in London over seventy years before. The text was Jeremiah 33:3: "Call unto me, and I will answer thee, and show thee great and mighty things, which thou knowest not" (KJV).

Grace Fuller later said: "When I called upon God in desperation in August 1933, he answered me by directing me *unmistakably* to the library shelf on which this book stood and to *this* sermon. It brought great comfort and enabled me to trust God and to await the unfolding of His plans for us."

God lifted her burden so remarkably that morning that when Charles returned exhausted later in the day, she told him, "Never mind how black things look now. God has assured me that He has great and mighty things in store for us for the future—things which we can't even imagine now."

So it happened. Charles Fuller began preaching on the radio in 1937. He helped pioneer radio evangelism, and his Old Fashioned Gospel Hour on the Mutual Broadcasting System (and later on CBS) was heard live from Long Beach every Saturday night on over six hundred stations. He became one of the most respected evangelists of his time, and he later helped found Fuller Seminary, which is named in his honor.

In one of his first broadcasts, Dr. Fuller said:

> I pass on to you a little of the comfort wherewith Mrs. Fuller and I have been comforted. We have come to know God in a new way because of the trials we have been going through these past three years. We have known what it is to have much sickness; financial losses; to have those turn against us and seek to hurt us who we thought were true friends; to have our only child brought down to death's door on two occasions, and to have gone before the microphone, after sleepless nights, so burdened and cast down I do not know whether I could preach—whether when I opened my mouth the words would come. Excuse these personal references, friends, I mention them only briefly as a testimony because I want to tell you that after going through all this and much more, Mrs. Fuller and I know that God is able— that His promises are true. We never could have known the sweetness of trusting God had we not come to the place where we ourselves could do nothing. We never could have known how precious it is to rest on [God's Word], and having committed all to Him and waiting to see Him work, if we had not been sorely tested.[2]

JANUARY 15, 2006

The Discipline of Destruction

Date preached:

By Dr. Denis Lyle

Scripture: 1 Kings 22:41–53; 2 Chronicles 20:35–37, especially 1 Kings 22:48:
Jehoshaphat made merchant ships to go to Ophir for gold; but they never sailed, for
the ships were wrecked at Ezion Geber.

Introduction: What particular object occupies most of your thinking, planning,
and energy? Chances are, we're like most people and spend our time thinking
about a house, a car, furniture, a bank account, an investment, property, land,
and so on. We are creatures committed to *things. Things* are marvelous servants
but terrible masters. Yes, often we get all wrapped up in *things,* and sometimes
God has to employ drastic methods to teach us invaluable lessons. He dashes
our hopes to the ground, using the discipline of destruction. Jehoshaphat, King
of Judah, experienced this, as we will see in this study.

1. **Do Not Initiate Selfish Schemes (1 Kin. 22:48).** Geographically, Ophir was
   probably located in southwest Arabia. Evidently gold reserves in Judah
   were low, and Jehoshaphat decided to build ships in order to send them
   to Ophir for gold. By importing more gold, Jehoshaphat thought he would
   strengthen his position financially and economically. Perhaps he desired
   to restore the glory of Judah as it was in the days of Solomon (see 1 Kin.
   9:26–28). Jehoshaphat was generally steadfast (see 1 Kin. 22:43, 2 Chron.
   17:3–6). In this case he got sidetracked. He began building ships right
   away (20:36) and initiated an alliance with Ahaziah (22:40), proving his
   ambition was materialistic (22:48). However, God had already laid down
   the law that the king should not ". . . greatly multiply silver and gold for
   himself" (Deut. 17:17). What schemes have you initiated in your heart?
   multiplying your wealth? attaining worldly possessions or power? Wealth
   and possessions are not wrong, but when they become master over you,
   the Lord may very well destroy what you put your faith in to redirect you
   to Himself, the only true treasure.

2. **The Message We Must Heed (2 Chron. 20:37).** Eliezer was God's "man on
   the spot." What a man and what a message! Commissioned by the Lord,

he came into the palace of Jehoshaphat and confronted the erring king. He was no crank or coward. Faithfully and fearlessly he delivered the divine message to Jehoshaphat. We notice that: *a ruin is predicted*, ". . . the Lord has destroyed your works." Secondly, *a reason is provided*, "Because you have allied yourself with Ahaziah . . ." This was the son of the notorious Ahab, Ahaziah "who did evil in the sight of the Lord" (1 Kin. 22:52–53). How often we lay aside our convictions for our comfort; we trade our morality for materialism! Is the Lord speaking to you this morning? Do you hear, and will you heed the message? Do not scheme with evil men for selfish gain!

3. **The Loss We Will Sustain (1 Kin. 22:48; 2 Chron. 20:37).** Notice the phrase, ". . . the ships were wrecked, so that they were not able to go" (2 Chron. 20:37). God was disciplining his wayward servant! The ships were built; their keels were laid; their hulls were formed; the masts were placed in position; the ships were fitted out; they were manned by the men of Judah. Before they could set sail for Ophir, they were destroyed on the rocks that lay in jagged ranges on each side of the port of Ezion-Geber. God's Word was fulfilled. What God did in the life of Jehoshaphat He has done and continues to do in the life of His children. He intervenes to break our pet schemes and our cherished intentions. He breaks them on the rocks of judgment. He permits storms to arise that wreak havoc with our selfish ambitions.

4. **The Profit We Can Derive (1 Kin. 22:49).** After the ships were broken at Ezion-Geber, Ahaziah approached his partner in the shipbuilding enterprise and urged Jehoshaphat to permit Ahaziah's servants to go with Jehoshaphat's servants in the ships. Apparently, Ahaziah wanted a new fleet built, but this one would be manned by Israelites. We read, ". . . Jehoshaphat would not" (1 Kin. 22:49). It seems that the king of Judah had learned his lesson. Perhaps some are here today who have been through this experience, or maybe you're being disciplined through destruction right now. The Lord offers His mercy to you.

Conclusion: Has God wrecked your ships? Broken your plans? Ruined your projects? Won't you step down off the throne of your life? Let's lay down our materialism and selfish ambition on the altar today and crown Jesus as our Lord, our Savior, and our treasure (Matt. 6:19–21).

STATS, STORIES AND MORE

Conviction or Convenience

The story is told of a farmer who one day happily told his wife and family that their best cow had given birth to twin calves, one brown and one white. He said, "You know, I suddenly had a feeling and impulse that we must dedicate one of these calves to the Lord. We will bring them up together, and when the time comes we will sell one and keep the proceeds, and we will sell the other and give the proceeds to the Lord's work." His wife asked him about which calf he was going to dedicate to the Lord. "No need to bother about that now," he replied. "We will treat them both in the same way, and when the time comes we will do as I say." In a few months the man entered his kitchen looking very miserable and unhappy. When his wife asked him what was troubling him, he answered, "I have bad news to give to you. The Lord's calf is dead."

My Ships

My ships are all broken, the ships I had planned
To bring me great riches from many a land.
They're battered and broken, the ships I had built
And now on the shore they lie covered with silt.

My ships are all broken. God stretched forth His hand
And now they lie shattered, all covered with sand
He smote them in judgment in order to show
His love will not let me in folly to go.

I will not doubt, though all my ships at sea
Come drifting home with broken masts and sails:
I shall believe the Hand which never fails.
From seeming evil all worketh good for me:
And though I weep because these sails are battered
Still will I cry, while my best hopes lie shattered,
I trust in Thee.
(Author unknown)

FOR THE BULLETIN

England's King Henry VIII declared himself the head of the English Church on January 15, 1535. He was a learned theologian who, in 1521, had written a book against Luther entitled *Defense of the Seven Sacraments*, for which Pope Leo gave him the title, "Defender of the Faith," which is still worn by the British monarchy. But in 1535, his struggles with the papacy led him to establish a national Catholic church independent of Rome with himself as "the only supreme head on earth of the Church of England." ✿ On January 15, 1559, Elizabeth I was crowned Queen of England. ✿ January 15, 1697 was set aside in Massachusetts as a day of fasting and repentance for the Salem witch trials. The edict said: "...so all of God's people may offer up fervent supplications unto Him, that all iniquity may be put away, which hath stirred God's holy jealousy against this land; that He would show us what we know not, and help us, wherein we have done amiss, to do so no more." ✿ The University of Notre Dame was chartered under Roman Catholic auspices in Indiana on this day in 1844. ✿ One of the most remarkable missionaries of the modern era, Mary Slessor, died on January 15, 1915. Hailing from Scotland, Mary sailed for Nigeria in 1876 and devoted her life to the physical, political, and spiritual needs of Africa. Her exploits are legendary. ✿ On this day in 1929, civil rights leader Martin Luther King, Jr. was born. ✿ Henry A. Ironside, popular Bible teacher and pastor of Chicago's Moody Memorial Church, died on this day in 1951.

APPROPRIATE HYMNS AND SONGS

All the Power You Need, Russell Fragar, 1995 Russell Fragar (Hillsong)

All Hail the Power of Jesus' Name, Edward Perronet / Oliver Holden/ John Rippon (adapt), Public Domain

Take My Life and Let It Be, Frances R. Havergal/ Henri A. Cesar Malan,

Take My Life, Scott Underwood, 1994 Mercy/Vineyard Publishing

Wherever He Leads I'll Go, B.B. McKinney, 1936, 1964 Broadman Press APR Distributed by Genevox Music Group

WORSHIP HELPS

Call to Worship
"Fight the good fight of faith, lay hold of eternal life, to which you were also called and have confessed the good confession in the presence of many witnesses" (1 Tim. 6:1).

Hymn Story
George Beverly Shea, famous soloist for the Billy Graham Crusades, wrote a book of hymn stories titled *How Sweet the Sound* in which he told of a meeting he never forgot. One day when he was eight years old, he was walking down the main street of Houghton, New York, with his father. Suddenly, Mr. Shea stopped and said to Bev, "Someone is coming toward us, an elderly lady I want you to meet. She is Mrs. Clara Tear Williams. She wrote number 368 in our hymnal, 'All My Life Long.'" Even at his young age, Bev was thrilled to meet a hymn writer, and he always looked on Mrs. Williams with awe. It was influences like this that led George Beverly Shea to become a famous writer and singer of hymns himself.[3]
The hymn, "All My Life Long" isn't well known today, but it should be. Its actual title is "Satisfied," and it reminds us that we should be content with what we have (1 Tim. 6:7–8). Written in 1875, the words say, in part:

All my life long I have panted
For a drink from some clear spring,
That I hoped would quench the burning
Of the thirst I felt within.

Hallelujah! I have found Him
Whom my soul so long has craved!
Jesus satisfies my longings,
Through His blood I now am saved.

Benediction
Bless us, O Lord, as we go our ways today. Use us, that when we meet again it shall be with testimonies of praise to You. In Jesus' Name, Amen.

Additional Sermons and Lesson Ideas

The Wrong Kind of Fellowship

By Dr. Denis Lyle

Date preached:

SCRIPTURE: Various, especially 1 Corinthians 6:14–17

INTRODUCTION: I wonder how many of us have allied ourselves with the world, as if the world can provide the abundance we crave. Let's remind ourselves today of what Scripture says about abstaining from evil.

1. Don't Have Fellowship with Unholy Practices (James 4:4).
2. Don't Have Fellowship with Unholy Pleasures (1 Cor. 5; Col. 3:5).
3. Don't Have Fellowship with Unholy Prophets (2 Cor. 6:15; Phil. 3:2).
4. Don't Have Fellowship with Unholy People (1 Cor. 5:11; 2 Thess. 3:6).
5. Don't Have Fellowship with Unholy Places (2 Cor. 6:16).

CONCLUSION: No doubt we will encounter ungodliness constantly in this world, and we must if we are to minister to the world. However, God's command is clear: "Come out from among them and be separate, says the Lord. Do not touch what is unclean, and I will receive you" (2 Cor. 6:17).

A Bird's Eye View of Romans

Date preached:

SCRIPTURE: Romans 1—16

INTRODUCTION: I'd like to cover an entire book of the Bible in one message to give you a "bird's eye view" of the greatest theological treatise ever written. After the prologue and theme (1:1–17), Paul describes the doctrine of justification by faith like this:

1. R - Ruin (1:17—3:20)—Our need for justification
2. O - Offer (3:21–31)—God's offer of justification by grace
3. M - Model (ch. 4)—Abraham, our model for justification
4. A - Access (5:1–11)—Access by faith: the benefits of justification
5. N - New Adam (5:12–21)—We are children of two "Adams"
6. S - Sanctification (ch. 6–8)—Struggle, sanctification, and victory

CONCLUSION: Romans 9—11 deals with the role of the Jews in God's redemptive plan for the world. And the great last section of Romans tells us how we live as those who are justified—as living sacrifices for Him who became a living sacrifice for us.

SANCTITY OF HUMAN LIFE SERMON

Thinking Biblically about Abortion

By Pastor J. David Hoke

Scripture: Psalm 139:13–16, especially verse 16:
Your eyes saw my substance, being yet unformed. And in Your book they all were written, the days fashioned for me, when as yet there were none of them.

Introduction: In 1973 the Supreme Court of the United States legalized abortion. Since that time, more than thirty million unborn children have had their lives snuffed out. This is sixteen times the total number of Americans lost in all of our nation's wars combined. Every day more than five thousand unborn lives are aborted in their mother's wombs. To say that abortion is a controversy is a gross understatement. Clear biblical thinking and positive biblical confrontation must be undertaken by the church if people are to know the truth.

I. **Issues to Confront.** Serious Christians must confront the fundamental issues that are raised by abortion.

   A. **The Right to Life Versus the Right to Choose.** In the abortion debate, there is certainly a lot of heat without light. Slogans abound. "A woman has the right to do what she wants with her own body." "Women should have the right to choose." "The fetus is not a baby." "Every child should be a planned and wanted child." Be careful to look behind the slogans to see whether they are based on the truth. Many of the slogans are simply based on what people want to believe is the truth. People choose to believe what they want to believe so they can have the kind of lifestyle they want. When we look at abortion, it becomes painfully evident that few care about the truth.

   B. **Pregnancy Is Often Viewed as a Problem to Be Fixed.** Abortion has now become one of the main methods of birth control. The issue for mothers of unwanted pregnancies is not whether the "product of conception" is really a baby. The issue for them is not whether they are killing a human life; they just don't want to be pregnant. They don't want to carry that baby to term. They want to have an abortion. Sometimes it's the pressure of the male involved who has the same selfish motives. This is the real driving force behind all the posturing and postulating about abortion. The goal is to be able to have an abortion at any time, and all the propaganda surrounding it is constructed to assure that the goal is achieved. Women are told their babies are "lumps of cells" and abortions are "simple medical procedures."

2. **Answers to Champion.**

A. **An Unborn Baby Is a Human Life Scientifically.** We come to the reality: during an abortion, more than an unformed clump of unwanted cells is removed. You see, these cells look very much like a little baby— a human baby! They don't look like a baby snake, or a baby fish, or a baby grasshopper, because they aren't. They are not deciding what to become, not simply because they cannot decide, but because there is no decision to make. Scientists are not anxiously standing around waiting to see what these cells become, because they already know. This is a little human baby developing into the only thing it can become, a more mature human being. It is not becoming a human; it already is. The doctors know this. But because we have chosen to close our eyes to the truth as we worship the god of self, we justify the killing of this life under the mantle of the law of the land as misinterpreted by the Supreme Court. Yes, killing is the right word. The doctor is not removing the life; he or she is killing it. We euphemistically call it "terminating a pregnancy."

B. **An Unborn Baby is a Human Life Scripturally.** The Word of God is full of evidence of the sanctity of human life! Genesis 1:26, 27 teaches us that humans are made in the image of God. Psalm 139 clearly states that God is already at work in an unborn child! Jeremiah 1:5 tells us God knows us before He formed us in the womb. Luke 1:41 uses the word for "baby" in reference to John the Baptist, the word used for both pre-born and post-born children.

3. **Actions to Consider**

A. **Do Justice.** We are to do justice by standing for the most helpless and defenseless among us—millions of unborn babies. There is something wrong with a society that closes its eyes to this injustice; something is gravely wrong with a church that does the same. How we choose to cry out for justice may differ. Some have chosen to take a very active role in picketing clinics and engaging in civil disobedience. Others consider such actions as unwise and counter-productive. It should be said that no form of violence against those who are pro-abortion is right. Christians should not fight fire with fire. Jesus did not. I have been personally impressed with what I feel is a more effective tactic. It is the approach of kindly but clearly sharing the truth via the mass media. The DeMoss Foundation is producing and airing many excellent television commercials concerning the sanctity of human life. They do not attack anyone, but they do present the truth concerning life inside the womb.

B. **Love Kindness.** We should be providing alternatives and care for those who choose to bring these unborn babies into the world. We cannot be those who simply curse the darkness. If all we do is piously denounce abortion, then we have not done enough. Those who have crisis pregnancies have great needs, and we must be there to help. We must provide help and counseling, housing, doctor's bills, and adoption to show the love of Jesus to those who are hurting and looking for an alternative to abortion. The fact is that every child is already a "wanted child." If the natural mother doesn't want the child, there are multitudes longing to adopt children. They want the child, and we must make sure that there are ways to bring them together.

Conclusion: We are living in a society that has closed its eyes to a major issue of inhumanity. There has been a devaluing of human life for the sake of convenience and comfort. There is much talk of rights, but what of the rights of the unborn? Who will stand for them? Will you?

Quotes for the Pastor's Wall

" I have noticed that nothing I never said ever did me any harm.

—Calvin Coolidge "

JANUARY 22, 2006

Intelligent Prayer

Date preached:

By Rev. Richard Sharpe

Scripture: Ephesians 1:15–23, especially verses 16–17
[I] do not cease to give thanks for you, making mention of you in my prayers: that the God of our Lord Jesus Christ, the Father of glory, may give to you the spirit of wisdom and revelation in the knowledge of Him. . . .

Introduction: Do you have a prayer list? What's your method of prayer, and why do you even pray? Christians often misrepresent the idea of prayer as a duty or as kind thoughts about someone. In our passage today, Paul displays for us the incredible importance and method of real, intelligent prayer.

1. **Preparation for Prayer (1:15).** When Paul began his prayer for the congregation of Ephesus, he mentioned that other disciples had reported the Ephesians' faith and love to him. This gave him a starting point for his prayer. This is a prayer of encouragement during difficulty. Remember that Paul was still in prison when he wrote this letter. His circumstances were incredibly difficult, but he was still willing to pray for others. Life will surely throw unpleasant circumstances at us too, but we must resolve to pray for others even during our own struggles.

2. **Purpose for Prayer (1:16–19).** Our passage beautifully outlines the purpose in Paul's prayer:

   A. **Thanksgiving (v. 16).** Paul wanted the Ephesians to realize that he was very thankful for their growth in the Lord. He was so thankful that he couldn't stop telling everyone he met about their growth. This especially motivated him to thank the Lord.

   B. **Wisdom and Revelation (v. 17).** The only way we can be intimately related to God is through good use of the disciplines of faith. Sometimes prayer needs to be accompanied by fasting. Meditation should be included in the study of the Word of God. Times of solitude from things and people are vital. When we become intimate with God, He reveals His will.

   C. **Understanding and Enlightenment (v. 18).** We always see things differently when we are intimate with God, for He wants us to see things from His perspective. Job had a problem with God taking all his children and possessions and sending him "friends" that had nothing but bad things to say about him. God answered Job by saying, "Where were you when I laid the foundations of the earth? . . ." (38:4). Job finally submitted to God's ultimate power and accepted God's plan for his life. What if we could live that way? Good or bad, we should submit to God's will for our lives and honor Him in all we do! Only if our eyes are enlightened by His Spirit through His Word can we see His perspective and live in His will.

D. **Knowledge and Hope of His Calling (v. 18).** God called the Christians in Ephesus to serve Him in their city. God had a plan for their lives before they were born, so the church at Ephesus could look toward the future with hope. They needed to keep looking up for direction. Every Christian's hope is based on the fact that Christ promised us victory in this world.

E. **Riches and Glory of His Inheritance (v. 18).** Paul told the Ephesians that in the future, after they were dead, they would receive an inheritance in heaven. We are told to store up for ourselves "treasures in heaven" (Matt. 6:20). Are we living for today or for eternity?

F. **Exceeding Greatness of His Power (v. 18).** In the present we need power to live each day for the Lord. He promises us His power in our lives. It is available to us when we are in the proper relation to Him. Our salvation is secure. Our service is a day-to-day relationship. Our growth in Christ is a process that goes on from the point of salvation until we die or Christ returns.

3. **Expectation of Prayer (1:20–23).** When Paul prayed for the Ephesian Christians, he expected that the Lord would grant his request. Paul gives Christ as the example of the *answer:* God has answered in the past, for He raised Christ from the dead. He set Christ at His right hand. He placed Christ above all the angels. He gave Christ all things under His feet. He made Christ the head of the church. If he did all those things for Christ, what will he do for us? We are His children in His service to reach the world for Him!

Conclusion: God wants His people to depend on Him. One of the ways that we show our dependence is to go to Him in prayer. He does know what we need and what our friends need, but He still wants us to ask. This powerful privilege is available to us. Are we using it for His glory?

STATS, STORIES AND MORE

More from Rev. Richard Sharpe

The Sermon on the Mount tells us that we need to enter our prayer closet and pray to the Lord who sees in secret and will reward us openly. The Pharisees liked to pray in public to be seen of men. They were fond of meaningless repetition. When the Lord prayed in the garden, He prayed three times for the cup to be removed. When Paul prayed regarding his thorn in the flesh, he prayed three times. Each received a "no" answer. We need to realize that when we pray for something, it has to be the will of the Lord for it to happen in the way we asked. We sometimes ask for things that are not the Lord's will. We have to accept the answer the Lord sends. When we pray in the Lord's will and receive a positive answer, we need to praise Him in our next prayer time. The Lord's prayer, which is really the disciples' prayer, teaches us most of the formula needed for our prayer lives. Christ gave further instructions before His death. We are to ask in His name. So the pattern for prayer would include the following:

1. Addressing the Father
2. Adoring God
3. Confessing sin
4. Thanksgiving for blessings
5. Petitioning for others
6. Petitioning for self
7. Closing in Jesus name

APPROPRIATE HYMNS AND SONGS

I Must Tell Jesus, Elisha A. Hoffman, Public Domain

Knockin' on the Door of Heaven, Steve Cantellow /Matt Redman, 1996 King's Ways Thankyou Music (Admin. by EMI Christian Music Publishing)

How Long Has It Been, Mosie Lister, 1956. Renewed 1984 Lillenas Publishing Company (Admin. by The Copyright Company)

May the Mind of Christ My Savior, Kate B. Wilkinson, Public Domain

The Lord's Prayer, Albert Hay Malotte, 1935 by G. Schirmer, Inc.

FOR THE BULLETIN

John Hooper, Reformation hero, was placed on trial on January 22, 1555. Born in Somersetshire and educated at Oxford, Hooper became an ardent supporter of the Reformation and was driven from the country by King Henry VIII. After Henry's death, he returned to England and became an Anglican bishop. When Mary ascended the throne, he was seized and imprisoned. Hooper described conditions in a letter: "On the one side is the sink and filth of the house, and on the other side the town-ditch, so that the stench hath infected me with sundry diseases—during which time I have been sick. . . . But I commit my cause to God, whose will be done, whether it be by life or death." He was burned at the stake. ✿ Today marks the death, in 1793, of John Berridge, vicar of Everton, who was sometimes called "God's Peddler." His tombstone reads:

> Reader art thou born again?
> No salvation without new birth.
> I was born in sin February 1716.
> Remained ignorant of my fallen state till 1730.
> Lived proudly on faith and works for salvation till 1754.
> Admitted to Everton vicarage 1755.
> Fled to Jesus alone for refuge 1756.
> Fell asleep in Christ 22 January 1793.

On January 22, 1882, the Fifth Street Presbyterian Church of Troy, New York, became the first church in America to be lit by electric lights. ✿ On January 22, 1973, the U. S. Supreme Court issued its Roe versus Wade decision, which legalized abortion in the United States.

Kids Talk

Take a megaphone with you (or make one out of a poster board). Ask the children how loud they would have to shout to be heard across the room? across the street? across town? across the nation? How loud would you have to shout to be heard all the way to heaven. Lift the megaphone toward the roof and say something like, "Hello, up there . . ." Explain to the children that when we pray, God is right beside us. He is close to us, and He hears every word, even if we whisper or even if we pray silently.

Call to Worship
Come, ye sinners, poor and needy,
Weak and wounded, sick and sore;
Jesus ready stands to save you,
Full of pity, love and power.
(Joseph Hart, 1759)

Responsive Reading (James 5:13; Ps. 108:1, 3; 55:17; Acts 16:25–26; Ps. 116:16–17)

Worship Leader:	"Is anyone among you suffering? Let him pray."
Congregation:	"Is anyone cheerful? Let him sing."
Worship Leader:	"I will sing and give praise . . . I will sing praises to You among the nations."
Congregation:	"Evening and morning and at noon I will pray, and cry aloud, and He shall hear my voice."
Worship Leader:	"But at midnight Paul and Silas were praying and singing hymns to God, and the prisoners were listening to them. Suddenly there was a great earthquake, so that the foundations of the prison were shaken; and immediately all the doors were opened and everyone's chains were loosed."
Everyone:	"O Lord, truly I am Your servant . . . You have loosed my bonds. I will offer to You the sacrifice of thanksgiving, and will call upon the name of the Lord."

Additional Sermons and Lesson Ideas

Defrauding God
By Rev. Peter Grainger

Date preached:

SCRIPTURE: Malachi 3:6–12

INTRODUCTION: I'm sure we're all guilty of holding back a little tithe when we need a little extra money. We often do not realize, however, that this is defrauding God. Israel was guilty of this sin:

1. The Lord's Complaint: "You have robbed me!" (v. 8). Israel was guilty of withholding the full tithe (Leviticus 27:30–32).
2. The Lord's Challenge: "Try me now in this" (v. 10). God challenged Israel with a test of faith during a time of need. His promise to them, should they obey His commands, was incredible and abundant blessing.
3. The Lord's Character: "For I am the Lord, I do not change" (v. 6). God is unchanging in both His character and in His plans for His people. He thus extended a gracious invitation for Israel to repent (v. 7).

CONCLUSION: Let us accept His invitation to repent. Let's give God what He deserves; surely He will bless us beyond what we deserve.

Verses to Sleep On

Date preached:

SCRIPTURE: Proverbs 6:20–22

INTRODUCTION: Do you have trouble sleeping? Many Christians have learned to relax their minds at night by mulling over some wonderful verses of peace and rest after they've turned off their lights. Sometimes a single verse of Scripture is better than a whole bottle of sleeping pills. Try memorizing and meditating on one of these verses:

1. Psalm 3:5–6. This was written as David was fleeing from Absalom his son.
2. Psalm 4:8. When we learn to rest our minds, we can rest our bodies.
3. Psalm 121:4–7. If God stays awake all night, we don't need to do the same.
4. Leviticus 26:6a. This is God's promise: "I will give peace in the land, and you shall lie down, and none will make you afraid." (See also Job 11:18–19.)
5. Proverbs 3:24. Sweet sleep comes to those who receive wisdom, understanding, and knowledge from the Lord (see vv. 19–23).

CONCLUSION: An Irish proverb says, "A good laugh and a long sleep are the best cures in the doctor's book." The verses listed above should be committed to memory to provide even better nocturnal medicines from the Great Physician.

A Morning Word after a Sleepless Night

I had a fitful night last night because of a situation causing me extreme anxiety. I think pastors are often special targets for this. Jesus warned Peter that Satan was attempting to sift him like wheat, and it was Peter's very role as the chief of the disciples that made him vulnerable.

Rising early this morning, I trudged to my desk with a cup of coffee and wrote out a prayer, asking God to forgive me for not trusting Him with sufficient faith. I had not rested in Him with perfect, abiding peace. I had committed the sin of unbelief, which is the very sin for which the ten spies had been condemned. They had discounted His presence, disregarded his promise, and disbelieved His power in handling their giants.

After writing my prayer, I decided at random to read a few pages from E. M. Bounds, the dean of American prayer writers. I soon realized it was no accident I had almost absently pulled this neglected volume off its place on my shelf. Chapter one of his book, *The Necessity of Prayer,* is entitled "Prayer and Faith." Though written in 1929, this was God's morning word for me after a sleepless night; and I've condensed the chapter below, for perhaps it is His word for you today, too:

In any study of the principles and procedure of prayer, of its activities and enterprises, first place, must, of necessity, be given to faith. It is the initial quality in the heart of any man who essays to talk to the unseen. He must, out of sheer helplessness, stretch forth hands of faith. He *must* believe, where he cannot prove. In the ultimate sense, prayer is simply faith, claiming its natural yet marvelous prerogatives— faith taking possession of its illimitable inheritance.

Faith does the impossible because it brings God to undertake for us and nothing is impossible with God. How great—without qualification or limitation—is the power of faith!

Prayer projects faith on God, and God on the world. Only God can move mountains, but faith and prayer move God.

Is faith growing or declining as the years go by? Does faith stand strong and foursquare, these days, as iniquity abounds and the love of many grows cold?

Faith is the foundation of Christian character and the security of the soul. When Jesus was looking forward to Peter's denial, and cautioning him against it, He said unto His disciple: "Simon, Simon, behold,

Satan hath desired to have you, to sift you as wheat, but I have prayed for thee, that thy faith fail not."

Our Lord was declaring a central truth; it was Peter's faith He was seeking to guard; for well He knew that when faith is broken down, the foundations of spiritual life give way, and the entire structure of religious experience falls. It was Peter's faith which needed guarding. Hence Christ's solicitude for the welfare of His disciple's soul and His determination to fortify Peter's faith by his own all-prevailing prayer.

The faith which creates powerful praying is the faith which centers itself on a powerful person. Faith in Christ's ability to *do* and to do *greatly,* is the faith which prays greatly.

It was to inspire faith in His ability to do that Jesus left behind Him that last, great statement, which, in the final analysis, is a ringing challenge to faith. "All power," He declared, "is given unto Me in heaven and in earth."

Yet faith is called upon, and that right often, to wait in patience before God, and is prepared for God's seeming delays in answering prayer. Faith does not grow disheartened because prayer is not immediately honored; it takes God at His Word, and lets Him take what time He chooses in fulfilling His purposes, and in carrying on His work. There is bound to be much delay and long days of waiting for true faith, but faith accepts the conditions—knows there will be delays in answering prayer, and regards such delays as times of testing, in the which, it is privileged to show its mettle, and the stern stuff of which it is made.

Fear not, O tempted and tried believer, Jesus will come, if patience is exercised, and faith holds fast. His delay will serve to make His coming the more richly blessed. Pray on. Wait on. You cannot fail. If Christ delay, wait for His own good time, He will come, and will not tarry.

Delay is often the test and the strength of faith. How much patience is required when these times of testing come! Yet faith gathers strength by waiting and praying. Patience has its perfect work in the school of delay. In some instances, delay is the very essence of the prayer. God has to do many things, antecedent to giving the final answer—things which are essential to the lasting good of him who is requesting favor at his hands.

If Jesus dwells at the fountain of my life; if the currents of His life have displaced and superseded all self-currents; if implicit obedience to Him is the inspiration and force of every movement of my life, then He can safely commit the praying to my will, and pledge himself, by an obligation as profound as His nature, that whatsoever is asked shall be granted.

Have faith in God.

JANUARY 29, 2006

SUGGESTED SERMON

The Occasion of Worship

Date preached:

By Dr. Melvin Worthington

Scripture: Exodus 20:8–11, especially verse 8
"Remember the Sabbath day, to keep it holy."

Introduction: The great American philosopher, Homer Simpson, said on one of his television shows: "I'm not a bad guy! I work hard, and I love my kids. So why should I spend half my Sunday hearing about how I'm going to hell?" He was actually asking these questions: Did God really mean it when He told us to set aside one day in seven for rest and worship? Did He really mean it when He told us not to forsake the assembling of ourselves together? Is there still any value to observing the Lord's Day?

From the very beginning, the Bible indicates that one day out of seven be set aside as a day of rest and reflection. In the Old Testament, judgment often fell on ancient Israel when the Sabbath was disregarded. In the New Testament, the Lord's Day became a weekly reminder of Christ's resurrection. Today our Sundays are filled with banking, shopping, sports, errands, church activities, school activities, drinking, and weekend pursuits. Even among Christians, work and athletics can interrupt our worship week after week until the basic habits of the Christian life fade from view. Does your view of the Sabbath center around the Lord who commanded to keep it holy, or do we treat this day as any other? Our text today is a powerful reminder of the importance of this sacred day.

1. **The Admonition in the Text.** We're to remember the Sabbath Day and keep it holy. The Sabbath Day is set apart to solemnly worship God. It has its own purpose and must not be alienated for our or other uses. The command "remember" shows our tendency to forget Sabbath holiness. We are thus reminded to sanctify the day.

Leslie Flynn told of seven unmarried brothers who lived together in a large house. Six went out to work each day but one stayed home. He had the place all lit up when the other six arrived home from work. He also had the house warm, and most importantly, he had a delicious, full-course dinner ready for his hungry brothers. One day the six brothers decided that the one who had been staying home should go to work. "It's not fair," they said, "for the one to stay home while the others slaved at a job." So they made the seventh brother find work too. But when they all came home the first night, there was no light, nor was there any warmth; and worst of all, there was no hearty dinner awaiting them. And the next night the same thing: darkness, cold, hunger. They soon went back to their former arrangement. "(It's) the day of rest and worship that keeps the other six bright, warm, and nourishing. When we desecrate the Lord's Day, we only hurt ourselves."4

2. The Analysis of the Text. There are six days in which we are to labor, though this is often ignored. In Old Testament times, the Sabbath was the last day of the week, or Saturday. The shift occurred as a result of the resurrection of Jesus Christ on the first day of the week. The early church began to celebrate the Sabbath as a day of rest and worship on the first day of the week. As Americans, how great a privilege it is that Sunday is a weekend day, the first day of the week in which we can both rest and commemorate! The *seventh day* commemorates God's creative work (Gen. 2:1–3); the *Sabbath day* commemorates God's redemptive work in delivering the Israelites out of Egyptian bondage (Ex. 31:13, 16, 17; Deut. 5:15); and *Sunday* (the first day) commemorates the resurrection of Christ our risen Redeemer (1 Cor. 16:1–2; Rev. 1:10). The *duties* of that day include:

A. Rest

B. Reflection

C. Relaxation

D. Reverence

E. Renewal

F. Restoration

3. The Application of the Text. One day out of seven belongs exclusively to God. Sunday is God's gift to the church. Sunday has been turned into a day for self or sports, which shows great disregard for our Sovereign God and His Word. Many people have rejected the infallible authority of Scripture on this issue, but God's people apply His Day to their lives for their own benefit (Hebrews 4:9).

Conclusion: Monday morning you wake up and hurriedly get ready for work. In what seems like a sprint, you run through your week: children, bosses, wives, husbands, grocery shopping, overtime, bills, errands, and so much more consume our time. As Friday approaches, the anticipation for a couple days off gets you through that last day. Saturday you take the kids to the park, wash the car, clean out the garage, and catch an evening movie or play a board game. Will you give the Lord what He asks? How important it should be to teach your children and to discipline yourself to rest from life's distractions by focusing on the One who granted us life and salvation.

STATS, STORIES AND MORE

Morbus Sabbaticus

"Morbus Sabbaticus"—better known as "Sunday Sickness"—is a disease peculiar to some church members. The symptoms vary, but these are generally observed:
1. It never lasts more than twenty-four hours.
2. It never interferes with the appetite.
3. It never affects the eyes. The Sunday papers can be read with no pain.
4. No physician is ever called.
5. After a few attacks at weekly intervals, it may become chronic.
6. No symptoms are usually felt on Saturday. The patient sleeps well and wakes feeling well. He eats a hearty Sunday breakfast, then the attack comes until services are over for the morning.
7. If there are church services scheduled for Sunday evening, the patient will have another short attack.
8. Invariably, the patient wakes up Monday morning and rushes off to work feeling refreshed. The symptoms will not recur until the following Sunday (unless another service is scheduled at church during the week).[5]

So They Won't Go Blind

In the old days, ponies and mules were used to haul out the coal in the mining camps. A man asked a little boy why there were so many ponies and mules out in the fields on Sunday. The little boy answered, "They work all week in the mines. We bring them up on Sundays so they won't go blind."

FOR THE BULLETIN

Today is the birthday of Martin Luther's remarkable wife, Katharina von Bora, who was born near Leipzig and at an early age was placed in a convent to become a nun. After the start of the Reformation, Katharina, along with several other nuns, escaped the convent in barrels used to transport herring. Martin Luther himself engineered their escape then proceeded to help the nuns find suitable husbands. In 1525, Luther, having tried and failed to secure a husband for Katharina, married her himself. They seemed perfectly matched for each other and worked side by side until Luther's death in 1546. Katharina lived another six years. ✿ Ulrich Zwingli defended his 67 theses on this day, January 29, 1523, before an audience of 600 at the first Zurich Disputation. ✿ The Edict of Nantes, which gave a measure of protection to French Protestants, was revoked on this day in 1685 by King Louis XIV. ✿ Today is the birthday of Swedish mystic Emmanuel Swedenborg. ✿ Thomas Shepherd, author of the hymn "Must Jesus Bear the Cross Alone?" died on this day in 1739. Today also marks the death, in 1904, of George Minor, who wrote the tune for the gospel song, "Bringing in the Sheaves." In 1880, hymn translator Frederick Oakeley passed away. He was the translator of the Latin Christmas carol, "O Come All Ye Faithful."

APPROPRIATE HYMNS AND SONGS

I'm Justified, Steve Cook/ Vikki Cook, 1991 PDI Worship (Admin. by Word Music Group, Inc.)/Word Music, Inc. (a division of Word Music Group, Inc.)

Into Your Courts, Dan Wilt, 1992 Mercy/ Vineyard Publishing (Admin. by Music Services)

A Mighty Fortress, Martin Luther, Public Domain

He Hideth My Soul, Fanny J. Crosby/William J. Kirkpatrick, Public Domain

Hide Me in the Cleft of the Rock, Dennis Jernigan, 1987 Shepherd's Heart Music, Inc. (Admin. by Word Music Group, Inc.)

WORSHIP HELPS

Call to Worship:
Let us hold unswervingly to the hope we profess, for He who promised is faithful. And let us consider how we may spur one another on toward love and good deeds. Let us not give up meeting together, as some are in the habit of doing, but let us encourage one another—and all the more as you see the Day approaching.
Hebrews 10:23–25 (NIV)

Scripture Reading - Psalm 92:1–6, 13–15
A Psalm. A Song for the Sabbath Day.
"It is good to give thanks to the Lord, and to sing praises to Your name, O Most High;
To declare Your lovingkindness in the morning, and Your faithfulness every night,
On an instrument of ten strings, on the lute, and on the harp, with harmonious sound.
For You, Lord, have made me glad through Your work; I will triumph in the works of Your hands. O Lord, how great are Your works! Your thoughts are very deep. A senseless man does not know, nor does a fool understand this... Those who are planted in the house of the Lord shall flourish in the courts of our God. They shall still bear fruit in old age; they shall be fresh and flourishing, to declare that the Lord is upright; He is my rock, and there is no unrighteousness in Him."

Offertory Comments:
Dr. J. Allen Blair once preached a sermon entitled, "Don't Bring Leftovers!" in which he said, "If you were to have a very special guest in your home, would you go to your refrigerator and pull out all the leftovers and warm them up?" No, he said, you would try to serve the best food you could. Yet when the offering plate is passed on the Lord's Day, many people just give God what's left.[6] The Bible says, "Honor the Lord will your possessions, and with the firstfruits of all your increase; so your barns will be filled with plenty, and your vats will overflow with new wine" (Prov. 3:9–10).

Additional Sermons and Lesson Ideas

Overcoming Impatience

By Rev. Todd M. Kinde

Date preached:

SCRIPTURE: James 5:7–12

INTRODUCTION: We often focus on the present so much that we forget the future God has revealed to us. He will punish the wicked when Christ returns, so let us be patient for Him. Now is the season for ripening the fruit of faith.

1. The Patience of the Farmer (5:7–8).
2. The Punishment of the Judge (5:9, 12).
3. The Perseverance of the Saints (5:10–11).

CONCLUSION: Are we living our lives in patient anticipation of Christ's return?

Don't Despair

By Joshua D. Rowe

Date preached:

SCRIPTURE: 1 Kings 17–19

INTRODUCTION: Do you ever struggle to provide for your family? Do you feel as if you're the only committed believer around? Or do you sometimes doubt God? Does life get the best of you? Elijah faced similar situations, and through them we learn about God's incredible provisions.

1. Times of Drought (17:1–16). Israel was facing a life-threatening drought, but God provided for both Elijah and an old widow and her family. He consistently gave them just enough to get by each day.
2. Times of Disbelief (17:17–18:46). The widow's son died and she immediately doubted God, but through Elijah her son was raised. The result was faith! In the same section, Israel turned to worship Baal, but God responded through Elijah and proved His power over false gods. The result was repentance!
3. Times of Discouragement (19:1–21). Elijah received a death threat and fled. He went into depression and felt abandoned. God spoke to Him, revealing that seven thousand others were true believers in Him. He then gave Elisha to him as his disciple.

CONCLUSION: When you struggle to make ends meet, trust God to provide each day. God knows what you are going through, and He can dispel all your doubts and reveal His great power. If you feel alone as a Christian, take comfort, for God will always have followers—even if there's only a remnant.

FEBRUARY 5, 2006

SUGGESTED SERMON

Record-Breaking Love

Date preached:

Scripture: Romans 4:1–25, especially verse 21
. . . being fully persuaded that God had the power to do what He had promised (NIV).

Introduction: In 1951, Sir Hugh Beaver, director of the Guinness Brewery, while on a hunting trip, became involved in an argument about the fastest game bird in Europe. It dawned on him that it would be helpful to have a book of world records; and thus was born the Guinness Book of World Records, which has been published regularly since 1955. It's remarkable what people do to get their names in that book. One man, for example, balanced on one foot for 76 hours and 40 minutes. A New Jersey couple set the record for kissing non-stop. It amounted to 30 hours, 50 minutes, and 27 seconds. There's one statistic, however, you'll never find in the Guinness Book of World Records. There has never been anyone strong enough, tall enough, or fast enough to jump into heaven on his or her own. Lots of people have tried, but there is none righteous, no, not one. We cannot qualify for heaven through our own efforts. Romans 1:18–3:20 stresses the fact that the world is "guilty before God" and that "by the deeds of the law no flesh will be justified in His sight" (3:19–20). Verses 21–22 say, "But now the righteousness of God apart from the law is revealed . . . even the righteousness of God, through faith in Jesus Christ." In Romans 4 Paul describes three incredible blessings to those who are justified by grace through faith.

1. **A Great Fact (Rom. 4:1–8).** This is a wonderful truth: salvation is by grace through faith. Everyone who goes to heaven—Jew and Gentile, whether in Old Testament times or New—does so on the basis of Christ's righteousness received by grace through faith. Exhibit A is Abraham. He was the most important figure in Jewish history, God's friend, and the father of the nation of Israel. What was the basis of his relationship with God? Was it his good life, excellent morality, perfect character, or likable disposition? No. He was a miserable sinner like us, but he believed God and it was counted to him as righteousness. Paul asserted that the doctrine of justification by grace through faith wasn't new or novel. It wasn't something he had dreamed up. Nor does it circumvent the truths of the Old

Testament. This is the way God has always worked. In every age, there has been only one way to be right with God—by God's grace through faith in God's Son.

2. **A Great Father (Rom. 4:9–18).** As a Christian, who is your spiritual father? God Himself is our Heavenly Father, but the Bible presents Abraham as the father of the Christian faith. Surprised? The sign of circumcision was given in Genesis 17, effectively establishing Abraham as the father of the Jewish race. But it was earlier, in Genesis 15, that "Abraham believed God, and it was accounted to him for righteousness" (Rom. 4:3; see Gen. 15:6), making him the father of all who believe.

3. **A Great Faith (vv. 19–25).** The last part of Romans 4 is among the most powerful passages about faith in the Bible. Paul gives us two things here— a *demonstration* of faith and a *definition* of faith. The demonstration of faith involves Abraham's trust in God's promise of an heir, though Abraham and his wife were old. Verse 21 provides a profound definition of faith: ". . . being fully persuaded that God had power to do what he had promised" (NIV). We are saved by this kind of faith, for none of God's promises can fail. We must come to Christ and we say, "I know I'm powerless to save myself. I can never get to heaven on the basis of my own works. But I believe Christ died and rose again, and I confess Him as Lord and Savior." And we rest in His merits, being fully persuaded that He can save us through his death and resurrection (vv. 24–25).

Conclusion: We don't know if we'll ever have another opportunity like this, to confess with our mouths Jesus as Lord and to believe in our hearts that God has raised Him from the dead. Today I'd like to invite you to turn from your own efforts and to come by simple faith to the cross of Christ to gain that righteousness that is by faith in Christ Jesus.

STATS, STORIES AND MORE

I dislike dealing with the subject of circumcision from the pulpit, but maybe that's because of my Southern sensibilities. In the ancient world, they didn't have any qualms talking about this subject, and neither did the writers of the Bible. So we don't have any choice but to mention it as it comes up on our Bible teaching. And here it is in Romans 4. God prescribed the act of male circumcision as the sign of the Abrahamic covenant. Why? Well, it's obvious. There is a sexual connotation to it. It was a matter of procreation. Every generation of Jews produced the next generation of Jews, and the seed of Israel was passed down from one generation to the next through the loins of the fathers, preserving the Messianic line. So circumcision became the sign of the Jewish people. But in Romans 4, Paul made an incisive observation about the story of Abraham in Genesis. He said that this act of circumcision had absolutely nothing to do with making Abraham righteous. It qualified no one for heaven. Circumcision was given in Genesis 17 as the sign of God's covenant with Israel, but it was earlier, in Genesis 15, where we see these critical words of the gospel: "And he [Abraham] believed in the LORD, and He credited it to him for righteousness" (Gen. 15:6). There's a powerful implication to this. Before he became the father of the Jewish nation, Abraham became the father of all who would be saved by grace through faith! He is the spiritual father of all who believe. He is our spiritual mentor, our model, and our father in the faith.

APPROPRIATE HYMNS AND SONGS

'Tis So Sweet to Trust in Jesus, Louisa M. R. Stead/ Steve Adams, 1981 Bridge Building Music (a division of Brentwood-Benson Music Publishing, Inc.)

Nothing But the Blood, Robert Lowry, Public Domain

Cornerstone, Lari Goss, 1976 HeartWarming Music (Admin. by Brentwood-Benson Music Publishing, Inc.)

His Grace is Sufficient for Me, Mosie Lister, 1965, Renewed 1993, Lillenas Publishing Company (Admin. by The Copyright Company)

In Jesus' Name, Randy Vader/ Jay Rouse, 1989 PraiseGathering Music ARR UBP of Gaither Copyright Management

FOR THE BULLETIN

According to *Foxes Book of Martyrs,* Agatha, a Christian woman, resisted the amorous approaches of Quintian, the governor of Sicily. Pursuant to his orders, she was scourged, burnt with red-hot irons, and torn with sharp hooks. Having borne these torments with admirable fortitude, she was laid naked upon live coals, intermingled with glass, and then, being carried back to prison, she died on February 5, A.D. 251. ❀ John Calvin preached his last sermon on February 5, 1564. ❀ February 5, 1597 marked the beginning of the Kiristan Holocaust in Japan. Twenty-six Christians were crucified on a hill in Nagasaki on this day, and over the next several decade tens of thousands of Japanese believers perished and the Christian church in Japan was virtually eliminated. ❀ On February 5, 1631, Roger Williams, an English preacher, arrived in America searching for religious freedom. When he was persecuted for his faith in Massachusetts, he stumbled through the wilderness until he founded and established Rhode Island, naming its capital Providence in honor of God's leading. ❀ Today marks the death of the German Father of Pietism, Philip Jakob Spener. It's also the birthday of Colonial Clergyman John Witherspoon, a signer of the Declaration of Independence. It's also evangelist D. L. Moody's birthday. ❀ On February 5, 1736, the Wesley brothers arrived in Georgia at the invitation of Governor James Oglethorpe. They hoped to be missionaries to the American Indians, but they returned to England as failures—seeking someone to convert *them.*

WORSHIP HELPS

Call to Worship:
(Christ Jesus) was delivered over to death for our sins and was
raised to life for our justification.
Romans 4:25 (NIV)

Hymn Story:
Today is a great anniversary in the history of hymns and gospel
songs. On February 5, 1864, the blind poet, Fanny Crosby, wrote
her first hymn. Fanny was born in a cottage in South East, New
York, in 1820. Six weeks later, she caught a cold in her eyes, and a
visiting doctor prescribed mustard poultices, leaving her virtually
blind for life. Growing into childhood, she determined to make the
best of it, writing at age eight: *O what a happy soul I am! Although I
cannot see, / I am resolved that in this world Contented I will be.*
Fanny spent many years in New York's Institution for the Blind,
first as a student then as a teacher and writer-in-residence. Her
career flourished. She recited her poems before Congress and
became friends with the most powerful people in America, including presidents. But not until 1851 did Fanny meet her greatest
friend, the Lord Jesus. While attending a revival meeting at John
Street Methodist Church in New York, she gave her life to Christ as
the congregation sang the hymn, "Alas! And Did My Savior Bleed?"
Fourteen years later she met the hymnist William Bradbury who
told her, "Fanny, I thank God we have met, for I think you can write
hymns." Bradbury suggested an idea for a song he needed, and on
February 5, 1864, Fanny, seizing his idea, wrote: *We are going, we
are going, to a home beyond the skies, where the fields are robed in
beauty and the sunlight never dies.* It was her first hymn, and she
was 44. But by the time she reached her "home beyond the skies"
fifty years later, she had written eight thousand more, including
"Blessed Assurance" and "All the Way my Savior Leads Me."

Additional Sermons and Lesson Ideas

Are You Singing?

By Rev. Richard Sharpe

Date preached:

SCRIPTURE: 1 Chronicles 16:1–4

INTRODUCTION: King David organized worship singers and their songs for three special purposes, described in our passage by three Hebrew words:

1. Blessings of the Past: Celebrate. The word *zakar* means "to commemorate, remember, bring to mind." Has the Lord blessed you in the past? Psalms 38 and 70 helped the Old Testament saints remember. What songs help you remember how great a God we serve?
2. Blessings of the Present: Thanks. The word *yadah* means "to give thanks, confess." To keep our relationship with God fresh, we need to confess our sins and thank Him for His daily provision of blessings and His help through every trial (Ps. 100). Are you thankful for His present help?
3. Blessings of the Future: Praise. The word *halal* means "to shine, praise, boast, or glorify." We see this in Psalm 113. The name "Jehovah" refers to a God who keeps promises. Do you praise God for His promises about your future?

CONCLUSION: God's Word tells us that a sign of being filled with the Holy Spirit is our dedication to worship through song and through giving thanks (Eph. 5:18–20). Are you singing to God?

Witnessing Effectively

By Dr. Timothy Beougher

Date preached:

SCRIPTURE: 1 Corinthians 2:1–5

INTRODUCTION: Someone once asked a Mercedes Benz spokesman why the company does not enforce its patent on the energy–absorbing car body, a design that has been copied by other car companies because of its success in reducing passenger injury in accidents. He replied, "Because some things in life are too important not to share." The same is true for the gospel of Christ. To be effective witnesses, we should:

1. Take the Initiative to Share (v. 1).
2. Focus on the Cross of Christ (v. 2).
3. Rely on the Holy Spirit's Empowerment (vv. 3-4).
4. Trust God for the Results (v. 5).

CONCLUSION: The gospel is too important to keep quiet, let's take the initiative, focus on the cross, and allow God to work through us to bring others to Himself!

CLASSICS FOR THE PASTOR'S LIBRARY
The Autobiography of Peter Cartwright

Christian filmmaker Ken Curtis once asked Professor Richard Heitzenreiter, a Wesleyan scholar at Southern Methodist University, how he aroused student's interest in Christian history. Heitzenreiter replied that he asked his students to open randomly a copy of *The Autobiography of Peter Cartwright* to just about any page. Inevitably, they would find there some fascinating anecdote that made them want to read more.

I recently purchased an old copy of Cartwright's *Autobiography* for a dollar at a library sale, and it's among the best bargains I've ever made.

Cartwright was converted as a teenager at the famous Cain Ridge Revival in Kentucky in 1801. Shortly thereafter he began preaching, and for seventy years (until his death at age eighty-seven), he traveled through Kentucky, Tennessee, Ohio, Indiana, and Illinois as a Methodist circuit-rider. He is remembered as one of America's most colorful and powerful evangelists.

Though poorly educated, he had a brilliant mind and strong opinions. Though often fatigued, he had a strong and rugged frame, and he didn't hesitate to interrupt his sermons, if necessary, to expel hecklers and rowdies. Cartwright's *Autobiography,* written in 1856, when he was 72, is among the most unique documents of American church history, laced with Cartwright's unvarnished convictions and stuffed with unusual stories.

For example, on one occasion when Cartwright was scheduled to preach near Nashville, only one man showed up for the service. Cartwright stood and preached a forty-five minute sermon to his one-man congregation. What followed is a miracle of grace that reminds us not to despise the day of small things.

On another occasion, when Cartwright was again preaching in Nashville, he sensed he was losing his audience. A distracting buzz of excitement rose from the crowd. The local pastor, seated on the platform behind him, whispered that General Andrew Jackson had slipped into the church. "General Jackson!" Cartwright roared, "General Jackson!"—and you can't imagine what came out of his mouth next.

At another time, as Cartwright was visiting a minister-friend whose wife was an embittered, loud-mouth cynic, he and the woman got into a terrible row. At the height of the argument the woman clenched her fist and made a threatening motion. Cartwright caught her by the arm, swung her in a wide circle, and sent her flying out the front door. Before she could pick herself off the ground, he slammed the door and locked her out of her own house. Would you believe it resulted in . . . her conversion?

On still another occasion, Cartwright sought lodging with a non-Christian family on the frontier, and at bedtime he asked permission to offer family prayers. The man of the house took him by lighted candle to the back of the house and said, "There, you can pray as much as you please," and shut the preacher in an empty bedroom. You'll have to read how Cartwright's unorthodox response resulted in . . . the conversion of the whole family.

Perhaps the most famous Peter Cartwright incident occurred as he was returning from a denominational convention in Baltimore. He arrived at an inn in the Cumberland mountains near bedtime. A dance was in progress, and the music, laughter, and liquor flowed in abundance. The preacher took a seat in the corner, and was approached by a ruddy young lady asking him to dance. Cartwright took her hand and walked with her to the middle of the dance floor. What happened next is one of the more remarkable stories in frontier evangelism. (I'll finish this one for you). Stopping the music, Cartwright explained that he never did anything of importance without first praying over it. He dropped to his knees and began vigorously praying aloud. The girl struggled to free herself, but his grasp was firm. The fiddler ran from the room, but most people were too shocked to move. As Cartwright continued praying, the sound of weeping was soon heard. The girl dropped to her knees, and so did others. The dance became a preaching service, resulting in over thirty conversions and the establishing of a church.

As you read *The Autobiography of Peter Cartwright,* remember that it was written in 1856 by an American original who had little schooling, was strongly opinionated, and who was deeply committed to Christ. Chapter titles include: "Itinerant Life," "Meeting in a Wagon," "Slavery in the Church," "Earthquake in the South," and "Camp Rowdies."

If you can't find an old copy of *The Autobiography of Peter Cartwright,* order a paperback version from Abingdon and read a chapter a day. Then pray for the fire to fall again from heaven as it did in the days of backwoods preacher Peter Cartwright.

FEBRUARY 12, 2006

SUGGESTED SERMON

The Seriousness of Shifting Standards

By Dr. Melvin Worthington

Date preached:

Scripture: Revelation 2:18–29, especially verses 25–26:
But hold fast what you have till I come. And he who overcomes, and keeps My works until the end, to him I will give power over the nations— . . .

Introduction: How do we guard against false teachers and corruption? Do we really take seriously the threat of false doctrines? The church we will study today was filled with corruptness, darkness, and effeminacy. Christ addresses the dangers of compromise for the church at Thyatira. This church's great fault was tolerance of false teachers, specifically, a woman called "Jezebel" who was allowed to teach heretical doctrines in the church. Jezebel was the heathen wife of Ahab, king of Israel, who brought these sins into Israel (1 Kings 16:31–33), which tells us what kind of woman this was in the church at Thyatira.

1. **The Inscription (v. 18).** *The Messenger:* The word "angel" refers to the pastor or bishop of this church. *The Assembly:* Acts 19:10 implies that Paul may have preached at Thyatira during his stay in Ephesus, although this is not certain. We do know that Christianity reached Thyatira at an early time. This church was guilty of compromise because of its sentimentality. *The Area:* Thyatira was a wealthy town in the northern part of the Roman province of Asia and derived its wealth from the Lycus valley. It was noted for its trade guilds, which were closely connected with Asiatic religion. *The Almighty.* Christ identifies Himself as the Son of God who has eyes like flame and feet like fine brass. The title "Son of God" conveys His deity. The Lord's "eyes of fire" indicate piercing insight into all persons and things, while "feet like fine brass" indicate strength and steadiness as He judges with perfect wisdom.

2. **The Inventory (v. 19).** The inventory covers their *performance, passion, participation, perception, patience,* and *progress.* Christ commends them for their love, service, faith, patience, and continued growth. The increase

in works implies that the church was making some spiritual progress. They were acting in accordance with their profession.

3. **The Indictment (vv. 20–21).** *The Presence of Corruption (v. 20).* This church was permitting an evil in its midst of a more serious character than had yet appeared. Christ charged the church with tolerating teachings and influence that led the church to commit fornication and eat things sacrificed to idols. Some believe that Jezebel was highly gifted and persuasive, artful, and resolute in the accomplishment of her purposes. She was ambitious in perpetuating her power and unscrupulous in the means she employed to accomplish her ends. The prophetess Jezebel encouraged believers in Thyatira to attend festivals in honor of false gods, which is idolatry. These festivals led to licentiousness and were attended by those who were gross and sensual in their daily lives. *The Patience of Christ (v. 21).* The wicked woman had been given opportunity to repent but had refused to do so. Jezebel showed no disposition to abandon her course, so it was proper for the Lord to rise in anger and cut her down.

4. **The Intention (vv. 22–23).** *The Punishment Described (v. 22).* Christ declared that His judgment would fall on Jezebel, those who participated with her, and on her children. The only way to avert swift, sure, and severe judgment was repentance. *The Purpose Declared* (v. 23a). Christ declared that He would kill her children and all the churches would know that He searches minds and hearts. The coming judgment would convince the church that Christ knows the hearts of all men, even the secret acts of wickedness that are concealed from human view. *The Plan Denoted (v. 23b).* Every man will be judged according to his works.

5. **The Incentive (vv. 24; 26–28).** The incentives include *The Full Burden (v. 24), The Future Blessings (vv. 26–27),* and *The Fortune Bequeathed (v. 28).* The *godly remnant* is given a special word of encouragement. The Lord did not intend to add to their burden nor did He expect them to lead reforms. The *gracious reminder* of the coming glory includes God's promise of final triumph and glory. Those who overcome are crowned with victory and will participate in the final triumph of the Lord.

6. **The Instructions (vv. 25, 29).** The instructions include *Hold steadfastly (v. 25)* and *Hear the Spirit (v. 29).* The church was exhorted to hold fast until Christ returns. He called their attention to what they had received so they

would hold fast their faith in good conscience. Until Jesus comes, the Word of God is our compass and enables us to chart our course. God's people live by faith and not by sight.

Conclusion: We must hold steadfastly to the Word of God. This means that we must not tolerate false teaching. We must live in obedience to the Word of God. Do our lives measure up to this standard?

STATS, STORIES AND MORE

Take any course in either the history of the Christian church or in the cults and you'll see how easily false teachings can derail a strong congregation. The history of the cults is filled with stories of men and women who deviated in their theology, and what began as a minor error became a major source of confusion and misdirection. In the overall history of Christianity, theological errors and false teachings have led to wars, wrongful martyrdoms, inquisitions, heresies, corruption in religion and government, and damned souls. The influence of German liberalism into the mainline denominations of Western Europe and America has resulted in the virtual death of evangelical Christianity in large parts of the western world and among many mainline denominations. The watered-down message of positive thinking has resulted in impotent preaching in many pulpits. No wonder Jude wrote, ". . . I found it necessary to write to you exhorting you to contend earnestly for the faith which was once for all delivered to the saints" (Jude 3). Vance Havner once wrote, "When we have room enough for any and every brand of doctrine, that's too much room. Can the same fountain send forth bitter water and sweet? Can two walk together except they be agreed? One scholar says that the early Christians condemned false doctrine in a way that sounds almost unchristian today."7

FOR THE BULLETIN

An eleventh-century church council tried to banish the deplorable habit of simony—the buying of church offices and positions. Pope Gregory, one of the worst offenders, abdicated and fled the country. In his place, an honest man named Suidger, bishop of Bamberg, was elected pope, but he lived less than a year. The next two popes also died quickly. Then Bruno, a good-looking, well-educated man of unblemished character and sincerity, was found. Summoned to Rome, he arrived barefoot, dressed as a pilgrim, and weeping. The people sang hymns of praise and consecrated him Pope Leo IX on February 12, 1049. ❀ Today is the birthday, in 1883, of the Puritan and Congregational minister, Cotton Mather. ❀ On February 12, 1797, Franz Haydn's "Austrian Hymn" was first performed. It later became the Austrian National Anthem, but was "stolen" during the Nazi era and is today the German National Anthem. It's also the tune for the majestic hymn, "Glorious Things of Thee Are Spoken." ❀ February 12, 1809 marks the birthday of Charles Darwin. It's also the date that the liberal theologian Friedrich Schleiermacher died in 1834. Henry Williams Baker, the author of "The King of Love My Shepherd Is," died on this day in 1877.

APPROPRIATE HYMNS AND SONGS

Because We Believe, Nancy Gordon/Jamie Harvill, 1996 Mother's Heart Music/ Integrity's Praise! Music (c/o Integrity Music, Inc.)/ Integrity's Hosanna! Music (c/o Integrity Music, Inc.)

The Solid Rock, Edward Mote/ William B. Bradbury, Public Domain

Standing on the Promises, R. Kelso Carter, Public Domain

Mighty is the Lord Our God, 1984 Sound III, Inc. (Admin. by MCA Music Publishing)/ Universal-MCA Music Publishing

Whom Have I in Heaven But Thee, Billy Luz Sprague/ Dave Durham, 1983 Meadowgreen Music Company (Admin. by EMI Christian Music Publishing)/ Straightway Music (a division of EMI Christian Music Publishing)

WORSHIP HELPS

Call to Worship:
. . . let all those rejoice who put their trust in You; let them ever
shout for joy. . .
Psalm 5:11

Word of Welcome
I'd like to take the opportunity to welcome all of you into our fellowship today. The message today will be from the Book of Revelation,
which is one of the most intriguing books in the Bible. Part of the
Scripture we'll examine today will come to us as a warning. We will
read that the church in Thyatira easily accepted false doctrines and
were led astray. In fact, the Old Testament is full of stories in which
false religions and teachers were constantly leading the Israelites
astray. What is our responsibility as church members or visitors in
trying to find truth? How can we distinguish truth from deception?
Follow the example of the Bereans. Listen as I read from Acts
17:10–11: "Then the brethren immediately sent Paul and Silas away
by night to Berea. When they arrived, they went into the synagogue of
the Jews. These were more fair-minded than those in Thessalonica,
in that they received the word with all readiness, and searched the
Scriptures daily to find out whether these things were so." You are
not only welcomed into our family of believers, but you are welcome
to search the Scriptures to be sure we are teaching what is true.
When you check the Scriptures, if a question ever arises as to the
validity of any teaching in this church, I encourage you to humbly
approach me or one of our leaders or members with your questions
and concerns. We will gladly approach the Lord together with you
and research the Scriptures to be sure we are on track. The Lord will
bless those who truly seek after truth (Matthew 7:7).

Benediction:
"Oh, love the Lord, all you His saints! For the Lord preserves the faithful, and fully repays the proud person. Be of good courage, and He
shall strengthen your heart, all you who hope in the Lord" (Psalm
31:23–24).

Additional Sermons and Lesson Ideas

The Poor in Spirit

Date preached:

By Pastor J. David Hoke

SCRIPTURE: Matthew 5:3

INTRODUCTION: As the crowd gathered toward Jesus, surely the people expected good preaching, but the beginning of His Sermon on the Mount may have shocked them (Matt. 5:3).

1. Our Poverty (v. 3a). Being "poor in spirit" means that we see our total spiritual poverty before God and our utter dependence on Him. Apart from Christ we are spiritually destitute. Have you seen your own poverty of spirit before God? Are you tired of trying to do it on your own?

2. Our Inheritance (v. 3b). The attitude of poverty of spirit brings us to the place where we can receive the kingdom from the King. Without being poor in spirit, a person cannot even come to Christ. But look at the magnitude of the blessing that we receive, the kingdom of heaven! What an inheritance!

CONCLUSION: It is to the poor in spirit that the promise comes of the kingdom of heaven. When we come to Christ with our hands empty, He will fill them with good things (Is. 57:15).

Currently Known as Prince

Date preached:

By Rev. Robert J. Morgan

INTRODUCTION: The artist formerly known as Prince recently he said he was going to stop writing explicit lyrics, because he didn't want his children listening to those kinds of songs. Well, we'll see. I don't have a lot of time for former princes. I'm too caught up in the real Prince. We often think of Jesus Christ as King of Kings, but He is also Prince of Princes:

1. The Prince of Life—Acts 3:15
2. Prince and Savior—Acts 5:31
3. Prince of the Host—Daniel 8:11
4. The Prince of Princes—Daniel 8:25
5. Messiah the Prince—Daniel 9:25
6. The Prince of Peace—Isaiah 9:6

CONCLUSION: "The prince of darkness grim, we tremble not for him; his rage we can endure; for, lo, his doom is sure. One little word shall fell him." (from Martin Luther's, "A Mighty Fortress Is Our God") Jesus is Victor—the King of Kings, Lord of Lords, and Prince of Princes!

Practice Makes Perfect

The other day I was talking with a well-known and highly respected minister who said something that surprised me. "Recently I've been preparing my sermons further in advance," he said, "and practising them in my study before I preach them on Sunday."

I found this affirming, for I've been practising my sermons for years before standing to preach them. As a teenager, I felt compelled to preach, but I had no one on whom to practice; so I learned to hike up the mountain behind our house, stand on an overhanging rock, and preach to the birds and squirrels in the hollow below. Now, three decades later, I still pace back and forth in my bathroom, bedroom, basement, or office every Saturday night, mumbling through my sermon, trying to force the current of my message to cut a channel through the shallow canyons of my brain.

Words tend to roll off the lips more easily the second time. Awkward phrases can be discarded, hard-to-pronounce names can be tackled in advance, and streams of thought flow more certainly the second time through.

Think of a wilderness guide; you'd probably rather travel with him over a trail he's traversed at least once before.

There are two ways of practising what you preach.

First, you can do it audibly. I have one young friend who goes into the chapel of his church and preaches away at his sermon, word-for-word, gestures and pauses and shouts and whispers and all. If the custodian or secretaries hear him, it doesn't faze him. He just preaches his whole sermon word-for-word in his best preaching voice. Truth be told, I did the same thing when I first started out.

Now I guard my voice from the strain of doing that by pacing back and forth in a more private spot, whispering or mumbling my message to myself. Sometimes I read through an illustration aloud, etching its details onto my memory. I even practice my welcome, announcements, prayers, and other pulpit utterances, for I've found I don't often speak well off the top of my head. Having gone through it at least once is a great help. I live in fear I'll tangle my words in some obscene way on any given Sunday. It's a little less likely if I've practised them first.

The second way of practising the sermon is doing it mentally. Today's best athletes have learned something similar in their respective sports. By working with team psychologists, they develop techniques of visualization. Studies have shown that athletes who spend all their time on physical conditioning may not have the mental stamina to make the big plays or win the big games. Instead, they supplement their training with a technique known as imaging in which they create vivid pictures in their minds of themselves performing smoothly and flawlessly during competition. They see themselves relaxed and confident and handling the ball or bat or puck with competence.

It's possible to do that with your sermon. Just visualize yourself preaching it, and listen to yourself in the silent chambers of your mind. It might help to divide your message into its individual segments, going over each one several times and paying attention to the transitions between the points.

One man wrote that he did this while walking, pretending that he was talking through his sermon with an imaginary friend. When he could explain it clearly and smoothly to his invisible friend, he felt ready to preach it to the congregation on Sunday. Another pastor did the same, but she recognized that invisible friend as the Lord Jesus Himself, and she preached it before the Lord in prayer before ever entering the pulpit.

Not everyone needs to do this. Some preachers are gifted with profluence, and they have only to mount the pulpit and open their mouths, and the words flow forth like a crystal river.

I've envious. For me, and for many of the rest of us, it helps if we practice what we preach.

FEBRUARY 19, 2006

Cult-Proof Your Loved Ones

Date preached:

By Dr. Dan Chun

Scripture: 2 Corinthians 11:1–6, especially verse 3:
But I fear, lest somehow, as the serpent deceived Eve by his craftiness, so your minds may be corrupted from the simplicity that is in Christ.

Introduction: This morning I want to give you preventive medicine on the markings of cults and how to stay out of them. This will be helpful, I believe, for all of us, no matter what age. Our young people, our adult children and our friends are all susceptible to cults if we are not trained in understanding them. The focus will be on the People's Temple, which was led by Jim Jones. By the end of this message you will know what some of the main marks of a cult are and how to avoid them.

1. **The Marks of a Cult**

    A. **Cult Members May Be Highly Educated.** Jean Mills was a seven-year member of the cult called the People's Temple. She said, "I could give you an answer from the Bible for any question. I know the Bible backward and forward."[8] The number two man of the same cult was Tim Stoen. Tim was a graduate of one of the most conservative evangelical Christian colleges in America, Wheaton College in Illinois. He was also a law graduate of Stanford University. He became the assistant district attorney for San Francisco. Then he resigned his district attorney position to go to Jonestown in 1977. His orthodox Christian roots and his brain finally alerted him that something was wrong with the People's Temple. He defected and tried to get his six-year-old son John out, but he was too late. Later, little Johnny was found dead near Jones's body in Guyana.

    B. **Cult Leaders Say Jesus Is not the Messiah, or He Is not the Only Messiah.** Jones believed that he himself was God's messenger. Cults may say that they believe in Jesus, but the leader often elevates himself to a place equal to Jesus or as the successor to Jesus. Cult leaders often adamantly refuse to be questioned about their authority and desire to be seen as perfect. Jones would stage fake healings in his worship services. Chicken parts were used to represent cancers he had extracted from sick people during his fake healing ministry.

C. Cult Followers Often Say They Weren't Loved in Their Previous Churches. Cults often create a warm and loving environment that is welcoming to most anyone. Hearing this should compel us to love our members so much that no one would feel so starved for love that they would seek a cult to join.

D. Cults are Often Attractive on the Surface but Abusive in Practice. We often see *abuse of authority*. Jim Jones rejected the authority of the Bible, claiming there were errors in Scripture. At least once, he threw a Bible on the floor and shouted at God, "If there is a God in heaven, strike me dead!" Often there is *abuse of time*. Jones kept his people in a state of exhaustion. He would have long worship meetings, organizational meetings, and long periods of ministry. *Abuse of money* is another key. Cults may try to keep their members in a state of poverty and dependence. They often have an unusually large proportion of income donated. There is *abuse of discipline,* including both psychological and emotional cruelty. Members may be disciplined for using the wrong toothpaste or voicing a disagreement with the leader. Unfortunately, there is often *abuse of sexuality*. Jones would order his members to have sex with people he designated, then he would abruptly switch and command total abstinence. Finally, there may be *abuse of intimacy*. Jones would only allow intimacy with him. Cult leaders often decide whom their followers marry, and this sometimes occurs even if the man and woman hardly know each other.

2. Application: Guard Against Cults

A. Let Our Children Know Cults Exist. They are on all of the campuses of the big schools. They infiltrate churches all the time. They are on our city streets. They often have names that sound Christian.

B. Make Sure Our Church is Authentic. We point to the truth of God and the love of God through His Son, Jesus Christ, but we must never think that we are a perfect church. Let our kids see the church as a place you can ask questions and share your doubts. Check our practices against Scripture and come to our leaders with any concerns.

C. Study Christianity. The best way for you and me and our kids to be invulnerable to cults is to study the real thing. Really study the Bible so when cult members come to you and try to persuade you to follow them, your Biblical cult detector activates and says, "No, that is not what the Bible says, and you are wrong. There is only one Bible. There is only one God. There is only one Messiah. There will never be another Messiah after Jesus Christ."

STATS, STORIES AND MORE

More from Dr. Chun

Some years ago, one of the top high school leaders in our youth group went off to a prestigious university. He had a heart for Christ and a passion to serve Him. We were later surprised to learn that he became involved with a cult. While at college, a group approached him, affirmed him and told him that they were a Christian group. He slowly got sucked into what was really a cult. Fortunately, he got out of it, but it took some time. It was because his "radar" was not finely tuned. He was not able to detect that what sounded like Christianity and a Christian community, was actually something radically different.

More on the People's Temple from Dr. Dan Chun

Here's a quote from Jeannie Mills, who worked at the People's Temple for fifteen years. Her husband, Al, left his Presbyterian church to join her. She said, "I was so turned off in every church I went to because nobody cared. Nobody cared that I, a human being with feelings and thoughts and emotions, came into their doors. And that is when I went to People's Temple. Everyone seemed so caring and loving. They hugged us and made us welcome. So many people said they liked us and wanted us to come back. After the first service, many peoples sent letters. The church even sent a box of candy to visitors."[9]

Jones knew people were looking for big displays of love, and here is a list of what he did. Would you be swayed in your thinking that maybe he and his church were genuine and really understood about God's love?

Jones counseled ex-prisoners and juvenile delinquents. He started a job placement center. He opened up rest homes and homes for the physically or mentally challenged. In San Francisco, he had a health clinic offering free diagnostic services. He had vocational training courses, a drug rehabilitation center, and free legal aid. His Temple Dining Hall fed eight hundred to eighteen hundred people a day.

Jones also founded a community center with a heated swimming pool, horses for underprivileged children to ride, college dormitories and tuition grants for students, homes for seniors, animal shelters, a drug rehab program that reportedly helped three hundred addicts, and legal aid to two hundred families a month.

FOR THE BULLETIN

On February 19, 843, Empress Theodora reintroduced icons in the Eastern churches, effectively ending the iconoclastic controversy but bringing about the eventual split with the Western church. ❁ On this day in 1377, John Wycliffe, the "Morning Star of the Reformation," was placed on trial in London. Though despised by the churchmen of the day for his early Reformation views and his attempts to translate the Bible into English, he was a popular professor and a beloved pastor. The authorities prohibited him from preaching. His writings were later burned, and in 1428 his body was exhumed and burned. His work on the English Bible, however, paved the way for many others well after his death. ❁ On February 19, 1401, William Sawtrey, one of Wycliffe's disciples, was burned at the stake, gaining the distinction of being the first in a host of English martyrs. ❁ It was also on this day in 1568 that Miles Coverdale passed away. He translated and published the first complete Bible in English, and he also edited the Great Bible. ❁ Scottish Covenanter, James Guthrie, was accused on February 19, 1651 of disloyalty, for he had preached that Christ, not the Scottish King, should rule the church. He was hanged, after which his head was hacked off and affixed on Netherbow Port. In coming months his small son, sneaking away to steal glances at his father's decaying head, would run home crying, "I've seen my father's head! I've seen my father's head!" ❁ On February 19, 1812, America's first missionaries, Adoniram and Ann Judson, sailed from Salem, Massachusetts. They were headed for India but settled in Burma.

APPROPRIATE HYMNS AND SONGS

Ancient of Days, Jamie Harvill/ Gary Sadler, 1992 Integrity Hosanna's! Music (c/o Integrity Music, Inc.)

Immortal Invisible, Walter Chalmers Smith/ John Robert, Public Domain

Great is the Lord, Steve McEwan, 1985 Maranatha Praise, Inc.

Rejoice the Lord is King, Charles Wesley/ John Darwall, Public Domain

I Exalt Thee, Pete Sanchez, Jr., 1977 Pete Sanchez, Jr. (Admin. by Gabriel Music)

WORSHIP HELPS

Call to Worship:
With what shall I come before the Lord, and bow myself before the High God? . . . He has shown you, O man, what is good; and what does the Lord require of you, but to do justly, to love mercy, and to walk humbly with your God?
Micah 6:6, 8

Suggested Scripture Reading:
Psalm 19
Luke 12:1–12
2 John 7–11

Offertory Comments:
Whether we consider it a law to obey or a pattern to keep, the concept of tithing has been important to Christians from the very beginning. If every believer gave ten percent of his or her income to the Lord's work, everything would be fully financed—both in our home churches and in our missionary and benevolent ministries. How close do we come to that? The most recent studies show that the average church attendee gave 2.62 percent of after-tax income to the Lord. That's a sixteen percent decline since 1968 when the average was 3.11 percent. Let's ask God for the faith to be faithful to His cause.[10]

Benediction:
Now to Him who is able to keep you from stumbling, and to present you faultless before the presence of His glory with exceeding joy, to God our Savior, who alone is wise, be glory and majesty, dominion and power, both now and forever. Amen. (Jude vv. 24–25)

Additional Sermons and Lesson Ideas

The First Cluster of Fruit
By Dr. Denis Lyle

Date preached:

SCRIPTURE: Galatians 5:22

INTRODUCTION: Paul talks about "the fruit [singular] of the Spirit," for he's thinking of qualities of character as a single cluster. They are like a cluster of grapes distinguishable and yet inseparable! The first three virtues express the God-ward aspects of the Christian life: love, joy, and peace.

1. Love. Of course love means different things to different people. The love that Paul is talking about here is unique. This is divine and unconditional love, which is God's gift to us (Rom. 5:5; Phil. 1:9). Are you someone who seeks the highest good of others regardless of their treatment of you?

2. Joy. Joy is inward peace and sufficiency that is not affected by outward circumstances. There's a difference between happiness and joy. Happiness is dependent on happenings, but true joy is not. It glows in the dark. Do you have joy regardless of your circumstances?

3. Peace. This is one of the great words of the Bible. The New Testament word for *peace* basically means "to bind together." A good way to describe peace is, "that tranquil serenity of heart which comes from the all-pervading consciousness that our times are in the hands of God."

CONCLUSION: Does your life radiate these qualities because of your ever-deepening relationship with God?

Conditions of Revival
Outline by W. Graham Scroggie

Date preached:

SCRIPTURE: Various

INTRODUCTION: The blessing of revival is conditional. God has made promises, but He has also given precepts that we must obey to receive the blessings. Let's look at some of these conditions:

1. There Must Be a Consciousness of the Need of Revival (Rev. 3:14–18).
2. There Must Be a Firm Belief in the Possibility of Revival (Matt. 21:22).
3. There Must Be a True Recognition that God Wills Our Revival (Is. 48:18; Ps. 81:13, 16; Hosea 11:7–8; 14:4).
4. There Must Be a Strong Sense of the Urgency of Revival (Rev. 3:19–20).
5. There Must Be an Earnest Desire for Revival (Ps. 103:5; Acts 1:7, 12–14).
6. There Must Be a Genuine Willingness to Pay for Revival (Matt. 10:17–23).
7. There Must Be a Determined Pursuit of Revival (Acts 1:12–26).

CONCLUSION: O Lord, help us to desire, understand, and pursue revival among Your people!

FEBRUARY 26, 2006

SUGGESTED SERMON

Covenant Renewal

Date preached:

By Rev. Todd M. Kinde

Scripture: Joshua 24, especially verse 14:
Now therefore, fear the LORD, serve Him in sincerity and in truth . . .

Introduction: When the Lord calls us to faith in Him, he gives us new life, another chance, and a new covenant. The final gathering in Joshua reminds us of how we should respond to God's covenant with us.

1. **Reviewing Our Past (vv. 1–13).** At Shechem Joshua began to recite the history of the Hebrew people from Abraham up to God's defeat of their enemies during the conquest. The history reflects God's redeeming His people and establishing a covenant relationship. Now the new covenant is entered through the blood of Christ Jesus. By grace through faith we become children of Abraham and thus rightful heirs of God's covenant. Our genetic makeup doesn't make us children of Abraham; the righteousness of Christ through faith does (Gal. 3:7–9). Since we who believe are children of Abraham, this history of the Old Testament becomes our history, our redemptive history.

2. **Renewing Our Piety (vv. 14–24).** We must embrace our history and renew our piety. Piety refers to that devotion, duty, loyalty, allegiance, and reverence to the God of our history. In verses 14–24 we find the renewal ceremony, a solemn ceremony that calls the people of God to fear the Lord and serve Him with all faithfulness (v.14). Joshua made a contrast between life on the old side of the River and life of the new side of the River (v.14). Joshua explained that Nahor and Abraham worshiped idols on the old side of the River but that the Lord brought Abraham from the land beyond the River to the Canaan land (see vv. 2–3). Verse 11 reveals that the whole nation was also brought across the River. Now the people must respond to the Lord's call to the new land this side of the River and serve Him, ridding themselves of idols. We too must throw away the idols once we have crossed into God's inheritance (1 Peter 4:3–4). We are freed from serving sin and self so that we might serve God (Rev. 1:5–6).

3. **Remembering Our Promise (vv. 25–28).** The Hebrew text literally says that Joshua "cut a covenant" (v. 25) so the people would remember God's promise. The idea of cutting portrays an animal sacrifice that represents the parties of the covenant ceremony. The servants who were committed to the king would walk between the cut halves of the animal to identify with the animal as an image of judgment and sacrifice. If someone broke a covenant with the king, he would be dealt with in the same manner as the animal. If you break a covenant, you will be broken (see Jer. 34:18–20). It doesn't take us very long as Christians to realize that we are not promise keepers but promise breakers. We have a God, however, who keeps His promises and made His covenant with us. He Himself walked between the pieces of the sacrifice (Gen. 15:17–18) and thus vowed to keep His word. Because we failed, God provided Jesus, the eternal Son of God, to take on the punishment of the covenant curse for those who would believe in Him.

4. **Remaining on Our Path (vv. 29–33).** The final statements of this chapter and book are a reminder of our continued journey of faith and a call to stay the course, to remain on the path. Joshua lived to be 110 years of age. Joseph had died in Egypt but left instructions that his bones be brought into the land and buried there. He was buried at Shechem, the place of the Lord's initial promise to Abraham concerning the land. Eleazar, the son of Aaron and the father of Phinehas, died and was buried in the hill country of Ephraim. These obituaries are a reminder to Israel and to us that all these lived as sojourners walking the path of faith (Heb. 11:13–16, 39–40; 12:1–4). The battle we fight is not against people and territories but against sin and self. The rest we seek is not to be found in temporal luxury but in eternal life through Christ Jesus our Lord.

Conclusion: Throughout the book of Joshua we see the destructive power of discontentment, disobedience, and disregard. These result in unrest and disorientation in the life of faith. It is time to review our history, renew our piety, remember our promise, and remain on our path.

STATS, STORIES AND MORE

More from Pastor Kinde

The Setting: The final gathering of Joshua chapter 24 occurs at Shechem. Shechem had a rich history for the people of Israel. It was at Shechem that God promised to give this land to Abraham (Gen. 12:6–7). At Shechem Jacob purchased a plot of ground and set up an altar to worship the Lord (Gen. 33:18–20). This may be the site where Dinah was raped and her zealous brothers destroyed the Shechemites as an act of revenge (Gen. 34:1–29). Here ten brothers betrayed Joseph and sold him to a slave caravan (Gen. 37:12–14). In this spot there are good memories and bad memories, memories of blessing and of cursing.

Our Heritage of Faith: The importance of having a history is great. Having a story that is older than I am and has roots in ancient times gives me a sense of belonging. I belong to a heritage of faith. Having a story rooted in ancient times gives me an identity. I gain perspective on who I am. I do not so much need to go off and discover myself as to get into the ancient Scriptures and discover who God's people are, and then I can begin to be shaped by God's Word.

Covenant Reflected in Ceremonies: In the covenant ceremony of the Old Testament, after the animal was cut into pieces and the members involved would walk between them, the cut animal would then be served as a meal as a demonstration of fellowship and peace. We also have a covenant meal in the Lord's Supper. This is the promise we remember: the death of Christ on the cross for us.

APPROPRIATE HYMNS AND SONGS

His Banner Over Me, Kevin Prosch, 1991 Mercy/Vineyard Publishing (Admin. by Music Services)

My Saviour's Love, Charles H. Gabriel, Public Domain

I Stand Amazed, Dennis Jernigan, 1991 Shepherd's Heart Music, Inc. (Admin. by Word Music Group, Inc.)

How Deep the Father's Love for Us, Stuart Townend, 1995 Kingsway's Thankyou Music (Admin. by EMI Christian Music Publishing)

He's Been So Good to Me, R. Douglas Little, 1978 HeartWarming Music Company/BMI

FOR THE BULLETIN

This is the traditional date, February 26, 398, in which the "Golden Mouthed Preacher," John Chrysostom, became bishop of Constantinople. ❁ On February 26, 1835, Christianity was outlawed in Madagascar. Despite the edict, the young church grew at a remarkable pace. ❁ Today is the birthday of hymnist George Stebbins (1846). Stebbins worked for years alongside evangelist D. L. Moody and composed several of our favorite hymn tunes. Included among them are the invitation hymns: "Have Thine Own Way, Lord," "Jesus is Tenderly Calling You Home," "What Will Ye Do with Jesus?" and "Jesus, I Come." ❁ Today is the birthday of Charles Sheldon in 1857, the author of "In His Steps," one of the most famous Christian novels of all times. The popular slogan "What Would Jesus Do?" arose from this book. ❁ February 26 marks the wedding anniversary of French missionaries Francois and Christina Coillard. Francois had arrived in Africa as a single, clean-shaven, young man. The Africans were perplexed, wondering how this beardless, wifeless youth could teach them anything. "Beards and wives are necessary for respect," they said. "We can't listen to one with neither hair nor helper." Hearing these whispers, Coillard immediately grew a fine beard, and on this day in 1861, he married Christina Mackintosh. For the next thirty years, the Coillards worked hand-in-hand establishing churches and sharing the gospel.

WORSHIP HELPS

Call to Worship:
Lift every voice and sing, till earth and Heaven ring . . .
Let our rejoicing rise, high as the listening skies
(James W. Johnson, 1899)

Responsive Reading from Deuteronomy 6:1–2, 4–7; Psalm 119:2

Worship Leader:	"Now this is the commandment, and these are the statutes and judgments which the Lord your God has commanded to teach you, that you may observe them in the land which you are crossing to possess, that you may fear the Lord your God, to keep all His statutes and His commandments which I command You, you and your son and your grandson, all the days of your life . . ."
Congregation:	"Hear, O Israel: The Lord our God, the Lord is one!"
Worship Leader:	"You shall love the Lord your God with all your heart, with all your soul, and with all your strength."
Congregation:	"And these words which I command you today shall be in your heart."
Worship Leader:	"You shall teach them diligently to your children, and shall talk of them when you sit in your house, when you walk by the way, when you lie down, and when you rise up."
All:	"Blessed are those who keep His testimonies, who seek Him with the whole heart!"

Benediction:
From every idol I have known now set my spirit free;
O make me worship you alone, and reign supreme in me
(William Cowper, 1772, O for a Closer Walk with God).

Additional Sermons and Lesson Ideas

The Father's Friend
By Dr. Melvin Worthington

Date preached:

SCRIPTURE: James 2:21–23; Hebrews 11:8–19

INTRODUCTION: Abraham was chosen by God to become the father of the faithful. He stands out as one of the most prominent characters in the Scriptures. In Genesis 12 Abraham received a distinct revelation from God regarding *His plan, purpose, people, and property.*

1. Abraham's Faith. Abraham's faith was *true faith, tested faith, tried faith, timid faith, tenacious faith, and triumphant faith.*
2. Abraham's Faults. Abraham's faults included *fear of famine* (Gen. 12:10–20), *fear of danger* (Gen. 20), *and fear for family* (Gen. 16:1–16; 17:1–27; 21:1–8).
3. Abraham's Future. Abraham's future includes *the covenant (Genesis 12; 17; 22), the conflicts* (Rom. 9 – past; Rom. 10 – present; Rom. 11– prospect), *and the consummation* (Matt. 24; Acts 1).

CONCLUSION: Abraham serves as a powerful illustration of one who believed God. *He believed the Word of God, he was beset by weaknesses, he was blessed with wealth and he was a beacon in witness.* He was *God's friend.*

Ultimate Fellowship
Adapted from Charles Haddon Spurgeon

Date preached:

SCRIPTURE: 2 Corinthians 6:16

INTRODUCTION: This verse tells us about the ultimate fellowship we have with God: "I will dwell in them and walk among them. I will be their God, and they shall be my people."

1. Here is Mutual Interest. Each belongs to the other. We find in God our chief possession, and He considers us His peculiar treasure.
2. Here is Mutual Consideration. God thinks of me all the time, and my thoughts ought to continually be on Him.
3. Here is Mutual Fellowship. God dwells in us, and we dwell in Him. We walk together.

CONCLUSION: Oh, for grace to treat the Lord as I should, to trust Him as I ought, and to serve Him as He deserves. Oh, that I could love, worship, adore, and obey the Lord in spirit and truth! This is my heart's desire. This is ultimate fellowship.

COMMUNION SERMON

"The Gift of Forgiveness"

By Dr. Timothy Beougher   *Date preached:*

Scripture: Isaiah 43:22–25, especially verse 25:
I, even I, am He who blots out your transgressions for My own sake; and I will not remember your sins.

Introduction: As we prepare our hearts to celebrate the Lord's Supper, I want us to look to the Old Testament Book of Isaiah—specifically Isaiah 43:25—to remind us of God's wonderful, powerful, amazing grace. Let's reflect on a few truths:

1. **God's Nature Is Forgiving.** In these verses of Isaiah, we learn that, although God had blessed His people, they were disobedient and unfaithful. Through a series of "nots" God reminds them of how they have ignored Him or outright rejected Him. They had not called on Him in prayer, not brought to Him their tithes and offerings, not honored Him with acceptable sacrifices in worship, and not offered Him their gratitude for His many blessings. God had not asked too much of them. His burden is always easy and His yoke is light. But instead of worshipping God with their sacrifices, they had weighed down God with their sins. But just at that moment, God displayed His grace and mercy. From a heart of love He declared that He would blot out their sin for His sake (v. 25). How could this possibly be? Israel deserved the judgment of God for ignoring Him, and they deserved His punishment for burdening Him with their sins. They could never possibly earn God's favor after all their sin and rebellion. Nothing but grace—pure, undeserved, unmerited favor—can explain God's forgiveness. God says in verse 25 that He forgives sins for His sake. The motive for forgiving sin is in the heart of God; He forgives not because we deserve it, but out of His sheer love and grace.

2. **Salvation Is from God.** Salvation is God-originated, God-empowered, and should result in praise and glory to God and God alone. Note the threefold repetition of God's name in verse 25 for emphasis. Not just anyone is declaring this gracious forgiveness and pardon; it is Almighty God! God did not have to forgive sin. He would have been completely just to let us all die in our

sin and spend eternity in hell apart from His presence, but God chose to provide forgiveness even when we were in rebellion against Him (Rom. 5:8). God bestows His grace upon us without *any* merit on our part. This wonderful truth sets Christianity apart from every other religion in the world. Every other religion approaches God through some kind of works-based system: if I will do this, God will do that. If I do enough good works, or perform enough religious ritual, or avoid enough bad deeds, then I will somehow earn God's favor. But our salvation can only come by grace through faith because even the best efforts we give God still fall short (Eph. 2:8–9).

3. **God Remembers Our Sins no More.** How can God remember our sins no more as verse 25 says? C.H. Spurgeon paints a masterful picture of how this might unfold at the judgment. He writes:

> The Christian will have many accusers. The devil will come and say, "'That man is a great sinner." "I don't remember it," says God. "That man rebelled against Thee. . ." says the accuser. "I do not remember it," says God, "for I have said I will not remember his sins." [The believer's own] conscience says, "Ah! But Lord, it is true, I did sin against Thee, and most grievously." "I do not remember it," says God—"I said, 'I will not remember your sins.'"

How did He do such a thing? Colossians 2:13–14 tells us that "He has made [you] alive together with Him, having forgiven you all trespasses, having wiped out the handwriting of requirements that was against us, which was contrary to us. And He has taken it out of the way, having nailed it to the cross." Scripture teaches that forgiveness is only through the blood of Christ: "And according to the law almost all things are purified with blood, and without shedding of blood there is no remission" (Heb. 9:22; see 1 Pet. 1:18–19).

Conclusion: Do you see why we celebrate the Lord's Supper? Do you see why it indeed is a celebration? Where else can we find such a picture of love and grace, of unmerited favor? In preparing to celebrate the Lord's Supper, it is not only a time to look back and be grateful for Christ's sacrifice, but it is also a time to look within, confess sin, and recommit to follow Him. As we prepare to receive the Lord's Supper, let's enter into a time of quiet meditation and reflection upon the truths of God's Word. If there is anything we need to confess to God during this time, let us do so to prepare our hearts.

MARCH 5, 2006

SUGGESTED SERMON

The Deadly Defect

Date preached:

By Dr. Melvin Worthington

SCRIPTURE: Revelation 2:1–7, especially verse 4:
But I have this against you, that you have left your first love.

Introduction: Staying busy with the Lord's work is an easy task for most of us. The challenge is maintaining the proper love and devotion to our Master. The letter to the church at Ephesus (Rev. 2:1–7) deals with backsliding. This church was endangered by its own success. It was industrious, orthodox, and faithful, but its love was cooling. Christ rebukes this church for allowing its early love to wane.

1. **The Inscription (v. 1).** *The angel:* The word "angel" refers to the pastor who was responsible for the spiritual condition of the church. *The assembly:* The letter was written to the church at Ephesus. *The area:* The church was located in the city of Ephesus in the province of Asia, which was noted for its idolatry, industry, and immorality. Paul did some of his greatest work in this wicked city. *The admonition:* John was instructed to write these things. *The Almighty:* each of the letters gives a portrait of our Lord Jesus Christ. He is presented in this particular letter in a three-fold manner. He is the one *heralding* the truth as He instructs the angel to write His words. He is the one *holding* the seven stars in His right hand. Christ is also the one *habitating* in the midst of the seven golden candlesticks, which represent the seven churches.

2. **The Inventory (vv. 2–3, 6).** Christ began this letter with a commendation. He declared that He had full knowledge of this church. He commended them for their *progressiveness, perseverance, patience, perception, purity,* and *possession.* Because He is omniscient Christ has infinite knowledge of all the deeds of His people. Christ found much to commend in this church. It almost seemed like a perfect church . . . but it wasn't.

3. **The Indictment (v. 4).** In spite of the commendable qualities of this church Christ declared, "But I have this against you, that you have left your first

love" (Rev. 2:4). This defect was not a trifling one, but a very serious and sobering one. They knew many things but their hearts were cold. They were in a state of decline, although they still maintained the doctrines of the faith and opposed the doctrines of error. This is not unusual in churches that begin in warm revival fires with zealous converts. The early zeal may die away, and the church, once full of life and love, may become cold. This church had not lost but had left its first love.

4. **The Instructions (v. 5).** *The Directive.* Christ counseled them to *remember.* They were to remember the state they once enjoyed. Recalling their former state of zeal, ardor, and love would fill them with happiness. Few things can cure a backsliding church than to remember its former condition—the happier days of piety. Christ counseled them to *repent.* Repentance was their duty and needed to include all areas in which they had erred. Christ counsels them to *repeat.* In other words, they were to manifest the zeal and love that were formerly evidenced in their lives. *The Danger.* If they ignored Christ's counsel, He would come in judgment and remove the church. The church gave light in Ephesus, and it was in danger of having the gospel light taken away and planted elsewhere. *The Decision.* This church was faced with a decision that it had to make: remember, repent, and repeat—or expect and experience removal.

5. **The Incentives (v. 7).** *Their hearing:* The expression, "He who has an ear, let him hear," occurs at the close of each of the addresses to the seven churches. Jesus frequently used this method in His personal ministry. It was designed to arrest attention and emphasize that the message was of special significance. *Their hope:* Those who conquered, repented, and turned back to their first love could eat of "the tree of life." *Their home:* "Paradise" refers to everything that God has in store for those who love him and live for Him.

Conclusion: We often stay busy in the Lord's work, substituting activity for adoration and affection. As we stand for that which is right, we must keep our hearts warm. Our heads might be right while our hearts are cold. The church today needs to be reminded of the danger of leaving its first love. If our love declines, Christ's anger burns. Christ notices every decline in our piety and will rebuke us without hesitation.

STATS, STORIES AND MORE

Revival

Duncan Campbell grew up in a Scottish village where he was known as the local musician. But one night during a concert he asked himself, "Is this all life offers a young man like me?" Excusing himself, he hurried home where his mother led him to Christ. He served the Lord in churches in his native Highlands until age 50 when he left as a missionary to the Outer Hebrides Islands.

A mission church had already been established on Lewis Island, and several of its members had been pleading for revival. One night in a prayer meeting, a young man rose and read Psalm 24:3, 4—"Who may ascend into the hill of the Lord? Or who may stand in His holy place? He who has clean hands and a pure heart . . ."

"Brethren," the man said, "it seems just so much humbug to be waiting and praying as we are, if we ourselves are not rightly related to God." Instantly the Christians began confessing their sins to God and to one another.

When Duncan Campbell arrived soon afterward, he went straight to the church and preached, then dismissed the service. The crowd filed from the building; but instead of going home, they stood under the stars, weeping, praying, and confessing their sins. The number soon swelled to six hundred, and all night the Holy Spirit moved through the village. Hundreds trusted Christ as Savior.

The revival spread to nearby villages, and Duncan traveled for three years, strengthening the converts. Night after night, churches were filled with worshippers, often until five o'clock the following morning. Duncan later said that during those days he could stop any passerby on the island and find him thinking about his soul.

APPROPRIATE HYMNS AND SONGS

The Heart of Worship, Matt Redman, 1997 Kingsway's Thankyou Music (Admin. by EMI Christian Publishing)

Have Thine Own Way, Adelaide A. Pollard/George C. Stebbins, Public Domain

Be Thou My Vision, Keith Landis/ Mary Byrne/ Eleanor Hull/ Carlton Young, 1964, 1994 Selah Publishing Company, Inc./Abingdon Press

As the Deer, Martin J. Nystrom, 1984 Maranatha Praise, Inc.

Seek Ye First, Karen Lafferty, 1972 Maranatha! Music (Admin. by the Copyright Company)

FOR THE BULLETIN

The first Christian magazine in America, "The Christian History," began publication on this day, March 5, in 1743. Editor Thomas Prince, a former missionary and the pastor of Boston's Old South Church, found a receptive audience in the multitudes coming to Christ during the Great Awakening.
❁ Today marks the death in 1778 of composer Thomas Augustine, who wrote the music to "Am I a Soldier of the Cross?" and "O for a Faith that Will Not Shrink." ❁ On March 5, 1834, George Müller and Henry Craik announced their intention to form a new society called "The Scripture Knowledge Institution, for Home and Abroad." Its purpose was to strengthen Sunday Schools, distribute Scripture, and help missionaries. ❁ America's first Methodist Episcopal Bishop, William McKendree, passed away on this day in 1835. He had fought in the Revolutionary War and came to Christ under Methodist preaching when nearly thirty years of age. His ministry helped spur on the Great Revival of the early 1800s, and he succeeded Francis Asbury as the Methodist Church's leading bishop in America. ❁ Today is the birthday, in 1850, of hymn composer Daniel Towner, who wrote the music to "At Calvary," "Marvelous Grace of our Loving Lord," and "Trust and Obey."
❁ Evangelist Sam Jones began a revival meeting in Toledo, Ohio, on March 5, 1899. The mayor of Toledo was also named Sam Jones, and the two men got into a public feud. Evangelist Sam Jones criticized Mayor Sam Jones over the high number of bars and saloons in Toledo. A great revival broke out in the city; yet the mayor won reelection the next month by a huge margin.

WORSHIP HELPS

Call to Worship:
God is here! we feel His presence
In this consecrated place;
But we need the soul refreshing
Of His free, unbounded grace.
(James M. Black, 1856–1938)

Scripture Reading Medley (Mark 12:30; 1 John 4:16, 19; John 21:15; John 14:15, 21; Psalm 18:1; Psalm 40:16)
"Love the Lord your God with all your heart, with all your soul, with all your mind, and with all your strength. This is the first commandment."
"God is love, and he who abides in love abides in God, and God in him. We love him because He first loved us. . . ."
" 'Simon, son of Jonah, do you love Me more than these?' He said to him, 'Yes, Lord; You know that I love You.' "
"If you love Me, keep My commandments. He who has My commandments and keeps them, it is he who loves Me. And he who loves Me will be loved by My Father, and I will love him and manifest Myself to him . . . ."
"I will love You, O Lord, my strength. The Lord is my rock and my fortress and my deliverer; My God, my strength, in whom I will trust."
"Let all those who seek You rejoice and be glad in You; Let such as love Your salvation say continually, 'The Lord be magnified.' "

Benediction:
Lord, we love You because You first loved us! You loved us first, last, and always. You loved us from the foundations of the world, to the depths of the cross, and to the endless reaches of eternity. May we go from this place with Your love in our heart to serve You this week. In Jesus' Name. Amen.

Additional Sermons and Lesson Ideas

Be a Man
By Rev. Billie Friel

Date preached:

SCRIPTURE: 1 Samuel 4:9

INTRODUCTION: The Philistine leaders rallied their fearful troops with the challenge: "Take courage and be men, O Philistines. . . " (v. 9). These words have been passed down through the ages, "Be a man." What does a real man look like?

1. Be a Protector. The "strong man" in each home (Mark 3:27) is the man, the husband, the father. He protects his family physically, morally, and spiritually.
2. Be a Provider. The real heroes in society are those men who earn their money through sweat (Gen. 3:19), pay their bills, and provide for the needs of their family. A man who doesn't provide for his family has denied the faith (1 Tim. 5:8).
3. Be a Partner. If married, a top priority for a real man is caring for his wife (Eph. 5:25). Men, honor your wives! (1 Peter 3:7).
4. Be a Priest. The priest represents God to man and man to God. Job was a priest to his home, offering sacrifices each day (Job 1:4). Men need to lead the family time of devotion. A real man prays daily for his family.

CONCLUSION: "Be on the alert, stand firm in the faith, act like men, be strong" (1 Cor. 16:13, NASB).

What About Israel?

Date preached:

SCRIPTURE: Romans 9—11

INTRODUCTION: Christians trace the roots of their faith to Israel, the nation chosen by God to bring the Messiah into the world. What is God's role for Israel now and later?

1. We Should Mourn Israel's Past Rejection of Christ (Rom. 9:1–4): "I tell the truth in Christ, I am not lying . . . I have great sorrow and continual grief in my heart. For I could wish that I myself were accursed from Christ for my brethren, my countrymen according to the flesh, who are Israelites . . ."
2. We Should Evangelize Because of Israel's Current Need for Christ (Rom. 10:9): ". . . if you confess with your mouth the Lord Jesus and believe in your heart that God has raised Him from the dead, you will be saved."
3. We Should Anticipate Israel's Future Glory in Christ (Rom. 11:25–26): ". . . blindness in part has happened to Israel until the fullness of the Gentiles has come in. And so all Israel will be saved . . ." (see Zech. 12:10; 13:1).

CONCLUSION: "Oh, the depth of the riches both of the wisdom and knowledge of God! . . . For of Him and through Him and to Him are all things, to whom be glory forever. Amen!" (Rom. 11:33, 36).

MARCH 12, 2006

SUGGESTED SERMON

A Foot in Two Worlds
Date preached:

Scripture: Romans 13, especially verse 1:
Let every soul be subject to the governing authorities.

Introduction: It's a vexing thing—being a Christian in this world. We're citizens of a nation here on earth, but Philippians 3:20 tells us that our citizenship is also in heaven. We have a foot in both worlds. Romans 13 helps us keep it all in balance. The apostle could have ended Romans with its theological section, drawing his book to a conclusion with chapter 11. It would have remained the greatest systematic theology on the doctrine of justification in human literature. But it would have been incomplete from God's perspective. Doctrine is never an end unto itself, for it provides vital teachings to apply to Christian living. The purpose of good doctrine is to produce happy, holy lives. Having given us such great theological truths in chapters 1–11, Paul devoted the rest of Romans to the implications of that theology in our daily lives. It's all about relationships. Romans 12 tells us about our relationship with God (vv. 1–2), ourselves (vv. 3–8), other Christians (vv. 9–16), and our enemies (vv. 17–20). Now Romans 13 continues along these lines.

1. **Listen to Your Leaders (vv. 1–7).** These verses addressed Christians in the imperial city of first-century Rome, telling them to be good citizens, to listen to their leaders, obey the laws, and pay their taxes. Paul gave two reasons: First, by doing so we stay out of trouble. Second, God built an authority structure into all the universe and ordained the concept of government. Without government we have nothing but anarchy. Regard for governing authorities implies respect for the authority of God Himself. Paul didn't deal here with what happens if the government violates our Christian rights and responsibilities. That principle is found in Acts 5:29. The emphasis in Romans 13 is on going as far as possible in respecting the government God has placed over us..

2. **Love Your Neighbors (vv. 8–10).** Christians should be developing pleasant souls. We should think more of other people and less about ourselves. Roland Hill used to say that he wouldn't believe a man to be a true

Christian if his wife, his children, the servants, and even the dog and cat, were not the better for it. Gordon MacDonald was walking down the street with a missionary friend when he made a derogatory comment about a mutual acquaintance. The missionary immediately rebuked him, saying: "Gordon, a man of God would not say such a thing about another person." MacDonald later wrote, "That rebuke stung and I lived with its pain for many days afterward. But I will always be thankful for that rebuke, painful as it was, because I hear those words every time I am about to embarrass myself with a needless comment about another person." That's a lesson we should all practice.

3. **Live Out Your Faith (vv. 11–14).** In verse 12, Paul tells us to put on the armor of light, and in verse 14 he tells us to put on the Lord Jesus Christ, making no provision for the flesh. Think of it as getting dressed in the morning. We should look into the mirror of His Word (James 1:23–25), and consciously "put on" Christ. Dr. Stephen Olford says that every morning he has a quiet time. "I have a simple procedure," he said. "I read from Genesis to Revelation. When I reach Revelation I go back to Genesis. Even though I have read it over the years, there's never a morning with God that He does not reveal something new to me. I let the Lord speak to me, showing me in His Word a promise to keep, a prayer to echo, a command to obey, a sin to confess, etc. I personalize it entirely and write in that form. And then I like to take what I have written and loosely turn that into prayer. There is a carry-over of the attitude of prayer that marks the rest of the day. I never pick up a telephone without a prayer. I never dictate a letter to my secretary without a prayer. I never let anybody out of my study without a prayer. It is literally praying without ceasing." That is putting on the Lord Jesus Christ, making no provision for the flesh to fulfill its lusts.

Conclusion: "I beseech you, therefore, brethren, by the mercies of God, that you present your bodies a living sacrifice, holy, acceptable to God, which is your reasonable service. And do not be conformed to this world, but be transformed by the renewing of your mind, that you may prove what is the good and acceptable and perfect will of God." (Romans 12:1–2)

STATS, STORIES AND MORE

From time to time, I've told some of my college-era stories about being in the home of Billy and Ruth Graham. I had the rare and wonderful opportunity of spending weekends in their home in Montreat, North Carolina. On my first visit there, I was sort of a pitiful young man, still trying to get established in my Christian life. Sometime during the weekend, I think it was Sunday afternoon, I walked by the den and Ruth had just sat down for the first time all weekend. She had been a beehive of activity, and there was an old movie on television. I knew that she rarely watched television, but she had sat down for a few moments to watch the old movie "Gigi." I didn't know any better, and I was full of questions about the Christian life. This was the first time I had seen Ruth alone, so I sauntered into the den and when she looked up, I said, "Ruth, can I talk to you for a few minutes." Instantly the television was off and I had her total attention. And the answers she gave me and the words she said have stayed with me all these years. But the older I get, the thing that impressed me was how quickly she dropped her own interests to attend to my needs. A few moments of relaxation instantly dropped in order to attend to my needs. I've never forgotten that. And sometimes I'm ashamed that I'm not as charitable with those who interrupt me as she was with me. The essence of love is putting the needs of another person—maybe your husband or your wife— before your own. And that is the fulfillment of the law.

APPROPRIATE HYMNS AND SONGS

A New Creature, L. O. Sanderson/Thomas O. Chisholm, 1935. Renewal 1963 L. O. Sanderson

All of Me, Mosie Lister, 1973 Lillenas Publishing Company (Admin. by The Copyright Company)

Call to Holiness, Dwight Liles/Niles Borop, 1985 Word Music, Inc. (a division of Word Music Group, Inc.)

I Will Follow, John Barbour/Anne Barbour, 1991 Maranatha Praise, Inc.

Channels Only, Mary E. Maxwell/Ada Rose Gibbs, Public Domain

Today is the birthday in 1607 of Paul Gerhardt, who might be called the "Charles Wesley of Germany," for he was a prolific hymnist who gave Lutheranism some of its warmest hymns. His hymnody reflects the shift from the rugged theological hymns of Luther to the more subjective, devotional songs of German Pietistic revival. Best known are "Give to the Winds Your Fears," "Jesus, Thy Boundless Love to Me," and "O Sacred Head, Now Wounded". ❀ On March 12, 1812, missionary Joshua Marshman entered a Calcutta classroom where William Carey was teaching. "I can think of no easy way to break the news," he said. "The print shop burned to the ground last night. Gone were Carey's massive polyglot dictionary, two grammar books, and whole versions of the Bible, along with sets of type for 14 eastern languages, 1200 reams of paper, 55,000 printed sheets, and 30 pages of his Bengal dictionary. Gone was his complete library. "The work of years — gone in a moment," he whispered. He took little time to mourn. "The loss is heavy," he wrote, "but as traveling a road the second time is usually done with greater ease and certainty than the first time, so I trust the work will lose nothing of real value. We are not discouraged; indeed the work is already begun again in every language. We are cast down but not in despair."

❀ Robert Lowry, American Baptist clergyman and hymn writer, was born on March 12, 1826. ❀ March 12, 1843, Robert Murray McCheyne preached his last sermon on this day. ❀ Father Gutilio Grande, one of the best known and loved priests of El Salvador, left home on March 12, 1977, to celebrate mass in an outlying church. His car was ambushed and he was killed, along with two companions. He has been called "El Salvador's First Christian Martyr."

WORSHIP HELPS

Call to Worship:
My voice You shall hear in the morning, O Lord; In the morning I will direct it to You, and I will look up.
Psalm 5:2

Pastoral Prayer:
Heavenly Father, So often we pray over our own requests and forget that You have made some prayer requests of Your own in Scripture. You've asked us, for example, to pray for our leaders and for those in authority over us. This morning we ask You to grant safety, strength, wisdom, and guidance to our president, to our congress, and to our Supreme Court. Give them the ability to see things from Your perspective and to make decisions that reflect Your standards of truth and righteousness. Bless the mayor of our city, and the members of our city council. Protect our service men and women scattered around the globe who are protecting the cause of freedom and advancing the cause of liberty. Protect our police officers, our emergency medical personnel, our public servants, and our local authorities. Bless our nation, O Lord, and raise up wise leaders. Send us revival. We pray in Jesus' Name, Amen.

Kids Talk

This would be a good Sunday to invite one of your members who is a police officer, fire fighter, paramedic, or local government official to join you with the children. Introduce the person and say a word about how important his or her job is. Tell the children that this person is serving the Lord just as much as a preacher or missionary (Rom. 13:1). Lead the children in praying for that person.

Additional Sermons and Lesson Ideas

Dealing with Satan's Strategy: Part 1

By Pastor J. David Hoke

Date preached:

SCRIPTURE: Various

INTRODUCTION: Do you feel like everywhere you turn there is another temptation? Does it seem like there's always an opportunity to make a quick and sinful decision? We learn in Genesis 3 that Satan is crafty. He often makes sneak attacks rather than head-on assaults. I want to share two short messages on how to deal with his strategy as we learn from Scripture.

1. Understand the Source (James 1:13–14). God does not tempt us in any way.
2. Understand the Power (James 1:14). The word in verse 14 for "enticed" is a fishing term for throwing out bait; Satan and our own evil desires "bait" the hook of sin to make it look harmless and appetizing.
3. Understand the Escape (1 Corinthians 10:13). No temptation is irresistible to the Christian. Christ in us is the way of escaping temptation!

CONCLUSION: God always provides a way to escape temptation in His grace. Keep your eyes fixed on Him.

Dealing with Satan's Strategy: Part 2

By Pastor J. David Hoke

Date preached:

SCRIPTURE: Various

INTRODUCTION: We often see and feel the effects of Satan's strategy to draw us into sin through the world and through ourselves. Understanding the source, the power, and the escape of Satan's strategy, we should also look at five ways to handle temptation as given in Scripture.

1. We Must Be Aware of His Strategy (2 Cor. 2:11). Don't be caught off guard; Satan is crafty and will trick you any way he can.
2. We Must Anticipate His Attacks (1 Peter 5:8). Don't allow the enemy to implement a surprise attack. Guard yourself in Christ at all times.
3. We Must Guard Our Minds (2 Cor. 11:3; 1 Peter 1:13; Rom. 12:2).
4. We Must Know Our Limitations (1 Cor. 1:12–13). Know your limitations and stay away from tempting situations.
5. We Must Depend on God's Resources (2 Cor. 10:3–5).

CONCLUSION: The next time Satan mounts an attack against you, see it for what it is and refuse to be fooled by his trickery. Instead, take your stand against him (Eph. 6:11).

CONVERSATIONS IN A PASTOR'S STUDY
The Pastor's Correspondence / Calvin Miller

The popularity of e-mail has made letter writing a lost art, but there's still a place for personal, hand-written notes in the pastor's ministry, isn't there?

Yes, there is. In fact, I believe there's a place for all kinds of personal correspondence that doesn't go through a keyboard or across a screen. There's something about holding a pen in your hand. The word is serif—the flourish that comes at the end of the line because you said something that needed to be said, and you held the ink when you said it—that's what's missing now. Electronic mail is busy and it's business—it doesn't have a heartbeat, it doesn't have perspiration. It's dead. And we read it as dead men, and then we pitch it.

How can pastors think through what they're saying so that every handwritten letter has its own individual touch?

I think the way to make that happen is to start with the life of the person you address. When our thank you notes, or any kind of correspondence, begin to get a commonality about them, it is because it arises from within us, not from beyond us. I think when we talk to a church member and we start from their orientation—what are they doing this morning, what's wrong with their lives—if we can write where they are, then our notes are all going to sound differently because they begin with the recipient and not the author.

Do you like to include Scripture in your notes?

Well, I am a very biblically oriented person and like to use Scripture when appropriate. If you refer to a Scripture and put the citation in parenthesis, your reader can look up the passage if he or she wants to. But the Scripture passage utilizes the voice of God.

A lot of pastors have to write church newsletters. What makes a monthly or weekly newsletter special, readable, or of interest?

The number one thing I'd say is that if you really want that newsletter article to be beautiful, don't make it promotional. Virtually every one I read involves the pastor's pushing something. He's pushing the program, the next picnic, the next *Forty Days of Purpose*; he's pushing some agenda. If you want it to be read, recount the stories of your love for the congregation or a hospital call with someone that week. I think it really works well when a pastor can get creative.

Sometimes in writing, less is more.

Less is more. It's interesting that for less to be more it has to be creative, maybe even poetic. A pastor who wants a short, readable column needs to struggle a little with verb usage and synonym siphoning. Learn to pick the most powerful words. Learn to become a creative writer. Then when less becomes more, people will read it and it will become memorable.

A lot of pastors would like to be published. Would you give two or three pieces of advice for someone who is just beginning to write for publication?

Well, I think when you're just beginning, write for a publication that's near at hand, if you can, like your city newspaper or if you have a friend within the denomination who is in charge of the denominational paper. If you do that, the likelihood of being published is a lot greater. Second, you probably know your audience, and therefore what you say is going to be pretty applicable. If you start sending in a huge column to one of the big magazines and aiming for that little window of acceptance, it can defeat you since they don't know you and you don't know them. Start somewhere close.

MARCH 19, 2006

Honoring Our Parents

Date preached:

By Dr. Melvin Worthington

SCRIPTURE: Exodus 20:12:
Honor your father and your mother, that your days may be long upon the land which the LORD your God is giving you.

Introduction: The first Commandment guards the unity of God, the second guards the spirituality of God, the third guards the deity of God, the fourth guards the day we worship God, and the fifth guards the ordained authority given by God. Parents are God's instruments to teach and train children. God's authority belongs to the parents. Our duty toward our parents is detailed in this Commandment. It is not an arbitrary but natural principle. The family, human government, and the church are three God-ordained institutions for the good of human society. The family is the foundation of society, and submission to authority begins in the family. Children have two responsibilities regarding their parents: (1) a temporary responsibility that requires obedience and (2) a timeless responsibility that requires respect. One is passing while the other is permanent.

1. **The Admonition in the Text.** The general principle enjoined is that we should feel and act in a loving manner, in a becoming manner toward our superiors. It is the will of God. The nature of the relationship and the moral order of society depend on submission to authority. Parents are *representatives of God, responsible to God,* and *a reflection of God.* Children who honor and obey their parents are promised *prolonged days, prosperous days,* and *pleasurable days.* Children who disrespect, disobey, and despise their parents will be judged by God.

2. **The Analysis of the Text.** The analysis deals first with the *representatives:* the children are addressed with a command. Often we view the Bible's mandates strictly in the sense of adults. Children of all ages also have responsibility to heed the words of Scripture. The *responsibilities* are noted in the text as well. The word "honor" commands a great deal of responsibility on behalf of the child. The parents, it should be noted, are

responsible to be honorable. The *rationale* and the *reward* for this command are simple. Children should honor their parents, otherwise a generation of unruly and ungodly people will arise. A child who never honors his parents is in danger much more often than not. In Moses' day one of the dangers of disobeying one's parents likely included wandering off into foreign territory. If a child were to play with a snake in the desert despite parental warnings, he or she might encounter a poisonous foe. The list could go on and on. In our culture, we see the deadly effects of not honoring one's parents. Increased suicide rates, drug use, sexually transmitted diseases, and many more dangers await those who go their own way rather than honoring their parents' instructions. God promised the Israelites who honored their parents a long life in the promised land. We too can experience this blessing through obedience to this command.

3. **The Application from the Text.** This command holds implications for parents as well as for children. Parents should be worthy of honor. They must learn to *listen, love, lead,* and *wisely lecture* their children. By *precept, promises,* and *pattern* parents can effectively bring up their children in the nurture and admonition of the Lord. There is an implication for very young children, and this is a great verse to teach to toddlers. Children should learn the importance of obedience early in life. In adolescence children are required to render *obedience to* their parents, though they are also becoming increasingly responsible for their own choices. There does come a time, as Scripture indicates, for children to move away from the rules of their parents' home and to begin their start home: "For this reason a man shall leave his father and his mother, and be joined to his wife; and they shall become one flesh" (Gen. 2:24). In adulthood, however, children are required to *show respect* to their parents.

Conclusion: The Lord Jesus Christ is our example of obeying this commandment (Luke 2:51; John 8:29). Children honor their parents when they love, respect, and obey them. Since all of us have parents, we must honor our parents all of our lives. Listen to the words of Scripture and honor your parents in whatever way you can.

STATS, STORIES AND MORE

"God's reason for giving the fifth Commandment was to train us to be honorable people. The first lessons are learned in the home and continue as a lifelong process. When we reach adulthood and begin to build our own homes as fathers and mothers, we still are obligated to honor the parents God gave us. The experience of the human family over the ages indicates that those who behave in an honorable manner toward their parents become honorable people in adulthood"—Stephen V. Rexroat, *For Our Good: The Ten Commandments from a Positive Perspective* (Issaquah, Washington: Sammamish Press, 1990, p. 59).

"Young man, if your parents are still living, treat them kindly. Do all you can to make their declining years sweet and happy. Bear in mind that this is the only command that you may not always be able to obey. As long as you live, you will be able to serve God, to keep the Sabbath, to obey all the other commandments; but the day comes to most men when father and mother die. What bitter feelings you will have when the opportunity has gone by if you fail to show them the respect and love that is their due! How long is it since you wrote to your mother?"—D. L. Moody, *On the Ten Commandments* (Chicago: Moody Press, 1896, p. 72).

"O children and young people, give serious thought to this solemn command in God's Word. You cannot afford to trifle with it. If you would enjoy the blessing of God, if you would please God, if you would partake of the promised reward of God, then I exhort you to give prayerful consideration to the instruction of your parents. Honor and reverence your father and your mother. They are God's gifts to you."—Lehman Strauss, *The Eleven Commandments* (Neptune, NJ: Loizeaux Brothers, 1946, p. 92).

APPROPRIATE HYMNS AND SONGS

Take Time to be Holy, William D. Longstaff/Shelly Hamilton, 1984 Musical Ministries, Inc. (a division of Majesty Music, Inc.)

Trust and Obey, Rev. John H. Sammis/Daniel B. Towner, Public Domain

With All My Heart, Babbie Mason, 1990 Word Music Group, Inc. (a division of Word Music Group, Inc.)

Yes Lord Yes, Lynn Keesecker, 1983 Manna Music, Inc. ARR UBP of Music Manna, Inc.

Purify My Heart, Jeff Nelson, 1993 Maranatha Praise Music, Inc./HeartService Music, Inc. (Admin. by Music Services)

On this day in 1229, during the sixth crusade, Holy Roman Emperor Frederick II entered the Church of the Holy Sepulcher and crowned himself king. But on the same day, the Catholic patriarch of Jerusalem pronounced an interdict over the city. Frederick was pelted with garbage as he made his way home. ❁ John Hopper, British Reformation hero, faced mounting persecution after the death of King Edward VI and the ascension of Queen "Bloody" Mary. He was seized and thrown into Fleet Prison. "I have been sick," he wrote, "the doors, bars, hasps, and chains, being all closed and made fast upon me. I have mourned, called and cried for help." After languishing in prison for eighteen months, he was called before five bishops and the Queen Commissioners on March 19, 1554, and stripped of his bishopric. He was later burned at the stake in front of seven thousand people. ❁ Today is the birthday, in 1589, of William Bradford. ❁ On March 19, 1711, clergyman and hymnist Thomas Ken, died in England. He is best known for writing an early English hymn for boys to sing at the opening and close of day during their personal devotions. The singing of public hymns was not yet popular in England. Ken's private hymn for boys ended with the words, "Praise God for whom all blessings flow . . ." and is today one of the world's best-known hymns—the Doxology. ❁ Missionary David Livingstone was born on March 19, 1813, and William Jennings Bryan was born on this day in 1860.

Call to Worship:
"You know me, Master GOD, just as I am. You've done all this not because of who I am but because of who you are—out of your very heart!—but you've let me in on it. This is what makes you so great, Master GOD! There is none like you, no God but you, nothing to compare with what we've heard with our own ears."
2 Samuel 7:21–22, the *Message*

Hymn Story: The Doxology
Thomas Ken died on this day, March 19, in 1711. He was the first of the great writers of English hymns, but he wrote his hymns at a time when English congregations only sang the Psalms of Scripture. As a result, he recommended his hymns for private use in one's personal daily devotions. In 1674, he wrote a book of suggested devotional helps for university students. Included was a great hymn entitled, "Awake My Soul and with the Sun." The last stanza of this hymn said: "Praise God from whom all blessings flow; praise Him all creatures here below; praise Him above ye heavenly hosts; praise Father, Son, and Holy Ghost." It was one of the first English hymns ever written, and it is still one of the best known. Unfortunately the great body of Ken's hymn has been largely forgotten, but it's a great poem for us on this Sunday morning. It says, in part:

Awake, my soul, and with the sun
Thy daily stage of duty run;
Shake off dull sloth, and joyful rise,
To pay thy morning sacrifice.

Lord, I my vows to Thee renew;
Disperse my sins as morning dew.
Guard my first springs of thought and will,
And with Thyself my spirit fill.

Direct, control, suggest, this day,
All I design, or do, or say,
That all my powers, with all their might,
In Thy sole glory may unite.

Additional Sermons and Lesson Ideas

Kept by God
By Rev. Billie Friel

Date preached:

SCRIPTURE: 1 Peter 1:5

INTRODUCTION: People are insecure. Many people protect themselves by elaborate alarm systems or sophisticated locks. What about our salvation—are we secure? The Bible says we are "kept by the power of God." We are "kept" by . . .

1. Christ's Promises. Note "not perish" in John 3:15, "lose nothing" in John 6:39, the seven-strand rope of security in John 10:28–30, and the seventeen things that cannot separate the believer from Christ in Romans 8:35–39.
2. Christ's Prayers. Jesus' effectual prayers enable believers to persevere (see 1 Peter 1:9, 11, 15). Believers are kept by Christ's prayers (see Luke 22:31–32).
3. Christ's Priesthood. Our Savior continues to support and sustain the saved through His priesthood ministry (Heb. 7:23–25). As our High Priest, Jesus continues forever and makes intercession for us.
4. Christ's Presence. Jesus would never leave or forsake us (Heb. 13:15). The believer, at salvation, is sealed with the Holy Spirit (Eph. 1:13) until the day of redemption (Eph. 4:30; see also John 14:15, 17).

CONCLUSION: Nothing is safe from loss except that which is kept by the power of God.

Honoring God with your Body
By Dr. Timothy Beougher

Date preached:

SCRIPTURE: 1 Corinthians 6:12–20

INTRODUCTION: If we were to add up the total number of sexual images we see every day, we would quickly realize that our culture is enslaved to sex. We aren't the first culture who had this infatuation, however. Let's look at how Paul addressed this problem in the Corinthian church.

1. Rationalizations for moral permissiveness (vv. 12–14)
   A. The argument from "liberty" (v. 12)
   B. The argument from "nature" (vv. 13–14)
2. Reasons for moral purity (vv. 15–20)
   A. The priority of our spiritual relationship (vv. 15–17)
   B. The prominence of sexual sin (v. 18)
   C. The presence of the Holy Spirit in our lives (v. 19a)
   D. The price of our redemption (vv. 19b–20)

CONCLUSION: Accept God's standards; they are for your benefit. God gives us His guidelines not to rob us of fulfillment but to lead us to true fulfillment, which ultimately is found only in Him.

MARCH 26, 2006

SUGGESTED SERMON

Cleansed by the Word

Date preached:

By Rev. Richard Sharpe

Scripture: John 15:1–11, especially verse 4:
Abide in Me, and I in you. As the branch cannot bear fruit of itself, unless it abides in the vine, neither can you, unless you abide in Me.

Introduction: Do you ever wonder how you could be more effective? Do you feel like your life is "dry," that you don't really accomplish much? Today we will study the words of Jesus as He walked with His disciples, teaching them how to remain fruitful. Perhaps this is just what you need to hear today. This passage is the last of the seven "I am" statements in John's Gospel. These were to show that Christ was equal with the "I am" of the Old Testament. This was to show that He is one Person of the Trinity—He was God the Son and equal with the Father. In this passage Jesus teaches us the importance of fruitfulness in the Christian life. Let's look at this word picture.

1. **No Fruit: Takes Away (vv. 2, 6).** In verse 2 "takes away" means that the branch can be raised up or lifted up. There have been many interpretations of this phrase. Verse 6 helps us understand a little more about what is being talked about in this verse: "If anyone does not abide in Me, he is thrown away as a branch and dries up; and they gather them, and throw them into the fire, and they are burned." One possible interpretation is that the individual in the verse is saved but stops being fruitful. The Father sees the unfruitful branch and has it removed. This individual is still saved but "so as through fire" (see 1 Cor. 3:15; 11:30; 1 John 5:16, 17; 1 Peter 4:17).

2. **Fruit: Prunes (vv. 2, 16).** The word translated "prunes" means "to make clean" and in a moral sense it refers to freeing us from sin's defilement. Jesus revealed that the cleansing agent is the Word of God (v. 3). Christ spoke the words of God to His disciples and they received cleansing through His words. We have the whole Bible to read; how much more will it cleanse us from our sins if we follow and apply it daily! Once we have produced fruit, the Father wants us to produce more fruit.

3. **More Fruit: Abide in Him (vv. 4–5).** The word "abide" means "to remain, tarry, stay." We are to remain in the presence of Christ on a regular basis. This is done through our reading and applying the Word of God. Our relationship with Christ is based on a daily commitment to take up our cross and follow Him. These verses make it plain that we can do "nothing" without the help of the vine, which is Jesus (v. 5). Christ is the vine in that He gives us life and energy. Without Him we have no life or energy. He is our source of strength; we need to trust in Him alone. Christ tells us that the way to remain or abide in Him is to obey the commandments He has given. Obedience is the key.

4. **Much Fruit: Father Glorified (vv. 7–8).** We have moved from no fruit to fruit to more fruit to much fruit. The process is hard. The pruning of the branches means there will be some times of suffering and sorrow for the individual Christian. However, this is the only way that a Christian can grow. If times are easy, we tend to trust in self rather than in God. He wants us to depend totally on Him. All of the children He has He prunes. Once He prunes us we will turn to Him on a regular basis. When we ask of Him, He will answer. When we see answered prayer, we are encouraged to move forward in our service to Him. He is glorified and we manifest his brightness to the world. We are the light of the world. We are His disciples.

Conclusion: As we produce fruit and see the Lord glorified, it brings us joy (v. 11). The Lord wants our joy to be full. He has promised that everything, good or bad, that happens to us is ultimately for our good. We need to be content with what He sends our way and have a simple desire to be fruitful for Him.

STATS, STORIES AND MORE

Hudson Taylor opened the interior of China to the gospel as no missionary had done before, but the effort brought him to the brink of collapse. A letter from fellow missionary John McCarthy turned the tide. The secret to inner victory, said McCarthy is "abiding, not striving nor struggling; looking off to Him, trusting Him for present power." Taylor read those words in a little mission station at Chin-kiang on an autumn Saturday in 1869, and "as I read, I saw it all. I looked to Jesus; and when I saw, oh how the joy flowed." John 15 took center stage in his life as he realized the joy of abiding in Christ. He later wrote: "As to work, mine was never so plentiful or so difficult; but the weight and strain are now gone. The last month has been perhaps the happiest in my life; and I long to tell you a little of what the Lord has done for my soul.

"As I read (McCarthy's letter) I looked to Jesus and saw that He had said, "I will never leave you." Ah, there is rest. For has he not promised to abide with me? As I thought of the Vine and the branches, what light the blessed Spirit poured into my soul!"

O to abide in Jesus,
Never to faint nor fall;
Clinging to Him Who loves me,
Trusting my all in all.
O for a heart to praise Him,
O for a tongue to sing
Glory to Him Who saves me,
Jesus my Lord and King.
(Fanny Crosby, 1896)

APPROPRIATE HYMNS AND SONGS

Thy Word, Amy Grant/Michael W. Smith, 1984 Meadowgreen Music Company (Admin. by EMI Christian Music Publishing)/Word Music, Inc. (a division of Word Music Group, Inc.)

Standing on the Promises, R. Kelso Carter, Public Domain

How Firm A Foundation, George Keith/ Anne Steele/ John Rippon/ Joseph Funk, Public Domain

The Word, Michael Card, 1988 Birdwing Music (a division of EMI Christian Music Publishing)/ Mole End Music (Admin. by EMI Christian Music Publishing)

Wonderful Words of Life, Philip P. Bliss, Public Domain

The first English-born Archbishop of Canterbury, Deusdedit, was born on March 26, 655. ❀ Cuthbert, a now-famous English monk, was born to a shepherding family in Northumbria about the year 630. Little is known of his early life until he entered a Scottish monastery in Melrose at about age 20. By 684, his reputation for holiness had become widespread; and on March 26, 685, Cuthbert was consecrated Bishop of Hexham. He spent his remaining days in public ministry, traveling around the diocese, preaching, converting sheep farmers in the Northumbrian hills, and distributing alms. ❀ On March 26, 1409, the Council of Pisa assembled in an attempt to solve the problem of two rival popes laying claim to the Western Christian world. Over 500 prelates attended. Both popes were deposed as heretics, and the Council elected a new pope, Alexander V. But the two existing popes, Gregory XII and Benedict XIII, refused to resign, resulting in three popes laying claim to Christianity. ❀ Today is the birthday, in 1700, of Nickolaus Ludwig von Zinzendorf, founder of the Moravians and the leader of the Moravian community at Herrnhut, famous for its missionary zeal. ❀ The first Sunday newspaper in Britain began publication on this day in 1780, the "British Gazette & Sunday Monitor." ❀ Today marks the death in 1831 of Richard Allen, the first African-American Methodist bishop in the United States. Allen had been born into slavery in Philadelphia in 1780. He was converted at age 17 and purchased his freedom some time later. He began preaching and was ordained in 1784. He later founded the African Methodist Episcopal Church and became the first black bishop in America. He was 71 when he died.

WORSHIP HELPS

Call to Worship:
How good it is to thank the Lord,
And praise to Thee, Most High, accord,
To show Thy love with morning light,
And tell Thy faithfulness each night.
From the Psalter (1912).

Offertory comment
Someone quipped, "The most expensive vehicle to operate per mile is—the shopping cart." As we receive this morning's tithes and offerings, it's a good time for us to remember that we are stewards. Our money all belongs to Him, and we should use it wisely that we may have more to give.

Hymn Story:
One of our greatest spiritual songs of guidance, "He Leadeth Me," was written on this day in 1862. The author, Joseph H. Gilmore, gave this account of how it came to be written:
"I was supplying for a couple of Sundays the pulpit of the First Baptist Church in Philadelphia. At the mid-week service, on the 26th of March, 1862, I set out to give the people an exposition of the Twenty-third Psalm, which I had given before on three or four occasions, but this time I did not get further than the words 'He Leadeth Me.' Those words took hold of me as they had never done before, and I saw them in a significance . . . of which I had never dreamed. It was the darkest hour of the Civil War. I did not refer to that fact—that is, I don't think I did—but it may subconsciously have led me to realize that God's leadership is the one significant fact in human experience. . . . At the close of the meeting . . . on a blank page of the brief from which I had intended to speak, I penciled the hymn, talking and writing at the same time, then handed it to my wife and thought no more about it.

Additional Sermons and Lesson Ideas

The Carpenter

Date preached:

SCRIPTURE: Mark 6:3

INTRODUCTION: Why a carpenter? He could have come as a king, a shepherd, a rabbi, a priest, or a physician. All would have been appropriate. But a carpenter?

1. He Came to Build a Gate to Heaven. It required hammers, nails, and the wood of the cross, the very implements Jesus knew so well.
2. He Came to Build a Temple in Three Days (John 2:19–22).
3. He Came to Build His Church (Matt. 16:18).
4. He Came to Build Us. We are God's building, His workmanship (1 Cor. 3:9).
5. He Came to Build Us an Eternal Dwelling Place (John 14:3; Heb. 11:10).

CONCLUSION: Visualize Him today, wearing His workman's apron, wielding hammers and nails, busy on your behalf—the Carpenter of Nazareth. He can straighten bent nails, sand rough surfaces, clean dirty timbers, and make a beautiful temple of your life. He who has begun a good work in you will carry it on to completion (Phil. 1:6).

Overcoming Ambiguity

By Rev. Todd M. Kinde

Date preached:

Scripture: James 5:12

INTRODUCTION: Do you ever get frustrated with "fine print"? Maybe you can't stand it when someone lies to you through a half-truth. James teaches us that simplicity and honesty of Christian speech honors the name of the Lord.

1. The Complexity of Speech (5:12a).
2. The Clarity of Speech (5:12b).

CONCLUSION: What is forbidden is an exaggerated defense of yourself to convince others that you are right. It is also not proper to speak with ambiguity and generalization so that no one knows what you really think or feel. The pattern of Christian speech is unconditional truthfulness with sincerity and simplicity, avoiding all deception. You will be judged for every word that comes from your mouth (Matt. 12:36–37).

HEROES FOR THE PASTOR'S HEART
Robert Raikes

For over two hundred years, Sunday schools have provided biblical training, fellowship, and pastoral care for millions of children, youth, and adults. It has been one of Christian history's greatest success stories, and much of the credit goes to Robert Raikes, an eighteenth century newspaper publisher.

Raikes was born in 1735 in Gloucester, England where his father published the *Gloucester Journal*. When the elder Raikes died in 1757, Robert inherited the newspaper at age twenty-two and immediately used it to crusade for moral reform. English prisons, for example, were inhumane places of misery where prisoners, crowded into tiny compartments with no ventilation or sanitary facilities, died of "gaol fever," a form of typhus. Raikes visited them, raised money for them, taught them to read, and provided books. His penetrating newspaper columns repeatedly called attention to their plight.

One Saturday afternoon in 1780, Robert discovered another cause to champion. He entered a slummy suburb of Gloucester to interview a prospective gardener. Swarms of children surrounded him, and Raikes recoiled in horror at their fighting, profanity, stench, gambling, and filth. He returned home deeply shaken and almost immediately conceived a plan for Sunday schools. Such schools had already been tried, but without widespread backing. Raikes hired four Christian women to open schools on Sunday. Why Sunday? Children worked in the factories the other six days of the week, but on Sunday they ran wild.

The portly Raikes, primly dressed and carrying an elegant snuffbox and tasseled cane, ambled through the ghettoes day after day recruiting pupils. The children began calling him "Bobby Wild Goose." But in his Sunday schools, they were taught to read and then they learned the Bible, catechisms, and other subjects. Sunday school began at 10 a.m. and continued until 5:30 p.m., with breaks for worship and meals.

Three years later, after the schools were clearly working, Raikes used his newspaper to promote them. On November 3, 1783, the Gloucester Journal published an article on the success of Sunday schools. To Raikes' surprise, London papers picked up the story and inquiries poured in from across England. The Sunday school movement spread rapidly.

Then Raikes had another idea. An annual festival was held near Gloucester, and it was always packed with hard-drinking, rabble-rousing crowds. Raikes distributed curious leaflets inviting the people to the festival to witness "a novel sight." On Sunday, September 24, 1786, the crowds flocked in. There, standing before the church, were 331 clean, well-dressed Sunday school children. Many in the crowd had never before seen a clean, well-dressed child.

Raikes had persuaded his friend, Dr. Samuel Glasse, to prepare a special address. Glasse rose, looked at the throng, and preached a sermon from Deuteronomy 31:12–13—"Gather the people together, men and women and little ones, and the stranger who is within your gates, that they may hear and that they may learn to fear the LORD your God and carefully observe all the words of this law, and that their children, who have not known it, may hear and learn to fear the LORD Your God as long as you live. . . ."

Dr. Glasse's sermon swept across England in printed form under the title, "The Piety, Wisdom, and Policy of promoting Sunday Schools." The Sunday School movement was soon established, and in various forms it is still flourishing around the world to this day.

APRIL 2, 2006

A Farewell Challenge

Date preached:

By Rev. Todd M. Kinde

Scripture: Joshua 23:1–16, especially verses 14 and 11:
Therefore take careful heed to yourselves, that you love the LORD your God. . . . Behold, this day I am going the way of all the earth. And you know in all your hearts and in all your souls that not one thing has failed of all the good things which the Lord your God spoke concerning you. All have come to pass for you; not one word of them has failed.

Introduction: What kind of legacy will you leave your family? Do you spend your time trying to advance yourself, or do you truly invest in the eternal future of others? Joshua was nearing his death (v. 14) when he assembled the leaders of Israel to ensure that they understood the way things were to continue. The purpose of this farewell, this last will and testament, was to ensure the faithfulness of future generations to the God who had been faithful to them. This is the character of a patriarch, a family leader, and we can learn from it. We can learn to pass on the heritage of the faith to the next generation of disciples.

1. **Confident Assurance (vv. 1–5).** With fatherly care, Joshua assured the Israelites of God's presence and help. He based this confident assurance in what God had already done for them. On the basis of God's work in the past, there is the full expectation that God will continue to prove faithful in the future (vv. 3–5). Is your goal to motivate and cultivate in others a confident assurance of faith in God? Have you told them the mighty work of God in your life? Have you told them how Jesus has transformed your temperament and personality with the fullness of the Holy Spirit? As Joshua stated that Yahweh would drive out the enemy and give Israel the possession of God's inheritance, so Jesus promised the Holy Spirit to convict, comfort, strengthen, and guide His people into all truth (John 16:8–13). We should be living in light of these truths daily and sharing them with others!

2. **Careful Obedience (vv. 6–13).** Joshua gave specific instructions about maintaining faithfulness to Yahweh in careful obedience. He commanded, "Be

strong", "Be careful to obey", and "Hold fast to the Lord your God" (vv. 6, 8; NIV). Obedience comes by careful attention to the written Word of God (v. 6). The Scriptures alone are our rule for faith and practice. Israel was not to associate with nations around them who worship false gods (v. 7). Rather, Israel was to love the Lord her God (v.11). This is not racism or prejudice; this does not attempt to portray the Israelites as better than any other nation. It is a clear mandate that Israel was to love only one God, whose name is Yahweh. The New Testament teaches the church the same truth. We are to be separate from the world around us so as to be devoted unto Christ alone (Matt. 6:24; Titus 3:10; 1 Cor. 5:11–13; 2 Cor. 6:14–7:1; Rev. 18:1–5).

3. **Certain Judgment (vv. 14–16).** Joshua concluded his monologue with the theme of judgment. Our culture isn't accustomed to ending with the negative. In fact, we tend to avoid the negative. Here, however, Joshua warned His people, as a good fatherly leader should, that any breach of covenant, any persistent disobedience, or any replacement of God from the center of life would result in destruction.

Application: As Christians, we are all to live a life of assurance and faith. We should be recognized by our consistent devotion to the gospel and to spreading it; this should be the legacy we leave behind. Our lives should not only consist of assurance of faith, but of obedience to the Word of God; otherwise we have no testimony to others.

We must also live with discipline. Parents, begin to teach your children the truth of God's judgment by your own consistent discipline. When you threaten your children with punishment for disobedience, you should follow through when that rule is broken. This will instill in them the reality of God's discipline and judgment and prepare them for true repentance, for a life of faithful obedience to the Lord. Children and young adults who are still at home should receive the discipline of their parents with a good attitude and a spirit of humility and honor, for it is far better to learn obedience through the chastisement of their parents than to suffer an eternity in hell apart from Christ because they never learned to be faithful and obedient to Him (Rom. 1:28–31; 2 Tim. 2:25–3:5).

STATS, STORIES AND MORE

More from Pastor Kinde:

I remember the last conversation I had with my father. I did not know it would be the last. It was a telephone conversation. I was in one of my melancholy moods in deep searching as to what the Lord would have for my life and ministry. I don't remember the content of our talk. If I knew it would form the last words I would hear from my dad, I would have paid closer attention to the particular words. I do remember the tone. Dad was ever patient and ever hopeful, always wanting God's best for me but never pushing me in a certain direction. Of course, we had had many talks throughout the years and I continue to follow his counsel today.

On one of our respites this summer we were boating. I was holding my two-year-old son as we cruised slowly around the lake. He grabbed my thumb with his hand, so I wrapped my hand completely around his hand, squeezed it, and then quickly released. He smiled and placed his hand inside my open palm wanting me to keep hold of his hand as we skirted the surface of the water. As I held this little hand, my mind and heart were flooded with the thought, "What will these hands do?" I determined to write down my thoughts so that when he is older and wondering what God may be calling him to do he would understand it to be a divine vocation—whatever it may be. I desire him to see it as a divine vocation and so glorify God in it with all skill and integrity.

APPROPRIATE HYMNS AND SONGS

Blessed Assurance, Fanny J. Crosby/ Phoebe P. Knapp/ Dougles E. Wagner, 1989 Lorenz Publishing (a division of the Lorenz Corporation)

Amazing Grace, John Newton/ Edwin Excell/ John P. Rees, Public Domain

Because He Lives, William J. Gaither/ Gloria Gaither, 1971 William J. Gaither, Inc. ARR UBP of Gaither Copyright Management

Forever, Chris Tomlin, 2001 worshiptogether.com songs/Six Steps Music (Admin. by EMI Christian Music Publishing)

Great is Thy Faithfulness, Thomas O. Chisholm/William M. Runyan, 1923. Renewed 1951 Hope Publishing Company

FOR THE BULLETIN

April 2, 742 marks the birth of Charlemagne, founder of Holy Roman Empire. ✹ On this day in 1521, Reformer Martin Luther bravely set out from Wittenberg to appear at the Diet of Worms to be questioned about his writings. ✹ On April 2, 1524, Swiss reformer Ulrich Zwingli, 40, publicly married the widow Anna Reinhard. On this same day in 1549, another reformer, John Calvin, publicly mourned for his wife, Idelette. He wrote to a friend, "I do what I can to keep myself from being overwhelmed with grief." ✹ On April 2, 1739, John Wesley began preaching in the open air in Bristol, England. "I could scarce reconcile myself to this strange way of preaching in the fields," he wrote. "On Monday, April 2, I submitted to be more vile, and proclaimed in the highways the glad tidings of salvation, speaking from a little eminence adjoining the city, to about 3,000 people. I preached on 'Come to me all ye that are weary and heavy laden, and I will give you rest.' My load was gone, and all my doubts and scruples. God shone upon my path, and I knew this was His will concerning me." ✹ Today is the birthday (1877) of American evangelist Mordecai Ham. Among his converts was Billy Graham. ✹ April 2, 1894 marks the death of the author of the hymn, "Take Time to Be Holy." His name was William Longstaff, and he was an English philanthropist and a close friend of evangelist D. L. Moody.

WORSHIP HELPS

Call to Worship:
Clap your hands, all you nations; shout to God with cries of joy.
How awesome is the Lord Most High, the great King over all the
earth!
(Ps. 47:1–2)

Offertory Comments:
The Bible says we should resist being pressed into the mold of our
culture. We're to be different from the world (Rom. 12:2). At some
point, every Christian—including me—needs to ask: "Does my
bank account reflect the values of the kingdom or just the con-
sumer-orientation of this world?" We miss a tremendous blessing
if we do not give our consistent offerings to the Lord, for God loves
a cheerful giver (1 Cor. 9:7), He promises to abundantly bless us for
our generosity (Mal. 3:10), and He uses our generosity to further
His kingdom (Phil. 4:14–19)!

Scripture Medley
You therefore, my son, be strong in the grace that is in Christ Jesus.
And the things that you have heard from me among many witnesses, commit these to faithful men who will be able to teach others also. (2 Tim. 2:1–2)

Only take heed to yourself, and diligently keep yourself, lest you
forget the things your eyes have seen, and lest they depart form
your heart all the days of your life. And teach them to your children
and your grandchildren. (Deut. 4:9)

A posterity shall serve Him. It will be recounted to the Lord to
the next generation, they will come and declare His righteousness
to a people who will be born, that He has done this. (Ps. 22:30–31)

Additional Sermons and Lesson Ideas

Overcoming Sickness
By Rev. Todd M. Kinde

Date preached:

SCRIPTURE: James 5:13–20

INTRODUCTION: Physical illness may be a result of sin and of wandering from the faith. Healing and forgiveness come through the power of the Name of the Lord.

1. Invitation to Prayer (5:13–14).
2. Healing Prayer (5:15–16).
3. Prevailing Prayer (5:17–18).
4. Preserving Prayer (5:19–20).

CONCLUSION: We must make strides to be a redemptive community where healing can occur. We should provide opportunities to seek forgiveness of one another and of God. We should have seasons of prayer for one another: for those of us who are sick and for those of us who are in any trouble. We should enjoy singing in praise along with those who are cheerful in the Lord.

Our Great Assurance

Date preached:

SCRIPTURE: 1 John 2:1

INTRODUCTION: Ever have trouble forgiving yourself of past regrets? This verse gives us a great assurance.

1. Our Great Adversary: Sin—"if anyone sins."
2. Our Great Adventure: Victory—"that you may not sin." It's possible to have consistent victory over known sin. Sin should not have dominion over us. While we can't be perfect in this life, we can have steadfast victory.
3. Our Great Advantage: Scripture—"These things I have written to you that you may not sin."
4. Our Great Advocate: "And in anyone sins, we have an Advocate with the Father."

CONCLUSION: The reason we can forgive ourselves of past mistakes and regrets is simply this—His forgiveness is all encompassing, total, eternal, and final. The blood of Christ so thoroughly expunges our sins that it's a sin to keep bringing them up. They're gone. As Eliza Hewitt put it, "I need no other argument, I need no other plea; / It is enough that Jesus died, and that He died for me."

APRIL 9, 2006

PALM SUNDAY SUGGESTED SERMON

Four Men Who Found Christ   *Date preached:*

By Dr. David Jeremiah

Scripture: John 1:34–51, especially verse 46: . . . "Come and see."

Introduction: Jesus entered Jerusalem on Palm Sunday so long ago. But He arose from the dead and is still alive, still seeking souls, and He wants to enter your heart today, on this Palm Sunday. It's exciting to see people come to know Christ as Savior. There's only one way to God—through Jesus; but the Lord uses many methods to bring us to Himself. I remember a doctor who came to church out of duty. One day, returning home, his son asked him, "Daddy, why don't we have any Bibles at home?" God used that question to prick that man's conscience and to ultimately save his soul. Today's passage displays four cases that teach us different ways in which people come to Christ.

1. **Salvation Comes Through The Preaching of the Word of God (vv. 34–39).**
    John the Baptist told the multitudes, "Behold! The Lamb of God who takes away the sin of the world!" (John 1:29). In verse 36, speaking to two men, he said the same. John only had one string on his violin, and he plucked it both publicly and privately. Wherever John went, his purpose was to point others to Jesus. Some of you who are hearing the gospel today need to come to the Lamb of God who can take away your sins.

2. **Salvation Comes Through Personal Witness about the Savior (vv. 40–43)**
    This text introduces us to Andrew. Whenever he appears in the Bible, he's bringing someone to Jesus (John 1:41; 6:8–9; 12:22). Andrew never did a better day's work than when he brought his brother Peter to Christ. In the Book of Acts we see Peter standing before thousands and preaching the gospel. From a human perspective, he never would have been there had it not been for Andrew's personal witness. I feel a sense of overwhelming anticipation when God allows me to lead someone to Jesus because you never know if one you've brought to Christ might be the next great world evangelist.

3. **Salvation Comes Through a Pointed Encounter with the Savior (vv. 43–44).** Jesus approached Philip without any human instrumentality. It just says, "Jesus found Philip." That was it—the direct approach. I think Philip was retiring and shy, and the Lord came to him as he was, saying, "Philip, I want you to follow Me." And he did. I've talked to people who have come to Christ like that. I remember a young man who got saved at three o'clock in the morning. Right in the middle of the night, he sat up in bed and said, "I've got to be saved." God isn't confined to bringing people to Christ on Sunday in a church building or on a Thursday night visit. God can encounter a person individually and just say, "Follow Me."

4. **Salvation Comes Through a Powerful Testimony from a Friend (vv. 45–51).** The fourth case proves the power of a friend's testimony. Philip told Nathanael, "We've found Him of whom Moses and the law and the prophets wrote" (v. 45). Nathaniel's response was interesting: "Can any good thing come out of Nazareth?" (v. 46). Philip didn't argue or explain. He just said, "Come and see" (v. 46).

In the hospital one night, I visited a young patient, and her first words were, "Pastor Jeremiah, I appreciate your coming to visit, but I'm an atheist, and I don't want to talk about any spiritual stuff." I said, "Well, that's alright. Could I ask you one question?" She said, "Sure." I said, "Have you come to the place in your spiritual life where you can say that you know for certain that were you to die tonight, you'd go to heaven?" She said, "No, sir, I haven't. You know, that really frightens me." I said, "Well, could I help you understand how I came to know that?" She said, "That'd be great." I spent the next hour going through the gospel, and she gave her life to Christ. The word atheist never came up again in the conversation. I learned long ago that, rather than spending my time trying to argue people into Christ, the main thing is to say, "Just come and see. Let me tell you what Christ has done for me." If you're saved today, find somebody and tell him what Jesus had done for you.

Conclusion: Do you need Christ? "Behold! The Lamb of God who takes away the sins of the world!" Are you already a Christian? Then who else are you bringing to Christ? To whom can you say, "Come and see"?

STATS, STORIES AND MORE

More from David Jeremiah

John 1:39 says, "it was about the tenth hour." I've read many commentaries on the Gospel of John, and it's amazing to me that the only thing that gets discussed on that phrase is whether it is Jewish or Roman time. I personally believe this is Roman time, but that's not the key issue. The key issue is that John, who wrote this book, is looking back on the experience when he spent a whole day with the Lord (I believe John was one of the two disciples in v. 35), and he pointed to a specific time when he came to know Christ in a personal way. He wrote in his journal, "It was about the tenth hour." It was ten o'clock in the morning. It's good to know the time of day that you became a Christian. I realize it is not imperative to know the exact time when you were saved in order to be saved. You may not have written it down. You may not remember the time or date. It's not as important to know *when* it was as it is to know there *was* a time and there *was* a date. But I feel good when someone opens the flyleaf of their Bible where they have recorded the date of their conversion. John the apostle was so thrilled that he wrote in his journal, "It was ten o'clock."

APPROPRIATE HYMNS AND SONGS

All Glory, Laud and Honor, Theodulph of Orleans; translated by John M. Neale, Public Domain

I Sing the Mighty Power of God, Isaac Watts, Public Domain

Come Let Us Praise the Lord, Timothy Dudley-Smith/John Darwall, 1984 Hope Publishing Company

Come Christians Join to Sing, Christian Henry Bateman, Public Domian

Majesty, Jack Hayford, 1981 Rocksmith Music (Mandina/Rocksmith Music [c/o Trust Music Management, Inc.])

April 9, 1761 marks the death of William Law, British devotional writer, best known for his book, *A Serious Call to a Devout and Holy Life.* ❋ Today is the anniversary of the African Methodist Episcopal (A.M.E.) Church. Richard Allen was instrumental in birthing this new denomination, which was founded in Philadelphia in 1816 by members of Saint George's Methodist Episcopal Church who withdrew in 1787 to protest racial discrimination. ❋ Joseph Parker was born on this day in Northumberland, England. He felt called to preach from childhood, and eventually became pastor of London's City Temple. He is best known for his printed volumes of sermons, *Joseph Parker's People's Bible.* ❋ On April 9, 1875, Dr. John Samuel Bewley Monsell was struck and killed by a piece of masonry while conducting an inspection on the renovations of his church. He wrote the well-known hymn, "Fight the Good Fight with All Thy Might." ❋ On April 9, 1906, William Seymour experienced the baptism of the Spirit in Los Angeles and began speaking in tongues, launching the famous Azusa Street Revival and the Pentecostal Movement. ❋ Bill Borden of Yale died on this day in 1913. Son of a wealthy Chicago family, Borden gave away much of his fortune and was appointed by China Inland Mission to evangelize Muslims in China. He died in Cairo of spinal meningitis. News of his death and the publication of his biography had a profound effect on twentieth century missions. ❋ On April 9, 1945, German pastor Dietrich Bonhoeffer was hanged by the Nazis at Flossenburg Concentration Camp.

WORSHIP HELPS

Call to Worship:
"Hosanna in the highest!" that ancient song we sing,
For Christ is our Redeemer, the Lord of heaven our King.
O may we ever praise Him with heart and life and voice,
And in His blissful presence eternally rejoice!
(Jeanette Threlfall, 1873)

Pastoral Prayer:
Lord of our songs and our souls, our minds roam back some two thousand years as we visualize the children of the Israelites, bringing You their palms and their psalms, praising their King who entered the holy city in humility, riding on the colt of a donkey. We ourselves cry, "Hosanna in the highest! Hosanna to the King!" We would ask for two things today. First, that our shouts of praise might be as memorable as those You heard that day in old Jerusalem. Second, that our commitments to you might last longer than those of the Palm Sunday crowd, who, by the following Friday, had decided to crucify their King. Lord, make our hearts steady, our commitments solid, and our obedience steadfast. As we enter this Holy Week, grant us the sobriety and the splendor that accompanies our calling. We pray in Jesus' name. Amen.

Kids Talk

A simple way to involve the children in today's Palm Sunday service is to have them join you during the service at the front of the auditorium, either on the floor or on the platform. Briefly tell them how the children waved their palm branches in honor of Christ. Then give branches to each child, and let them wave them back and forth as the congregation sings a verse of a Palm Sunday hymn.

Additional Sermons and Lesson Ideas

Hosanna in the Highest

Date preached:

SCRIPTURE: Matthew 21:1–9

INTRODUCTION: The word "Hosanna" was a word that originally meant "Oh, save!" Later it came to be an exclamation of praise. For our purposes, we can consider it an acrostic giving us the various elements of worship and praise for our Lord Jesus.

H—Heart. Real worship must bubble up from a sincere heart.

O—Offering. Worship should be rendered sacrificially as an offering. The Bible talks about the sacrifice of praise.

S—Singing. Worship in the Bible was often accompanied by song.

A—Appreciation. Real worship involves thanksgiving and gratitude.

N—Now. Every moment of life is an opportunity for praise.

N—New. The Bible tells us to sing to the Lord a new song. This means that our worship should always be fresh. Every time we sing to Him, it should be as though we were singing that song for the first time.

A—Adoration. Only those who are in deepest love with Jesus can richly worship Him.

CONCLUSION: Is your life a constant source of *Hallelujah* and *Hosanna* to the King?

The Palm Sunday Commands

Date preached:

SCRIPTURE: Mark 11:1–3

INTRODUCTION: Jesus gave His disciples four commands in verse 2 concerning the donkey He needed for His trip into Jerusalem. He commands us in exactly the same way concerning the people around us.

1. Go (v. 2)
2. Find (v. 2)
3. Loose (v. 2)
4. Bring (v. 2)

CONCLUSION: So many people are tied down by sin, but the Lord has need of them. We must go, find them, loose them by the power of the gospel, and bring them to the Master who wants to use them for His glory.

APRIL 16, 2006

EASTER SUNDAY SUGGESTED SERMON

Because He Lives   *Date preached:*

Scripture: John 14:19: ". . . Because I live, you will live also."

Introduction: Easter is the oldest of our Christian holidays. It's been celebrated annually from the days of the church fathers, but there's also a sense
in which we celebrate Easter every week. When Jesus rose from the dead, the
first day of the week suddenly became the Christian Lord's Day. One of the
most remarkable aspects of Christian history is how a group of Jewish believers immediately shifted their day of worship from the seventh day to the first
day of the week. Every Sunday became a celebration of our risen Lord who
said, "Because I live, you will live also." Because He lives, we have:

1. **Healing.** I read about a Russian thief named Sasha who attempted to
   break into a Russian Orthodox Church. According to Outreach to the
   Nations, a publication of Derek Prince Ministries, he fell from the dome
   and broke both legs. Sasha's whole life flashed before his eyes as he fell,
   but he later said, " I heard an audible voice saying that I would not die."
   As he lay on the ground waiting for the police to come, he studied the biblically themed paintings and artwork that adorned the church walls. He
   saw the stained glass that spoke of Christ and His Resurrection. Shortly
   afterward, he gave his life to Christ. Then another miracle occurred.
   Sasha's crime usually carries a sentence of ten to fifteen years, but his case
   became bogged down in the bureaucracy. By the time officials were ready
   to prosecute a year later, Sasha's life had changed so dramatically that the
   case was dismissed. He now helps run a Russian Correspondence Bible
   School.[11] You may feel like Sasha—mixed up, on the wrong road, stumbling, falling, tumbling downward, hurting. But because Christ is alive,
   He can bring healing to your heart, your life, and even to your circumstances. Because He lives, you can live also.

2. **Hope.** One of our most popular gospel songs is based on today's text.
   Written by Bill and Gloria Gaither, it says, "Because He Lives, I can face
   tomorrow." In the late 1960s and early 1970s, America was in turmoil

with a bloody war in Southeast Asia and riots at home. At the same time, Bill contracted mononucleosis, which left him exhausted. When they suddenly discovered they were expecting another baby, Bill and Gloria asked themselves, "If this world is like this now, what will it be in fifteen or sixteen years for our baby? What will this child face?" While grappling with that question, they realized that the power of the Resurrection of Jesus Christ gives hope for tomorrow, whatever the circumstances. Thus their wonderful song reflects the truth about Easter: Because He lives, you can face tomorrow.

3. **Holiness.** Paul wrote, "[Christ] was delivered over to death for our sins and was raised to life for our justification" (Rom. 4:25, NIV). The blood of Jesus and the power of His Resurrection provide the necessary ingredients for our justification. We're made holy in God's sight through Him that we might be qualified through His merits for eternal life.

4. **Happiness.** In the Upper Room on the eve of His crucifixion, Jesus warned the disciples, "In a little while you will see me no more, and then after a little while you will see me... I tell you the truth, you will weep and mourn while the world rejoices. You will grieve, but your grief will turn to joy... You will rejoice, and no one will take away your joy" (John 16:19–20, 22, NIV). Imagine the grief of the disciples as the shadows of evening fell on crucifixion Friday. Imagine their incredible joy when they saw Jesus alive again two days later. That's the joy that we carry in our hearts to this day.

5. **Heaven.** According to Philippians 3:20–21, when Jesus comes again, our bodies will be transformed and glorified after the pattern of His own Resurrection body, fitted for eternity, equipped for everlasting life in His mansions of glory.

6. **Him.** Best of all, because of Easter we have Him. Jesus said on our text today, "I will not leave you as orphans" (John 14:18). Easter tells us that I serve a risen Savior; He's in the world today. He walks with me and talks with me along life's narrow way.

Conclusion: No wonder Easter is our greatest day. Because He lives, we can face tomorrow. Because He lives, we have healing, hope, holiness, happiness, heaven, and Him. Because He lives, we will live also. Come to Christ today! Come, and welcome!

STATS, STORIES AND MORE

Herman Melville's great classic, *Moby Dick,* is packed with biblical themes and allusions. For example, there is a character aboard ship named Queequeg, who was beloved by the crew. When he was seized by a serious fever, everyone tended him carefully and he recovered, but the illness left him worried about his future. Calling the ship's carpenter, Queequeg requested a coffin be made for him in the shape of a canoe. The carpenter took Queequeg's measurements, marshaled his planks and tools, and set to work. Soon it was finished. Little more is said of the strange coffin, and, as the book progresses, the story returns to Captain Ahab and his fatal obsession with the great whale, Moby Dick.

In the novel's dramatic climax, Captain Ahab finds Moby Dick, but the great whale overcomes the captain, smashing the boat to pieces, killing Ahab and tossing the crew into the sea to eaten alive by sharks.

Ishmael, the storyteller, found himself floundering in the water, being sucked into the vortex of the sinking ship, circling in a fatal eddy, prey for the sharks. Suddenly a "black bubble" burst from the water, liberated from the depths by its own buoyancy. It shot up with great force and landed near Ishmael. It was the canoe-shaped coffin. Climbing into it, Ishmael floated for a day and night until he was rescued by a passing ship.

Because of Easter, our coffins are nothing more than canoes bearing us across the Jordan to a wonderful world on high.

APPROPRIATE HYMNS AND SONGS

Christ the Lord is Risen Today, Charles Wesley, Public Domain

He Lives, Rev. Alfred H. Ackley, 1933 Homer A. Rodeheaver. Renewed 1961. Word Music, Inc. (a division of Word Music Group, Inc.)

Come Christians Join to Sing, Christian Henry Bateman, Public Domain

In Christ Alone (My Hope is Found), Stuart Townend/Keith Getty, 2002 Thankyou Music (admin. worldwide by worshiptogether.com Songs; admin. in the U.K. and Europe by Kingsway Music)

Thank You Lord, Dennis Jernigan, 1991 Shepherd's Heart Music Inc. (Admin. by Word Music Group, Inc.)

FOR THE BULLETIN

Peter Waldo, founder of the Waldenses, died on or near this day in 1217. He was a merchant in Lyons who become a preacher and read Scripture in the vernacular, a practice that led to his condemnation by the Church. ❀ Martin Luther entered the city of Worms, Germany, on this day in 1521, to appear before the Imperial Diet to defend his views on salvation. ❀ On April 16, 1529, Protestantism got its name as Luther's followers protested a ruling by the Diet of Speyer forbidding the teaching of Lutheranism in Catholic states—although Catholic doctrines were allowed to be taught in Lutheran states. ❀ Sir John Franklin, Christian explorer, was born on April 16, 1786. In 1845, he sailed from England to look for the Northwest Passage and to explore the Arctic. Two letters came from him, then news ceased, and Franklin's fate was unknown. His wife spent a fortune searching for him. Finally a boat was found frozen in the north. In it were two skeletons and Sir John Franklin's Bible. ❀ On April 16, 1858, John Paton sailed from Glasgow to the New Hebrides Islands (modern Vanuatu) as a missionary. His wife and newborn son soon perished, but Paton pressed on to do a great work in the South Pacific. ❀ On April 16, 1963, Martin Luther King, Jr., wrote a letter from a Birmingham jail to ministers who had criticized his involvement in their city. "You deplore the demonstrations taking place in Birmingham," he wrote. "But your statement, I am sorry to say, fails to express a similar concern for the conditions that brought about the demonstrations."

WORSHIP HELPS

Call to Worship:

Why do you seek the living among the dead? He is not here, but is risen! Remember how He spoke to you when He was still in Galilee, saying, "The Son of Man must be delivered into the hands of sinful men, and be crucified, and the third day rise again." And they remembered His words.

Luke 24:5–8

Pastoral Prayer:

Lord, this prayer would be wasted and useless, an exercise in futility and emptiness, were it not for Easter. But because of the risen Christ, we have access to You for salvation, for sustaining grace, for joy and peace, for prayer and petition. We serve a risen Savior, and because He lives we live also! We praise and thank You. We adore You. We extol You. We worship You. We render to You our lives, our love, and our lips. We are not our own, for we have been bought with a price, therefore we glorify God on this Easter Sunday. We say with the hymnist of old:

Hallelujah! hallelujah!
Heart and voice to Heaven raise,
Sing to God a hymn of gladness,
Sing to God a hymn of praise;
He Who on the cross a ransom
For the world's salvation bled,
Jesus Christ the King of glory
Now is risen from the dead.
(Christopher Wordsworth, 1807–1885)

Benediction:

May the risen Christ strengthen your hearts, fill your soul, replenish your joy, renew your spirit, and bless your efforts for His glory today, this week, and until we meet again.

Additional Sermons and Lesson Ideas

Easter: How Do We Know and Why Does It Matter
By Dr. David Jeremiah

Date preached:

SCRIPTURE: Luke 24:25–27

INTRODUCTION: In this great Easter text, Jesus chided the disciples for being slow of heart to believe. He also explained the importance of His Resurrection and the Old Testament witness about Himself.

1. How Do We Know the Resurrection Really Happened?
   A. The soldiers—Matthew 27:62–66
   B. The seal—Matthew 27:66
   C. The stone—Matthew 27:59–60; 28:2
   D. The sepulcher—Matthew 28:5–6
   E. The shroud—John 20:3–8
   F. The scars—John 20:26–28
   G. The sightings—1 Corinthians 15:3–8
   H. The survival of the church
   I. The Sunday worship
2. Why is the Resurrection Important Today?
   A. The Resurrection of Jesus Christ is about our past (saved from our sins).
   B. The Resurrection of Jesus Christ is about our present (saved to serve Him).
   C. The Resurrection of Jesus Christ is about our future (saved to be with Him forever).

CONCLUSION: Have you considered inviting Him into your life to take control?

It was Necessary

Date preached:

SCRIPTURE: Luke 24:46–49

INTRODUCTION: Crucifixion was the most horrible kind of execution ever conceived. After His resurrection, Jesus spoke of:

1. The Necessity (v. 46)—It was necessary for Christ to suffer.
2. The Need (v. 47)—Repentance and remission (forgiveness) should be preached.
3. The News (v. 48–49)—We are witnesses, endued with power from on high to share this message with others

CONCLUSION: Every human being either needs the gospel, or needs to be sharing the gospel with others.

MISSIONS SERMON

Mission Motivations

By Rev. Todd M. Kinde   *Date preached:*

Scripture: Matthew 10:26–39, especially verses 38, 39:
And he who does not take his cross and follow after Me is not worthy of Me. He who finds his life will lose it, and he who loses his life for My sake will find it.

Introduction: Jesus gives us instructions about the nature of our mission and that it will be filled with travels and troubles. All this talk of travel and trouble can lead us to be filled with hesitation and fear to move out into the mission to which He calls us. Jesus may be calling you beyond this church, even to an unreached part of the world. Whatever mission field He is calling you to, it requires courage. Courage is not the absence of fear. Courage and fearlessness are not the same thing. Courage is the virtue of acting properly and punctually in the face of fearful circumstances. Not many are what we might truly call fearless, except perhaps the truly foolish. No, we all have fear. Some fears are greater than others. And it is these greater fears, not courage, that most often drive us to overcome the lesser fears. The virtuosity and nobility of our courage is measured not by our fearlessness but by the worthiness of that which we fear most. So, whatever the mission field God is calling us to, He has given us these principles as we go forth:

I. **Fear God (10:26–33).** You must ask yourself this simple yet profound question, "What do you fear most?" Jesus instructs us that a disciple is to have but one fear: the fear of God. Fear of God will drive all other fears away and display the most noble and most virtuous courage that is possible. No amount of dramatic bravado comes close to comparing to the courageous actions taken by those who fear nothing in this created universe as much as they fear God.

A. **The Unworthy Fear of Man (vv. 26, 27, 32).** Fear of man causes us to hide truth and conviction. But when you fear man, you will hide your conviction about the truth of the gospel. Fear of man produces a low estimation of God's care and control (vv. 28–31). Fear of man betrays our lack of trust in God's sovereignty. Not a single sparrow falls and dies without the knowledge and direction of God. No one can do anything to you that God does not allow. No one can get to you without going through God first.

B. **The Freedom of Fearing God (v. 28).** The healthy fear of God gives freedom from man's expectations and limitations. If sinful man values most highly this life in this world in this body, then fear of losing it will drive them to do anything to exploit it and keep it. But if your greatest fear is God, then you are free from the bondage of living up to everyone's expectations. Fear of God gives freedom to live in God's favor (vv.32–33). When you are free from the fear of losing your body, then you are also free to witness boldly and to live heartily for the sake of God's kingdom. The Body of Christ is more important to you than your own body. When you are free from the cares of this life, then you are free to receive the favor of God in heaven.

2. **Follow Christ (10:34–37).** Next after the fear of losing our own lives or reputation is the fear of losing those we hold most dear. The gospel of Christ brings division among the most precious and intimate relationships. Following Christ helps us let go of the worldly things we hold most dear. Do you remember the call that came to the disciple in Matthew 8:21? That man valued pleasing His father more than pleasing Christ; he found it more desirable to follow in the footsteps of dad than to follow Christ. The setting of this Scripture passage is one of overt persecution for the faith. From all around the world come missionaries' stories about those who become followers of Christ and are killed by their own family members for doing so. Many profess Christ and are baptized in the Triune Name of God only to be slaughtered for it. They loved Christ more than life itself— more than family ties. Following Christ means we must take up the cross. Verse 38 tells us that we all have a cross to bear. Whatever it is, it will be the death of us—the death of self. To follow Christ is to walk in the way of the cross. We will follow our Master all the way or not at all. Where is He leading you? Is your workplace or school a mission field full of lost and hurting people? Has the Lord been calling you to support a missionary or missions agency, or to go overseas yourself? Are you willing to go no matter where He leads?

3. **Find Life (10:38, 39).** We are never more living than when we lose our life, when we are dead to self (v. 39). Life is not about self-preservation. We are to

be about self-denial. The progression of thought in this passage seems to be the reverse of our way of thinking. In Christian discipleship we are to fear God, to follow Christ, and then we will find life. If we attempt to find life first, we will lose it. Life begins with God, and if we are to find it we must begin with Him.

Conclusion: Where is your mission field? Do you fear God enough to respond? Have you heard the call of Christ in your life to take up your cross, to be willing to die for Him? We live in a world of people who fear so many things rather than God, who follow other gods and philosophies; they ultimately find death. Won't you fear the God of their judgment? Won't you follow Christ who desires their salvation? Won't you embrace the self-denying life, and follow Him to the mission field no matter where it may be?

Quotes for the Pastor's Wall

" If you can't preach like Peter,

If you can't pray like Paul,

Just tell the love of Jesus,

And say He died for all. **"**

—from "There is a Balm in Gilead," an African-American spiritual

APRIL 23, 2006

SUGGESTED SERMON

The Temptation in Worship

Date preached:

By Dr. Melvin Worthington

Scripture: Exodus 20:4–6:
You shall not make for yourself a carved image—any likeness of anything that is in heaven above, or that is in the earth beneath, or that is in the water under the earth; you shall not bow down to them nor serve them. . . .

Introduction: When you think of the Ten Commandments, which one do you think is the most difficult to keep? Often, we think of commands against lying, coveting something of our neighbors, committing adultery, or neglecting the Sabbath. We're prone to overlook the commandment against idolatry. We consider idolatry a sin most often seen in other cultures; but in fact, idolatry is all around us. On magazine stands we see idols of our culture. One popular TV show names the next "American Idol," and many lives here today are plagued with the worship of possessions. The other day I saw a Hollywood awards show, and I noticed how similar the presentations were to what I'd envision for an idol—little golden statues that dominate one's life and career. Paul warns in 1 Corinthians 10:14, "Therefore, my beloved, flee from idolatry"; and in Colossians 3:5 he broadens the definition of idolatry: "Therefore put to death your members which are on the earth: fornication, uncleanness, passion, evil desire, and covetousness, which is idolatry." God is to be adored in the heart, and He alone is to be enthroned in the core of our lives. Anything that we love more than Him is an idol, for idolatry is essentially anything that comes before Him in our lives. Let's look at each aspect of this commandment together.

1. **The Admonition in the Text.** There are several elements of admonition here. Whether the images and idols are visible (like an image hanging on the wall) or invisible (like a drive, a goal, or a dream), we must keep them out of our lives. We must not *build or construct* graven images. We must not *bow or commit* to graven images. We must not *believe or give creditability* to graven images. We must not *bestow or conform* to graven images. It's possible to worship the wrong God, and it is equally possible to worship the true and living God in the wrong way. Jesus said, "God is Spirit and those who worship Him must worship in spirit and truth" (John 4:24).

2. **The Analysis of the Text.**

   A. The requirements: The worship of idols is denounced.

   B. The reason: God is a jealous God and a God of judgment.

   C. The repercussions: God's favor is on His obedient children. God's fury is poured out on those who disregard and break this commandment. How wonderful it is that our God is a jealous God and willing to discipline us when we disobey.

3. **The Application from the Text.**

   A. This commandment may be broken by *ritualistic practices.* Our church traditions and rituals have their place, but when we just go through the motions of worship, depending on the forms instead of on the Father Himself, it amounts to idolatry. Many churches are guilty of bowing down before their creeds, ceremonies, candles, and crosses. A ritual can become a substitute for a relationship. Images and idols can be substitutes for Christ. All idolatry and image worship is truly satanic.

   B. This commandment can be broken by the *revival of pantheism.* The worship of nature violates this commandment.

   C. This commandment can be violated by the *revival of personalities.* The hero worship of today—following cultic personalities—violates this commandment. We become like what we worship; thus we must worship the true and living God and do so in spirit and truth.

   D. This commandment can be violated by the *relishing of possessions* (Col. 3:5).

Conclusion: God calls us into His own presence, to immediate worship. We worship—not merely by listening to a sermon or being distracted by the form and fashion of music—but by coming face-to-face with the God of Scripture. When we stop short of face-to-face worship of the Eternal God, we are ruining our own character, because we are breaking this commandment. God's purpose in worship is to cause us to be Christ-like. The design of worship is that we might grow in grace and that the image of Christ might grow in us. Simple obedience to His Word and true worship by His Spirit bring you closer to Him than any idol ever could.

STATS, STORIES AND MORE

The famous London pastor, T. DeWitt Talmage, once used this illustration in a sermon. Suppose you have rented or purchased a whole house, and the former owner comes to you with the keys. There are twelve rooms in the house and he gives you six of the keys. You say: "Where are the other keys?" "Oh," he says, "you can't have them! There is a room on the second floor you can't have, and there is a room on the third floor and a room on the fourth floor you can' t have, and there is a dark place in the attic you can' t have, but here are the keys for the others." But you say: "I purchased the whole house, and I want all the keys, or I don't want any of them."

Christ will take everything, from cellar to attic—all the keys to all your affections, all your hopes, all your ambitions, all your heart, all your life, or He will not take one key.[12]

Any key that isn't yielded to Christ is your idol.

No God but God

"The Lord would rather have one person who is 100 percent committed to him than one hundred people who are only 75 percent committed."—Anonymous

"I guess the reason is because God has all there is of me."—William Booth when asked by Queen Victoria for the secret of his ministry

"If Jesus Christ be God and died for me, then no sacrifice can be too great for me to make for him."—C. T. Studd

"All there is of God is available to the person who is available to all there is of God."—Major Ian Thomas

APPROPRIATE HYMNS AND SONGS

Famous One, Chris Tomlin/Jesse Reeves, 2002 worshiptogether.com songs/Six Steps Music (Admin. by EMI Christian Music Publishing)

Blessed Be the Lord God Almighty, Bob Fitts, 1984 Scripture In Song (a division of Integrity Music, Inc.)

Majesty, Jack Hayford, 1981 Rocksmith Music (Mandina/Rocksmith Music [c/o Trust Music Management, Inc.])

We Will Glorify, Twila Paris, 1982 Singsparation Music (Admin. by Brentwood-Benson Music Publishing, Inc., 741 Cool Springs Boulevard, Franklin, TN 37067)

FOR THE BULLETIN

April 23 was established at the Council of Oxford in 1222 as the Feast Day of St. George, "Protector of the Kingdom of England." According to tradition, George was persecuted by the Emperor Diocletian, reportedly on April 23, 304, by being tied to a cross and his skin scraped with iron combs. ❀ On April 23, 1538, John Calvin and William Farel were banished from Geneva, Switzerland for refusing to administer the Lord's Supper of Easter Sunday. They claimed that the city was too sinful to partake of the sacrament. Calvin later returned to Geneva and established it as the center of his Reformation Movement. ❀ April 23, 1564, was the birth date of William Shakespeare ❀ Today is also the birthday, in 1586, of Martin Rinckart, German clergyman and hymnist, author of the hymn "Now Thank We All our God." Having endured the horrors of the Thirty Years' War, he wrote this hymn in commemoration of its conclusion. ❀ The author of the gospel song, "Jesus Savior, Pilot Me," Edward Hopper, died on April 23, 1888. ❀ On April 23, 1942, during World War II, William Temple was appointed Archbishop of Canterbury. He is fondly remembered for his classic definition of worship: "To worship is to quicken the conscience by the holiness of God, to purge the imagination by the beauty of God, to open the heart to the love of God, and to devote the will to the purpose of God."

Call to Worship:
Sing to God, you kingdoms of the earth; Oh, sing praises to the Lord. To Him who rides on the heaven of heavens, which were of old. . . . Blessed be God!
Psalm 68:32–33, 35

Responsive Reading

Worship Leader:	Who may ascend into the hill of the Lord? Or who may stand in His holy place?
Congregation:	He who has clean hands and a pure heart, who has not lifted up his soul to an idol, nor sworn deceitfully.
Worship Leader:	What profit is the image, that its maker should carve it, the molded image, a teacher of lies, that the maker of its mold should trust in it, to make mute idols?
Congregation:	Woe to him who says to wood, 'Awake!' To silent stone, 'Arise! It shall teach!' Behold, it is overlaid with gold and silver, yet in it there is no breath at all. But the Lord is in His holy temple. Let all the earth keep silence before Him.
Worship Leader:	When Christ who is our life appears, then you also will appear with Him in glory.
Congregation:	Therefore put to death your members which are on the earth: fornication, uncleanness, passion, evil desire, and covetousness, which is idolatry.
Worship Leader:	Little children, keep yourselves from idols.
All:	For all the gods of the peoples are idols, but the Lord made the heavens. Honor and majesty are before Him; strength and beauty are in His sanctuary.

(Ps. 24:3–4; Hab. 2:18–20; Col. 3:4–5; 1 John 5:21; Ps. 96:5–6)

Additional Sermons and Lesson Ideas

Overcoming Death
By Rev. Todd M. Kinde

Date preached:

SCRIPTURE: James 5:19–20

INTRODUCTION: Wrong thinking and wrongdoing lead to death, while discipline leads to life.

1. The Stray (5:19).
2. The Searcher (5:20).

CONCLUSION: To turn from the error of your ways is to repent. Repentance is to be overwhelmed with godly sorrow, to confess your attitudes and actions of sin, to pray and ask God for wisdom and grace, to live a life of faith bearing the fruit of the Spirit and of righteousness. Whoever leads someone who has strayed down this path of restoration will save that person from death and bring that him or her into the realm of forgiveness.

Celebrating Life
By Rev. Richard Sharpe

Date preached:

SCRIPTURE: Various

INTRODUCTION: How often do we celebrate life? Let's look at three Biblical examples of celebrating life in various circumstances.

1. Miriam (Ex. 15: 20, 21). Miriam made up a song in celebration of the Israelites' rescue from the Egyptians. It was a time when all Israel saw the mighty hand of God defeat the army of the Egyptians by drowning them in the Red Sea. Are you praising Him for your salvation?
2. David (2 Samuel 6:12–15). David was bringing the ark of the covenant into Jerusalem the right way. He was sacrificing offerings to the Lord all along the way. He was dancing before the Lord. Do you rejoice to see the Lord glorified?
3. Paul and Silas (Acts 16:25). Paul and Silas were in prison with chains on their feet. They had been stripped and beaten. What was their reaction? They prayed and sang praises so everyone heard. The end result was the salvation of the jailer and his family!

CONCLUSION: Whether motivated by the Lord's works, character, salvation, or any aspect of His glory, the important thing is to celebrate Him!

APRIL 30, 2006

SUGGESTED SERMON

Lights Out

Date preached:

Scripture: Romans 1:18—3:20, especially 3:10:
... "There is none righteous, no, not one."

Introduction: Suppose you came upon a man hammering pieces of lumber together. "What are you doing?" you ask. Suppose he replies, "I'm building a ladder to reach to the moon." You'd think him mad. No one can build a literal ladder to the moon. Nor can we build a ladder of good works that will take us to heaven. Many believe if they live a good life, God will let them into heaven. But a large segment of the book of Romans refutes this. Romans is the Bible's most systematic presentation of God's plan of salvation. Before we can know how to be saved, we must have some sense of our sinfulness, some idea of the holiness and wrath of God, and some understanding of our total inability to save ourselves. Romans 1:18—3:20 tells us that we can never go to heaven on the basis of good works. We can never establish our own righteousness before God by keeping the law. We're all in moral and spiritual darkness. In this extended passage, the Lord tells us it's "Lights Out" for the Gentiles, for the Jews, for everyone.

1. **Lights Out for the Gentiles (1:18—2:16).** This section falls into two parts. First, it's "Lights Out" for the masses of people among the Gentiles, for ourselves and our society as a whole. Second, it's "Lights Out" for the moral people of our society, for those individuals who think they're in pretty good shape morally and spiritually.

   A. **The Masses of People (1:18–32).** Here Paul gives a brilliant description of the way a culture collapses. There are five downward stages that always occur when a society begins to erode morally.

   (1) **Rejection of Creationism (vv. 18–20).** The wrath of God will be revealed from heaven against any society that refuses to acknowledge the obvious fact that God is the Creator of the universe. He specifically made the vast, endless ocean of stars, the splendors of the solar system, the burning sun, the glowing moon, and the

beautiful earth to show us His invisible power and divine nature. When we refuse to acknowledge that, we've taken the first step in a downward slide that leads to utter ruin.

(2) Idolatry (vv. 21–23). When we reject the true Creator, we begin making our own gods. Today our gods aren't typically images of birds, animals, and reptiles. We're a more sophisticated society; our idols are pleasure, ambition, and materialism.

(3) Immorality (vv. 24–25). When we erect our own gods, we can write our own rules, and such a society increasingly becomes immoral and sexually permissive.

(4) Homosexuality (vv. 26–27). The fourth step involves the homosexualization of society. It increasingly becomes a seedbed for homosexual activity and acceptance.

(5) Total Moral Collapse (vv. 28–32). The remainder of the chapter describes a society that is unraveling at the seams. It is moral meltdown. This five-stage pattern is as true for modern America as it was for ancient Sodom, Greece, and Rome.

B. The Moral People (2:1–16). Yes, yes, you say. This society is going to the dogs. It's terrible what these people do. There's no excuse for it. But keep reading! Paul isn't just referring to the masses of immoral people; he's also talking about the individuals within that society who think they are morally upright. We're all sinners facing the wrath of God. We have all done the same things—actually, mentally, or potentially.

2. **Lights Out for the Jews (2:17—3:8).** "This doesn't apply to me," some might say. "I'm not just a moral person; I'm a religious person." That's what Paul's Jewish listeners thought, but he said that it's "Lights Out" for them, too.

3. **Lights Out for Everyone (3:9–20).** Paul sums it all up by assembling verses from Psalms, Proverbs, Isaiah, and Ezekiel, the theme being the exceeding wickedness of each and every person in God's sight.

Conclusion: Of course, we can't leave it there. The next two verses take us to the heart of the gospel: "But now the righteousness of God apart from law is revealed. . . even the righteousness of God, through faith in Jesus Christ to all and on all who believe" (Rom. 3:21–22). The Lord Jesus, seeing our condition, came and shed His blood to make atonement for our sins that through Him we might have eternal life. He bids us proclaim Him Savior and Lord. It may be "Lights Out" for the world, but the Light of the world is Jesus.

STATS, STORIES AND MORE

Forty miles south of London is a village named Piltdown. One day in 1908, a lawyer named Charles Dawson, a member of the British Geological Society, claimed to have discovered an ancient skull. Suddenly the world had "proof" of Darwin's theory of evolution—Piltdown Man. The scientific literature about Piltdown Man is enormous, with over five hundred doctoral dissertations written about the discovery. School children were shown "pictures" of how Piltdown Man fit into the evolutionary chain.

Sir Arthur Keith, one of the world's greatest anatomists, wrote more about Piltdown Man than anyone else. He based a lifetime of thinking on his fascination with Piltdown Man.

Sir Arthur was a frail eighty-six years old when two scientists paid a visit to his home. They were breaking the news that after a half-century of study, Piltdown Man was a hoax—an old human skull, the jawbone of an orangutan, and a dog's tooth.

"Keith was a rationalist and a pronounced opponent of the Christian faith," wrote Marvin L. Lubenow in *Bones of Contention*. "Yet in his autobiography he tells of attending evangelistic meetings in Edinburgh and Aberdeen, seeing students make a public profession of faith in Jesus Christ, and often feeling 'on the verge of conversion.' He rejected the gospel, because he felt that the Genesis account of Creation was just a myth and that the Bible was merely a human book. It causes profound sadness to know that this great man rejected Jesus Christ, whose resurrection validated everything He said and did, only to put his faith in what proved to be a phony fossil."

FOR THE BULLETIN

On April 30, 304, Emperor Diocletian issued the most destructive edict in his campaign again Christians. For seven years, believers were subjected to unimagined terrors. Christians were dismissed from their positions, their civil rights suspended. Church buildings were set afire. Copies of the Scriptures were burned in the marketplaces. Pastors and church leaders were rounded up and executed, many by lions in the coliseums. The prime instigator of the campaign, Augustus Galerius, disheartened and embittered, finally issued an edict of toleration on April 30, 311, setting the stage for the recognition of Christianity by Emperor Constantine. Some five days after he signed the edict, Galerius died of a disease that caused him to be eaten by worms. ✿ On April 30, 1532, James Baynham, a lawyer, confessed under questioning to owning five copies of the books of Bible translator William Tyndale, but he recanted under pressure. Later that day, he entered a church carrying Tyndale's writings for all to see and publicly withdrew his recantation. As a result, he was burned at the stake on April 30, 1532. As he died, he reportedly said, "Ye look for miracles; here now may you see a miracle; for in this fire I feel no more pain than if I were in bed; for it is as sweet to me as a bed of roses." ✿ On April 30, 1598, Henry IV of France issued the Edict of Nantes, granting religious toleration to the Huguenots (French Protestants). ✿ April 30, 1854 marks the death of journalist and hymnist James Montgomery. His best known hymn is the Christmas carol "Angels from the Realms of Glory."

APPROPRIATE HYMNS AND SONGS

You are My King, Billy James Foote, 1999 worshiptogether.com songs (Admin. by EMI Christian Music Publishing)

Amazing Love, Graham Kendrick, 1989 Make Way Music (Admin. by Music Services)

A Broken Spirit, Don Harris/Martin J. Nystrom, 1993 Integrity's Hosanna! Music (c/o Integrity Music, Inc.)

How Deep the Father's Love for Us, Stuart Townend, 1995 Kingsway's Thankyou Music (Admin. by EMI Christian Music Publishing)

At Calvary, William R. Newell/Daniel B. Towner, Public Domain

WORSHIP HELPS

Call to Worship:
I will praise the name of God with a song, and will magnify Him with thanksgiving . . . Let heaven and earth praise Him, the seas and everything that moves in them. (Ps. 69:30, 34)

Benediction:
Behold, the eye of the Lord is on those who fear Him, on those who hope in His mercy, to deliver their soul from death, and to keep them alive in famine. Our soul waits for the Lord; He is our help and our shield. For our heart shall rejoice in Him, because we have trusted in His holy name. Let Your mercy, O Lord, be upon us, just as we hope in You.
(Ps. 33:18–22)

Kids Talk

Find a long, open space that everyone can see. Have the children gather around facing you. Ask for a volunteer. Have the volunteer stand in place and give him a spot far enough away that he cannot possibly jump there. Ask him to attempt to jump to that spot. When he cannot, turn to the children and say, "Maybe if we all tell him he can get there and cheer him on he can make it." When he fails once more under these conditions, ask the children why. When they answer that it's impossible to jump that far, explain that heaven is too far away for us to ever reach on our own,

Additional Sermons and Lesson Ideas

Thankful for Affliction
By Rev. Billy Friel

Date preached:

SCRIPTURE: 2 Corinthians 4:7–18

INTRODUCTION: If you were to name what you are thankful for you would probably name the good things, the things we would call blessings. Would anyone be thankful for affliction? Here are four reasons we are thankful for affliction:

1. Affliction Makes Us Appreciate the Treasure, Not the Vessel (v. 7). Most people focus on the body, not the soul. Spiritual priority returns through affliction.
2. Affliction Makes the Treasure Spill on Others (vv. 10, 11). The life of Jesus will be manifested when we suffer. Affliction causes our light to shine (Matt. 5:16). Anyone can be happy when all is well—affliction reveals our faith walk (Gal. 2:20).
3. Affliction Makes the Spiritual World Real to Us (v. 18). Affliction strips away pride, independence, and self-sufficiency. It also produces humility and repentance.
4. Affliction Demonstrates God's Love (v. 17). God does not delight in judgment (Ezek. 33:11), and He deals with us as sons.

CONCLUSION: Are you spiritual enough to be thankful for affliction and judgment? Thank God that He loves you enough to permit affliction and bring judgment.

Do You Want to be Truly Wise?
By Dr. Timothy Beougher

Date preached:

SCRIPTURE: 1 Corinthians 2:6–13

INTRODUCTION: In today's information age, we have more information available to us than to any other people in history. So how can we discern true wisdom? Our passage today speaks of wisdom not of the world; let's look at true Biblical wisdom and how to attain it.

1. Understand the Nature of True Wisdom (vv. 6–7).
   A. Wisdom Is a Mystery (v. 7).
   B. Wisdom Was Designed for Our Glory (v. 7).
2. Recognize the Source of True Wisdom (vv. 6–7).
   A. It Does not Come from Human Reason (v. 6).
   B. It Originates with God (v. 7).
3. Realize How to Obtain True Wisdom (vv. 8–13).
   A. It Cannot be Found by Human Senses (vv. 8–9).
   B. It Is Given by Divine Revelation (vv. 10–13).

CONCLUSION: Let's seek true wisdom from its source, God Himself.

They Found the Secret
By V. Raymond Edman

V. Raymond Edman intended to spend his life in missionary service among the Indians of the Andes, but in 1928 his health broke. Seeking recovery, he took a Pacific voyage aboard a Dutch freighter. Even aboard ship, however, he labored intently over the lectures he hoped to give at his Ecuadorian Bible institute.

As he outlined 2 Corinthians, he reached chapter 2, and read the words, "Now thanks be to God who always leads us in triumph in Christ" (v. 14). He was staggered, sensing a great contrast between that verse and his condition. Here he was, broken in health, unsure of the future, and anxious about his ministry. Yet to Paul, life was an ongoing, unbroken triumph! Edman walked to the deck and began praying for a triumphant spirit. Quickly and quietly, the Lord seemed to whisper, "But are you willing to go anywhere for Me?"

"Yes, Lord, anywhere in Ecuador Thou mayest send me."

"I did not say in Ecuador."

Edman gazed across the Pacific, conscious that the Lord was standing beside him, awaiting an answer. Finally in deepest sincerity, Edman replied, "Yes, Lord, anywhere Thou sayest I will go, only that my life may be always a constant pageant of triumph in Thee."

It was the beginning of a life of profound fruitfulness that reached its apex years later when Edman served as President of Wheaton College.

He was long gone from Wheaton when I arrived as a graduate student in 1975, but stories about him lingered, passed down from class to class. I remember hearing, for example, how Edman, as president of the college, would arise in the early hours, walk to each student dormitory, lift up his hands, and pray for God's blessings on the students that day.

I recall hearing how he had guided a young Wheaton student named Billy Graham into the ministry of evangelism.

I recall hearing how in 1967 V. Raymond Edman, then chancellor of Wheaton, was to preach in chapel. Rising to the pulpit, he told the students he wanted to take them into the presence of the King of kings. Then he slumped to the floor, dying instantly of a massive heart attack.

He left a mark behind him—circled, underlined, and highlighted. His contagious Christian influence as missionary, pastor, and college president touched thousands of lives, and his writings on the victorious Christian life moved millions more.

Among Edman's books is a little, easy-to-read classic that I frequently pull from my bookshelf. The title is *They Found the Secret,* a collection of biographical gems telling how twenty people discovered the secret of the victorious life. In the introduction Edman explains that every now and then a Christian passes our way who is more radiant than most. Some Christians seem to harbor an inward, wonderful secret that gives them a supernatural bounce. That secret, explains Edman, is the work of the Holy Spirit in fully surrendered lives, the very lesson Edman himself had learned in 1928.

Most of his twenty examples were well-known Christians in their own day, but many are no longer familiar to us. Reading this book is a pleasant stroll through 19th and early-20th century church history. Here you'll read the deeper experiences of J. Hudson Taylor, Amy Carmichael, Oswald Chambers, Charles Finney, A. J. Gordon, Charles Trumbull, Walter Wilson, D. L. Moody, and twelve more men and women who learned the secret of the overcoming life. Each story is short, colorful, and challenging.

I've not only read and re-read them, but I've recycled the stories into sermons and books of my own.

Hardback editions of *They Found the Secret* must be furrowed out of used book stores, but paperback editions are still in print. It's worth almost any price. Read a story a day, Monday through Friday, for four weeks, and at the end of the month you'll be a different person.

MAY 7, 2006

The Discipline of Disappointment *Date preached:*

By Dr. Denis Lyle

Scripture: 2 Samuel 7; 1 Chronicles 17, especially 2 Samuel 7:12–13: "When your days are fulfilled and you rest with your fathers, I will set up your seed after you, who will come from your body, and I will establish his kingdom. He shall build a house for My name, and I will establish the throne of his kingdom forever."

Introduction: When nothing in life seems to go as planned, how do you react? Sometimes disappointment so crushes a person that he is emotionally handicapped for life, and yet the Lord wants us to live in victory over circumstances. David is a great inspiration to those of us who have or will encounter the discipline of disappointment.

1. **A Holy Resolve.** David had big dreams to do something great for God who had been so good to him. The kingdom had been united. Jerusalem had been taken. The Philistines had been defeated. David sat in a beautiful new palace that was built for him by King Hiram of Tyre (2 Sam. 5:11). He considered the goodness of God in giving him rest from his enemies (7:1). The ark was brought to its new home in Jerusalem (6:17). Then the thought struck him, "Here I sit in a luxurious home while the ark rests in that drab tent. God deserves better." The plan begins to formulate with a number of elements involved:

   A. A Practical Element. David's desire to build a house for the Lord was to some extent dictated by circumstances. The ark of the Lord had been brought to Jerusalem, which naturally brought many people to worship. All of the gatherers needed accommodation, and this no doubt moved David to make such a decision.

   B. A Devotional Element. When David thought of everything God had done for him, he poured out his heart in adoring gratitude to the Lord. Do you ever sit in the presence of the Lord and ponder His blessings to you?

   C. A Spiritual Element. Since Nathan was God's spokesman, David decided to bounce a new idea off him. In effect, he says, "Nathan, I'm troubled that I have a nicer house than the ark does" (2 Sam. 7:2). It was unthinkable to him that the symbol of the Presence of God, the ark of the covenant, should still have only the trappings of Israel's long-past nomadic existence (1 Chron. 16:1).

2. A Heavenly Response. The same night Nathan told David to build the temple, God spoke to him as Nathan laid down to sleep (2 Sam. 7:4–16). Nathan realized that he had spoken too soon. Now he would have to admit to David that he had been wrong. What man proposes, God disposes! How did God handle David's proposal? Well, notice:

A. God Responded Negatively. God's refusal to let David build a house for the ark was based on four reasons. First, no precedent had been established (2 Sam. 5:6). God had never dwelt in a permanent building—only a tent. Second, no request had been made by God for such a building (2 Sam. 7:7). These plans were David's initiative, not God's. Thirdly, no man of war could build this house, for this was to be a house of peace (1 Chron. 22:8; 28:3). Finally, no safety for the ark could yet be assured since Jerusalem was not completely fortified against her enemies (1 Kin. 5:3–4). There was nothing wrong with David's dream. His motives were pure and his intentions were pleasing to God (2 Chron. 6:8), but he was not the right man to carry out the job.

B. God Responded Positively (2 Sam. 7:12–13). God told David that his son Solomon would build the Lord's House (1 Chron. 28:6). Initially, David's plans had been cancelled; now they were to be carried out in splendor. When God says no, it's because He has a better plan. He never intends to frustrate or disillusion us.

C. God Responded Superlatively. Rather than David building a house for God, God promised to build a house for David. Prophetically, this is known as the Davidic covenant in which the Lord ultimately promised an eternal heir, Jesus Christ, who would come through David's family line.

3. A Humble Reaction. How did David react? There's a beautiful statement in 2 Samuel 7:18, ". . . David went in and sat before the LORD . . ." The word "sat" means "tarry" or "linger." David did not complain because his desire had been refused; instead, he reflected on the goodness of God.

Conclusion: Has God said no to you? Before you turn away, before there creeps into your life some bitterness, just sit down before the Lord and think about His goodness to you! Rest in His promises, and He will readjust you to His purposes.

STATS, STORIES AND MORE

A Poem on Disappointment:
Disappointment—His Appointment
Change one letter, then I see
That the thwarting of my purpose
Is God's better choice for me.
His appointment must be blessing,
Tho' it may come in disguise,
For the end from the beginning
Open to His wisdom lies.

Disappointment—His Appointment
Whose? The Lord, who loves me best,
Understands and knows me fully,
Who my faith and love would test;
For, like loving earthly parent,
He rejoices when He knows
That His child accepts, UNQUESTIONED,
All that from His wisdom flows.

Disappointment—His Appointment
"No good thing will He withhold,"
From denials oft we gather
Treasures of His love untold,
Well He knows each broken purpose
Leads to fuller, deeper trust,
And the end of all His dealings
Proves our God is wise and just.
—Edith Lillian Young

FOR THE BULLETIN

The Great Schism (the breach between the Western Catholic Church and the Eastern Orthodox Church) was a primary hindrance to global Christian unity in the Middle Ages. On May 7, 1274, the Synod of Lyons sought to end the Schism. Pope Gregory X also wanted to use the Synod to liberate the Holy Land and reform morals in the church. ❀ On May 7, 1318, four Franciscans were burned at the stake at Marseilles at the order of Pope John XXII. And on this day in 1355, twelve hundred Jews were killed in Toledo, Spain. ❀ A Mr. Sharpe of Bristol, England, was burned at the stake on May 7, 1556, for his reformation views. He had entered the church one Sunday during mass, and, standing in the choir loft, had said: "Neighbors, bear me record that yonder idol (pointing to the altar) is the greatest and most abominable that ever was." His words were not well received, and he was bound back-to-back with Thomas Hale, another reformer, and burned to death. ❀ On May 7, 1631, Samuel Rutherford, a seventeenth-century Scottish pastor who was exiled for non-conformity, wrote in a letter, "Daily I receive from Him who is made of his Father a running-over fountain, at which I and others may come with thirsty souls and fill our vessels. Long hath this well been standing open to us." ❀ Today is the birthday of hymnist Elisha A. Hoffman (1839), author of "What a Wonderful Savior," "I Must Tell Jesus," "Are You Washed in the Blood?" "Glory to His Name," "Down at the Cross," and "Leaning on the Everlasting Arms."

APPROPRIATE HYMNS AND SONGS

It is Well with My Soul, Horatio G. Spafford/ Philip P. Bliss, Public Domain

You are Holy, Marc Imboden / Tammi Rhoton, 1994 Marc Imboden

Great is Thy Faithfulness, Thomas O. Chisholm/ William M. Runyan, 1923. Renewed 1951 Hope Publishing Company

Day by Day, Wendell P. Loveless, 1946 Wendell P. Loveless. Assigned to Hope Publishing Company

Firm Foundation, Nancy Gordon/ Jamie Harvill, 1994 Integrity Hosanna! Music (c/o Integrity Music, Inc.)/ Integrity Praise! Music (c/o Integrity Praise, Inc.)

WORSHIP HELPS

Call to Worship:
Sing to God, sing praises to His name; extol Him who rides on the clouds, by His name YAH, and rejoice before Him.
Psalm 68:4

Offertory Comments:
In our passage today, we will study a portion of David's life in which He planned to build a temple for the Lord. You see, David had a beautiful palace built for him, sparing no expense. As he sat looking around him, he realized there was something wrong with such luxury when the ark of God, the symbol of God's Presence, was enclosed with a simple tent. A tent was the lodging place of a nomad, who was the lowest and least significant member in the social structure of the Hebrew people. David must have thought, Surely the ark was worthy of a permanent building. Do you ever think like that? Are we ever convicted between what we spend on our homes and what we give to God's cause? Is there a striking contrast between what we spend on ourselves and what we offer to the Lord? Do we spend more time building up our own possessions than building up the kingdom of God? To do less for God than we do for ourselves shows where our hearts are. As a servant David wished to honor his Master; as a saint he wished to glorify his God; as a steward he wished to dedicate his possessions to the Lord. Don't offer your tithe out of guilt, and don't serve the Lord out of duty. Let our hearts be filled with worship and gratitude toward God for all His blessings; let that be our motivation in this service as we give.

Additional Sermons and Lesson Ideas

A Precious Promise
By Dr. Denis Lyle

Date preached:

SCRIPTURE: 2 Samuel 7:10–16

INTRODUCTION: After being denied his desire to build the Lord's temple, the Lord in turn made a covenant with David. Five promises were made to David and Israel:

1. A Promise of Residency (7:10).
2. A Promise of Security (7:10).
3. A Promise of Posterity (7:11–12).
4. A Promise of Authority (7:13).
5. A Promise of Perpetuity (7:16).

CONCLUSION: God ultimately promised an eternal heir from David's line. The fulfillment of these promises is in Jesus Christ (Luke 1:30–33; 3:31; Rev. 22:16). Even when we are denied of our dreams or desires as David was, we can rest in the precious promises of Christ. He does exceedingly abundantly above all that His people ask or think (Eph. 3:20).

Faithfulness
By Pastor J. David Hoke

Date preached:

SCRIPTURE: Various

INTRODUCTION: "He who is faithful in what is least is faithful also in much; and he who is unjust in what is least is unjust also in much" (Luke 16:10).

Let me suggest several ways in which we must be faithful as believers.

1. Be True To Your Word (Matt. 5:37).
2. Honor Your Marriage (Heb. 13:4).
3. Use Your Talents (1 Pet. 4:10).
4. Guard Your Tongue (James 3:6, 8–10).
5. Manage Your Money (Luke 16:11).
6. Be Committed To Your Church (John 13:35; Rom. 12:5; Heb. 10:25).

CONCLUSION: Jesus is coming again, and He will bring His reward with Him. It is my prayer that we will all hear the words, ". . . Well done, good and faithful servant; you were faithful over a few things, I will make you ruler over many things. Enter into the joy of your lord" (Matt. 25:21).

Dear Pastor . . . You Stink!

Ah, those letters. Little sharp daggers. Tipped in poison. What pastor hasn't felt their barbs? I've actually received five of them in the last two weeks (three were from the same person).

I suppose I should begin by saying I'm blessed with a wonderful congregation of loving people, most of whom are affirming and cheering. I've been their pastor for over twenty-five years, and every week I receive notes of encouragement and letters of support.

Having said that, not all my correspondents are of the positive variety. Two weeks ago, for example, I ran into a woman at the library. She had left our church last year in a huff over a number of things. She had never approached me directly with her complaints, but had sent her husband to detail my faults so as to make sure I didn't miss any of them. After joining another church, this woman had placed calls, seeking to lure families from our congregation. In a few instances, she succeeded.

I had borne it with heroic silence; and when I ran into her in the library, I decided that silence was still the safest route. I spoke to her briefly and formally—that is, with the required civility, but I didn't chat. The next week I received her letter. It was obvious, she said, that while she harbored no ill will toward me, I certainly had an appalling attitude toward her. Though she had lovingly sought to bring my faults into the clear daylight of her opinions, I had not listened. And more's the pity—since we'd be living together forever in heaven, shouldn't I get my heart right with the Lord and with her?

I wrote back a simple message: "Dear so-and-so. I received your letter. I'm very sorry you were offended by our chance meeting. Please forgive me."

So far, I've heard no more from her, though I do look both ways now before ducking into the library.

My second correspondent appeared a week later. This time the missives came electronically. I received a series of e-mails excoriating me on a host of issues. Some were valid; some weren't. My friend complained, for example, about my frequent absences from the pulpit. I wrote back pointing out that so far this year—it was now August—I had only been away one Sunday.

I know this member quite well, and were I to answer him in his own tone, he would be deeply offended. In fact, even my gentler tone offended him, and he wrote a second letter telling me so.

My third letter came anonymously. It was sent to both my wife and me, hand-addressed to our home. Opening it, I found a sheet of paper on which were written the words: "Repent—or Else."

My wife didn't like the looks of it, but I reminded her of that old story about the preacher who received a letter containing only one word: FOOL. The next Sunday, he rose in his pulpit and said, "I've occasionally received letters in which the writer wrote the message but forgot to sign his name. This is the first time I've gotten a letter in which the person signed his name but forgot the message."

None of this would matter very much except that many pastors in America are utterly worn out and badly discouraged. Our critics seldom realize the burdens we bear. Our churches are filled with pesky, problem-prone people. Our congregants come from many backgrounds, have thousands of opinions, and possess varying levels of maturity. Furthermore, our biggest problems are frequently lodged inside our own chests.

Our disparaging, nit-picking, judgmental, holier-than-thou correspondents (of course, I love every one of them in my heart) don't realize that many pastors are already afflicted with a low self-image, and that those letters hurt.

Well, what do we do?

First, thank God for the hands that held the pens. I happened to receive my most recent batch of fan mail while reading Bill Bright's book, *The Journey Home,* in which he wrote of dying of pulmonary fibrosis. I'd been deeply moved by his attitude during his illness, expressed in a little phrase he frequently used: "Thank you, Lord."

When the doctor told him he was dying, his reply was, "Thank you, Lord. I'll get to see Jesus sooner than I thought." When his disease sent him to the hospital suffering from suffocation, his response was, "Thank you, Lord. Now I have a better idea of what Jesus endured on the cross for me."

So, reading my malevolent mail, I just said, "Thank you, Lord. I get so much encouragement from so many people that a negative letter now and then balances things out and keeps me from pride."

Second, don't answer too quickly. Give yourself a few days. Your initial response is usually not your wisest one, for we tend to react defensively and emotionally. It's perilously easy to make bad matters worse—the old "from the frying pan to the fire" routine.

Third, show the letter to a trusted, objective friend. "Here's a letter that came today," I told a buddy who walked innocently into my office. "Read it and tell me what you think." My friend's response was quite

THOUGHTS FOR THE PASTOR'S SOUL

different from mine. "I sense some sincerity here," he said. "I think you might be a tad defensive. This person doesn't want to cause trouble; it's a cry for help." That helped me form my response.

Fourth, if it's really bothering you, lay the letter before the Lord as Hezekiah did in Isaiah 37:14 when Sennacherib sent his threatening letter: "And Hezekiah received the letter from the hand of the messengers, and read it; and Hezekiah went up to the house of the Lord, and spread it before the Lord."

Fifth, decide whether the letter merits an answer. Some letters should either be burned or banned. And sometimes the Lord may prompt us to pick up the phone and call the person directly. "Jim, I just received your letter. I can see you have some concerns. Is this a good time to talk, or would you like to suggest a better time and place?" Often, the person doesn't know what to do at that point. They hadn't expected to account for themselves so quickly, and their tone changes, sometimes for the better.

Sixth—and this is very hard—try to detach emotionally and look at the whole issue objectively. Frankly, I'm not good at this; but I do recognize it as a vital skill that can be cultivated. By the very nature of their calling, pastors tend to be emotional people of deep feelings who labor with enormous passion under great pressure and who are deeply loyal—and thereby easily hurt. To wriggle out of that mindset long enough to be dispassionate is a challenge. But it's the essence of wisdom. If we're just a bundle of reactions (as I tend to be), we'll seldom offer a wise response, and we'll frequently make things worse.

Finally, don't take yourself too seriously, and don't become too wrapped up in those letters. For several years I enjoyed telling people of a highly critical letter I once received. My writer questioned my judgment in several areas, sprinkling his comments with the pepper of pomposity.

"It was a seven-page, single-spaced letter!" I bragged at pastor's conferences. Smugness was in order, after all, for after the man left our church, he tried pastoring himself with predictable results.

No long ago, I found the letter. To my surprise, it wasn't seven pages, but only three-pages. And it was double-spaced. Furthermore as I reread the letter, I was surprised to find that the man wasn't completely wrong in what he wrote. I should have read it, smiled, separated the wheat from the chaff, recognized it as a series of honest differences, and gone on loving him anyway.

Of course, some people are just mean-spirited, and their letters should be filed roundly. I have one denominational critic whose integrity I don't trust enough to answer. Whatever I say, he'll find a way to distort. So when he recently e-mailed me questions with an accusatory tone, I just answered like this: "Hi. Got your e-mail! Have a good day." Underneath my name, I put a Scripture reference: Nehemiah 6:3. If he bothered to look it up, he would have read these words: "I am doing a great work, so that I cannot come down. Why should the work cease while I leave it and go down to you?"

I smiled about it all day long.

Come to think of it, I'm still smiling.

So let'er come. We know that all letters work together for good to those who love the Lord and are called according to His purpose.

MAY 14, 2006

MOTHER'S DAY SUGGESTED SERMON

God's Word to Parents

Date preached:

By Dr. Timothy Beougher

Scripture: Psalm 127—128, especially Psalm 127:1 and 128:1:
Unless the Lord builds the house, they labor in vain who build it. (127:1) Blessed is every one who fears the Lord, who walks in His ways. (128:1)

Introduction: There's a Mother's Day card that, on the front, reads: *"Mom, I remember that little prayer you used to say for me every day."* When opened, the inside reads: *"God help you if you ever do that again!"* Kids can be challenging, but they are precious gifts from God. As we celebrate Mother's Day today, moms, I'm not going to focus just on you this morning. The message this morning is for moms and dads. If you're not a parent yet, don't check out on me, because some of these principles will apply to you even if you don't have children. Let's look at God's Word to us in Psalms 127 and 128.

1. **Dedicate Your Home to God (127:1).** Why must we dedicate our home to God? Because God created the family; it's His design and He knows how it will best function. The building of a house illustrates the creation of a family. The point is that if it is to be done right, God must inspire and empower the building efforts. Are you trying to build your home in your own strength? Take heed to the words of verse 1; the Lord must build your home. Turn your life, including your home, over to the Master Builder.

2. **Trust God to Provide for Your Family (127:2).** The point in this verse is that God doesn't intend for us to work 24/7. If we are to build our family, we must make them a priority. Children need our *presence* more than our *presents*. Moms and dads, do you need to refocus? You may need to take out your calendar this afternoon and take a long, hard look at your schedule. Are you making your family a priority? No one ever said on his or her deathbed: "I wish I'd spent more time at the office!"

3. **Recognize Children as God's Blessing (127:3–5).** I don't have to tell you that in our society not everyone recognizes children as a blessing; some see them as a burden. We all must admit raising kids isn't easy. Kids can

be challenging! The Bible doesn't specify how many children you should have, but it does say children are a blessing. You and your spouse need to seek God together about this issue; and if you have children, realize from the start that they are blessings from God.

4. **Prepare Your Children to Make a Difference (127:4–5).** What is the purpose of arrows? To shoot them! Arrows are designed to fly. Remember the saying, "Give your children roots and wings." You raise them up so one day you can launch them out. If our kids are to make a positive difference, we must make sure they are aimed properly. In teaching our children to make a difference, we as parents need to play both defense and offense. Playing defense means you work to direct your child away from getting into serious trouble. Teach them what to avoid. We need to raise our children to play offense, to learn how to change the world for Jesus Christ. Train your children to make an impact on the world, to count for something in God's kingdom.

5. **Model Godliness in Your Family (128:1).** We need to model before our families that true happiness and true fulfillment in life come from following Christ. Billions are searching for happiness in all the wrong places; true happiness comes in obeying our Creator! Parents, we must communicate this truth not only by our words but also by our actions. If we are to model godliness, then we must have a close relationship with the Lord.

6. **Rejoice in God's Blessing (128:2–6).** Husbands and fathers, your wife is a fruitful vine not only in childbearing but in all areas of home life. Parents, your children are "olive shoots," plants that will in time bear their own fruit. With these blessings, we should always live with a proper fear of God, for God's blessings will ultimately rest on those who walk in His ways.

Conclusion: In light of these two Psalms, we have a choice to make this morning. We can either try to rely on our own feeble resources to build our homes, or we can surrender our false sense of control to a powerful and loving heavenly Father. He gives us His promise: if we dedicate our homes to Him, He will build our families and protect our families.

STATS, STORIES AND MORE

Survival of the Fittest

Some moms have come up with a great idea for the next reality show. Six men will be dropped off on an island for six weeks with one mini-van and four kids each. Each kid must play two sports and take either music or dance lessons. Each man must take care of his four kids, keep his assigned hut clean, do laundry, correct homework, and prepare meals. Each man must attend a weekly PTA meeting and make a miniature Indian hut from four toothpicks, two paper clips, and a flour tortilla. They must make a four-year old eat an entire serving of peas. The kids get to vote them off the island based on their performance. The surviving winner gets to go back to his job.

Priceless Time

A little boy asked his dad, "Daddy, how much money do you make every hour at work?" The dad said, "Son, I don't get paid by the hour but I figure I make about twenty dollars an hour based on a forty-hour work week." The little boy left the room and came back a few minutes later with his hands filled with quarters from his piggy bank. He said, "Daddy, here's ten dollars. Can I buy half an hour of your time—just for you to be with me?"

Building a Home

Have you ever built or remodeled a house? There are four principles:

    1) It will take more time than you planned.
    2) It will cost much more than you figured.
    3) It will be messier than you anticipated.
    4) It will require more patience than you thought possible.

Building a home has the same four principles.

FOR THE BULLETIN

Today marks the death in A.D. 964 of Pope John XII, the first pope to change his name upon assuming the papacy (which he did at age 18). ❀ Today is the birthday in 1752 of Timothy Dwight, grandson of Jonathan Edwards. Dwight was a revivalist who helped usher in a period of revival and awakening, especially on college campuses. He served as President of Yale University from 1795 until his death from cancer in 1817. He was also a hymnist who penned the words to "I Love Thy Kingdom, Lord." ❀ On May 14, 1759, John Berridge began preaching outdoors. "After dinner," he wrote, "I went into the yard, and seeing nearly a 150 people, I called for a table and preached for the first time in the open air. We then went to Meldred, where I preached in a field to about 4000 people." His remaining thirty years found him preaching the gospel in the open air. He was known as the Whitefield of the English countryside. ❀ On May 14, 1883, Charles Spurgeon helped his parents celebrate their golden wedding anniversary. He wrote, "On Monday, May 14, our honored father and mother were spared to celebrate their Golden Wedding Day with us... All their children and grandchildren were present with the exception of our beloved son, Thomas, and the company consisted of 32 persons in all. Of this household seven are preachers of the gospel. Very gracious has the Lord been to us as a family." ❀ May 14, 1948 is remembered for the establishment of the modern state of Israel. David Ben-Gurion stood before a small crowd in a Tel Aviv art museum and declared Israel's independence.

APPROPRIATE HYMNS AND SONGS

For Future Generations, Dave Clark/ Don Koch/ Mark Harris, 1994 First Verse Music (Admin. by Brentwood-Benson Music)

Gentle Shepherd, William J. Gaither/Gloria Gaither, 1974 William J. Gaither, Inc. ARR UBP of Gaither Copyright Management

House of the Lord, John Darin Rowsey, 1994 Centergy Music (Admin. by Integrated Copyright Group, Inc.)

Let Us Praise God Together, Richard D. Baker, 1988 McKinney Music, Inc. ARR distributed by Genevox Music Group

Make Us One, Jeff Switzer, 1987 A Mission In Music

WORSHIP HELPS

Call to Worship:
Brethren, we have met to worship and adore the Lord our God;
Will you pray with all your power, while we try to preach the Word?
All is vain unless the Spirit of the Holy One comes down;
Brethren, pray, and holy manna will be showered all around
—George Atkins and William Moore, "Brethren We Have Met to Worship"

Scripture Reading:
Who can find a virtuous wife? For her worth is far above rubies. . . . She also rises while it is yet night, and provides food for her household, and a portion for her maidservants. . . . She extends her hand to the poor, yes, she reaches out her hands to the needy. . . . Strength and honor are her clothing; she shall rejoice in time to come. She opens her mouth with wisdom, and on her tongue is the law of kindness. She watches over the ways of her household, and does not eat the bread of idleness. Her children rise up and call her blessed; her husband also, and he praises her: "Many daughters have done well, but you excel them all." Charm is deceitful and beauty is passing, but a woman who fears the Lord, she shall be praised. Give her of the fruit of her hands, and let her own works praise her in the gates.
(Prov. 31:10, 15, 20, 25–31)

Suggested Scriptures:
Deuteronomy 4:9–10; 6:6–9
Proverbs 13:24; 19:18; 22:6, 15; 29:15–17, 31:10–31
Psalm 78:5–6
Ephesians 4:29–32; 5:1–2, 22–33; 6:1–4
Titus 2:1–5

Additional Sermons and Lesson Ideas

The Challenge of Children

Date preached:

By Rev. Peter Grainger

SCRIPTURE: Various Proverbs

INTRODUCTION: I must begin with a statement by an unnamed person: "I once had no children and six theories on child-rearing. Now I have six children and no theories on child-rearing." Parents surely can identify with the challenge of raising children. The Book of Proverbs contains invaluable guidance for parents and children.

1. The Responsibility of the Parents. This includes teaching (Prov. 1:8; 4:1–4; 22:6), discipline (Prov. 13:24; 19:18; 22:15; 29:15), and accepting the Lord's discipline of you (Prov. 3:11–12; c.f. Heb. 12:1).
2. The Response of the Child. Children are to show obedience (Prov. 1:8–9; 3:1–2; 4:1) and wisdom in character and actions (Prov. 10:10; 13:1; 15:20; 17:25).

CONCLUSION: As mothers and fathers, we are to train our children according to the Lord's ways, since we are under His authority. Children, good and godly parents don't automatically mean you are good and godly; you have a responsibility to your parents and to the Lord about your conduct.

When God Calls Your Name

Date preached:

By Rev. Mark Hollis

SCRIPTURE: Genesis 12:1–9 and 22:1–18

INTRODUCTION: It may not have been a thundering voice from heaven, but at some point you have probably heard God speak. Maybe it was through Bible reading, a sermon, a song, or a prayer. What do you do when God calls your name?

1. When the future looks bright—Obey! (Gen. 12:1–9)
   A. Start Walking (Gen. 12:1–9)
   B. Expect God to Show Up (Gen. 21:1–5)
2. When God's command makes no sense—Obey Anyway! (Gen. 22:1–12)
   A. Start Walking (Gen. 22:1–5)
   B. Expect God to Show Up (Gen. 22:6–12)
3. When God shows up—Celebrate! (Gen. 22:13–18)
   A. He provides a substitute (Gen. 22:13–14)
   B. There is hope for the future (Gen. 22:15–18)

CONCLUSION: What do you do when God calls your name? Start walking. Expect God to show up. When he does there is hope for the future!

YOUTH SERMON

SUITABLE FOR A GRADUATION EVENT

Dare to Be a Daniel

Date preached:

By Rev. Timothy Beougher

Introduction: Different countries have different cultural norms, and what is appropriate in one culture may be offensive in another culture. For example, you should never touch a person's head in Thailand; the head is considered sacred. In Portugal you should never write anything in red ink; it is very offensive. Chewing gum is illegal in Singapore and can result in a large fine. In our message today Daniel illustrates for us how to live when we "leave home" or encounter new situations. While this message is focused especially on those graduating from high school, it applies to all of us. Anytime something changes in our lives (a new job, a new house, a new school, a new stage of life), we face challenges to our faith. Daniel illustrates how to live when we leave what is familiar to us and encounter new situations.

1. **You Will Face a Test: To Walk with God in a "Strange" Land.** Daniel 1:3–7 introduces us to Daniel and three of his friends who were carried off in captivity to Babylon. They are called "young men," a phrase used to describe teenagers between the ages of twelve and fifteen. These young men had grown up around Jerusalem. There they were constantly reminded about God through His Word and worship at the temple. Instead of being surrounded by a culture that supported walking with God, they found themselves in a pagan nation surrounded by pagan practices and people. Verse 4 introduces us to the king's reprogramming effort; Daniel was enrolled at Babylon State University on a full scholarship. He was in a new location; no one was watching him and his actions. His parents weren't there; his pastor wasn't there. The opportunity for temptation was great. But Daniel remembered that God was there! The Babylonians gave them new names to fit that culture. Do you see the challenge that Daniel faced? He was thrust into a pagan culture in this strange land and was expected to conform. But Daniel was a teenager with convictions. He made a choice: "I'm going to walk with God even in a strange land." Just because your circumstances have changed doesn't mean God has changed.

2. **You Must Fight the Temptation to Compromise Your Convictions.** Verses 5 and 8 tell us about the food and wine at the king's table, but Daniel resolved not to defile himself. We are not sure why the food represented a compromise for Daniel, but it is clear Daniel drew a line in the sand. As we encounter new situations, we must fight the temptation to compromise our convictions. Some of you will be going to schools where you will experience what one pastor has called "cultural brainwashing." You will be challenged to abandon your beliefs, to become like everybody else. Don't give in! Determine not to conform (Rom. 12:2). The decisions you make over the next few years will greatly impact the rest of your life. There are three key issues:

A. **Truth Issue: What is Truth?** The Babylonians sought to educate Daniel and his friends in their history and culture. Education is not evil; it's good and important to learn. But as we learn, we need wisdom to sort out truth from opinion. Daniel and his friends were being challenged to accept a pagan view of life. The key is that they mastered the material, but it never mastered them. The world will try to get you to adopt their view of truth. You will face the temptation to become intellectually sophisticated. You will be pressured to conform! Don't compromise your convictions! Do not determine what is right based on cultural norms. There are absolutes in God's Word. The bottom line is that it doesn't matter what others say; ultimately, what really matters is what God says.

B. **Identity Issue: Who am I?** Daniel means "God is judge." Hananiah means "The Lord is gracious." Mishael means "Who is like God?" Azariah means "The Lord helps." They were given new names: Daniel became Belteshazzar, "Bel will protect" (Babylonian God). Hananiah became Shadrach, "command of Aku" (a Babylonian moon god). Mishael became Meshach, "who is like Aku?" (Babylonian god). Azariah became, Abednego, "servant of Nebo" (another god). The identity issue is a key issue. By what name will others know you? Teenagers, college students, graduate students, adults, you're going to have to make a choice. Are you willing to be called a Christian in your culture? You must deal with the temptation to compromise your identity. Take a stand! Be proud of being a Christian!

C. Morality Issue: How Will I Live? Daniel had to decide whether to obey King Nebuchadnezzar and live like him, or to follow the King of kings and obey Him completely. Will we adopt the world's immorality or live by God's morality? You must fight the temptation of compromising your convictions.

3. You Can Triumph by Staying Pure in a Fallen World. The Babylonians changed these young men's homes, their names, and their education, but they couldn't change their hearts! These young men had decided to follow God no matter what the cost. They didn't give in to the voices: "It's okay—everybody else is doing it." "I'll just keep my faith to myself—after all, faith is a private matter."

"When in Rome, do as the Romans do." They requested a different diet and God honored them. God honored Daniel and his friends: they became healthier (vv. 15, 16) and wiser (vv. 17–20) than the others. When your heart truly belongs to God, you can be in any location and in any situation and still do the right thing.

Application: First, *commit to walk with God* (see v. 8). Let people know you're a Christian from the moment you set foot on that campus or the first day on your new job. Second, *spend time with the Lord each day in the Word and in prayer.* Either the Bible will keep you from sin or sin will keep you from the Bible. Next, *memorize key verses to deal with temptation* (see Ps. 119:11) and *develop a bond of accountability* (see Eccl. 4:9, 10). Graduates can find a campus fellowship (see Heb. 13:3). It's also necessary to find a good church, so don't sleep in! Finally, *trust God* (Prov. 3:5, 6). In 1873 hymn writer Philip Bliss wrote a gospel song about this story called "Dare to be a Daniel." We should all heed these words of wisdom:

Dare to be a Daniel.
Dare to stand alone!
Dare to have a purpose firm!
Dare to make it known.

Quotes for the Pastor's Wall

" Never think of giving up preaching! The angels

around the throne envy your great work. **"**

—Alexander Whyte to Rev. E. Jenkins,
a Methodist pastor who was discouraged and thinking of resigning.

MAY 21, 2006

When God Doesn't Answer Our Prayers

Dr. Woodrow Kroll *Date preached:*

Scripture: James 4:1–6, especially verse 3:
You ask and do not receive, because you ask amiss. . . .

Introduction: I want to address the question of God not answering your prayers. What are some of the roadblocks that may keep God from answering your prayers? It's so sad to see people reaching out to God, then wondering if He even heard their prayers at all. I've made a list of things that came to my mind out of God's Word about why God might not answer my prayer. I've put them in the form of questions we should ask ourselves.

1. **"Have I actually prayed about this?"** God may not answer my prayer if I forget to ask Him. The greatest reason for unanswered prayer is you and I don't remember to pray. James 4:2 says, ". . . you do not have because you do not ask." Dr. F.B. Meyer once said, "The great tragedy of life is not unanswered prayer but unoffered prayer." We just forget to ask. Billy Graham once quipped that heaven is full of answers to prayers for which no one has ever bothered to ask.

2. **"Am I cherishing sin so that God isn't going to want to hear my prayer?"** See Isaiah 59:1–2 and Psalm 66:18. One of the reasons God chooses not to answer prayer has a lot to do with what's in our lives. We have to have clean hands and a pure heart (Ps. 24:4). Is there a little corner of your mind that says, "Lord, you can have everything except that one corner. You can have every part of my life except this little closet." Is there something in your life that would keep God from answering your prayers?

3. **"Am I treating God well enough for Him to want to answer my prayer?"** Ezekiel 8:18 says, ". . . though they cry in My ears with a loud voice, I will not hear them." That's talking about God's chosen people, Israel (see also Mic. 3:4; Zech. 7:13; Jer. 7:11–16; 14:11–12). The Israelites were treating Him as just another god who often got in the way. I have to tell you in the

love of the Lord, friends, that God will not be treated that way. Sometimes we treat God so poorly that He isn't prone to listen to our prayers.

4. **"Are my motives correct?"** (James 4:2). It's important to ask for the right things for the right reasons. You may ask for the right thing but for the wrong reason, causing God to still say no.

5. **"Am I asking for the right reasons but asking the wrong things?"** Sometimes we ask God for things that He is never going to give to us for He knows those things would be harmful. James 4:15 says, ". . . you ought to say if it is the Lord's will we will live or do this or do that." My friends, when you ask according to the will of God, you will get the answer that goes with God's will (1 John 5:14–15).

6. **"Am I quitting too soon?"** Jesus encouraged His disciples to be persistent in prayer. (Luke 11:5–10; 18:1). Sometimes when you ask, you just have to hang in there. I read a story about an old man who had been ungodly all his life. There were a revival meeting in the town, and one night he trusted Christ as his Savior. Another man jumped from his seat and came down, tears in his eyes. This second man turned to the audience and said, "You wouldn't know this, but fifty years ago, twenty-five men including myself decided we would pray for our friend to come to know Christ as Savior. I am the only one left alive to see our prayers answered."

7. **"Am I taking advantage of all the things that unblock prayer?"** Do you find time every day for consistent Bible study and prayer? You need to have a regular place to meet God each day.

Conclusion: God wants to hear your prayers and answer them more than you want Him to. But often there are things that cause roadblocks, and we need to address the roadblocks, remove them, ask the right questions, and make sure we have clean hands and a pure heart. Then we can talk to God in intimacy and in full assurance that He will hear us and answer our prayers according to His will.

STATS, STORIES AND MORE

In the wonderful old classic, *The Christ Life for Your Life,* Dr. F. B. Meyer told this story:

My friend, Dr. Harry Grattan Guinness, told me once that all the water supply had become choked out of their college in Derbyshire, England. They could not obtain one drop of water from the bottom to the top of the house. They searched the cisterns, and inspected the taps and the whole machinery, and found no cause. At last they went to the junction between the main reservoir-pipe and their house-pipe, and there in the orifice, in the joint between the two, squatted a huge toad, which (as they were told) had probably come in as a tadpole, had fed upon the water, and had grown to this size, so that the whole water was stopped because it choked the orifice. Your life has been dry latterly; no tear, no prayer, no fervor. You have not met Christ, and you have not seen His face for many a long day. He has not used you. It must be because there is something in your heart, innocent once but injurious now. May God show you what it is . . . ! Cast yourself down in some solitary place before God and say, "May God forgive me! May God show me my sin, show me what it is that hinders me."[13]

APPROPRIATE HYMNS AND SONGS

Think About His Love, Walt Harrah, 1987 Integrity Hosanna! Music (c/o Integrity Music, Inc.)

God Leads Us Along, G. A. Young, Public Domain

I Will Celebrate the Goodness of the Lord, Dennis Jernigan, 1994 Shepherd's Heart Music, Inc. (Admin. by Word Music Group, Inc.)

He is Good, Jeff Nelson/ Frank Hernandez, 1996 Birdwing Music (a div. of EMI Christian Music Publishing)/His & Hernandez Music

Isn't He Good, Beverly Darnall, 1992, 1993 Maranatha Praise, Inc.

On May 21, 1382, in London at a synod meeting of Blackfriars who had assembled to condemn Wycliffe and his followers, an earthquake struck. The terrified clergymen fled. Wycliffe later claimed that God sent the earthquake "because the friars had put heresy upon Christ. The earth trembled as it did when Christ was damned to bodily death." This gathering became known as the "Earthquake Synod." ❁ On May 21, 1527, Michael Sattler, spokesman for the Anabaptists, was burned at the stake in Rottenburg, Germany. ❁ William Tyndale is a towering figure in English church history. As a young man, he developed a passion for translating the Bible into English, an idea fiercely opposed by the official Church. Forced to flee to mainland Europe, he was betrayed, ambushed, and arrested on May 21, 1535. The next year he was executed. ❁ May 21, 1607, marks the death of John Rainolds, one of the translators of the King James Version of the Bible. ❁ On May 21, 1738, Charles Wesley, who was to co-found Methodism with his brother John, converted to Christianity while sick with pleurisy. He wrote in his journal: "Sunday, May 21st, 1738. I rose and looked into the Scripture. The words that first presented were, 'And now, Lord, what is my hope? Truly my hope is even in Thee. . . .' I now found myself at peace with God, and rejoiced in hope of loving Christ. . . . I saw that by faith I stood. . . . I went to bed . . . confident of Christ's protection." ❁ Today is the birthday of the following: Elizabeth Fry (1780) who gained fame for her efforts to reform British prisons; Robert Murray McCheyne (1813), Scottish preacher; and Hudson Taylor (1832), missionary to China.

WORSHIP HELPS

Call to Worship:
Oh, worship the Lord in the beauty of holiness! . . .
Psalm 96:9

Pastoral Prayer:
Our Lord and our God, you have told us to call You our Father. You have told us to call you our Friend. Yet we acknowledge you as King of Kings, Lord of Lords, Prince of Princes, and God of all Gods. We thank you today for the rain that falls from heaven, for the winds that blow over the earth, for the lakes and seas and rivers that provide us with both beauty for our eyes and water to quench our thirst. We thank you for the clothes we wear, the cars we drive, the food we eat, and for the money in our pockets. All we have comes from you, and we ourselves belong to you. For the earth is the Lord's and the fullness thereof. And for that reason, Lord, we have come to worship you today. We worship You Father, Son, and Holy Spirit. Amen.

Kids Talk

Ask the children, "What are the best words you can say to your mother or father? Is it "Daddy, I want more toys! I want more money! I want more this or that!"? No, sometimes we may need to ask our parents for something; but the best words are, "I love you." The same is true when we talk to our Father in heaven. It's all right to ask Him to do things, for He invites our requests. But it's a good idea to always begin our prayer by saying, "I love You," and "Thank you, Father."

Additional Sermons and Lesson Ideas

Barriers Broken Down
By Charles Haddon Spurgeon

Date preached:

SCRIPTURE: Romans 10:1–3

INTRODUCTION: If you really desire others to be saved, pray for them, then labor for souls (v. 1). As you do so, you will find three barriers to their conversion.

1. Ignorance (v. 2)—The vast majority of people are not aware of how perfect and how complete their righteousness must be for God to accept it; nor do they know that God has provided a righteousness through Jesus Christ. They do not know Christ, and they do not know the excellence of the gospel.
2. Self-Will (v. 3a)—The vast majority of people try to get by on a righteousness of their own. They set up an idol in their hearts and live self-centered lives.
3. Flat Rebellion (v. 3b)—The vast majority of people have not submitted to God. This is a strange word, a searching word, and a suggestive word. But it is also a cheering word, for it tells us that all we have to do is to submit ourselves. That is all. Say: "Lord, if my soul be sent to hell, I deserve it. I submit, and I plead for mercy. I plead the precious blood of Christ as my righteousness."

CONCLUSION: Beloved friend, may the Holy Spirit lead you to submit. You have been kicking and struggling; now submit.

Early in the Morning

Date preached:

SCRIPTURE: Mark 16:1–2

INTRODUCTION: It took effort for the women in Mark 16:1–2 to rise in the chilly, early morning darkness, but it was worth it. The Bible speaks frequently of the blessings of the morning hours.

1. It's a Time for Devotion (Mark 1:35; Luke 21:38; Ps. 5:3; 88:13; Is. 26:9).
2. It's a Time for Singing (Ps. 59:16).
3. It's a Time for Executing God's Commands (Gen. 22:3; Josh. 3:1).
4. It's a Time for Going About our Daily Duties (Prov. 31:15).

CONCLUSION: Proverbs 6:9–11 warns about wasting the morning hours. Start every day on the right foot. Begin every morning by saying, "This is the day that the Lord has made!"

MAY 28, 2006

When God Answers Our Prayers Differently Than We Had Expected
Date preached:

Scripture: Romans 15:14–33, especially verse 29:
But I know that when I come to you, I shall come in the fullness of the blessing of the gospel of Christ.

Introduction: Has God failed to answer your deepest prayers as you had hoped? You prayed with intensity, but just the opposite occurred. Why does God not answer our prayers?

1. **Background: Review the career of the apostle Paul.** He set out in Acts 13 on his first missionary journey, traveling to Cyprus and Asia Minor. His second journey took him further west, to Greece; and his third journey covered much the same territory. His first two trips had a single purpose—to plant churches; but his third had several purposes. He wanted to preach and plant churches, but he also wanted to encourage those he had previously planted. He also wanted to collect an offering from the Gentile churches of Europe for the impoverished Jewish churches in Judea. So in Acts 20, carrying this offering, Paul began wrapping up his third journey. On his way to Jerusalem, he stopped in Corinth for three months of prayer and planning (Acts 20:2–3), staying in the villa of his friend Gaius. There he wrote the book of Romans. He decided to launch a fourth journey, one that would allow for a layover in Rome, but then Paul would press on to Spain (Rom. 15:22–29). One reason he wrote Romans was to pave the way for this fourth journey.

2. **Romans 15:19–33.** Here Paul disclosed his plans to the Romans. These verses are a prayer request for God's blessing on his plans, asking that he be spared problems in Jerusalem. But that isn't what happened. Paul's careful strategy blew up in his face, and his prayerful plans fell apart. God didn't answer as he had hoped or requested.

3. **Acts 21:30–34.** Paul was seized in Jerusalem, and it would be years before he would again see freedom. Was he disappointed? angry? confused? Probably. I don't think Paul was particularly happy with being seized, beaten, and arrested. But as he sat in that prison cell, he had a visitor. Acts

23:11 says, "But the following night the Lord stood by him and said, 'Be of good cheer, Paul; for as you have testified for Me in Jerusalem, so you must also bear witness at Rome.' " Notice the three lessons for us.

A. The Lord stands by us in times of seemingly unanswered prayer.

B. The Lord tells us to be of good cheer even when He doesn't answer as we wish.

C. The Lord reminds us that He knows what He's doing.

Sometimes when I order plants from a nursery, there's a box on the order form saying, "If we are out of the item you want, may we substitute one of equal or greater value?" I always say no, because the boys in the warehouse know what's best for my garden. But with the Lord, we should always say, "Yes! Yes, Lord! You may substitute!"

4. **Philippians 1:13–14.** Later, after Paul could see things in retrospect, he told the Philippians: "I want you to know, brethren, that the things which happened to me have actually turned out for the furtherance of the gospel, so that it has become evident to the whole palace guard, and to all the rest, that my chains are in Christ; and most of the brethren in the Lord, having become confident by my chains, are much more bold to speak the word without fear." Paul was able to evangelize the Imperial Guard, the upper echelons of the government of the mighty Roman Empire, and his example inspired hundreds of Christians to jump in and take his place in preaching the gospel. It had all worked out for good.

Conclusion: The hymnist Fanny Crosby wrote thousands of poems and hymns, and many of them were lost. A few years ago Dr. Don Hustad compiled a book called *Fanny Crosby Speaks Again.* He had uncovered a number of unpublished Fanny Crosby poems. And among them was this one:

> God does not give me all I ask,
> Nor answer as I pray;
> But, O, my cup is brimming o'er
> With blessings day by day.
> How oft the joy I thought withheld
> Delights my longing eyes,
> And so I thank Him from my heart,
> For what His love denies.

STATS, STORIES AND MORE

Aurelius Augustine, in his *Confessions,* tells about his wild and ungodly youth. For many years, he ran from the Lord. He was a brilliant, immoral, and pagan young man. But his mother Monica prayed and prayed and prayed for him. They lived in North Africa, and one day Augustine decided to move to Italy. Monica was distraught but prayed earnestly that he would not go to Italy. Yet he went. But it was there that Augustine found the Lord as His Savior under the preaching of Bishop Ambrose of Milan. Here is what Augustine later wrote (addressing his comments to God) about his mother's prayers: "But You, taking Your own secret counsel and noting the real point of her desire, did not grant her what she was then asking in order to grant to her the thing that she had always been asking."

Ruth Bell Graham wrote something similar in her book on prodigals: "How often has God said no to my earnest prayers that He might answer my deepest longings, give me something more, something better."

Vance Havner wrote: "God wants us to trust him, no matter what He does. There is a heavenly carelessness that leaves it all with Jesus and doesn't become upset when He does things contrary to what we expected."

APPROPRIATE HYMNS AND SONGS

O the Deep Deep Love of Jesus, Tom Fettke / Samuel Trevor Francis, 1986 Word Music, Inc. (a div. of Word Music Group, Inc.)

Trust His Heart, Eddie Carswell/ Babbie Mason, 1989 Dayspring Music, Inc. (a div. of Word Music Group, Inc.)/May Sun Music (Admin. by Word Music Group, Inc.)/Word Music, Inc. (a div. of Word Music Group, Inc.)/Causing Change Music (Admin. by Word Music Group, Inc.)

He Brought Me Ought, Henry J. Zelley/ Henry L. Gilmour, Public Domain

Who Can Satisfy My Soul Like You, Dennis Jernigan, 1989 Shepherd's Heart Music, Inc. (Admin. by Word Music Group, Inc.)

FOR THE BULLETIN

On May 28, 1533, the English reformer and church leader, Thomas Cranmer, Archbishop of Canterbury, declared that King Henry VIII's marriage to Anne Boleyn was valid, having earlier approved his divorce from Catherine of Aragon. Cranmer went on to advance Protestant views and develop the Prayer Book for the Church of England. Under the reign of Queen "Bloody" Mary, he was arrested and sent to the Tower of London. He was burned at the stake in Oxford in 1556 for his Protestant convictions. ✱ James Guthrie was a Scottish Covenanter preacher and pastor who was converted under the ministry of the famous Dr. Samuel Rutherford. On May 28, 1661, Guthrie was condemned for his faith, and he was executed on June 1, 1661. His head was cut off and nailed to Netherbow Port, where it remained for 27 years. ✱ Joseph Alleine was non-conformist Puritan preacher in the 1600s. The restoration of England's monarchy in 1662 resulted in the Act of Uniformity, removing two thousand preachers from their pulpits in a single day. Most of them preached their farewell sermons on August 17, 1662. Joseph, however, continued preaching. The authorities descended, and on May 28, 1663, he was thrown into prison. His health soon declined, and he died on November 17, 1668, at the age of thirty-four. He left behind a Puritan classic entitled *Alleine's Alarm*. ✱ Today is the birthday in 1836 of Annie Hawks, American homemaker, and the author of the hymn, "I Need Thee Every Hour." ✱ On May 28, 1954, the phrase "under God" was added to the Pledge of Allegiance by a bill signed by President Dwight Eisenhower.

WORSHIP HELPS

Call to Worship:
. . . "If anyone thirsts, let him come to Me and drink. He who believes in Me, as the Scripture has said, out of his heart will flow rivers of living water."
John 7:37–38

Readers' Theater (May be adapted as a responsive reading)

Reader 1:   We give You thanks, O Lord God Almighty, the One who is and who was and who is to come, because You have taken your great power and reigned.

Reader 2:   We give thanks to the God and Father of our Lord Jesus Christ.

Reader 1:   I will give thanks to You, O Lord, among the Gentiles, and sing praises to Your name.

Reader 2:   I will give thanks to You forever.

Reader 1:   At midnight I will rise to give thanks to You, because of Your righteous judgments.

Reader 2:   We give thanks to You, O God, we give thanks! For Your wondrous works declare that Your name is near.

Reader 1:   Oh, give thanks to the Lord, for He is good! For His mercy endures forever.

Both: And whatever you do in word or deed, do all in the name of the Lord Jesus, giving thanks to God the Father through Him.

(Rev. 11:17; Col. 1:3; 2 Sam. 22:50; Ps. 30:12; Ps. 119:62; Ps. 75:1; Ps. 136:1; Col. 3:17)

Benediction:
Blest be the dear uniting love,
That will not let us part!
Our bodies may far off remove,
We still are one in heart.
—Charles Wesley, 1742

Additional Sermons and Lesson Ideas

Encouraging Words
By Rev. Mark Hollis

Date preached:

SCRIPTURE: John 13:31—14:14

INTRODUCTION: The disciples were about to face their darkest hour of grief. Jesus words in this passage offered hope for them and for us.

1. Lord, where are you going? (John 13:31–38; 14:1–4). Though the coming days would be dark, Jesus encouraged His disciples not to be troubled. He was going away to get a place prepared for them. He would come back to take them there.
2. How can we know the way? (John 14:5–7) If we want to go there, Jesus is the way!
3. Lord, show us the Father (John 14:8–14). Do you want to know the Father? Know Jesus. He is the radiance of God's glory and the exact representation of His being (Heb. 1:3).

CONCLUSION: Jesus has gone to that land that is fairer than day to prepare us a dwelling place there. Yet He dwells within every believer and walks with us through our greatest difficulties.

Praise & Worship
By Pastor J. David Hoke

Date preached:

SCRIPTURE: John 4:24

INTRODUCTION: What is all the fuss about praise and worship? Are praise and worship really that important for the believer? Let's look at what Scripture has to say about this aspect of the Christian life.

1. The Imperative (John 4:23–24). Praise and worship is an imperative for every Christian. This means that they are absolutely essential for us to engage in praise and worship. Both are essential because God created us to praise and worship Him.
2. The Implications. Why do we need to praise and worship God? First, God commanded it (John 4:24). Second, God is worthy of praise and worship (Rev. 4:11). Third, they bring us into His presence (Ps. 100:4). Fourth and fifth, they give us His perspective on our situation and they change us (Ps. 73).

CONCLUSION: At all times we ought to be people of praise and worship, because our God is worthy of both and because we receive so much through them. Make both of them your priority.

JUNE 4, 2006

Keeping in Step

Date preached:

By Dr. Denis Lyle

Scripture: Galatians 5:13–26, especially verse 25:
If we live in the Spirit, let us also walk in the Spirit.

Introduction: On this Pentecost Sunday, I'd like to ask this question: As one living in the age of the Christian church, are you keeping in step with the Holy Spirit? What is He doing in your life? How can we keep in step with something invisible? Some think we are to *imitate* the life of Christ. But keeping in step in the Christian life is not done through *imitation* but by *identification*. We don't live the Christian life by trying to imitate the lifestyle of Christ; rather, He lives His resurrected life through us because we have received Him by faith! How can a believer learn to keep in step with the Savior? The answer is found in our passage today in which Paul deals with this subject; he emphasizes three things.

I. **The Conflict (Gal. 5:16–21).** There is a war going on inside the believer. The Greek word for "contrary" means "to be opposite" or "to be in continual opposition." The old you and the new you don't get along at all. The flesh and the Spirit are mortal enemies. Civil War? Yes! Soon after we become Christians and begin to discover the role of the Holy Spirit in our lives, we make a starling discovery. We find that we have all kinds of opposition. A number of enemies will try to keep us from walking in the Spirit. These enemies will hinder our attempt to live the victorious Christian life!

    A. **The External Enemy: The World (1 John 2:15).** John tells us not to love the world. The Greek word for "world" can mean several things: the earth (Acts 17:24), the human race (John 3:16), and the evil system opposed to God (1 John 2:15). Living the Christian life involves carefully interacting with the world but not being submerged in it.

    B. **The Infernal Enemy: The Devil.** Peter warns believers that Satan prowls around as a lion seeking to devour someone (1 Pet. 5:8). Satan should not be regarded lightly, for on our own, we are no match for him. Remember that the devil will seek to hinder you in every way possible.

C. **The Internal Enemy: The Flesh (Gal. 5:16–21).** The human body is not sinful; it's neutral. If the Holy Spirit controls the body, then we walk in the Spirit; but if the flesh controls the body, we walk in the lusts or desires of the flesh. The flesh stands for that part of man's nature wherein his natural desires have free rein. Sometimes the Bible refers to this flesh nature as the old man or the old nature. Something wonderful happens when we receive Christ as our Savior; at that moment we receive a new spiritual nature. The Bible refers to this new nature as the new man. Paul explains the contrariness of these (5:17).

2. **The Contrast (Gal. 5:19–23).** God wants us to walk in the Spirit (v. 16), but when we attempt this, a contrast occurs between the works of the flesh and the fruit of the Spirit. Paul talks about the negative first, listing sensual sins, superstitious sins, and social sins as works of the flesh. He then explains the fruit of the Spirit. The contrast between "works" and "fruit" is important. A machine in a factory works and turns out a product, but it can never manufacture fruit. Fruit must grow out of life, and in the case of the believer it is the life of the Spirit.

3. **The Conquest (Gal. 5:24–26).** Paul brings us to the point of victory here in this matter of walking in the Spirit! Is the victorious Christian life possible? Yes! But there are certain factors we need to take on board. We must consider the *historical aspect,* that is, that we died to sin and are now alive in Christ because of His sacrifice and resurrection. The *mental aspect* must penetrate our minds so that we know we are truly dead to sin (Rom. 6:11). The *practical aspect* must penetrate our lives; we must walk in the Spirit, meaning we must keep in step with the Spirit. This involves the Word, prayer, worship, praise, service, and fellowship with God's people.

Conclusion: The secret to avoiding temptation and living a fruitful life in the will of God is simple: keep in step with His Spirit. Count yourself dead to sin and alive in Christ; don't simply imitate Jesus—die to yourself and allow Him to *live* through you!

STATS, STORIES AND MORE

More from Denis Lyle

"When a boat is in the water, there's no problem, but when the water is in the boat, you've got problems. It's all right for a Christian to be in the world, but it's not very good for the world to be in the Christian."

Keeping in Step

Charlie never learned to keep in step. He was in the high school band for four years. He played the trumpet. Everyone tried to help him keep in step. The frustrated band conductor used to march right beside him in the practices. Other members of the band offered their help. But Charlie just couldn't do it. It got to be a quite a show every time the band performed. During the annual festivals the band would march in the downtown parade, and there was Charlie, out of step, out of time. All the half-time marching for the football season featured the same comic mistake. Charlie couldn't keep in step. It's not like he didn't try. He was always attempting to do better. Sometimes he would skip along trying to get in step. Other times, he would hold his left foot high, and hop on his right one, trying to find the correct time to put down the left one. But he never found it. He just didn't have a sense of timing.

In many ways Charlie reminds me of many believers who try to live the Christlike, Spirit-filled life. They want to be in step. They just can't seem to pull it off. They hear the beat, they try to imitate the band, but they just can't keep it. Perhaps if Charlie allowed the music to penetrate his mind beyond the technical aspects of marching, he would find the music beginning to manifest itself in his movements, allowing him to keep in step naturally. Perhaps if we gave up imitating what we think is a correct way to live and allowed the Spirit to live through us, we would be much more victorious as Christians!

APPROPRIATE HYMNS AND SONGS

Channels Only, Mary E. Maxwell/ Ada Rose Gibbs, Public Domain

Breathe On Me, Edwin Hatch/ B. B. McKinney, 1937. Renewed 1965 Broadman Press ARR Distributed by Genevox Music Group

Holy Spirit Thou Art Welcome, Dottie Rambo/ David Huntsinger, 1977, 1983 John T. Benson Publishing Company (Admin. by Brentwood-Benson Music Publishing, Inc.)

FOR THE BULLETIN

On June 4, 1568, the leaders of the Flemish opposition to the Spanish Inquisition were beheaded as traitors at Brussels, an event that precipitated a revolt by the Lowlands lasting eighty years. ❀ The old Trinity Lutheran Church of Wilmington, Delaware, was dedicated on this day in 1699; and the first German Bibles were printed in America on this day in 1743. ❀ In the 1760s a bitter battle was brewing in Virginia over religious freedom. Episcopal clergy and representatives of the British Crown sought to outlaw dissenters. In Spotsylvania County on June 4, 1768, five Baptist ministers were arrested and charged with disturbing the peace. "They cannot meet a man upon the road," it was charged, "but they must ram a text of Scripture down his throat." Due to public clamor, the five were shortly released. ❀ Today is the birthday in 1822 of Elvina M. Hall. She was a member of the Monument Street Methodist Church in Baltimore, Maryland, for over forty years, and she is best known as the author of the hymn, "Jesus Paid It All." ❀ June 4, 1900 is the birthday of Jewish Archaeologist Nelson Glueck. ❀ The British completed the "Miracle of Dunkirk" by evacuating over 300,000 troops on June 4, 1940. ❀ The Far East Broadcasting Company went on the air on June 4, 1948. Robert H. Bowman and John Borger founded it in 1945. Today FEBC broadcasts 560 hours of programming each day in 150 languages, much of it beamed into restricted access nations.

WORSHIP HELPS

Call to Worship:
Before His presence let us come
With praise and thankful voice;
Let us sing joyful psalms to Him,
With grateful hearts rejoice.
(From The 1912 Psalter)

Suggested Scriptures:
1 Samuel 10:9–10
Psalm 51:10–13
Acts 2:1–11
Ephesians 5:15–21

Offertory Comments:
Many years ago, two brothers grew up in New England. One
became a famous poet and the other a well-known hymnist. The
older brother was the poet Henry Wadsworth Longfellow. His
younger brother Samuel became a hymnist of note. On one occasion he wrote a simple one-verse hymn to use for the collecting of
the Sunday offering. It will do nicely for our offertory prayer today:
Bless Thou the gifts our hands have brought;
Bless Thou the work our hearts have planned.
Ours is the faith, the will, the thought:
The rest, O God, is in Thy hand.

Kids Talk

This is a good Sunday to get a microphone and
interview the children about their summer plans.
Are they taking a vacation? visiting grandparents?
attending summer school? Take the opportunity to
tell them about the church's summer program for children—camp, Vacation
Bible School, summer classes, choirs, etc. End with prayer for the children's
ministry for the summer months.

Additional Sermons and Lesson Ideas

Are You Filled?

Date preached:

By Rev. Richard Sharpe

SCRIPTURE: Ephesians 5:16–21

INTRODUCTION: Our passage gives us three signs of the filling of the Holy Spirit:

1. Speaking in Spiritual Songs (v. 19). The Spirit fills the heart of the believer so that it's full of song. We don't have to sing on key to do this type of singing. We are to sing to the Lord. If our hearts have a spiritual song, we are on our way to being filled with the Spirit.

2. Giving Thanks (v. 20). We remember that everything that comes our way is from the Lord. He wants us to grow. The flat tire and the weather are from the Lord. Everything is sent our way so that we can give thanks.

3. Submitting (v. 21). The Spirit fills us with the ability to listen to others and respect their opinion, even if it doesn't agree with ours. Are we listening to one another? No one has to be boss. We are all servants.

CONCLUSION: With all the evil that exists in the world, how can we really make a difference? Paul tells us the only way is to be filled with the Holy Spirit on a daily basis.

Kingdom Workers: Part One

Date preached:

By Dr. Timothy Beougher

SCRIPTURE: 1 Corinthians 3:5–9

INTRODUCTION: Throughout history there have been many occupations with different titles used to describe these vocations. There is one title that God has given to every single believer—"Kingdom Worker."

1. The Description of Kingdom Workers (v. 5a).
2. The Ministry of Kingdom Workers (v. 5b).
3. The Individuality of Kingdom Workers (v. 5c).
4. The Focus of Kingdom Workers (vv. 6–7, 9).
5. The Unity of Kingdom Workers (vv. 8, 9a).
6. The Reward of Kingdom Workers (vv. 8b).

CONCLUSION: Are you doing your part? All believers are called to be kingdom workers, to build the kingdom of God (Eph. 2:19–22).

JUNE 11, 2006

SUGGESTED SERMON

Christis: The Eternal Reality

Date preached:

By Dr. David Jackman

Scripture: Philippians 1:12–26, especially verse 20: . . . in nothing I shall be ashamed, but with all boldness, as always, so now also Christ will be magnified in my body, whether by life or by death.

Introduction: How do we stay firm under pressures when our faith is being tried and tested? What convictions will keep us standing firm for Christ in the gospel? Paul had been imprisoned and faced possible death in Rome. We can learn from his words to the Philippian church.

1. **Reflection on the Present Situation (vv. 12–18).** What looked like reversal to the Philippians was in fact advance (v. 12). Verses 13–18 explain what Paul meant by this. This paragraph makes clear that Paul's means of assessing the situation was far different than the world's criteria for assessment. At the end of the paragraph, he rejoiced because Christ was being preached (v. 18). Paul was imprisoned for preaching Christ; to ensure his freedom he needed only to stop preaching. The gospel was more important than life to Paul, so Christ would continue to be preached! How did this happen?

    A. **Paul Was Able to Preach to an Otherwise Impenetrable Group (v. 13).** Paul explained that the Praetorian Guard knew why he was in chains. This group consisted of veteran military men who could be trusted as the Emperor's personal guards; these guards were also in charge of those awaiting trial by the Emperor. For two full years while under house arrest Paul had many visitors and preached the gospel boldly and without hindrance (Acts 28:31). These guards surely noticed Paul's Christ-centered life and that the only real chains that bound Paul were the chains of love that bound Him to Christ. Gospel messengers are never without work to do.

    B. **Others Began to Preach Christ who Otherwise Wouldn't Have (vv. 14–18).** The circumstances hadn't gotten easier for the Christians, but

Paul's imprisonment had somehow made them bold preachers despite the circumstances (v. 14). Verses 15–18 tell us that there were mixed motives in this preaching. One group preached to advance the message in Paul's stead, the other to cause him more trouble and strife. We'd expect Paul to be angry, but he rejoiced because the gospel was being preached. It wasn't the motives or the messenger that concerned Paul, but the message. Of course, our motives do matter; we should search our hearts to be sure our Christian service isn't driven by selfish ambition, but we should rejoice when the gospel is spread!

2. **Focusing on the Future (vv. 19–26).** What looked like disaster was in fact deliverance. The same Christ whose gospel had become central in Paul's life is the Savior whom Paul desired to see glorified, whether that meant Paul's freedom or martyrdom (v. 20). The Greek word translated "exalted" literally means "made large" or "magnified." The one thing a magnifying glass never magnifies is itself. Paul thus would not magnify himself but Christ, whether in life or in death. Whenever we put Christ above ourselves, Christ is magnified there, for we show that Christ matters more than we do. That's the sort of gospel living that penetrates the world. Paul had no illusions about the cost. He prayed for courage (v. 20), but as he was up against the ultimate test that may take his life, he was confident for two good reasons:

A. **The Prayers of His Fellow Christians (v. 19).** Paul knew the Christians in Philippi were praying for him, and he expressed gratitude to them and thanks to God for his coming deliverance in answer to their prayers, whether the deliverance was release from prison or release from this life into Christ's presence (v. 21).

B. **His Eternal Perspective (v. 21–24).** We have trouble identifying with the idea that dying is gain because, in practice, we don't identify with living being Christ! For Paul, Christ was more important than life itself: Christ is the eternal reality. Death in Paul's mind meant immediate transport to the presence of Christ who meant everything to him. It can only be better by far to die and be with Christ, if here and now to live IS Christ. What looked like the disaster of martyrdom was actually deliverance and salvation. That's where Paul's heart was.

Conclusion: Two appointments exist that we cannot put on our calendars or in our diaries: death and judgment. How do you view them? Are they deliverance or disaster? The answer depends on what Christ means to you now. The real challenge to us is this: if to live is mainly the pursuit of my personal ambitions (my career, my family, my status, my wealth, or whatever), then of course death is the prince of terrors. That's why our culture is so terrified of death and won't talk about it. But if my life is Christ—all my energies are devoted to His gospel and its advancement—then no matter what the circumstances may be I'm always a winner. Even the removal of life itself, which to the world is the greatest horror, is in fact the greatest blessing (v. 22).

STATS, STORIES AND MORE

More from Dr. Jackman

I was once walking along the South Bank and I crossed the so-called "wobbly bridge," which is certainly still wobbly. Looking at that magnificent structure so strikingly designed, the construction appears most impressive. I remember, however, that when it was put to the test, it wobbled. It wobbled so alarmingly and with such potential danger that it had to be closed. It reminded me that we don't know how strong anything is until it's really tested. That's true not only of bridges but of every human resolve, every commitment, every friendship, every marriage, every business contract; they are only sure when they've been tested. This is equally true of faith in Jesus Christ, that it becomes sure through testing.

Look at what happened to the church in China during the last twenty to thirty years. From time to time there's been very severe persecution and tremendous opposition, and yet there's very reliable evidence that the church continues to grow. Why? Because hundreds of Christians have courageously, sensitively, fearlessly, and yet without compromise, shared the Word of God to their friends, their colleagues, and their neighbors. Though they may have served some time in prison for these actions, when the messengers were imprisoned, the Word wasn't fettered. What looked like a reversal was actually an advance. God is all-powerful and nothing can stand in His way. The gospel will continue to spread. Even if all we do is sit on the sidelines and neglect the spread of the gospel, it still remains true that God doesn't depend on us for the spread of the gospel in the world; He will raise up gospel workers. What a privilege it is to be one of those workers, whether in the neighborhood, the office, the school, or the church. We are incredibly blessed to be a part of the preaching of Christ.

FOR THE BULLETIN

Today marks the death in 1294 of Roger Bacon, a Franciscan monk and professor at Oxford. He was a creative genius, predicting the development of aircraft, submarines, suspension bridges, and engines. He sought to relate all lines of scientific inquiry to the Scriptures. ✿ Today is the anniversary of the ordination in 1799 of Richard Allen, the first African American Methodist bishop in the United States. ✿ June 11, 1869 marked the birth of Charles Hurlburt, who served as general director of the Africa Inland Mission from 1897 to 1925. Today is also the birthday in 1912 of American publisher David C. Cook. ✿ In 1907, missionary Jesse Brand, young and unmarried, left for India. He was joined later by Evelyn Harris, and the two were married in 1913. The Brands labored tirelessly, giving medical aid to thousands. Jesse took every opportunity to share Christ, in one year preaching four thousand times in ninety villages. Their son Paul was born and taught by his mother under a tamarind tree. His nature-loving dad showed him the wonders of termite mounds, bee swarms, and bird nests. At age nine Paul was sent to England for formal education, and his parents pressed on alone. In the spring of 1928 Jesse contracted blackwater fever. His condition worsened throughout May, but he continued working. On June 11, 1928, his temperature reached 106 degrees, and he was forced to bed and soon died. Evelyn remained in India and became a legendary figure since she hiked over the mountains with her walking stick doing the Lord's work. "Granny Brand" lived to see her son, Dr. Paul Brand, become a famous missionary-physician who excelled in the treatment of leprosy.

APPROPRIATE HYMNS AND SONGS

Immortal, Invisible, Walter Chalmers Smith/John Robert, Public Domain

Ancient of Days, Jamie Harvill/Gary Sadler, 1992 Integrity's Hosanna! Music (c/o Integrity Music, Inc.)

Awesome God, Rich Mullins, 1988 BMG Songs, Inc. (Admin. by BMG Music Publishing)

God is in Control, Twila Paris, 1993 Ariose Music (Admin. by EMI Christian Music Publishing)/ Mountain Spring Music (Admin. by EMI Christian Music Publishing)

How Great Thou Art, Stuart Hine, 1941, 1953, 1955, Stuart K. Hine, Renewed 1981 Manna Music, Inc. ARR UBP of Manna Music, Inc.

WORSHIP HELPS

Call to Worship:
In God we boast all day long, and praise Your name forever
Psalm 44:8

Invitation:
If you believe in the gospel, I invite you right now to pray. Ask the Lord to give you the boldness to preach the gospel and to make Him the most central reality in your life. If you're somewhere in between, perhaps like the "wobbly bridge"—a Christian who started out well but who is now a bit out of focus and wobbly—this is the way to get the stability back. Let's pray that our lives would be Christ, so that death may be gain. Won't you give yourself completely to Him and what He has for you and give up your selfish motives, ambitions, and worldly desires? If you do not believe in the gospel, let me challenge you today to ask yourself, *Why do I not? What's keeping me from making Christ the central reality of my life now and forever?* Meet with me or one of our church leaders today, or come to the front at the end of the service. Christ wants to pull you from your temporary life full of striving and self-motivation into the eternal reality of Jesus Christ.

Pastoral Prayer:
We ask, our gracious God, that these words that you inspired Paul to write would be written not only on our minds as we understand them, but in our hearts and that they may motivate our wills. We ask you to forgive us when we become gospel people as a hobby rather than making it the center of our lives. So give us, Lord, confidence in the gospel and in the Lord Jesus that He may be the eternal reality, the center of our personal lives and of our life as a congregation, so that together we may make Him known and see the gospel advance in our day and generation. We ask for the glory of Your Name, Amen.

Additional Sermons and Lesson Ideas

When God Turns Scoundrels into Saints
Date preached:
By Rev. Mark Hollis

SCRIPTURE: Genesis 25–35

INTRODUCTION: Jacob was a scoundrel that God turned into a saint. There are four phases to his spiritual journey.

1. "I'll do it my way!"
   - A. Attitude toward God—Independence (25:29–34)
   - B. Emotion—Defiance (27:18–24)
   - C. Personal Crisis—Death threat (27:41)
   - D. Encounter with God—Dream (28:10–15)
2. "If God will bless me, then I will honor Him."
   - A. Attitude toward God—Testing (28:18–22)
   - B. Emotion—Ambivalence (28:18–22)
   - C. Personal Crisis—Reunion (32:9–12)
   - D. Encounter with God—Wrestling Match (32:22–25)
3. "I will not let go until You bless me!"
   - A. Attitude toward God—Determination (32:26)
   - B. Emotion—Resolute (32:26)
   - C. Personal Crisis—Name Change (32:27–28)
   - D. Encounter with God—Touched Jacob's Hip (32:25, 31, 32)
4. "Lord, I am yours no matter what!"
   - A. Attitude toward God—Surrender (35:1–4)
   - B. Emotion—Peace (35:5)
   - C. Personal Crisis—Worship (35:6–7)
   - D. Encounter with God—Blessing (35:9–13)

CONCLUSION: Where are you in your spiritual journey?

Focus on Faith
Date preached:
By Dr. Denis Lyle

SCRIPTURE: 1 Thessalonians 3:1–13

INTRODUCTION: It was Charles Spurgeon who said, "A little faith will bring your soul to heaven, but a great faith will bring heaven to your soul." Paul teaches us to focus on faith:

1. Our Faith Needs to Grow (vv. 1–2).
2. Our Faith Needs to Know (vv. 3–5).
3. Our Faith Needs to Show (vv. 6–13).

CONCLUSION: Is your faith growing in the Lord? Do you know how to react to trials and temptations? Is your faith showing?

CONVERSATIONS IN A PASTOR'S STUDY
An "Interview" with Martin Luther

How do you inwardly strengthen yourself against your critics?

When I find myself assailed by temptation, I forthwith lay hold of some text of the Bible, which Jesus extends to me; such as this one: that he died for me, from which I derive infinite hope.

Do you have other favorite Scriptures that help you in times of distress?

The Psalms of David. The second Psalm is one of the best Psalms. I love that Psalm with all my heart. The 110th is very fine. It describes the kingdom and priesthood of Jesus Christ, and declares him to be the King of all things, and the intercessor for all men. It is a noble Psalm; if I were well, I would endeavor to make a commentary on it.

You have written many commentaries. How important are commentaries in one's study of the Bible?

When I was young, I read the Bible over and over and over again, and was so perfectly acquainted with it, that I could, in an instant, have pointed to any verse that might have been mentioned. I then read the commentators, but I soon threw them aside, for I found in them many things my conscience could not approve as being contrary to the sacred text. It's always better to see with one's own eyes than with those of other people. We must make a great difference between God's Word and the word of man. A man's word is a little sound that flies in the air and soon vanishes; but the Word of God is greater than heaven and earth.

How does that view of Scripture influence your preaching?

God very wonderfully entrusts His highest office to preachers that are themselves poor sinners who, while teaching it, very weakly follow it. When I preach, I sink myself deep down. I regard neither the doctors nor politicians, of whom there are in this church over forty; but I have an eye to the multitude of young people, children, and servants, of whom are more than two thousand.

What would you tell a discouraged pastor?

As long as we live in this vale of misery, we shall be plagued and vexed with flies, with beetles and vermin, that is, with the devil, the world, and our own flesh; yet we must press through, and not allow our-selves to retreat or recoil.

What would you say to an angry pastor, seeing that you've had the reputa-tion of being somewhat, well . . . irritable.

I never work better than when I am inspired by anger; when I am angry, I can write, pray, and preach well, for then my whole tempera-ment is quickened, my understanding sharpened, and all mundane vex-ations and temptations depart.

What is the role of prayer in the pastor's life?

No one can believe how powerful prayer is, and what it is able to do, but those who have learned it by experience. It is a great matter when in extreme need to take hold on prayer. I know, whenever I have earnestly prayed, I have been amply heard and have obtained more than I prayed for. God, indeed, sometimes delayed, but at last He came. The ancients ably defined prayer as *Ascensus mentis ad Deum*—a climbing into the heart of God Himself.

What other qualities should characterize an effective preacher?

A good preacher should have these virtues: First, [the ability] to teach systematically; secondly, he should have a ready wit; thirdly, he should be eloquent; fourthly, he should have a good voice; fifthly, a good mem-ory; sixthly, he should know when to end his sermon; seventhly, he should be sure of his doctrine. The defects in a preacher are soon spot-ted. Let a preacher have ten virtues, and but one fault, and yet this one fault will eclipse and darken all his virtues and gifts. Dr. Justus Jonas has all the good virtues and qualities a man may have; yet merely because he hums and spits, the people cannot bear him.

—Martin Luther's quotes are taken from *The Table Talk of Martin Luther*

JUNE 18, 2006

Training Our Children in the Way They Should Go

Date preached:

By Dr. Woodrow Kroll

Scripture: Proverbs 22:3–6, especially verse 6:
Train up a child in the way he should go, and when he is old he will not depart from it.

Introduction: What is our greatest legacy? Investing in our children is the most important investment we ever make, so I want to talk with you about an important verse; then we'll see how to invest our time in other people, specifically our children and grandchildren.

Biblical Study: The Hebrew word for "train up" in Proverbs 22:6 can also be translated "dedicate." The same word is used in 1 Kings 8:63 when Solomon dedicated the temple to the Lord. When you train up a child you dedicate that child to the Lord. I'm not just talking about a ceremony performed in church once when the child is an infant. I'm talking about getting up every morning and looking for opportunities to give that child to the Lord that day (see Deut. 6:5–9). Notice the context. Proverbs 22:3 warns us to foresee evil and hide from it. Verse 4 says that humility and godly fear bring prosperity to our lives. Verse 5 warns that thorns and snares entangle the perverse, but those who guard their souls are safe. Then comes verse 6, which tells us to train up our children. In other words, we're to instill within them the ability to foresee evil, exercise humility and godly fear, and avoid thorns and snares in life. If we do, as our children grow older, they will not depart from it. If you train children early in the moral things they need to know, then what you've instilled in them will still be there after they are grown. That's God's promise. Now, this verse doesn't promise that our children will not wander from the Lord. What it does promise is that if we put the right things in, the right things will be there when our children need them. We should train our children when they're young because:

1. **They Are Imaginative.** Children are bundles of imagination. I love to watch my grandchildren play. They're in another world all the time. But the same imagination that brings the kind of mischief that little kids get

into is the imagination that produces humility and godly fear. Ninety percent of a child's imagination decreases between ages 5 and 7. I'd hate not to use that imagination to spark some innate God-consciousness. It's the perfect time to involve yourself in your children. It's a wonderful opportunity to help them to begin well.

2. **They Are Teachable.** Children have just about everything in life to learn. One of the things they need to learn is how to live before the Lord. They need to know about the thorns and snares, about humility and the fear of the Lord. Don't be afraid to instill the morality of God's Word into your kids. If you don't do that by the time they go off to school, somebody else will be waiting to take over the job.

3. **They Are a Garden for Satan's Cynicism.** If we don't invest in our children when they're young, they will become cynical because Satan will find ways to take over their little minds. I remember a story by the English preacher William B. Riley. He was taking a vacation on the premises of a Scottish sheepherder. His host met him at the station, but the drive to the ranch was somber. The old shepherd finally said, "I lost sixty-five of my best lambs last night. The wolves got in." Riley expressed grief over the loss, and then asked how many total sheep the wolves killed. The shepherd looked surprised and said, "You don't know? A wolf never takes an old sheep when he can get a lamb." Satan is looking for the lambs, my friends. You can end your life well by helping them begin theirs well. Don't miss this opportunity. "Train up a child in the way he should go, and when he is old, he will not depart from it."

Conclusion: If your children are older, I can tell you it's not too late to do the right thing. Your influence may not be as strong as it would have been years ago, but as long as there's breath, there's influence. Don't curse the past; seize the day. Take every opportunity to make things right, to start over again. No matter what stage of life we're in, we can have a significant influence in the spiritual life of others.

STATS, STORIES AND MORE

Runs in the Family

The minister asked a group of children in Sunday School class, "Why do you love God?" He got a variety of answers, but the one he liked best was from a boy who said, "I guess it just runs in our family."

Don't Forget the Ministry of Grandparenting!

"Over the mountains," the old song says, "and through the woods, to grand-mother's house we go." More and more grandparents are finding that their greatest legacy is in their love and influence with their grandchildren. "The bond between a child and a grandparent is the purest, least psychologically complicated form of human love," says Dr. Arthur Kornhaber, author of several books on grandparenting. He claims that grandparents can offer an emotional safety net when parents falter. They pass on traditions in the form of stories, songs, games, skills, and crafts. And they have another magical ingredient that parents often lack—time. What many grandchildren appreciate most is the relaxed rhythm of life at the home of their grandparents. Kornhaber has found that children who are close to at least one grandparent are more emotionally secure than other children, and they have more positive feelings about older people and about the process of aging. Grandparents are, after all, *grand* parents. And in the dictionary the word *grand* means: *having more importance than others; foremost; having higher rank; large and striking in size, scope, extent, or conception; lavish, marked by regal form and dignity; intended to impress; very good; wonderful.*

APPROPRIATE HYMNS AND SONGS

Cry of My Heart, Terry Butler, 1991 Mercy/Vineyard Publishing (Admin. by Music Services)

I Need Thee Every Hour, Annie S. Hawks/Robert Lowry, Public Domain

The Potter's Hand, Darlen Zschech, 1997 Darlene Zschech (Hillsong) (Admin. in U.S. & Canada by Integrity's Hosanna! Music)

Lead Me Lord, Wayne Goodine/Elizabeth Goodine, 1994 New Spring Publishing (a div. of Brentwood-Benson Music Publishing, Inc.)

Take My Life and Let It Be Consecrated, Frances R. Havergal/ Ovid Young, 1984 Laurel Press (a div. of the Lorenz Corporation)

The final charges against Bohemian Reformer John Hus were presented by the Council of Constance on June 18, 1415. He was condemned and burned at the stake, but his death sowed the seeds for the coming Protestant Reformation. ✿ On June 18, 1464, Pope Pius II died, having launched a final crusade against the Turks. His death brought the era of the crusades to an end. ✿ On June 18, 1528, an arrest warrant was issued for William Tyndale by Cardinal Thomas Wolsey. For several years, Tyndale lived in hiding before being ambushed and seized outside Brussels in 1535. ✿ Thomas Kyme kicked his wife, Anne Askew, out of the house when she became a Protestant. The loss of home, husband, and two children was only the beginning of sorrows, for she soon faced trial for denying the doctrine of the mass. She was taken to the Tower of London and tortured on the rack until she was crippled. On June 18, 1546, she was officially condemned. A month later she was carried to Smithfield, chained to the stake, and burned as a heretic. ✿ Life Insurance was invented on this day in 1583, when Richard Martin of London took out a policy on William Gibbons. ✿ Today is the birthday, in 1830, of Elizabeth C. Clephane, Scottish poet and author of "Beneath the Cross of Jesus" and "The Ninety and Nine." ✿ On June 18, 1873 Susan B. Anthony was fined a hundred dollars for attempting to vote for president. ✿ Dawson E. Trotman, founder of the Navigators, died on June 18, 1956, while trying to save a drowning victim at Schroon Lake in the Adirondacks.

WORSHIP HELPS

Call to Worship:
Come and welcome, come and welcome,
That's our call to you today.
Worship Father, Son, and Spirit,
Come and worship and obey!

Worship Idea:
If you have the technical resources in your church, arrange a surprise phone call from a far away son or daughter to an unsuspecting father in the congregation. This will require the cooperation of family members, but the entire church will be blessed by hearing an American serviceman overseas suddenly come on the line to wish his dad a Happy Father's Day.

Scripture Medley:
O God, You have taught me from my youth; and to this day I
declare Your wondrous works.
Every day I will bless You, and I will praise Your name forever and
ever.
This is the day the Lord has made; we will rejoice and be glad in it.
Through the Lord's mercies we are not consumed, because His
compassions fail not, they are new every morning; great is your
faithfulness.
Goodness and mercy shall follow me all the days of my life.
So this day shall be to you a memorial; and you shall keep it as a
feast to the Lord throughout your generations.
From this day I will bless you.
I am the God of your father Abraham; do not fear, for I am with
you. I will bless you.
(Ps. 71:17; 145:2; 118:24; Lam. 3:22–23; Ps. 23:6; Ex. 12:14; Hag. 2:19;
Gen. 26:24)

Benediction:
Now, Lord, we leave this place, but we continue in worship by going forth with Your voice ringing in our hearts, Your songs pealing in our souls, Your power surging through our lives, and your Word guiding our steps. Amen.

Additional Sermons and Lesson Ideas

Is the Bible the Word of God?

Date preached:

Adapted from W. Graham Scroggie

SCRIPTURE: Psalm 119:89

INTRODUCTION: To the question, "Is the Bible the Word of God?" we can give a three-fold answer:

1. It Seems to Be.
   A. Its origination
   B. Its preservation
   C. Its circulation
2. It Claims to Be.
   A. In the Old Testament: See Psalm 19:7–11.
   B. In the Testimony of Jesus: See John 10:35.
   C. In the New Testament: 2 Timothy 3:16.
3. It Proves to Be
   A. The Witness of Individuals. The testimony of millions is a witness to the Bible's authority.
   B. The Witness of the Church. The origination, progress, preservation, and influence of the church bear witness to the Bible's authority.

CONCLUSION: Being of divine origin, the Bible speaks with sovereign authority and demands we take its precious teachings into our hearts and lives as a standard for faith and practice.

Three Important Words for Dads

Date preached:

SCRIPTURE: Various

INTRODUCTION: Several verses in the Bible address fathers specifically, and these are of utmost importance to those who are privileged to be called "Dad."

1. 1 John 4:13, 14—Fathers should know Him who is from the beginning (Jesus) so they can teach their children to know Him too.
2. Colossians 3:21—Fathers should not discourage their children.
3. Ephesians 6:4—Fathers should raise their children in the nurture and instruction of the Lord.

CONCLUSION: By knowing Him who is from the beginning, fathers will have the resources needed to encourage their children and to raise them in the nurture and instruction of the Lord.

JUNE 25, 2006

The God-Planned Life

Date preached:

Scripture: Various New Testament passages on "the will of God"

Introduction: Who would you like to plan your life? You say, "Well, I want to plan my own life." But we can't really do that, because we don't know what the future holds and there's no way we can plan for all the contingences that may come our way. George Herbert said, "Life is half spent before we (even) know what it is." In some cultures, the parents plan out their children's lives. In communist and other totalitarian nations, the government plans a person's life. But what if the all-good, all-loving, all-wise, wonderful God offered to plan your life for you. Well, He does! I want to show you some Scriptures today that use a phrase that's found twenty-five times in the New Testament—"the will of God."

I. **Mark 3:31–35.** This story seems a little strange at first. Why wouldn't Jesus acknowledge His family who had come to visit Him? The answer is found earlier in the chapter. Verse 21 says: "But when His own people"—His family, His relatives—"heard about this, they went out to lay hold of Him, for they said, 'He is out of His mind.' " His mother, brothers, and sisters had showed up because they thought He had lost His mind, and they were trying to lure Him out so they could take Him away and have him committed to a hospital for the mentally ill! Of course, they didn't have any such hospitals in that day, but you know what I mean. They thought, "He's gone bonkers. He's off His rocker. He's lost His marbles. He's not right in the head. He doesn't have both oars in the water." Jesus, however, knew exactly what He was doing, and He wasn't about to be lured out. Instead, He said something very wonderful that has a direct meaning to you and me: "I want to be your Brother. I want to be your Son. I want to be your Father. I want to be your Best Friend. I want you to be My family. I want to be in an intimate, personal, daily, family relationship with you. But there's one thing that's necessary. You must be committed to doing the will of God in your life."

2. **Luke 7:30.** Let's take this a little further and look at another passage in the Gospels. Here, Jesus was commenting on the role of John the Baptist: "But the Pharisees and lawyers rejected the will of God for themselves, not having been baptized by him." God has a plan for our lives, but He isn't going to force it. He has a will for us, but He says it's optional. You can either accept it or reject it.

3. **Ephesians 5:17.** Our great need, then, is to be wise and not unwise, understanding "what the will of the Lord is." In other words, there are two ways to live—wisely and foolishly. There are two kinds of people—the wise and the foolish. What's the difference? The foolish reject the will of God. The wise understand what the will of the Lord is, which implies that the will of the Lord is understandable. We can find it for our lives if we want to. God will reveal it to us if we meet certain conditions. What are these conditions? Well, that brings us to our last passage.

4. **Romans 12:1–2.** This is the Bible's classic three-point sermon. These two verses give us three ways of finding God's will. First, we must offer our bodies as living sacrifices; then we must make a break from the world around us; and finally, we must get the Bible into our minds and be transformed by God's Word. What does God want from my life? He wants my whole life. He wants my entire life—not fifty percent, eighty-five percent, or even ninety-nine percent. He wants all there is of you.

Conclusion: Luke 9:59 records an encounter Jesus had with a would-be disciple: "He said to another, 'Follow Me.' But he said, 'Lord, let me first go and bury my father.' " Do you see the problem here? "Lord, me first." That's a contradiction. You can't say, "Lord, me first"! If Jesus is Lord, He *is* first. He has got be first in our lives; our bodies must be living sacrifices to Him; our lives must be divorced from the world; our minds must be renewed by the Scriptures. The Bible says, "Trust in the Lord with all your heart and lean not unto your own understanding. In all your ways acknowledge Him, and He will direct your paths" (Prov. 3:5, 6). This takes discipline and commitment. But it leads to living a God-planned life.

STATS, STORIES AND MORE

In his autobiography, the great Christian composer John W. Peterson wrote that he grew up in church; then at a certain point in his life, he invited Jesus to be his Savior. As a young man, someone gave him a copy of a book about John and Betty Stam, missionaries to China who were martyred for their faith. Their story of dedication and sacrifice had a profound effect on Peterson. He couldn't put the book down, and he couldn't get it out of his heart. He knew Christ was commanding him to offer his life fully in devotion to God—no matter the cost. Hours passed, and John struggled with the decision. Finally the last wall of his resistance crumbled, and he cried out, "Here I am, Lord. I don't know what You want of me, but even if it's China and martyrdom, I'm willing." That became the defining moment of his life. He later explained that there were three phases of his understanding of Christianity. The first was as a child, when Christianity was little more than stained glass windows, going to Sunday School, and being a good boy. The second was his conversion when he began to understand the Christian life. But then he saw that Christianity was something more: Jesus Christ was to be Lord of all his life. What about you? Are you at the stained glass stage? Or have you had a real encounter with God through Jesus Christ? Or are you at the Lordship stage when you're beginning to understand that God wants to be the Lord of all there is of you. It's at that stage that we begin to understand and to prove the good and acceptable and perfect will of God.

APPROPRIATE HYMNS AND SONGS

How Firm a Foundation, George Keith/Anne Steele/John Rippon/Joseph Funk, Public Domain

The Lord Has a Will, Mike Hudson/Barbara Hudson, 1977 Word Music, Inc. (a div. of Word Music Group, Inc.)/Wordspring Music, Inc. (Admin. by Word Music Group, Inc.)

What a Friend We Have in Jesus, Joseph M. Scriven/Charles C. Converse, Public Domain

In Christ Alone, Shawn Craig/Don Koch, 1990 Paragon Music Corporation (Admin. by Brentwood-Benson Music Publishing, Inc.)

FOR THE BULLETIN

On June 25, 1178, five Canterbury monks reported something exploding on the moon. It became known as the "Canterbury Event," and it was thought to be a cataclysmic result of a collision between the Moon and some large object flying through space. The monks probably observed a collision between the moon and an asteroid that carved out the lunar crater now known as Giordano Bruno, named for the Italian heretic who was burned at the stake for believing in the existence of inhabited planets other than earth. ❁ The Augsburg Confession was presented to Emperor Charles V on this day in 1530. Written by Philip Melanchthon at age thirty-three while in consultation with Martin Luther, it was a detailed explanation of Lutheran doctrine. ❁ On June 25, 1812, John Jasper, the prodigal son of a Baptist slave in Virginia, was converted to Christ. Jasper became a prominent African-American preacher and the founder of the Sixth Mount Zion Baptist Church in Richmond, Virginia. ❁ On this day in 1823, Charles Finney, an attorney in New York, applied for ordination into the Presbyterian ministry and was taken under the care of the St. Lawrence presbytery. He was ordained on July 1, 1824. He became one of the most successful revivalists in American history. ❁ The China Inland Mission was founded by English missionary J. Hudson Taylor on this day in 1865. ❁ William Simpson grew up in Tibet where his parents were missionaries. He was later sent there himself as a young evangelist with the Assemblies of God. He poured his life into gospel labors on the border with China, traveling hundreds of miles on horseback and seeking to plant the seeds of the gospel in the remote villages. He also established a mission station at Labrang, Tibet. One June 25, 1932, he was killed by a horde of Muslims.

WORSHIP HELPS

Call to Worship:
. . . I have trusted in Your mercy; my heart shall rejoice in Your salvation. I will sing to the Lord, because He has dealt bountifully with me (Ps. 13:5, 6).

Benediction:
For you were once darkness, but now *you are* light in the Lord. Walk as children of light (for the fruit of the Spirit *is* in all goodness, righteousness, and truth), finding out what is acceptable to the Lord (Eph. 5:8–10).

Kids Talk

Take a bottle of bubbles and tell the children, "You know, I really might need some help here. I bought this bottle of bubbles, but I think they're broken. See, I can pull out this wand and see the liquid, but they don't do anything. Why is that?" Allow the children to answer that you must blow into the wand. "Oh, so you're telling me that they don't work by themselves, that air must be provided to make them float around and act like bubbles." After blowing some bubbles, continue, "You know what that reminds me of? There's a verse in the Bible that tells us that we are like dead people because of sin, but if Jesus is in us, His Spirit gives us life (Rom. 6:10, 11). So, we're kind of like these bubbles. When someone adds air to them, they do what bubbles are supposed to do. When Jesus is in our hearts, He adds His Spirit so that we can do what He wants us to do."

Additional Sermons and Lesson Ideas

Body Life

Date preached:

By Pastor J. David Hoke

SCRIPTURE: Ephesians 4:15b–16

INTRODUCTION: The church is not a building. If the room is full of Christian people, it may simply be a Christian crowd; it may not be a church at all. Let's look at what
the body of Christ should look like:

1. Our Source: The head is Christ (v. 15b).
2. Our Work: Every part contributes to the growth of the body (v. 16a).
3. Our Goal: The whole body is edified by love (v. 16b).

CONCLUSION: Are you beginning to understand what body life is all about? We are
a community of God's people who have been brought into a living union with God
and with one another. The body of Christ is a living organism submitted to Christ as
the Head, composed of many individual parts, yet all working together in harmony
through an exercise of the gifts given to each one so that we might all grow together
in love to be more like Christ. That is what body life is all about.

The Marks of a Mighty Church

Date preached:

By Dr. Rev. Denis Lyle

SCRIPTURE: 1 Thessalonians 1:1–10

INTRODUCTION: You may remember using your hands to this little poem: "This
is the church and this is the steeple. Open the door and see all the people." Paul opens
the church of Thessalonica to show us the marks of a mighty church:

1. An Energetic Church (v. 3)
   A. The Elements of the Christian Life: Faith, Love, Hope
   B. The Evidences of the Christian Life: Work, Labor, Patience
2. An Elect Church (v. 4)
3. An Exemplary Church (vv. 6–7)
   A. Eagerness for the Word of God (v. 6)
   B. Eagerness to Be Workmen of God (v. 6)
   C. Eagerness to Do the Work of God (v. 7)
4. An Evangelistic Church (v. 8).
5. An Expectant Church (v. 9–10).

CONCLUSION: Ask yourselves, "What kind of church would mine be if every member were like me?"

Henry Crowell

When Henry Crowell was nine his father died from tuberculosis, and when he was seventeen Henry himself contracted the disease. Though he appeared to be dying, he mustered his strength to attend D. L. Moody's campaign in Cleveland, Ohio. He listened carefully as Moody thundered: "The world has yet to see what God can do through a man fully dedicated to him."

Crowell determined to be God's man. "To be sure, I would never preach like Moody. But I could make money and support the labors of men like Moody. I resolved, 'Oh God, if you preserve my life and allow me to make money to be used in your service, I will keep my name out of it so you will have the glory.' "

Shortly thereafter Henry found Job 5:19: "He shall deliver you in six troubles, yes, in seven no evil shall touch you." The Lord seemed to assure him of healing through that verse.

Henry grew stronger and began honing his business instincts, shrewdly investing his family's wealth. He started companies, purchased properties, and introduced innovations to the marketplace. When a mill owned by nearby Quakers became available, Henry purchased it and began dreaming of modern cereal products for American homes. Thus Quaker Oats Company was born.

The money rolled in—and it rolled out. Henry consistently gave sixty-five to seventy percent of his income to Christian causes. Millions of dollars flowed to churches, schools, and missions. He worked tirelessly for the new, fledgling Moody Bible Institute of Chicago. Under his vision, MBI escaped financial ruin and became a powerful training center. He helped start Moody Press, Moody Magazine, and Moody radio ministries.

And he was still dreaming at age 89. Shortly before his death, he spoke to the Board of Moody Bible Institute, complimenting them for their vision but telling them to "think in terms of still greater things for the glory of Christ."

PRAYERS FOR A PASTOR'S CLOSET

I would not have the restless will
That hurries to and fro,
Seeking for some great thing to do
Or secret thing to know;
I would be treated as a child,
And guided where I go.

Wherever in the world I am,
In whatsoe'er estate,
I have a fellowship with hearts
To keep and cultivate;
And a work of lowly love to do
For the Lord on Whom I wait.

So I ask Thee for daily strength,
To none that ask denied,
And a mind to blend with outward life
While keeping at Thy side;
Content to fill a little space,
If Thou be glorified.

—Anna Waring

JULY 2, 2006

Sacrifice: The Authentic Demonstration

By Dr. David Jackman

Date preached:

Scripture: Philippians 2:5–18, especially verse 5:
Let this mind be in you which was also in Christ Jesus. . . .

Introduction: Self-preservation is all-important in our culture, whereas self-sacrifice is not so highly regarded. Our passage today teaches us, however, that self-sacrifice is the very heart of the Christian faith.

I. **Jesus Embodies the Essence of the Gospel (vv. 5–11).** Central to Paul's theology is the idea that what we think determines how we will act. The New Testament uniformly teaches that behavior is the product of belief. If we are to become effective Christians in the world, we need to become more and more like the Christ we serve. For this reason the little phrase "in Christ" occurs often in Paul's writings. When you become a Christian, you do not simply make an intellectual assent to a God who is "out there," but an actual uniting to Christ through faith. Then all of His benefits become yours: His death becomes a death for you; His resurrection becomes a new life for you; His Holy Spirit lives in you, giving you victory as you grow in Christ-likeness. Verse 5 could be paraphrased, "Develop this Christ-like mindset in your congregation," for the statement here is plural, focusing on the church in Philippi. Paul was saying that the genuine example of the gospel is seen in Jesus and needs to be exemplified in us. The implication of that is that all forms of pride are absent in God's people. In verses 6–8 there are two key verbs that explain what that meant for Jesus and what it means for us.

A. **Jesus as God: He Made Himself Nothing (v. 6–7).** Verse 6 does not mean that Jesus ceased to be fully God but that He chose not to guard His rights as the Son of God and His heavenly position at all costs. Instead, Jesus emptied Himself. He didn't empty himself of deity but of dignity. He didn't empty Himself of divine attributes, but He did take on a human nature. He looked and seemed like a normal human

(v. 7–8). Jesus was, however, unlike any other human because He was fully God—yet He became a servant.

B. Jesus as Man: He Humbled Himself (v. 8). Throughout His life Jesus demonstrated loving service to God and to His fellow man. Do you see how this is the polar opposite of Adam and of the fallen human nature we received from him? Jesus was ready to leave His heavenly status and become man, but Adam wanted that heavenly status: to be equal with God. Adam's rebellion resulted in a death sentence for all of humanity, whereas Jesus' life of humility and loving obedience resulted in His becoming the atoning sacrifice for the whole world! When we think of the Cross of Jesus—the pain, the shame, the rejection, and the amazing love and grace for us—how can we be anything other than humbled into the dust that God should do that for us?! The inevitable outcome of the Cross is embodied in verses 9–11: Jesus is exalted as Lord of all.

2. **Christians Exemplify the Lifestyle of the Gospel (vv. 12–18).** Paul would come to us, as he wrote to the Philippians, and say, "My dear friends who have gathered for this service today, have you received this great salvation that the Lord Jesus brought you? Very well, then, *work it out.* Carry it out. Do it through your continued obedience in awe, in trembling, and in love to such a great Savior. When you look at Christ, you see the exalted God who is full of glory and strength. When you look at yourselves, you see weakness and pride. Jesus willingly left all His glory to rescue you, so won't you work out your humility in your lives and work out that salvation?" Verse 13 turns despair into possibility. We can have confidence that God will accomplish this in us. God never calls you to do anything without providing you the means to do it. Paul then explains what humility looks like practically—even through offering himself as a sacrifice— should the gospel require martyrdom (vv. 14–18).

Conclusion: How we live will either commend or deny the gospel we preach. If unbelievers find the same pride and self-centeredness in us that they see in the world, why should they take the gospel seriously? Why should the world think that Christianity has any relevance at all if they see the church divided? Jesus came and emptied Himself to bring people like us into His own likeness.

STATS, STORIES AND MORE

More from David Jackman

Verses 6–11 are in poetic form. This passage is one of the great hymns in the New Testament. It's a great Christological poem. It's one of the most profound expositions of Christ and the gospel found in the whole of Paul's letters. In context, however, this passage is not just abstract theological theory. It has a motivational application to your everyday life and to mine. We miss the whole point of the passage if we don't see how it challenges our attitudes and our behavior.

Someone Once Said...

"We often settle for a Christian veneer of humility. It reminds me of the best-selling author whose book was entitled, *Humility and How I Achieved It*."—Dr. David Jackman

"First, humility. Second, humility. Third, humility"—Augustine, when asked to list the principles of the Christian life

"That any good man should be willing to humble himself in this way for the blessing of others is breathtaking, but that the offended One, the Lord of Glory, should willingly enter into such humiliation, should bring . . . adoration to our hearts."—Sinclair Ferguson

In the book, *Ruth Bell Graham: Celebrating an Extraordinary Life,* neighbor Betty Frist tells of a visitor who went to the Graham home and found Ruth in the kitchen, cradling a strange baby in one arm, fixing breakfast with her free hand, and trying to shut the oven door with her foot. The baby's parents were young missionaries home on furlough and were desperate for sleep because of the travel-worn, upset baby. So Ruth had taken the baby into her room for an all-night stand while the parents caught up on their sleep.[14]

APPROPRIATE HYMNS AND SONGS

Trust and Obey, Rev. John H. Sammis/Daniel B. Towner, Public Domain

With All My Heart, Babbie Mason, 1990 Word Music, Inc. (a div. of Word Music Group, Inc.)

You Are Holy, Marc Imboden/Tammi Rhoton, 1994 Marc Imboden

Purify My Heart, Jeff Nelson, 1993 Maranatha Praise, Inc./HeartService Music, Inc. (Admin. by Music Services)

Make Me A Servant, Kelly Willard, 1982 Maranatha! Music (Admin. by The Copyright Company)/Willing Heart Music (Maranatha! Music [Admin. by The Copyright Company])

FOR THE BULLETIN

The English church leader, Thomas Cramner, was born on July 2, 1489. He became the first Protestant Archbishop of Canterbury and a crucial figure in the English reformation. Cramner promoted the circulation of the Scriptures in the vernacular. He was also the primary author behind the English Prayer Book and "The Thirty-Nine Articles." When Queen Mary came to the throne in 1553, Cramner was sent to the tower of London. Under great pressure he recanted his Protestant convictions, but then publicly renounced his recantations and died heroically by being burned at the stake in Oxford in 1556.

✽ On July 2, 1505, Martin Luther, age 21, was caught in a thunderstorm and made his famous vow to become a monk. ✽ William Tyndale, the great English Bible translator and martyr, was awarded his Master's Degree at Oxford on this day, July 2, 1515. ✽ The English Civil War between King Charles I and the Parliamentarian Troops began in the late summer of 1642. It appeared that Royalist forces would prevail, but the intervention of Scotland turned the tide. The Parliaments of England and Scotland made an agreement to adopt a uniform religion "according to the Word of God and the example of the best reformed churches." On July 2, 1644, the Royalist forces of King Charles I were defeated in the Battle of Marston Moor. Within two years, the royal army completely collapsed, and Charles I was beheaded on January 30, 1649. ✽ Pastor and hymnist, Washington Gladden, died on this day in 1916. He is chiefly remembered for his "Social Gospel" and for writing the hymn, "O Master, Let Me Walk with Thee."

WORSHIP HELPS

Call to Worship:
Blessed is the man You choose, and cause to approach You, that he may dwell in Your courts. We shall be satisfied with the goodness of Your house, of Your holy temple.
Psalm 65:4

Pastoral Prayer:
Father, we thank you for the statement in Philippians 2:13 that says ". . . for it is God who works in you." Lord Jesus, we praise You for all You've accomplished through Your death for us on the Cross. Thank you for Your obedience which brought You into our world. Thank You for the humility that took You in obedience to death, even death on the Cross. We worship You as our Lord and our ascended King. We rejoice, therefore, that You have been raised to the Father's right hand, and we look forward to the day that every tongue confesses that Jesus Christ is Lord. You have given us days to live in between now and then in which we want to be more like Jesus. We want our church to reflect the realities of the gospel more and more, that people will know there is a supernatural power that can transform human lives. We want to love one another more and to serve one another more. We ask You to keep us from the negativity, the grumbling, and the complaining that is truly selfish. Write on our hearts a desire to be more like Jesus, pure and blameless, that the light may shine from us onto our wicked and warped generation. Help us toward that end, we pray. Work in us. Give us both the will and the ability to do it for Your name's sake. Amen.

Additional Sermons and Lesson Ideas

The Problem of Anger
Date preached:

By Rev. Peter Grainger

SCRIPTURE: Various Proverbs

INTRODUCTION: Have you ever lost your temper? I'm sure all of us here regret unkind words or actions that resulted from our anger. The book of Proverbs offers practical wisdom for the problem of anger:

1. Controlling Anger. Practice self-control (Prov. 16:32) through the Spirit (Gal. 5:19–22), being slow to become angry (James 1:19–20).
2. Confronting Anger. Anger is often our natural reaction. Scripture gives us an alternative: "A soft answer turns away wrath, but a harsh word stirs up anger" (Prov. 15:1; see also Prov. 19:11; Matt. 6:12).
3. Expressing Anger. The Bible doesn't condemn the act of anger, but the attitude of the angry (Prov. 14:29) that results in the sin of anger (Eph. 4:26–27).

CONCLUSION: My challenge is to memorize some of these verses. The next time you feel your blood pressure rise, recite and meditate on Scripture's approach to anger.

Living the Happy Life
Date preached:

SCRIPTURE: Romans 5:1–11

INTRODUCTION: Matthew Perry, popular star of the TV show *Friends,* said, "I had all this money and fancy cars and beautiful girlfriends, but it wasn't making me happy." I wish I could sit down and share the book of Romans with him, because there we find the secret of happiness. The first three chapters of the book tell us about our faults and failures, and about God's answer—justification by grace through faith. Chapter 4 explains that faith more fully, and then Romans 5:1–12 gives the benefits of being saved by grace through faith.

1. Joy in God's Grace (vv. 1–2)
2. Joy in Suffering (vv. 3–5)
3. Joy in God's Love (vv. 6–8)
4. Joy in God's Deliverance (vv. 9–10)
5. Joy in God's Son (v. 11)

CONCLUSION: The joy of the Lord is our strength—and this is why we should rejoice. May God give us a heart overflowing with His joy today!

PATRIOTIC SERMON

I Pledge Allegiance to Jesus Christ

By Rev. Richard Sharpe   *Date preached:*

Scripture: Various, especially Matthew 10:32: Therefore whoever confesses Me before men, him I will also confess before My Father who is in heaven.

Introduction: When I was in seminary, one of the students was from Russia. The one thing that surprised her the most was that we had the American flag in our churches. She said that they would never have the Russian flag in their churches. We are so used to having our flag in our churches we don't even think about what it means. We say our pledge to the American flag in our churches because we believe that we are "one nation under God." That has changed over the years. It seems that America is trying to deny its Christian heritage. Can we still confess that we are "one nation under God," or should we take the American flag out of our churches? Where is our allegiance? The word "confess" means praise, acknowledge, agree, say the same thing, promise, or admit. When we study confession, we will realize that our allegiance needs to be to Jesus Christ. We need to give Him our full attention. Let's look at some verses that will help us realize these facts.

1. **I Pledge Allegiance to Jesus Christ as My Savior (Romans 10:9, 10; 1 John 4:15).** The first step in our personal life with Christ is to agree that we are sinners in need of a Savior. There are many who claim to be saviors in the world, but there is only one that is presented in the Word of God. That Savior is Jesus Christ. He died on the Cross for our sins. He was buried and then raised from the dead. No other religion can claim a risen Savior; their leaders are all still dead. We need to confess or agree with God that Jesus is the only way to heaven. We have to not only say it with our mouths, but we also have to believe it in our hearts for salvation to take place. If we believe it in our hearts, then we will pledge allegiance to Jesus Christ to everyone we meet. We will tell them that Jesus is the only Son of God who died on the cross for their sins and that they need to accept Him as their personal Savior. Our allegiance belongs to Jesus as our Savior.

2. **I Pledge Allegiance to Jesus Christ My Shepherd (John 10:9, 11; Ps. 23:1).** Once we have Christ in our hearts, we can realize that He is the Shepherd of our lives. He leads us in the direction we need to go. He gives us a guidebook called the Bible. In His Word we find all we need to live the Christian life. However, we have to go to Him in prayer to understand His guidebook. The

Holy Spirit, the third Person of the Trinity, was given to us at the point of salvation to help us understand His guidebook. The Holy Spirit indwells us, baptizes us, fills us, and seals us at the point of salvation. The passage in the Gospel of John informs us that Christ's sheep hear His voice and listen. We need to be listening to our Savior's voice on a regular basis. That can only be done through a regular, daily meditation on the Word of God. As our Shepherd, Christ is by our side in every circumstance we face. Some of the problems we have are because of our own sins, but some are trials that are sent our way to make us more Christ-like in the way we live. We need to enjoy our Shepherd on a daily basis and remember that He is always with us.

3. **I Pledge Allegiance to Jesus Christ My High Priest (Heb. 2:17, 18; 3:1, 2; 4:14–16; 1 John 1:9).** Finally, once we have accepted God's gift of salvation, once we realize that we need daily instructions on how to live the Christian life, then we will also realize that we sin even after we have Christ in our lives. What are we to do with this sin? If all our sins are forgiven when we accept Christ as our Savior, why do we have to do anything about them? At the point of salvation all our sins, including all our future sins, were covered by the blood of the Lamb. That is justification. The Father looks at us through the blood of Jesus and sees only Jesus and none of our sins. That gives us access to heaven—only because of what Christ has done for us. First John 1:9 addresses the doctrine of sanctification. Sanctification is an ongoing process that ends when we die. During this process we are growing in grace and the knowledge of the Lord Jesus Christ. During this time we sin on a daily basis because we still have a tendency to sin that is not fully removed until after we die. We have to do something with our sins after salvation, so we can have daily fellowship with Christ. Our eternal life is settled. Our daily fellowship is in need of confession. John the apostle teaches us to confess our sins and that God is faithful to forgive us when we do. Jesus has been given the responsibility of being our High Priest. The responsibility of a High Priest was to go before the Father with a sacrifice to confess the sins of the people. Christ died on the cross and brings His blood to the Father so that we can have a continual relationship with Him. The blood only needs to be brought once. Our allegiance belongs to our High Priest!

Conclusion: Who has our allegiance on a daily basis? Is it Christ? Is it our money? Is it our possessions? Is it our jobs? Is it our family? We love our nation and we're thankful for our freedom. But the Bible says that our allegiance or confession needs to start with Jesus Christ. He is the author of our salvation. He is our Shepherd. He is our High Priest. If we start each day in a right relationship with Christ, then all the other things will fall into line. If we put other things in front of Christ, then everything will fall apart. The choice is ours.

JULY 9, 2006

The Discipline of Disqualification *Date preached:*

By Dr. Denis Lyle

Scripture: Jeremiah 15:10–21, especially verse 19b–c:
If you return, then I will bring you back; you shall stand before Me; if you take out the precious from the vile, you shall be as My mouth.

Introduction: What are servants of the Lord to do when they face exhaustion or exasperation because of His work? Perhaps Jeremiah helps us to answer this question. Almost every servant of God, like Jeremiah, has had a spell when he was ready to resign but knew all the time that he couldn't. Let's look at Jeremiah's case:

1. **The Pressure that Crushed Him.** Here is a servant of God under severe strain. Indeed he had broken down under the burden of his responsibility. Why was he ready to give up?

    A. **Unceasing Opposition (v. 15).** Jeremiah's prayer in 15:15 reveals his frustration with opposition. The people of Anathoth, Jeremiah's hometown, attempted to assassinate him (11:18—12:6). Everyone's hand was against the prophet. The princes, prophets, priests, and people of his land were against him (26:8). Jeremiah was hated and despised because of his message and ministry. Sensitive to his people's response, Jeremiah felt keenly the attitude of his people. Could this be the cause of your spiritual breakdown? Are you experiencing the pressure of unceasing opposition in the home, office, firm, or university? We must deliver the message despite how unwelcome it may be.

    B. **Unrelieved Isolation (vv. 16–17).** As he recounted his past experience, Jeremiah said, "Your words were found . . . O LORD God of Hosts" (v. 16). This is an obvious allusion to his call related in chapter one. He then mentioned the cost of answering that call: ". . . I sat alone because of your hand . . ." (v. 17). The Book of Jeremiah reveals that, while there were several individuals who befriended the prophet in a time of dire need, very few stood with him in his testimony against the sins of the people. As a prophet, Jeremiah was called to walk a narrow path in solitude.

C. **Undisciplined Thinking (v. 18).** Jeremiah permitted himself to indulge in thoughts that led to the volcanic eruption of verse 18. What was Jeremiah saying? He was laying the blame for his circumstances at God's door. He openly accused God of having failed him in the hour of his need. He charged God with being a liar and compared Him to a mirage in the desert. Compare verses 16 and 18; how can it be the same man speaking? One moment Jeremiah was most orthodox and a few seconds later was accusing God of deception and failure. Don't we do the same? One moment we express our confidence in God; the next moment our unbelieving hearts lay charges against him.

2. **The Possibility that Challenged Him (v. 19).** How does God deal with a student in His school who wants to quit? How does God deal with a saint in His family who accuses Him of breaking His Word? Well, this spiritual breakdown automatically disqualified Jeremiah from continuing as the Lord's messenger! While in a state of criticism and faithlessness, he could not represent God. Verse 19 records the Lord's response:

A. **God's Concern for Jeremiah's Restoration (v. 19a).** When Jeremiah was initially called to the prophetic office, the Lord told him He would put His words into Jeremiah's mouth (1:9). Now, because of his criticisms of God's dealings, he had disqualified himself from being the Lord's messenger, but God is always ready to restore and re-commission (Is. 55:7).

B. **God's Restoration Dependent on Jeremiah's Repentance (v. 19b).** The metaphor is that of a smelter. Jeremiah is urged to purify his thoughts, to separate the precious gold of the divine Word from the worthless slag of sinful human ideas.

3. **The Peril that Confronted Him (v. 19c).** The Lord basically said, "Jeremiah you're going to be confronted again by the people of Jerusalem and Judah. They want flattering messages, and they want prophecies that will promise peace and judgment. But you are by no means to lapse again in heart and mind so that you revert back to the place of failure and defeat. Take your stand for Me and with Me."

4. **The Promise that Comforted Him (vv. 20–21).** Along with a warning there came encouragement. Notice the threefold promise in these verses: "I will make you . . . I am with you . . . I will deliver you . . . I will redeem you."

Conclusion: Jeremiah was warned about being set aside as a prophet of the Lord. Have you also questioned the goodness and wisdom of God? Have you also criticized God's dealings in your life? The Lord calls you to repent, to return, and to be reinstated in His service. Will you respond to His appeal?

STATS, STORIES AND MORE

More from Denis Lyle

Have there been times when you felt like quitting and running away? Resigning from your church, giving up your Sunday School class, or leaving that committee will never solve the problems or meet the needs in your heart. You'll probably meet the same situation and the same people (with different names) in the next church you'll join. Why? Because God won't let His servants run away (Jon. 1—2). Every servant of God is human and subject to the weakness of human nature. Moses became discouraged and wanted to die (Num. 11:10–11). Joshua was ready to quit and leave the Promised Land (Josh. 7:6–9). Elijah even abandoned the place of duty and wanted to die (1 Kin. 19:1–4). Jonah became angry at God for saving the despised Assyrians in Nineveh (Jon. 4:1). Jeremiah poured out his discontent and angry heart to God. God's answer may have shocked the prophet, for the Lord told him he needed to repent (Jer. 15:19). Because of his attitude toward God and his calling, Jeremiah was about to forfeit his ministry! A great preacher of a former day was discouraged and thought of resigning when he received this impression from the Lord. "What you need is not to resign your commission, but to have your commission re-signed." One thing is certain: a minister may have his study walls lined with diplomas: a sheaf of recommendations from the mighty of the land, but if the stamp of heaven on his commission is faint and fading, he had better take time out until he can return to his pulpit with a brand new autograph from God. And when he is thus re-signed, he will be reassigned, like Elijah, like Jonah, like Peter, and so many others.

FOR THE BULLETIN

The Byzantine emperor Anastasius I died on this day in A.D. 518 at the age of 88 after a 27-year reign. He was succeeded by his uneducated Illyrian body-guard, who was 68, and who took the name Justinus I. ✿ Stephen Langton, Archbishop of Canterbury, died on July 9, 1228. He is chiefly remembered for his role in the adopting of the English Magna Carta and for dividing the Old Testament into chapters. ✿ Bartholomew Ziegenbalg arrived as a mission-ary to India on July 9, 1706. As a four-year-old, he had stood by his dying mother's bed as she whispered, "My dear children, I have a great treasure for you," pointing to the Bible. Bartholomew never forgot his mother's words, and at age 12, he received Christ as his Savior. As a missionary, he estab-lished the first Protestant church for Indian nationals and completed the translation of the New Testament into Tamil, along with Luther's catechism, a Danish liturgy, and some German hymns. ✿ On July 9, 1827, the Scottish missionaries to India, Alexander Duff and Anne Scott Drysdale, were married. They served the Lord together for nearly fifty years. ✿ Sir Robert Grant died in India on this day in 1838. He is the author of the hymn, "O Worship the King." On the same day, hymnist Philip Bliss was born. He wrote such famous gospel songs as "I Will Sing of My Redeemer" and "Man of Sorrows, What a Name!"

APPROPRIATE HYMNS AND SONGS

Be Thou My Vision, Eleanor Hull/Mary E. Byrne, Public Domain

I Give You My Heart, Reuben Morgan, 1995 Reuben Morgan (Hillsong) (Admin. in U.S. & Canada by Integrity's Hosanna Music)

Guide Me O Thou Great Jehovah, William Williams /Harry E. Fosdick/John Hughes/Peter William, Public Domain

Change My Heart Oh God, Eddie Espinosa, 1982 Mercy Vineyard Publishing (Admin. by Music Services)

I Offer My Life, Don Moen/Claire Clonginger, 1994 Juniper Landing Music (Admin. by Word Music Group, Inc.)/ Word Music, Inc. (a div. of Word Music Group, Inc.)/ Integrity's Hosanna! Music (c/o Integrity Music, Inc.)

WORSHIP HELPS

Call to Worship:
Lord, this day Thy children meet
In Thy house, with willing feet;
Unto Thee this day they raise
Grateful hearts in hymns of praise.
—William H. How, 1864

Reader's Theater:

Reader 1:   My soul loathes my life; I will give free course to my
              complaint, I will speak in the bitterness of my soul. I
              will say to God, 'Do not condemn me; show me why
              You contend with me. Does it seem good to You that
              You should oppress, that You should despise the work
              of Your hands, and smile on the counsel of the wicked?

Reader 2:   The Lord answered Job out of the whirlwind, and
              said: "Who is this who darkens counsel by words
              without knowledge? Now prepare yourself like a man;
              I will question you, and you shall answer Me . . .
              Would you indeed annul My judgment? Would you
              condemn Me that you may be justified? Have you an
              arm like God? Or can you thunder with a voice like
              His? Then adorn yourself with majesty and splendor,
              and array yourself with glory and beauty. Disperse the
              rage of your wrath; look on everyone who is proud,
              and humble him . . . Then I will also confess to you
              that your own right hand can save you.

Reader 1:   Then Job answered the Lord and said: ". . . You asked,
              'Who is this who hides counsel without knowledge?'
              Therefore I have uttered what I did not understand,
              things too wonderful for me, which I did not know.
              Listen, please, and let me speak; You said, 'I will ques-
              tion you, and you shall answer Me.' I have heard of You
              by the hearing of the ear, but now my eye sees You.
              Therefore I abhor myself, and repent in dust and ashes."
              (Job 10:1–3; 38:1–3; 40:8–14; 42:1–6)

Benediction:
Take words with you, and return to the Lord. Say to Him, "Take
away all iniquity; receive us graciously, for we will offer the sacrifices of our lips" (Hos. 14:2).

Additional Sermons and Lesson Ideas

Winning Our Spouses to Christ
By Rev. Billie Friel

Date preached:

SCRIPTURE: 1 Peter 3:1–7, 12

INTRODUCTION: Are you, as a Christian, married to a non-Christian? The Bible devotes a special paragraph to telling wives how to win their husbands to Christ. The same principles work for husbands wanting to win their wives.

1. Our Pleasantness (v. 1). Instead of defiance or bitterness, the Christian spouse is to be humble. Instead of nagging, our pleasant attitudes can win our spouses "without a word."
2. Our Personality (vv. 2–4). The spiritual beauty of a "gentle and quiet spirit" will radiate Christ and last forever.
3. Our Performance (vv. 5–9). Sarah is a good model for us. We must embody the behavior found in verses 8–9.
4. Our Prayer (v. 12). Pray for your spouse daily. Involve godly people in praying. Psalm 51:17 tells us that God will reward your burden.

CONCLUSION: When a person lives with a sermon, talks with a sermon, sleeps with a sermon, and sees a sermon, he or she will be won to Christ!

Remain in Me!
By Rev. Mark Hollis

Date preached:

SCRIPTURE: John 15:1–8

INTRODUCTION: As Jesus and His disciples walked from the upper room to the Mount of Olives, they must have passed many grape arbors. Perhaps it was at one of those that Jesus stopped and—pointing at the vines—offered the words of John 15:1–8.

1. The Analogy (v. 1).
   A. Jesus is the Vine.
   B. We are the Branches.
   C. The Father is the Gardener.
2. The Teaching (vv. 2–4).
   A. The Unfruitful Are Cut Off.
   B. The Fruitful Are Pruned.
   C. The Pruning Is through God's Word.
   D. The Fruit Comes as We Remain Connected to the Vine
3. The Warning (vv. 5–6).
   A. Those Who Remain Connected to Jesus Will Bear Much Fruit.
   B. Those Who Do Not Remain Connected to Jesus Will Be Thrown Away, Wither, and Burn.
4. The Promise (vv. 7–8).

CONCLUSION: How is God at work pruning me? Have I become unfruitful? Have I become disconnected? How might I revitalize my relationship?

A Covenant of Failure

Discouraged? Thinking it's time to move on, to try another field, to seek another work? I'd like to suggest a novel approach to the problem. Why not make a special agreement with God, a covenant of failure?

This was the attitude of the great Methodist leader, Samuel Logan Brengle, a leader of the early Salvation Army movement in America. Brengle (1860–1936) was a powerhouse of spiritual energy, and his writings on holiness are among the richest on my bookshelves. As a young, newly married Christian, he was attacked in Boston by a group of thugs, and his head was nearly bashed in by a brick. It took almost two years for Brengle to recover enough to resume his ministry; and as he did so, he offered God a new kind of covenant—a consecration for failure.

It came to him like this. As he resumed his work, he began to worry about what his superiors in the Salvation Army would think of him as he tried to rebuild his ministry. He was concerned about how his reputation would fare and about the perceived successes and failures that others would attach to his labors. Finally he knelt in prayer and made an agreement with the Lord in which he accepted perceived failure in advance, should it come.

"Lord," he prayed, "take away this restlessness and fear of what men may think or do. I am willing, Lord, to go around this division and preach holiness and salvation to the very best of my ability. But if I don't see a tear shed, a sinner saved, a backslider reclaimed, or a Christian sanctified, I will still rejoice in Thee."

As Brengle pursued his ministry, some of his assignments proved fruitful, but other times he labored with all his heart and saw few apparent results. When tempted with depression, he would remember his covenant and make up his mind to rejoice in the Lord anyway.

Habakkuk made a similar covenant with God, saying, "Though the fig tree does not bud and there are no grapes on the vines, though the olive crop fails and the fields produce no food, though there are no sheep in the pen and no cattle in the stalls, yet I will rejoice in the Lord, I will be joyful in God my Savior" (2:17, 18, NIV).

If it's good enough for Brengle and Habakkuk, it's good enough for us; but there are several things to keep in mind about making such a covenant. First, from God's long-term perspective, there is no failure for those in His will, and our labor is never in vain in the Lord.

Sometimes we're planting rather than harvesting. After studying the lives of pioneer missionaries, Dr. A. J. Gordon of Boston made an interesting observation in his book, *The Holy Spirit and Missions.* It took seven years before William Carey baptized his first convert in India. It was seven years before Adoniram Judson won his first disciple in Burma. Robert Morrison labored for seven years before bringing the first Chinese soul to the Lord. Robert Moffat declared that he waited seven years to see the first moving of the Spirit among the Bechuana of Africa. Henry Richards worked seven years in the Congo before the first convert was gained in Banza Manteka.

Fredrick Batsch, pioneer missionary with the Gossner Mission among the Kohls of India, wrote, "We are now seven years in this land, but through these long years it was but trial of our patience and endurance. . . . Everything seemed in vain, and many said the mission was useless. Then the Lord Himself kindled a fire before our eyes; and it seized not only single souls, but spread from village to village."

In summarizing his observations, Dr. Gordon wrote, "It has seemed almost as though God had fixed this sacred biblical number as the term of the missionary's apprenticeship, as I have found it recurring again and again in the story of the planting of the Gospel. But how rich his reward who has waited patiently till the seed should spring up . . . !"[15]

Our results are seldom immediately apparent, and sometimes a single sermon that seemed ineffective at the moment of delivery will bear a great harvest in coming years. I once read about a man who was converted at the advanced age of 116 by recalling a sermon he had heard one hundred years before when he was sixteen. Biblical Spirit-filled sermons have a very long shelf life.

The second thing to remember is that our primary joy isn't found in our work *for* the Lord, but in our walk *with* the Lord. There is great joy, of course, when one sinner is converted, and Paul referred to his disciples as his "joy and crown" in Philippians 4:1. But only three verses later, he reminds us to "rejoice in the Lord always." We can't always rejoice in our circumstances, in our ministries, in our people, or in our own efforts. But we can always rejoice in the Lord, in His presence, in His promises, in His provisions, and in His praises.

The final thing to remember is that making a "covenant of failure" with the Lord is not a license for laziness. It doesn't mean we accept a fruitless ministry with resignation and complacency. One of the reasons we sometimes harvest little is because we sow little, and the diligent pastor knows the truth of 2 Corinthians 9:6, "Remember this:

THOUGHTS FOR THE PASTOR'S SOUL

Whoever sows sparingly will also reap sparingly, and whoever sows generously will also reap generously" (NIV).

When, however, we have tried our best and prayed our hardest, we must then leave the matter with God. Success or failure in the eyes of others is not our concern. Statistics are an unreliable gauge of success in God's work. He pays no attention to fame, fortune, or failure; but faithfulness is paramount in His sight.

If you're discouraged today, consider making the following "consecration of failure" suggested by two old preachers, Samuel Logan Brengle and the ancient prophet Habakkuk: "Lord, take away this restlessness and fear of what others may think. I am willing, Lord, to go around preaching and working to the best of my ability. But if I don't see a tear shed, a sinner saved, a backslider reclaimed, or a Christian sanctified, I will still rejoice in Thee. Even if there are no grapes on the vines, cattle in the stalls, or people in the pews, I will still be joyful in God my Savior."

Quotes for the Pastor's Wall

---

66 That was quite a good sermon you gave this evening, but it was a topical sermon, and if you are going to make topical sermons your model, you will presently come to the end of your topics, and where will you be then? I advise you to do as I have done for the last thirty years—become an expositor of Scripture. You will always retain your freshness and will build up a strong and healthy church. 99

—Rev. Charles M. Birrell, to his young assistant, F. B. Meyer, as they walked home after a service. The advice set the direction of Meyer's ministry.

JULY 16, 2006

I'll Shout it from the Mountaintop

Date preached:

Scripture: Romans 1:1–17, especially verse 16
I am not ashamed of the gospel of Christ. . . .

Introduction: I'm convinced the Lord wants to use us more than we realize, and He wants to accomplish more with us than we know. As we look at the history of the Lord's church in this world, there's something about the Book of Romans that has often been the spark that gets the fire going. So today, let's look at the prologue of this great book. It provides three insights for those wanting to change their world.

1. **Respond to Your Calling (vv. 1–7).** We're called to be conveyers of the gospel. In these verses, Paul introduced himself and greeted the church in the city of Rome. In doing so, he used the word "call" four times. The first is in verse 1: "Paul, a bondservant of Jesus Christ, called to be an apostle." He goes on to say that through Christ he has received "grace and apostleship for obedience to the faith among all nations for his name . . ." (v. 5). Then he says: "...among whom you also are the called of Jesus Christ; to all who are in Rome, beloved of God, called to be saints." We are called, we are called to call others, we are the called of Jesus Christ, and we are called to be saints. It's as though the Lord is leaning over the balustrades of heaven, calling down to you and me, saying, "Hey, you! Hey you over there. Go in that direction. Go tell those people. There's someone for you! That's your assignment." You never know when God may use you to plant a life-changing seed in someone's heart, for that's our calling.

2. **Pray and Plan for Open Doors (vv. 8–15).** In the second paragraph, we learn something else. We can't just wait around for witnessing opportunities to happen by accident. We need to be intentional about our witnessing, and we need to pray for open doors. Paul was strategic. In brief, we can say that from about A.D. 47 to 57, Paul evangelized the eastern half of the Roman Empire during three great missionary tours. As he finished

his last tour (Acts 20), he stopped in Corinth where he rested for three months in the villa of a Christian friend named Gaius, and there he planned his next move. Paul had dreamed of evangelizing the western half of the Empire, so he devised a plan to go to Rome and from there on to Spain. So in Corinth he composed the book of Romans and sent it on his way to prepare them for his visit (see also 15:22–24). He was praying for open doors. He was asking God to send him to Rome, to Spain, to the West. He was pleading for more opportunities to share the gospel. What does all this mean to us? If you have never shared Christ with another person, let me suggest this prayer: "Lord, show me an open door. Lord, open my eyes to the person you want me to evangelize. Lord, give me a soul." Pray for open doors. Make it an earnest, daily prayer. Then begin thinking strategically. Begin planning. Say to yourself: "Next Christmas, as I send out Christmas cards, is there a way to use them to evangelize my unsaved family. As I select birthday gifts for my friends this year, can I give them something containing the gospel? As I think about Easter, are there people I can round up and bring with me to church?"

3. **Share the Gospel Without Shame (vv. 14–17).** It would have been easy for Christians in first century Rome to have felt embarrassed about the gospel, because they were such a strange little group. Just a few years later, in fact, Emperor Nero would blame them for burning part of the city of Rome, and they would be viciously persecuted. But Paul said, "It doesn't matter what others think. I am a debtor. I have an obligation. I owe it to my Lord and to the world around me to share the gospel." Specifically, Paul stated what every believer should be able to say: "For I am not ashamed of the gospel of Christ for it is the power of God to salvation for everyone who believes, for the Jew first and also for the Greek" (v. 16).

Conclusion: So respond to your calling, plan and pray for opportunities to evangelize, and share the gospel without embarrassment. Be proud of the Lord. Boast in Him. Brag about Him. Tell others of Him. You never know what's going to happen when you share the gospel like that. As one gospel song says:

> I'll shout it from the mountaintop,
> I want my world to know.
> The Lord of Love has come to me.
> I want to pass it on.

STATS, STORIES AND MORE

F. F. Bruce once said, ""There's no telling what may happen when people begin to study the Epistle to the Romans." Here are three examples: Augustine: Aurelius Augustine was born in North Africa in the fourth century. His town sat among the woods near the Mediterranean. His father was a pagan, but his mother Monica was a devout Christian. Augustine was an undisciplined child who became an immoral young adult. He also joined a cult, and for years he broke his mother's heart. Monica prayed for him ceaselessly, and one day in Milan, Italy, as Augustine sat in a friend's garden, he heard a child singing, "Take up and read!" He opened the Bible near him and read a verse from Romans 13. By the time he finished the sentence, he later said, he was converted. He went on to become one of the greatest leaders of the early church.

Martin Luther: In the late fifteenth century, a Catholic monk in Germany named Martin Luther tried to find inner peace. He had done everything he could to fulfill the requirements of his Augustinian order, yet he was a tormented man. But he had a mentor named Johann von Staupitz who knew that Luther's problem was that he didn't understand the power of the gospel. So he sent Luther to the German town of Wittenberg to teach at the university. And his subject? The Book of Romans. As Luther came to Romans 1:16–17, his eyes were opened and he became a transformed man. Out of that transformation came the great cries of "Scripture Alone! Grace Alone! Faith Alone!"

John Wesley was a miserable failure as he sat in a Moravian meetinghouse on Aldersgate Street in London listening to the reading of Luther's preface to the Book of Romans. But that night as he listened to Romans explained, Wesley's heart was strangely warmed and he was transformed into a great force of revival in this world.

FOR THE BULLETIN

Today is a pivotal date in Christian history. On this day in 1054, the two major branches of Christianity—the Roman Catholic Church based in Rome and the Eastern Orthodox Church based in Constantinople—excommunicated each other, resulting in the "Great Schism" between East and West. ✱ This is also a famous day in the history of Catholic missions in America. On this day in 1769, Father Serra founded Mission San Diego, the first permanent Spanish settlement on the west coast of America. ✱ On July 16, 1805, missionary Henry Martyn sailed for India. Though lonely and melancholy, he labored faithfully in street preaching in India and Persia. He is especially remembered for translating the New Testament and the Prayer Book into Hindustani and the New Testament and Psalms into Persian. He died of fever and tuberculosis in 1812. ✱ Today is the birthday in 1863 of Howard K. Smith, composer of the melody for the gospel song "Love Lifted Me." ✱ Missionary C. T. Studd, one of the famous "Cambridge Seven" and a zealous missionary to China, India and Africa, died on this day in 1931. As a young man, C. T. Studd had been one of England's most popular cricket players. He was converted under the preaching of D. L. Moody. So great was the change in him that he gave away much of his vast inherited wealth and dedicated himself to missionary service. His conversion had a great impact on the British Isles. ✱ The first atomic bomb was detonated on July 16, 1945, in the desert near Alamogordo, New Mexico.

APPROPRIATE HYMNS AND SONGS

Christ For the World We Sing, Samuel Wolcott/ Felice De Giardini, Public Domain

Friend of a Wounded Heart, Wayne Watson/Claire Cloninger, 1987 Word Music, Inc. (a div. of Word Music Group, Inc.)

Get All Excited, William J. Gaither/Gloria Gaither, 1972 William J. Gaither, Inc. ARR UBP of Gaither Copyright Mangagement

Go Light Your World, Chris Rice, 1995 BMG Songs, Inc. (Admin. by BMG Music Publishing)

I Am Not Ashamed, Dawn Thomas, 1989 McSpadden Music (Admin. by Integrated Copyright Group, Inc.)

WORSHIP HELPS

Call to Worship:

But I will sing of Your power; yes, I will sing aloud of Your mercy in the morning; for You have been my defense and refuge in the day of my trouble. To You, O my Strength, I will sing praises; for God is my defense, my God of mercy.

Psalm 59:16–17

Offertory Comments:

Malachi 3:8–10 (*The Message*)

Do honest people rob God? But you rob me day after day.

"You ask, 'How have we robbed you?'

"The tithe and the offering—that's how! And now you're under a curse—the whole lot of you—because you're robbing me. Bring your full tithe to the Temple treasury so there will be ample provisions in my Temple. Test me in this and see if I don't open up heaven itself to you and pour out blessings beyond your wildest dreams."

Kids Talk

If you have elementary age children, it's time for them to realize they can be "evangelists." Take a large marker board (or you can use a power point presentation) and spell out the word evangelism. Then break it apart: EV – ANGEL – ISM. Ask, them if they knew there was an "angel" in the middle of evangelism. Explain that the word "angel" means "messenger," and that the prefix "ev" means "good." So the word means: "Good-message-ism." An Ev-angel-ist is someone who shares the good message with someone else. And that can be a child! Have the children suggest

Additional Sermons and Lesson Ideas

Peace

Date preached:

By Pastor J. David Hoke

SCRIPTURE: Various

INTRODUCTION: Do you ever turn on your TV only to be discouraged at the lack of peace in this world? Let's reflect on what Scripture has to say about peace:

1. The Perversion of Peace. The world's idea of peace is often off base (Ezek. 13:10), focusing on external perceptions. Jesus distinguishes the peace that only He can give from the world's perverted idea of peace (John 14:27).
2. The Provision of Peace. The key to peace is to trust the source, God Himself (Is. 26:3). David certainly knew conflict, so the true peace of God was evident to him (Ps. 4:8; 29:11). The greatest provision is through Christ (John 16:33; Phil. 4:7; Col. 3:15).
3. The Process of Peace. Through the work of Christ in us and as we grow in Him and walk in His ways, His Spirit guides us through the process of peace (Gal. 5:22–23). Prayer and praise are an integral part of this process (Phil. 4:6–7).

CONCLUSION: "The Lord will give strength to His people; the Lord will bless His people with peace" (Ps. 29:11).

Kingdom Workers: Part Two

Date preached:

By Dr. Timothy Beougher

SCRIPTURE: 1 Corinthians 3:10–15

INTRODUCTION: In 1 Corinthians 3:5–9, Paul described working in the kingdom through the use of agricultural metaphors. In verses 10–15 he turned to the world of construction, as he pictured the church being built as an edifice with God as the divine Architect and with every believer working on the construction crew.

1. Recognize the Foundation of Kingdom Ministry (vv. 10–11).
2. Build on the Foundation Carefully (vv. 10b, 11–12).
3. Reflect on the Testing of Your Labors (vv. 13–15).

CONCLUSION: "And behold, I am coming quickly, and My reward is with Me, to give to every one according to his work" (Rev. 22:12).

JULY 23, 2006

The Message of Instruction

Date preached:

By Dr. Stuart Briscoe

Scripture: Haggai 2:10–19, especially verse 19:
. . . As yet the vine, the fig tree, the pomegranate, and the olive tree have not yielded fruit. But from this day I will bless you.

Introduction: The Book of Haggai is composed of messages the prophet Haggai preached to a remnant of the Jews who returned to Jerusalem after the exile to Babylon. They returned to rebuild the temple, but they became discouraged and gave up the project. For eighteen years, nothing was done. Then in 520 B.C., a man called Haggai showed up and challenged the people. He said, "You're saying you don't have time to build the Lord's house. How come you find time to work on your own houses?" So poignant was his challenge that the people responded positively and set to work rebuilding the temple of the Lord. Haggai 2:10 contains the prophet's subsequent message of instruction. The questions he asked in the text sound very complicated, but let me put them in modern English. The two questions Haggai posed were these. Number one: Is holiness contagious? This question can also be put this way: Can you catch holiness just by being in touch with something holy? The answer is no. Number two: Is uncleanness contagious? The answer is yes. Haggai's point was that the people had accepted the challenge to rebuild their holy temple, and accordingly, because they were involved in a "holy" work, they assumed that it made them holy. Haggai challenged them on this because that is not necessarily the case. However, conversely, if we engage in the work of the Lord and our lives are defiled, is it possible the defilement is contagious? In other words, can we defile the work of the Lord if our own lives are unclean? The answer is yes. Why is this important? Why was holiness such a big deal to the children of Israel? Is holiness a subject we should be concerned about? The answer is emphatically, "Yes!" Leviticus 19:2 says, "You shall be holy, for I the Lord your God am holy." Holiness is the overarching characteristic of God, and it is to be the overarching characteristic of the covenant people of God.

1. **God Is Holy.**

   A. **He is exalted in His transcendence.** To ascend means to go up. To descend means to go down. To transcend means to go across. Holiness means that God goes across or overarches. This is His over-arching attribute. When we ask someone what is the greatest characteristic of God, we get answers like His love, His grace, His mercy, His forgiveness. The actual fact is that his holiness defines His other attributes. His love is a holy love. His grace is a holy grace. His mercy is a holy mercy. He is holy.

   B. **He is awesome in power.**

   C. **He is glorious in appearance.**

   D. **He is pure in character.** One aspect of His other-ness or separate-ness is that, while we are fallen and sinful, He is pure and sinless.

2. **We are to be Holy.**

   As far as the children of Israel were concerned, they were to be holy because that was the overarching characteristic of their God. By the way they behaved, by the way they conducted themselves, by the way they lived distinctively among the other nations, they were to demonstrate something of the beauty and power and purity of God Himself. But Haggai wanted the people to realize that holiness isn't just a matter of being engaged in activities such as rebuilding the temple. It came from their own relationship with God. He wanted them to realize that it was perfectly possible for them to go through all their externals and rituals but be totally devoid of any holiness. We must make sure that we're not just involved in the work and worship of the Lord without being deeply committed in obedience to the Lord to whom our work and worship is rendered.

Conclusion: In 2 Corinthians 7:1, we read: "Therefore, having these promises, beloved, let us cleanse ourselves from all filthiness of the flesh and spirit, perfecting holiness in the fear of God." That pretty well summarizes what we've been talking about. Haggai tells us to never underestimate the holiness of God, nor devalue the sinfulness of humanity, nor neglect the wonders of grace, nor take your own spirituality carelessly. We're to be holy for He is holy.

STATS, STORIES AND MORE

Someone Once Said

"As I read the Bible, I seem to find holiness to be His supreme attribute."

—Billy Graham[16]

"It does not seem proper to speak of one attribute of God as being more central and fundamental than another; but if this were permissible, the scriptural emphasis on the holiness of God would seem to justify its selection."

—Louis Berkhof in Systematic Theology

"Lower our sense of holiness, and our sense of sin is lowered."

—Dan DeHaan[17]

"Neither the writer nor the reader of these words is qualified to appreciate the holiness of God. Quite literally a new channel must be cut through the desert of our minds to allow the sweet waters of truth that will heal our great sickness to flow in. We cannot grasp the true meaning of the divine holiness by thinking of someone or something very pure and then raising the concept to the highest degree we are capable of. God's holiness is not simply the best we know infinitely bettered. We know nothing like the divine holiness. It stands apart, unique, unapproachable, incomprehensible and unattainable."

—A. W. Tozer

Holy, Holy, Holy

Philadelphia pastor James Montgomery Boice once spoke to a discipleship group on the attributes of God. He began by asking them to list God's qualities in order of importance. They put love first, followed by wisdom, power, mercy, omniscience, and truth. At the end of the list they put holiness.

"That did surprise me," Boice later wrote, "because the Bible refers to God's holiness more than any other attribute."

The Bible doesn't refer to God as "Loving, Loving, Loving!" or "Wise, Wise, Wise!" or "Omniscient, Omniscient, Omniscient!" But we do read the cry of the angels, Holy, Holy, Holy![18]

FOR THE BULLETIN

On July 23, 1518, Philip Melanchthon was called to the University of Wittenberg as a professor. ✿ John Day died at Walden, Essex, England, on this day in 1583. He was born during the reign of Henry VIII and entered his profession at age twenty-two during Edward's brief Protestant rule. He became the most prominent publisher of Protestant materials in London, and was appointed at age thirty by King Edward to publish Poynet's Protestant catechism. During the reign of Queen Elizabeth, Day became the first to print music and to use Anglo-Saxon type. His most famous book was John Foxe's *Book of Martyrs,* which went through repeated printings and became the most important book of its time. The sign in front of John Day's shop featured a man pointing to the sun, saying, "Arise, For It Is Day." ✿ On July 23, 1727, Count Nicolaus Ludwig von Zinzendorf stirred the Moravians at Herrnhut with the story of a liberated slave named Anthony who was burdened for his unevangelized family on the island of St. Thomas. Two men offered themselves as missionaries, sparking the Golden Age of Moravian Missions. ✿ Today is the birthday in 1846 of William R. Featherstone, a Canadian Methodist about whom little is known except that he wrote the probing words to the hymn, "My Jesus, I Love Thee," at the surprising age of sixteen. ✿ James Hannington of Brighton, England, arrived as a missionary on the African coast on July 23, 1884. He started inland toward Uganda but was seized by warriors. His small diary is among the most moving missionary documents on record. He was killed on October 29 of that year.

APPROPRIATE HYMNS AND SONGS

O Word of God Incarnate, William Walsham How/ Felix Mendelssohn, Public Domain

Because We Believe, Nancy Gordon/Jamie Harvill, 1996 Mother's Heart Music/Integrity's Praise! Music (c/o Integrity Music, Inc.)/Integrity's Hosanna! Music (c/o Integrity Music, Inc.)

Thy Word, Amy Grant/Michael W. Smith, 1984 Meadowgreen Music Company (Admin. by EMI Christian Music Publishing)/Word Music, Inc. (a div. of Word Music Group, Inc.)

Wonderful Words of Life, Phillip P. Bliss, Public Domain

Call to Worship:
The four living creatures . . . do not rest day or night, saying: "Holy, holy, holy, Lord God Almighty, Who was and is and is to come!"
Revelation 4:8

Hymn Story: "Holy, Holy, Holy"
Following his graduation from Oxford University, Reginald Heber succeeded his father as the local pastor in an English village. There he had plenty of time to compose poems and write hymns. In fact, it was during his sixteen years in the obscure parish of Hodnet that Heber wrote all fifty-seven of his hymns, including the great missionary hymn, "From Greenland's Icy Mountains." That hymn represented an earnest desire for Reginald, for he felt God was calling him as a missionary to "India's coral strand." His desire was fulfilled in 1822, when, at age forty, he was appointed to oversee the Church of England's ministries in India.

Arriving in Calcutta, he set out on a sixteen-month tour of his diocese, visiting mission stations across India. In February of 1826 he left for another tour. While in the village of Trichinopoly on April 3, 1826, he preached to a large crowd in the hot sun, and afterward he jumped into a pool of cool water. He suffered a stroke and drowned.

After his death his widow found his fifty-seven hymns in a trunk and had them published in a book called, *Hymns Written and Adapted to the Weekly Service of the Church Year.* In this volume was the great Trinitarian hymn based on Revelation 4:8, "Holy, Holy, Holy."

Additional Sermons and Lesson Ideas

A Purple Thread of Promise

Date preached:

SCRIPTURE: Romans 8:28

INTRODUCTION: The King of kings, whose sovereign reign over all provides Providence for His people, has given us a promise that all things work together for good. In its various forms this promise is found in:

1. Romans 8:28
2. Genesis 50:20
3. Nehemiah 13:2b
4. Ephesians 1:11
5. Philippians 1:12

CONCLUSION: This is the Christian's basis for optimism, the reason we can "be glad" and "be of good cheer."

New Testament Missionaries
Adapted from a sermon by A. B. Simpson

Date preached:

SCRIPTURE: Various

INTRODUCTION: Let me present a group of New Testament missionaries who stand out in bold relief in the story of early Christianity:

1. Philip, the Missionary Evangelist (Acts 8)
2. Barnabas, the Consecrated Business Leader (Acts 4:36–37; 13:1–3)
3. Gaius, the Missionary Host (3 John)
4. Epaphras, the Missionary of Prayer (Col. 4:12–13)
5. Luke, the Missionary Writer (Luke 1:1–4)
6. Aquila and Priscilla, the Missionary Couple (Acts 18:26)
7. Timothy, the Missionary Helper (Acts 16:1–5)
8. Paul, the Missionary Pioneer (2 Cor. 5:20)

CONCLUSION: May God fire us up, whatever our station or status, and make us His missionaries!

JULY 30, 2006

When The Wall is Broken

Date preached:

By Rev. Charles McGowan

Scripture: Nehemiah 1:1–11, especially verse 4:
So it was, when I heard these words, that I sat down and wept, and mourned for many days; I was fasting and praying before the God of heaven.

Introduction: The book of Nehemiah is about a broken wall and the man God raised up to rebuild it. The great wall of Jerusalem was demolished by King Nebuchadnezzar in the sixth century B.C. as he finally gained complete victory over Judah. After the Babylonian captivity had ended, Nehemiah became cupbearer to the Persian king. God gave him an important task. In fifty-two days (Neh. 6:15) the wall around the entire city of Jerusalem was completely rebuilt. Do you have any walls that need to be rebuilt? God can restore that which is broken. He not only rebuilds broken walls, but broken marriages, broken families, and broken relationships. The pattern for his work is found in the Nehemiah story. For the one who yearns to be a participant in God's restoring work, the principles begin to be laid out in chapter 1.

1. **Obtain Accurate Information (vv. 2–3).** To participate in God's restorative work, we must seek the truth.

   A. **Be Hungry for Truth.** The opening verses of chapter 1 describe a man hungry for the truth. Hanani, who had just returned from Jerusalem, provides it in vivid detail. The news is both good and bad. The people in Jerusalem are in great distress, but there is a remnant there with whom to work.

   B. **Face the Realities.** The walls of Jerusalem were torn down and the gates were burned with fire! Rather than turning a blind eye, facing reality was necessary if Nehemiah was to take part in God's restoration. Often, it's easy for us to gloss over the ugly aspects of the picture. It is easier yet to be so self-absorbed or so busy that we do not listen or care. Nehemiah was not too busy to care. He was absorbed in the news brought by Hanani. With a clear picture of the desperate situation in

Jerusalem, he was prepared to be a useful instrument in the hand of God.

2. **Be Burdened for the Loss (v. 4).** Notice Nehemiah's reaction to what he was told by Hanani. The weight of the information caused him to sit down and weep. With the passage of time the burden seemed to become heavier and more intense. It affected his every countenance, which was noticed by the king (Neh. 2:2). He carried it for four months before things began to happen. Burdens are important. For Nehemiah, his burdens are the beginning point of ministry. They are developed by a clear picture of what is against the backdrop of what God intends. The call to action is related to the burden, not the need. When God places a burden on one's heart, the question before him is whether he is willing to do something about it.

3. **Fast and Pray (vv. 4–11).** The first thing to do with a burden is to bring it to before the Lord. As Nehemiah went into the presence of God, he focused first of all on God's faithfulness (v. 5), which brings assurance. Then he focused on the failures of God's people, and he included himself by confessing his own sins (vv. 6–7). Hope and healing begin with brokenness. Then Nehemiah focused on God's promises (vv. 8–9). While sin brings consequences and almost always leaves a scar, God's promise is to restore. There are no hopeless cases with God. Finally, Nehemiah concluded his prayer on a reverent note of hope (vv. 10–11).

Conclusion: Nehemiah's reaction to his burden was not worry, panic, or the development of a brilliant plan of action. His hope was not in his ability or influence. His only hope was in God. This prompted him to lay his burden down in the presence of God. So what do we do with a broken wall? What do we do when the circumstances of our lives, our families, and our churches seem hopeless? Do we frantically attempt to fix it? Do we give up and look for another place to start over? Do we sit and wallow in despair? Our text offers us a word of hope in the pattern Nehemiah set. We should fall on our faces before our God who is faithful. There we discover hope because God delights in restoring broken walls. In doing so He is glorified.

STATS, STORIES AND MORE

From Charles Spurgeon:

Nehemiah and his companions . . . had not only to build the wall of Jerusalem, but to watch against their enemies at the same time. Their case is ours. We have to work for Christ. I hope that all of us who love him are trying to do what we can to build up his kingdom; but we need also to watch against deadly foes. If they can destroy us, of course they will also destroy our work. They will do both, if they can. The powers of evil are mad against the people of God. If they can in any way injure or annoy us, you may rest assured that they will do so. . . .

Nehemiah was well qualified for his work. He gave the Jews very shrewd, sensible, and yet spiritual advice, and this was a great help to them in their hour of need. Beloved, we have a better Leader than Nehemiah; we have our Lord Jesus Christ himself, and we have his Holy Spirit, who dwells in us, and shall abide with us. I beg you to listen to his wise and good advice. I think that he will give it to you through our explanation of the text. He will say to you what Nehemiah, in effect, said to these people, "Watch and pray." Although the adversaries of the Jews conspired together, and came to fight against Jerusalem, and to hinder the work of rebuilding the wall, Nehemiah says, "Nevertheless, we made our prayer unto our God, and set a watch against them day and night, because of them." In the text, I see *two guards;* first, *prayer:* "We made our prayer unto our God." The second guard is *watchfulness:* "We set a watch."

APPROPRIATE HYMNS AND SONGS

Forever, Chris Tomlin, 2001 worshiptogether.com songs/Six Steps Music (Admin. by EMI Christian Music Publishing)/(Admin. by EMI Christian Music Publishing)

Standing on the Promises, R. Kelso Carter, Public Domain

He Leadeth Me O Blessed Thought, Joseph H. Gilmore/ William B. Bradbury, Pulbic Domain

Open Our Eyes, Bob Cull, 1976 Maranatha! Music (Admin. by The Copyright Company)

Take My Life, Scott Underwood, 1994 Mercy/Vineyard Publishing (Admin. by Music Services)

FOR THE BULLETIN

Robert Barnes was an early English Reformer who had come to Christ due to the testimony of "Little" Thomas Bilney. As he advanced the Reformation message, he was seized and taken to London to be questioned before Cardinal Thomas Wolsey and then imprisoned. After his release he became a chief distribution agent for Tyndale's English Bibles, which were being smuggled into the country. He was eventually captured and burned at the stake on this day in 1540. ✿ Ignatius Loyola, founder of the Jesuit order, died on July 30, 1556. And on this day in 1715, Nahum Tate passed away. He was an Irish hymnist who wrote, "While Shepherds Watched Their Flocks by Night." William Penn, founder of Pennsylvania as a colony for Quakers, died on this day in 1718. ✿ On July 30, 1806, the melancholy missionary, Henry Martyn, proposed to Lydia Grenfell with whom he was deeply in love. Lydia, who had no desire for Asian missionary, had previously refused to accompany Martyn to India. On July 30, 1806, after much deliberation, he wrote, proposing marriage. Letters traveled slowly, and a year passed before he received Lydia's newest refusal. Martyn's health, always frail, began to falter. He wrote asking her to reconsider. She would not, though she agreed to correspond friend-to-friend. Martyn accomplished great things for Christ but died in loneliness at age thirty-one. ✿ On July 30, 1839, slave rebels took over slave ship Amistad. ✿ July 30, 1976 marks the death of German theologian, Rudolf Bultmann, at age ninety-two.

WORSHIP HELPS

Call to Worship:
Stand up and bless the Lord your God forever and ever! Blessed be Your glorious name, which is exalted above all blessing and praise! You alone are the Lord; You have made heaven, the heaven of heavens, with all their host, the earth and everything on it, the seas and all that is in them, and You preserve them all. The host of heaven worships You.
—Nehemiah 9:5b–6

Reader' Theater (May be adapted for a Responsive Reading)

Reader 1:	Unless the Lord builds the house, they labor in vain who build it.
Reader 2:	Unless the Lord guards the city, the watchman stays away in vain.
Reader 1:	It is vain for you
Reader 2:	to rise up early
Reader 1:	to sit up late
Both:	to eat the bread of sorrows
Reader 1:	for He gives His beloved sleep.
Reader 2:	Come to Me, all you who labor and are heavy laden, and I will give you rest.
Reader 1:	Take My yoke upon you and learn from me, for I am gentle and lowly in heart,
Both:	And you will find rest for your souls. For My yoke is easy, and My burden is light.
	(Ps. 127:1–2; Matt. 11:28–30)

Benediction:
Show Your marvelous lovingkindness by Your right hand, O You who save those who trust in You from those who rise up against them. Keep me as the apple of Your eye; hide me under the shadow of Your wings.
(Ps. 17:7–8)

Additional Sermons and Lesson Ideas

A Model for Ministry

By Dr. Denis Lyle

Date preached:

SCRIPTURE: 1 Thessalonians 2:1–12

INTRODUCTION: It's not an easy task to be the Lord's workers. What does an effective ministry look like? Paul gives us a model for all of us who serve the Lord. It involves three pictures of ministry:

1. A Faithful Steward (vv. 1–5). Paul was entrusted with the gospel, so he was bold in manner (v. 2), clear in message (v. 3), pure in motive (v. 5), and true in method (v. 3).
2. A Helpful Mother (vv. 7–8). Paul had a caring ministry (v. 7) and a costly ministry (v. 8).
3. A Dutiful Father (vv. 9–12). Paul's work for the Thessalonians was priceless (v. 9), his walk before them was consistent (v. 10), and his words to them were convicting, comforting, and challenging (v. 11–12).

CONCLUSION: God has entrusted us with the gospel of Christ; let us be good stewards—caring, speaking, working, and walking before others as if they were our own children.

The Tri–Unity: God in Action

Adapted from an outline of George W. Noble

Date preached:

SCRIPTURE: 2 Corinthians 13:14

INTRODUCTION: The subject of the Trinity is beyond our comprehension, but we are given several pictures of the three Persons' joint activity on our behalf. We see Father, Son, and Holy Spirit in divine cooperation:

1. In Creation (Gen. 1:1; John 1:3; Job 26:13)
2. In Incarnation (John 3:16; Heb. 10:5; Luke 1:35)
3. In Redemption (Heb. 9:14; 1 Pet. 3:18; Gal. 2:20)
4. In Salvation (Eph. 1:4, 7, 13)
5. In Communion (Eph. 2:18; Rom. 8:27; 2 Cor. 13:14)
6. In Glory (Rev. 1:4–5; Phil. 3:21; Jude 23)

CONCLUSION: Hail! Father, Son, and Holy Ghost, One God in persons Three; Of Thee we make our joyful boast, our songs we make of Thee.

—Charles Wesley

AUGUST 6, 2006

Testing, Teaching, and the Transfiguration

By Joshua D. Rowe   *Date preached:*

Scripture: Mark 8:27—9:12, especially 9:7:
And a cloud came and overshadowed them; and a voice came out of the cloud, saying,
"This is My beloved Son. Hear him!"

Introduction: I'm sure many of you here had or have favorite school subjects and teachers. Some of you aced English, but math perplexed you. Some of you whizzed through science but slept through history. One common name for Jesus in Scripture is "Teacher." The disciples faced many of Jesus' tests and lessons; let's look at how the disciples reacted and how we should react to these most crucial teachings and tests.

1. **We Must Embrace Christ's Identity (8:27–30).**

   A. **The Teaching (1:1—8:26).** Mark's Gospel, from chapter 1 to 8:26, focuses on the person of Jesus. The events of Jesus' life up to this point clearly display His identity as the Messiah (see 1:7–8, 11; 6:1–6). The accounts of His public ministry include teaching, healing, exorcism, and miracles, and they also point to His identity (see 1:23–24; 2:5–12, 27–28; 3:11, 35).

   B. **The Test (8:27–30).** Jesus asked the disciples who others thought He was; the popular opinion then was the same as it often is today: just a good teacher or a prophet. Having taught and shown the disciples the truth, He asked: "But who do you say that I am?" (v. 29). Peter passed this test with flying colors, "You are the Christ" (v. 29). Who do you think Jesus is? Is He just a prophet or a teacher, or is He the Messiah: the Savior, the Son of God, and the Lord of your life?

2. **We Must Accept Christ's Sacrificial Purpose (8:31–33).**

   A. **The Teaching (vv. 31–32a).** Peter aced his first test! Jesus then went on to His next lesson: "And He began to teach them that the Son of Man must suffer many things . . . and be killed, and after three days rise again" (v. 31).

B. **The Test (vv. 32b–33).** Have you ever seen a contestant on "Family Feud" buzz in too early? They lack information, so their answer is always wrong. Peter buzzed in too early, rebuking Jesus for prophesying His own death. Jesus rebuked him in turn, for Peter was thinking like Satan, not like God, who had in mind salvation and His own glory!

3. **We Must Be Willing to Lay Down Our Lives as Christ's Disciples (8:34—9:1).**

   A. **The Teaching (8:31—9:1).** This section of Scripture could be an entire sermon series, but we'll summarize the passage in a sentence: Jesus requires no less than the very life of His servants, devotion so strong that *we* would suffer death on a cross for following Him.

   B. **The Test (John 6:60–66).** In John 6:22–66, Jesus gave a similar teaching to test the disciples. Using the graphic imagery of eating His flesh and drinking His blood, He illustrated His requirements of complete devotion to and dependence on Him. Their response: "This is a hard saying; who can understand it? . . . From that time many of His disciples went back and walked with Him no more" (vv. 60, 66). Are you willing to follow with complete devotion and dependence?

4. **We Should Worship in Christ's Glory (9:2–12).**

   A. **The Transfiguration.** With all the teaching of His suffering and death, the disciples needed a glimpse of His ultimate purpose. Jesus "was transfigured" (v. 2) before the disciples, dazzling and bright, which perhaps was a glimpse of His heavenly form, and He was speaking face to face with Moses and Elijah!

   B. **The Teaching.** Jesus told the disciples about His resurrection (8:31, 9:9) and spoke with Moses and Elijah of His "departure" (Luke 9:31, NIV), perhaps referring to His ascension. This teaches us that the torturous death of Christ was not without its ultimate purpose: Jesus' resurrection and ascension and ultimate glory! The second lesson comes from God Himself, "This is My beloved Son. Hear Him!" (v. 7).

   C. **The Test.** God told the disciples to listen to Christ. As they descended the mountain, Jesus taught again about His upcoming death and resurrection. How did they react? They were stuck, unable to answer. The rest of Mark shifts focus from Jesus' public ministry to His teaching the disciples, repeatedly prophesying His suffering, death, and resurrection in preparation for their ultimate test: their response to His death and resurrection.

Conclusion: The ultimate test for us is the same. First, we must answer that Jesus truly is the Messiah, the Son of God, the Savior of our souls, and the Lord of our lives. Second, we must not reject His purpose, that He suffered a cruel death for us by crucifixion. Third, we must be willing to follow Him to the cross, to lay down our own lives and follow Him. Finally, we must recognize His glory, that He truly did rise again, ascend into the heavens, and currently sits at God's right hand until He comes again. These are lessons straight from Christ Himself; listen to Him! Only when we pass these tests can we "come down off the mountain" to teach others the same lessons that they too might pass life's most important tests.

STATS, STORIES AND MORE

Why Moses and Elijah? There are striking similarities between Jesus and these two:

Moses died on a mountain, Mount Nebo (Deut. 34:1–5); Jesus died on a mountain, Calvary (Luke 23:33) and ascended to heaven from the Mount of Olives (Acts 1:9–12).

Elijah miraculously and visibly ascended in the presence of Elisha (2 Kin. 2:11–12); Jesus ascended visibly in the presence of His disciples (Acts 1:9).

Moses and Jesus had divine knowledge of their imminent deaths (Deut. 32:48–50; Matt. 16:21); Elijah and Jesus had divine knowledge of their imminent ascensions to heaven (2 Kin. 2:1–3; Mark 8:31).

The Holy Spirit upon Moses was given to his successor, Joshua (Deut. 34:9); the Holy Spirit upon Elijah was given doubly to his successor, Elisha (2 Kin. 2:9–15); the Holy Spirit upon Jesus was given to His followers at Pentecost (Acts 2:1–4) and to us who share in His salvation (Rom. 8:9).

Also, Moses, Elijah, and Jesus each represent a different portion of Scripture. Moses represents the Old Testament Law, the written moral code by which Israelites were to live. Elijah represents the Prophets, the divine representatives of God. Jesus is the ultimate fulfillment of both (see Luke 24:25–27) and established the new covenant (or New Testament) in His blood (Luke 22:20).

Finally, the subject of conversation during the transfiguration is significant. Luke 9:31 tells us that Jesus spoke about His "departure" (NIV). Although this word is often interpreted as His death, it's the Greek word for "exodus." While it may refer to His death, perhaps in His transfigured form Jesus spoke to Moses—who led the Israelite's glorious Exodus from Egypt—and to Elijah—who ascended into heaven—about His own upcoming "exodus," His glorious ascension from the Mount of Olives.

FOR THE BULLETIN

On August 6, A.D. 258, the Bishop of Rome, Sixtus II, was seized during services in the catacombs and executed under orders of the Roman Emperor Valerian. ❀ On August 6, 1749, David Brainard's prayers and preaching sparked a revival among Native Americans. His diary for that date says: In the morning I discoursed to the Indians at the house where we lodged. Many of them were then much affected and appeared surprisingly tender, so that a few words about their souls' concern would cause the tears to flow freely and produce many sobs and groans. In the afternoon . . . I again discoursed to them. There were about fifty-five persons in all. . . . There appeared nothing very remarkable except their attention, till near the end of my discourse. Then divine truths were attended with a surprising influence, and produced great concern among them. There were scarce three in forty that could refrain from tears and bitter cries. . . . " ❀ On August 6, 1801, the Revival at Cain Ridge began. For a full week, thousands of people descended on this little hamlet twenty miles west of Lexington, Kentucky. No one knows the exact attendance figure, but estimates vary from ten thousand to twenty-five thousand. It triggered a wave of revivals and camp meetings that changed the complexion of the American culture of the nineteenth century. ❀ John Mason Neale died on August 6, 1866. He was an Anglican preacher who worked tirelessly to translate ancient Latin hymns into English. We appreciate his service whenever we sing, "Good Christian Men, Rejoice," "O Come, O Come, Emmanuel," and "All Glory, Laud, and Honor." ❀ On August 6, 1978, Pope Paul VI died of heart attack at his summer residence at the age of eighty.

APPROPRIATE HYMNS AND SONGS

Rejoice the Lord is King, Charles Wesley/John Darwall, Public Domain

Holy and Anointed One, John Barnett, 1988 Mercy/Vineyard Publishing (Admin. by Music Services)

I'd Rather Have Jesus, Rhea F. Miller/George Beverly Shea, 1922, 1950 Renewed 1939, 1966 Word Music, Inc. (a div. of Word Music Group, Inc.)

As the Deer, Martin J. Nystrom, 1984 Maranatha Praise, Inc.

Turn Your Eyes Upon Jesus, Helen H. Lemmel, Public Domain

WORSHIP HELPS

Call to Worship:
Oh, give thanks to the Lord, for He is good! For His mercy endures forever.
(Ps. 136:1)

Welcome:
Today we celebrate the Transfiguration, the day that Jesus appeared bright and dazzling before the disciples as He spoke upon a mountain with Moses and Elijah. Jesus invited certain disciples to see Him in His glory, to teach them, and to be in intimate fellowship with them. We'd like to welcome you today to worship Jesus with us, to learn with us from His Word, and to have joy in the intimate fellowship you find here.

Kids Talk

Bring a small washtub with a pitcher of water, some bleach, a white t-shirt, and some cranberry juice. Tell the children, "You know, I saw a commercial once that taught me about bleach. It said that bleach can get stains out of clothing. So, let's take this white t-shirt, spill some juice on it . . . and then try to wash it with bleach here in this tub." Allow the children to get involved and tell you whether they can still see the red spot. Continue, "You know, sometimes bleach can help get stains out, and sometimes it just doesn't work. Did you know we all have stains in our lives too? Because all of us have sinned, it's as if we have red stains on us that God can't bear to look at, but there's someone who can help wash us. In fact, the story of the Transfiguration that we celebrate today tells us Jesus' clothes once turned whiter than anyone in the world could bleach them; He looked clean before God. Jesus can do that for the stains in our lives too! The Bible also says, even though your sins are like scarlet, He can wash you as white as snow! Let's ask Jesus to forgive the sins in our lives and wash us, better than any bleach ever could."

Additional Sermons and Lesson Ideas

Accent the Ascension

Date preached:

By Dr. Melvin Worthington

SCRIPTURE: Acts 1

INTRODUCTION: Christianity rests upon clear historical facts: the incarnation, the crucifixion, the resurrection, and the ascension of Christ. Consider the following truths regarding the ascension:

1. The Record Viewed. Acts 1:9–11 records the dramatic ascension of Christ. It is simple but specific. The ascension provided the apostles with an explanation of where Jesus was and confirmed the truth of Christianity.
2. The Reasons Verified. Christ ascended because He had completed His earthly ministry and was ready to begin his heavenly ministry. He also ascended so that the Holy Spirit might come down and perform His part in the work of redemption. Further, He ascended in order to prepare us a heavenly home (John 14:1–3).
3. The Revelation Validated. While the disciples looked toward heaven, two angels appeared to comfort them and to clear up any misapprehensions regarding Christ. The angels emphatically declared that this same Jesus would return in the same manner He ascended: visibly, personally, and bodily.

CONCLUSION: When we celebrate the Lord's Resurrection, let us also accent His ascension and anticipate His second advent.

Change is Good!

Date preached:

Adapted from the writings of Thomas Watson

SCRIPTURE: Acts 9:21

INTRODUCTION: When we come to Christ, we become new creatures (2 Cor. 5:17). Paul was so changed after his conversion that people did not know him. Oh what a metamorphosis does grace make! When we come to Christ, He changes us in many ways. Here are three of them:

1. He Changes our Understanding (Eph. 5:8). Before conversion, there was ignorance; darkness was upon the face of the deep. Now there is light. The first work of God in the creation of the world was light; so it is in the new creation.
2. He Changes our Will (Acts 9:6). Before conversion, the will was an iron sinew; afterward it is like melting wax. It asks, "Lord, what do you want me to do?"
3. He Changes our Conduct (Eph. 5:1–21). Those who are called of God walk contrary to their former conduct.

CONCLUSION: Are you living a changed life? Is God so effectively changing you that people can scarcely recognize you?

Spurgeon's Sermons

In recent years, Charles Haddon Spurgeon has been much maligned by postmodern, seeker-friendly preachers who brag about never quoting him.

Well, he's still worth quoting—and worth reading. He'll forever be, after all, the Prince of Preachers, and his story is remarkable. When he was seventeen years old, Spurgeon was asked to pastor a small congregation in Waterbeach village. His first sermon there was to a dozen people. Soon hundreds were attending each week, and the doors and windows of the church were left open so the overflow could hear. Two years later, he moved to London. Despite his youthful appearance, he set the city afire, packing London's greatest auditoriums and preaching to thousands without aid of microphone or amplification.

I like Spurgeon's sermons so much better than his writings. He himself once admitted that writing was difficult for him, but his sermons poured from his mouth in remarkable bursts of seemingly spontaneous oratory. He used no pulpit, and his eloquent discourses were preached with only a few notes on a table beside him as he stood at the platform railing. He did little formal preparation for his sermons. Throughout the week, he read and studied like a rabid dog thirsting for water, then on Saturday night he collected his thoughts, determined his subject, and sketched out a few notes. The next morning, hearing him preach was akin to visiting Niagara Falls. It was a veritable cataract of eloquence and enlightenment.

If you're not well acquainted with Spurgeon, start with one of his many biographies. A unique new volume is out, published in England, that combines his story with a travel guide of sites associated with his ministry. It is called *Travel with C. H. Spurgeon: in the Footsteps of the Prince of Preachers,* by Clive Anderson (published by Day One Publications as part of a series of Christian travel guides). I enjoyed it so much I almost wept when I came to the last page. Another new biography is *The Unforgettable Spurgeon* by Eric Hayden, which draws heavily on Spurgeon's writings in his magazine, *The Sword and the Trowel.*

Older, classic biographies of him include the ones by W. Y. Fullerton, Richard Ellsworth Day, and J. Manton Smith.

Then plunge into his sermons. The collected sermons of Charles Spurgeon fill sixty-three volumes and represent the largest set of books by a single author in church history. Many of these sermons are now posted at www.spurgeon.org; you can use the search function to locate specific phrases, passages, and words.

Here's a Spurgeon sermon sampling. Shortly after he arrived in London, Spurgeon preached a sermon entitled "The Tomb of Jesus." It was on April 8, 1855, and Spurgeon was, incredibly, only twenty years old.

It is a fact we do not often think of, that we shall all be dead in a little while. I know I am made of dust and not of iron; my bones are not brass, nor my sinews steel; in a little while my body must crumble back to its native elements. My friends, there are some of you who seldom realize how old you are, how near you are to death. Sometimes I have tried to think of the time of my departure. I do not know whether I shall die a violent death or not; but I would to God that I might die suddenly; for sudden death is sudden glory.

Die I must—this body must be a carnival for worms; it must be eaten by those tiny cannibals; the constituent particles of this my frame will enter into plants, from plants pass into animals, and thus be carried into far distant realms; but, at the blast of the archangel's trumpet, every separate atom of my body shall find its fellow; like the bones lying in the valley of vision, though separated from one another, the moment God shall speak, the bone will creep to its bone; then the flesh shall come upon it; the four winds of heaven shall blow, and the breath shall return.

So let me die, let beasts devour me, let fire turn this body into gas and vapor, all its particles shall yet again be restored; this very self-same, actual body shall start up from its grave, glorified and made like Christ's body, yet still the same body, for God hath said it.

Christ's same body rose; so shall mine. The grave—what is it? It is the bath in which the Christian puts the clothes of his body to have them washed and cleansed. Death—what is it? It is the waiting-room where we robe ourselves for immortality; it is the place where the body, like Esther, bathes itself in spices that it may be fit for the embrace of its Lord. Death is the gate of life; I will not fear to die.

AUGUST 13, 2006

Living Uprightly

Date preached:

By Rev. Richard Sharpe

Scripture: Various, especially 2 Corinthians 11:2b:
For I have betrothed you to one husband, that I may present you as a chaste virgin to Christ.

Introduction: When you hear the word *chastity*, what comes to mind? Often we think of sexual purity or abstinence. The Greek word for pureness can be translated "cleanness, blamelessness, pureness, uprightness of life, without moral defect, or chastity." It actually deals with the way we live towards God. Paul said in 2 Corinthians 11:3 that he feared the church would be deceived and thus lose its purity. Let's look at how we can live a consistent life of chastity before the Lord.

1. **We Must Have a Proper Love for the Lord and Others (Matt. 22:34–40).**

   A. **Types of Love.** Three types of love are mentioned in the New Testament. The first is concerned with only the sexual side of life. The second type of love is one involving the emotions and the mind. The third type of love is called *agape*. This type of love involves the emotions, mind, and will of the person. This type of love loves people who hurt the person loving. God loves us this way. God wants us to *agape* Him and one another.

   B. **Teachings of Love.** Two commandments deal with love: Christ told the Pharisees and Sadducees that there are two commandments that all the law and the prophets hang on (Matt. 22:34–40). The first commandment is that we are to *agape* the Lord our God with all our heart, and with all our soul, and with all our entire mind. The second commandment is that we are to *agape* our neighbors as ourselves.

   C. **Testimonies of Love.** In the book of Genesis we find a man named Enoch who is said to have walked with God and then simply was no more, "for God took him" (5:24). Enoch was so close to the Lord that he never died because his life was one that manifested the love of God.

Think of Noah: the whole world he lived in was only happy when they were eating, drinking, and partying. Noah was not like that. He was one who found grace in the eyes of the Lord because he walked with God (6:8–9). Both of these men were sinners, but they made choices that honored God and that God honored. He recognized that they loved Him with all their hearts, souls, and minds.

2. **We Must Have a Proper Hatred of Sin (1 John 2:15).** The Bible tells us that we are not to *agape* the world. There are three areas where we are not to love the world. These ideas are found in 1 John 2:16, Genesis 3:6, and in Matthew 4:3–10.

   A. **The Lust of the Flesh.** This is the one sin where we usually associate chastity. We must not desire people of the opposite sex or of the same sex as we would our spouses. A person's spouse should be the only object of his or her sexual love.

   B. **The Lust of the Eyes.** We must remember that we start our wrong thoughts with our eyes. We see something that we want, and then we dwell on that lust until it affects other areas of our lives.

   C. **The Pride of Life.** If we love ourselves more than we love God, we are in trouble. This is a real problem when we are confronted by others about sin in our lives. We need to lose the pride if we are to have an upright life in the eyes of the Lord.

3. **We Must Renew Our Commitment Daily.** Each day we have a new choice to make about what thoughts we will follow. In order to live a life of purity, we need to realize that choices come on a daily basis. There are many verses that deal with this daily choice: *We must take up our crosses daily* (Luke 9:23; Matt. 10:39); *we must ask for daily bread* (Matt. 6:11); *we must choose to serve daily* (Josh._ 24:15); *we must search the Scriptures daily* (Acts 17:11); *we must exhort one another daily* (Heb. 3:13).

Conclusion: To truly live a life of chastity and purity before God, we must love the Lord our God with all our hearts, minds, and souls. We must hate the lust that is found in the world, and with the Lord's help we can overcome temptation. We must be people who choose daily to walk with God.

STATS, STORIES AND MORE

You've probably never heard the name Geoffrey Anketell Studdert-Kennedy. He was a British soldier in World War I, a Christian young man who was given the name "Woodbine Willy" for his habit of distributing Woodbine cigarettes to soldiers. He was decorated for his bravery under fire. On one occasion, he ran heedlessly into no-man's land to comfort and help his injured compatriots. Woodbine Willy was a devoted Christian who often wrote poems and hymns for his fellow soldiers. His poems became so popular that they were printed and distributed to the troops. One of them was on our subject today—God's love channeled through us to others. Woodbine Willy wrote:

Awake, awake to love and work!
The lark is in the sky;
The fields are wet with diamond dew;
The worlds awake to cry
Their blessings on the Lord of life,
As He goes meekly by.

Come, let thy voice be one with theirs,
Shout with their shout of praise;
See how the giant sun soars up,
Great lord of years and days!
So let the love of Jesus come
And set thy soul ablaze.

To give and give, and give again,
What God hath given thee;
To spend thyself nor count the cost;
To serve right gloriously
The God Who gave all worlds that are,
And all that are to be.

FOR THE BULLETIN

Maximus Confessor led the fight against a heresy called monothelitism — the teaching that Christ had a divine, but no human, will. At the age of 73, he was placed on trial in Constantinople and banished to a remote spot where he suffered greatly from cold and hunger. The emperor offered Maximus great rewards to convert to monothelitism, and great suffering if he refused. He refused and was beaten, spat on, robbed of his possessions, imprisoned for six years, then flogged. His tongue and right hand were chopped off. He died August 13, 662, at age eighty-two, but his sufferings paved the way for the triumph of his doctrine. ❀ On August 13, 1587, Manteo, the first Native American convert to Protestantism, was baptized. ❀ Today marks the death in 1667 of Jeremy Taylor, a renowned British preacher. ❀ Though he died at age twenty-nine, Robert Murray McCheyne is remembered as one of the most powerful preachers in evangelical Scottish history. On August 13, 1836, he preached a trial sermon at St. Peter's Church in Dundee. He made a powerful impression upon the church and was installed as pastor three months later. Here he served until his death in 1843. ❀ Several hymnists have died on this day. The author of "More Love to Thee, O Christ," Elizabeth Prentiss, died on August 13, 1878. Ira Sankey, the song leader for D. L. Moody and the leader of the Gospel Song movement, died on this day in 1908. And Howard K. Smith, who composed the music to "Love Lifted Me," passed away on this day in 1918. ❀ Today is the wedding anniversary of Billy and Ruth Graham, who exchanged vows on August 13, 1943.

APPROPRIATE HYMNS AND SONGS

Holy, Holy, Holy, John B. Dykes/ Reginald Heber, Public Domain

How Deep the Father's Love for Us, Stuart Townsend, 1995 Kingsway's Thankyou Music (Admin. by EMI Christian Music Publishing)

I'll Live for Him, Ralph E. Hudson/ C.R. Dunbar, Public Domain

Giving My Best, Mark Condon, 1992 Brooklyn Tabernacle Music (Admin. by Integrated Copyright Group, Inc.)/Dayspring Music, Inc. (a div. of Word Music Group, Inc.)

Jesus Paid It All, Elvina M. Hall/ John T. Grape, Public Domain

WORSHIP HELPS

Call to Worship:
I wait for the Lord, my soul waits, and in His word I do hope. My soul waits for the Lord more than those who watch for the morning—yes, more than those who watch for the morning.
(Ps. 130:5, 6)

Pastoral Prayer:
Thank You, heavenly Father, for another Lord's Day in which we can celebrate the first day of the week—the day of Jesus' Resurrection—the day of Easter. Remind us that we're to live as though every day were Easter, for we live every moment in the presence of our risen Savior. We praise You for that, and we pray that the love, joy, peace, and patience of our risen Christ might seep deeply into our personalities that we might be more like Him. Is anyone here sad today? Lord, give him good cheer. Is anyone here sick? Lord, give him strength. Is anyone here confused? Lord, grant him wisdom. Is anyone bored and wishing he were somewhere else? Lord, awaken him to the splendor of Your holiness. You inhabit the praises of Your people; so we praise and sing and thank You today. We love you, and we ask that the love of Jesus Christ might be shed abroad in our hearts through the Holy Spirit. In Jesus' Name. Amen.

Scripture Medley from 1 John
He who says he abides in Him ought himself to walk just as He walked. . . . He who says he is in the light, and hates his brother, is in darkness until now. . . . little children, abide in Him. . . . believe on the name of His Son Jesus Christ, and love one another. . . . let us love one another, for love is of God; and everyone who loves is born of God and knows God. . . . In this is love, not that we loved God, but that He loved us and sent His Son to be the propitiation for our sins. Beloved, if God so loved us, we also ought to love one another.
(1 John 2:6, 9, 28; 3:23; 4:7, 10, 11)

Additional Sermons and Lesson Ideas

Worshipping God by Name

By Dr. David Jeremiah

Date preached:

SCRIPTURE: Psalm 23

INTRODUCTION: The Old Testament people of God knew how to celebrate Him, and they can teach us the wonderful secret of worshipping Him by name.

1. Jehovah-Rohi—The Lord My Shepherd (Ps. 23:1)
2. Jehovah-Jireh—The Lord Will Provide (Gen. 22:14)
3. Jehovah-Rophe—The Lord Who Heals (Ex. 15:26)
4. Jehovah-Nissi—The Lord Is My Banner (Ex. 17:15)
5. Jehovah-Mekaddesh—The Lord Who Sanctifies (Lev. 20:8)
6. Jehovah-Shalom—The Lord Is Peace (Judg. 6:24)
7. Jehovah-Tsidkenu—The Lord Our Righteousness (Jer. 23:6)
8. Jehovah-Shammah—The Lord Is There (Ezek. 48:35)

CONCLUSION: Notice how all these names of God are descriptive of the unfolding ministry the Lord provides us in Psalm 23. He meets all our needs, and He is the object of all our praise.

Kingdom Workers: Part Three

By Dr. Timothy Beougher

Date preached:

SCRIPTURE: 1 Corinthians 3:16–23

INTRODUCTION: Have you ever been driving when all the sudden a sign catches your eye: "WARNING, left lane closed 500 feet ahead!" If you don't take heed, you're headed for a crash. In this section Paul gives three warnings to kingdom workers, three caution signs, three things we need to avoid.

1. Damaging Behavior (vv. 16–17). We are to build up, not tear down. Are you seeking to build up?
2. Deceptive Attitudes (vv. 18–20). Are you marching to the drumbeat of this world, or are you allowing God's Word to transform your way of thinking?
3. Misplaced Devotion (vv. 21–23). Are you rejoicing in all that you have in Jesus Christ?

CONCLUSION: As God's kingdom workers, we should heed His warnings and commit ourselves to His Word.

CLASSICS FOR THE PASTOR'S LIBRARY

The Knowledge of the Holy

A. W. Tozer isn't for cowards. There's something very intense about his writings. His words are pungent. Warren Wiersbe, who heard him many times in person, said that listening to Tozer preach was about as safe as "opening the door of a blast furnace." But if you want to know God better, live straighter, think clearer, and meet problems head-on, take a deep breath and open one of his books.

You might start with *The Knowledge of the Holy.*

I've read it repeatedly and often quote from it in sermons. It is perhaps the best devotional treatment of the attributes of God to be found. The preface alone is worth memorizing. Tozer says: "It is impossible to keep our moral practices sound and our inward attitudes right while our idea of God is erroneous or inadequate. If we would bring back spiritual power to our lives, we must began to think of God more nearly as He is."

Tozer explains that we tend by a secret law of the soul to move toward our mental image of God. We are becoming whatever we envision God as being. Knowing God theologically, personally, and accurately is therefore the most important thing about us.

So what is God really like? Tozer describes God's self-sufficiency, His infinitude, His wisdom, His goodness, His mercy, His justice, His holiness.

Here is a sampling:

To say that God is omniscient is to say that He possesses perfect knowledge and therefore has no need to learn. But is it more: it is to say that God has never learned and cannot learn. . . . God knows instantly and effortlessly all. . . .

With the goodness of God to desire our highest welfare, the wisdom of God to plan it, and the power of God to achieve it, what do we lack?

The Lord God omnipotent can do anything as easily as anything else. All His acts are done without effort. He expends no energy that must be replenished.

The vague and tenuous hope that God is too kind to punish the ungodly has become a deadly opiate for the consciences of millions.

[The holiness of God] stands apart, unique, unapproachable, incomprehensible, and unattainable. The natural man is blind to it. He may fear God's power and admire His wisdom, but His holiness he cannot even imagine.

Because we are the handiwork of God, it follows that all our problems and their solutions are theological.

Aiden Wilson Tozer (1897–1963) grew up on a farm in Pennsylvania, where as a boy he put in long hours of physical labor. His education was limited. Economic pressures forced the family to move to Akron, Ohio when he was fifteen, and there he began working for the Goodrich Rubber Company. Walking home after work one afternoon, Tozer heard a street preacher say, "If you don't know how to be saved. . . just call on God." After arriving home, Tozer crawled into the attic and asked Jesus Christ to be his Savior and Lord.

Shortly after, he joined the Missionary Alliance Church. He then was ordained and began ministering in the Christian and Missionary Alliance denomination. From 1928 to 1959, he pastored the Southside Alliance Church in Chicago where his congregation grew from eighty to eight hundred. But his greatest and most lasting ministry was arguably as editor of the *Alliance Weekly*. His words were read, re-read, re-printed, and re-published. Many people subscribed to the magazine just to read his editorials. By the time he died of a heart attack at age 66, his columns, articles, and sermons had become best-selling books.

"It is not a cheerful thought," says Tozer, "that millions of us who live in a land of Bibles, who belong to churches and labor to promote the Christian religion, may yet pass our whole life on this earth without having once thought or tried to think seriously about the being of God."

The Knowledge of the Holy aims to correct that.

Among Tozer's Other Books :

The Pursuit of God—written in the late 1940s aboard a train en route to McAllen, Texas. Tozer wrote all night, the words coming to him as fast as he could put them down. It's considered a classic now, with over one million copies in print.

Born After Midnight—"Revivals are born after midnight," writes Tozer. "[They] require a serious mind and a determined heart to pray past the ordinary into the unusual."

We Travel An Appointed Way—One of several volumes of Tozer's collected editorials in *Alliance Weekly*. The opening segment says, "To the child of God, there is no such thing as accident. He travels an appointed way."

That Incredible Christian—Another collection of Tozer's articles and editorials, these focus on the overcoming power of the Christian who lives by obedience and faith.

AUGUST 20, 2006

The Virtue of Marriage

By Dr. Melvin Worthington   *Date preached:*

Scripture: Exodus 20:14: You shall not commit adultery.

Introduction: Life is full of temptations. Some of the most tragic cases of falling to temptation are those of marital infidelity. Have you known a situation like this? Scripture gives us strong warnings to avoid this particular sin. Let's look at the seventh commandment and some of its supporting Scriptures.

1. **The Admonition in the Text.**

   A. **This Commandment Recognizes the Institution.** Marriage is the oldest, ordained, and ordered institution (Gen. 2:7–25; Matt. 19:3–10; John 2:1–11; 1 Cor. 7:2; Eph. 5:22–33; Col. 3:18–19; 1 Tim. 4:3; 5:14; Heb. 13:4; 1 Pet. 3:1–7). Marriage is *established by the Sovereign, emphasized in Scripture, essential for society,* and *exists for siblings* as a place of *safety, security, and support.*

   B. This Commandment Reveals the Intention. God designed marriage for *pleasure, passion, partnership, procreation, prevention, purity, protection, and as a portrait.*

   C. This Commandment Requires Integrity and Intimacy (Prov. 4:21, 23; 1 Cor. 6:17, 18; 7:2; Heb. 13:4). Successful marriages require *honor, humility, honesty, and holiness* on the part of the husband and the wife.

   D. This Commandment Rebukes Impurity and Immorality. Violation of this commandment results in defilement, disease, destruction, and debasement. We should be as much afraid of that which defiles our body as that which destroys it.

2. **The Analysis of the Text.** This commandment prohibits unchastity in thought and desire (see Prov. 4:18; Matt. 5:28), unchastity in conversation (Eph. 5:3, 4), and sensuality in all its forms and actions (Prov. 6:13; Is. 3:16;

2 Pet. 2:14). Impurity defiles, destroys, debases, and damns. Adultery is a *heinous sin* because it breaches the marriage oath; it is done deliberately; it is needless; and it dishonors, displeases, and disobeys God. Its consequences are devastating for the individual, the family, society, the nation, and the human race. Adultery is a *hideous sin* because it is a thievish sin, it debases a person, it pollutes, it drains the purse, it is destructive to the body, it destroys one's reputation, and it impairs the mind. Without repentance it can damn the soul, and the adulterer is abhorred by God. Adultery is a *health-related sin* because of the physical, psychological, practical, and personal consequences. Purity is the highest, happiest, healthiest, and the holiest standard of living.

3. **The Application from the Text**. Adultery encompasses one's appetites, acts, apparel, and associations. Few that are entangled in the sin of adultery recover out of the snare, for pleasures harden the heart. Therefore we should be sober and temperate, modest, and circumspect in marriage and chaste in society. We should flee all occasions and incentives to uncleanness, begin with our own hearts, make a definite choice, and be satisfied with what we have. We must beware idleness, fear God, and set our delight in the Word of God. Those who are married should love their own spouses. It is not the having of a spouse, but the loving of one's spouse, that makes a person live chastely. He who loves his wife, whom Solomon calls his fountain, will not go abroad to drink of muddy, poisoned waters. We need to be reminded that God sees this act of sin and that this sin is very hard to overcome. If we are to keep our bodies pure, our souls must remain pure.

Conclusion: Our passions and desires are God given. When we control them, they make our firesides places of comfort and cheer. When we don't control them, they consume our homes and leave us miserable wanderers. Now we may approach the subject of marriage. A high ideal for marriage is a great incentive to purity of heart. If young people anticipate a pure marriage, every step toward it must be in the way of virtue. If you wish to win a pure person as your lifelong companion, you should be unwilling to give less than you wish to receive. You will keep your own soul sweet and clean.

STATS, STORIES AND MORE

Two Important Strategies

If you feel you're falling out of love with your husband or wife, here's a suggestion: Act like you love each other. Just start acting like you love each other. Admittedly, there are some days when we don't feel as much love as on others. I read about one young preacher's wife who stood up in a marriage retreat and began nervously to share her testimony. She said, "The Bible promises, 'No good thing does the Lord withhold from them that walk uprightly.' " "Well," she said sincerely, "my husband is one of those 'no good things'!" We all feel that way at times. But if you act *as if* you feel a certain way, sooner or later you will actually begin filling that way. William James, the father of American psychology, concluded that we become how we act. As he put it: "By regulating the action . . . we can indirectly regulate the feeling."

Avoid platonic friendships with members of the opposite sex. Platonic friendships seem to be normal, natural, and innocent. But most affairs begin as platonic, innocent relationships that, without either partner realizing it, begin to develop a life of their own. We can't isolate ourselves from members of the opposite sex, nor should we, but we need to be cautious and keep the boundary lines in place. Anytime you find yourself telling a member of the opposite sex something that you wouldn't want your spouse to know—that's dangerous. Anytime you find yourself wanting to spend time with a member of the opposite sex besides your husband or wife—that's dangerous. Anytime you find yourself alone with a member of the opposite sex—that's dangerous. Have rules for yourself, and avoid being drawn into relationships that may divert your emotional energy and attention from your marriage.

APPROPRIATE HYMNS AND SONGS

Redeemed, Fanny J. Crosby/Aubrey L. Butler, 1966, 1967 Broadman Press ARR Distributed by Genevox Music Group

Sanctify My Heart, John Chisum/Gary Sadler, 1994 Integrity's Hosanna! Music (c/o Integrity Music, Inc.)

In the Cross of Christ I Glory, John Bowring/Ithamar Conkey, Public Domain

Sacrifice of Love, John Barnett, 1990 Mercy/Vineyard Publishing (Admin. by Music Services)

You Are My King, Billy James Foote, 1999 worshiptogether.com songs (Admin. by EMI Christian Music Publishing)

FOR THE BULLETIN

The hermit Celestine, nearly eighty years old, was consecrated as Pope Celestine V on this day in 1294. He accepted the papacy against his better judgment, was unhappy in the papal chair, and resigned four months later to return to a life of solitude. ❀ On August 20, 1636, Scottish pastor and theologian Samuel Rutherford was exiled to Aberdeen, Scotland, and forbidden to preach. His letters from exile became a classic in Christian history. ❀ Today marks the birth in 1745 of the Methodist leader Francis Asbury. During his lifetime he traveled nearly three hundred thousand miles by horseback, overseeing the establishment of Methodism in America. ❀ On August 20, 1866, President Andrew Johnson formally declared that the Civil War was over. ❀ Today is the birthday in 1884 of the German scholar and theologian Rodolf Bultmann, who attacked the evangelical gospel by seeking to "demythologize" the Bible. This is also the birthday of another German theologian, Paul Tillich, who was born on this day in 1886. ❀ William Booth, founder of the Salvation Army, was promoted to glory on this day in 1912. ❀ Haralan Popov of Bulgaria, a converted atheist, was serving as a pastor and evangelist when the Communists invaded his country in 1944. Popov was arrested and subjected to torture. On August 20, 1948, a guard put a gun to his head and threatened to kill him. The guard didn't pull the trigger, but Popov remained in prison for over thirteen years, where he worked tirelessly in bringing other inmates to faith in Christ.

WORSHIP HELPS

Call to Worship:
I will abide in Your tabernacle forever; I will trust in the shelter of Your wings. . . . So I will sing praise to Your name forever . . . (Ps. 61:4, 8a).

Reader's Theater (May be adapted as a Scripture Reading Medley):

Reader 1: And the LORD God said, "It is not good that man should be alone; I will make him a helper comparable to him."

Reader 2: Marriage is honorable among all, and the bed undefiled; but fornicators and adulterers God will judge.

Reader 1: Husbands, love your wives, just as Christ also loved the church and gave Himself for her, that He might sanctify and cleanse her with the washing of water by the word, that He might present her to Himself a glorious church, not having spot or wrinkle or any such thing, but that she should be holy and without blemish. So husbands ought to love their own wives as their own bodies; he who loves his wife loves himself.

Reader 2: Wives, likewise, be submissive to your own husbands, that even if some do not obey the word, they, without a word, may be won by the conduct of their wives, when they observe your chaste conduct accompanied by fear. Do not let your adornment be merely outward—arranging the hair, wearing gold, or putting on fine apparel—rather let it be the hidden person of the heart, with the incorruptible beauty of a gentle and quiet spirit, which is very precious in the sight of God.
(Gen. 2:18; Heb. 13:4; Eph. 5:25–28; 1 Pet. 3:1–3)

Benediction:
And God is able to make all grace abound toward you, that you, always having all sufficiency in all things, may have an abundance for every good work (2 Cor. 9:8).

Additional Sermons and Lesson Ideas

The How and Why of Giving

Date preached:

By Pastor J. David Hoke

SCRIPTURE: 2 Corinthians 8:1—9:15

INTRODUCTION: Since we live in a world that places such a high value on money, why should anyone want to give it away? What does generosity look like?

1. Thankful Giving (2 Cor. 9:15). The basis for true thanksgiving is God's gift of Jesus Christ. As we get to know Jesus better, we will find that our gratitude grows; our giving should reflect our gratitude.

2. Cheerful Giving (2 Cor. 9:7). The Greek word for "cheerful" in 2 Corinthians 9:7 is the basis for our word *hilarious*. God loves a giver who gives joyously, "hilariously," or delightfully.

3. Liberal Giving (2 Cor. 9:6). Although you can't out-give God, many Christians certainly under-give him.

4. Sacrificial Giving (2 Cor. 8:1–4). Most people give only out of their surplus; God rejoices in the person who gives generously.

CONCLUSION: As you are faithful in your giving, God will be faithful to bless you with such abundance in your life that you will wonder why you didn't do it sooner.

Heaven Inspired Living in a Hell–Bent World

Date preached:

By Rev. Mark Hollis

SCRIPTURE: John 14:15–27; 15:26—16:15

INTRODUCTION: How are Christians to live in a society that is hell-bent on being hell-bound? The Holy Spirit is our resource.

1. He Is the Counselor Who Is with Us Forever (14:15, 16).
2. He Is the Spirit of Truth (14:17a).
3. He Is the Means by which Jesus Indwells Believers (14:17b–18 and 23, 24).
4. He Teaches, Reminds, and Gives Peace (14:25–27).
5. He Testifies about Jesus (15:26—16:4).
6. He Is the Presence of Christ in Our World (16:5–7).
7. He Convicts the World of Guilt in Regard to Sin, Righteousness, and Judgment (16:8–11).
8. He Guides into All Truth and Tells what Is to Come (16:12, 13).
9. He Brings Glory to Jesus (16:14–15).

CONCLUSION: Jesus' departure meant the coming of the Holy Spirit. The Spirit works to prepare the world for the message of the gospel and within us that we might live with heavenly values in a hell-bent world.

AUGUST 27, 2006

Praying like Jesus

Date preached:

By Dr. Ed Dobson

Scripture: John 17:6–19, especially verse 17:
Sanctify them by Your truth. Your Word is truth.

Introduction: Do you ever kneel or close your eyes to pray for someone and just not know what to say? Jesus gives us wonderful insight into how we should pray for others.

1. Verse 6 says, "I have manifested Your name to the men whom You have given Me out of this world." The Greek word for "manifested" literally means "to make clear, to make visible," that is, to make something so plain that everyone can see it and understand it exactly. Jesus basically said, "While I have been with these disciples whom You've given me, my first task was to reveal You—to make You clear, to make You plain, to make You understandable." He gives a footnote, that they "kept" His Word. This Greek verb means to stand guard over someone, to prevent them from escaping. Do we keep His Word? Do we watch over it, guard it, and obey it?

2. Verse 8 says, "For I have given to them the words which You have given Me and they have received them. . . ." In John 6:21, after Jesus had just walked on the water, the text explains that the disciples "received" Jesus into the boat. The same word for "received" is used in both texts. This word means to receive something personally and individually so you can incorporate it into your life.

3. Verse 9 says, "I pray for them. . . ." This is the heart of the passage. Before we read it, Jesus prayed for two things specifically. Number one, He prayed that the disciples would be protected from the world. Number two, He prayed that they would be sanctified. Jesus meant something like this: "My prayer, since I'm leaving the world and I'm going to You, is that You would guard them and protect them from the world so that they might be one as we are one." Jesus completed His thought in verse 17 when He asked God to sanc-

tify the disciples by His truth, that is, His Word. The only successful way to be protected from the world is through God's Word.

4. Verse 18 says, ". . . I also have sent them into the world." Jesus meant something like this: "I'm going away, I want them to be one with You, so that they will be protected from the world." He then finished His prayer with, "Yes, I want them to be protected from the world, but not withdrawn from the world. In fact, I am sending them into the world." What is our mission to the world? It's not to live only on the defensive, nor is it to actively condemn the world. Our mission, rather, is to bring a message of hope, salvation, forgiveness, and deliverance to the world (John 3:16–17).

Application Questions:

1. How Do We Glorify God? Verse 4 reveals that Jesus brought God glory through doing His work. We can glorify God in two ways: first, by making God clear to those around us, that is, by explaining God to them; second by sharing God's Word.

2. How Should We Respond to God's Word? Two verbs we looked at help us with this question. First, I'm to guard God's Word and protect it. Second, I'm to receive it into my life.

3. How Should We Pray for Ourselves and for Others? We ought to be praying for at least two things: protection from the world and sanctification through the truth. Praying for others should sound something like, "Lord, protect them from the world, and protect them from the evil one. Make them holy through Your Word."

4. How Do We Overcome the World? Get as close to God as you possibly can. Jesus said something like this, "Protect them by the power of Your name so that they may be one, one with the Father against the world, one with the Father overcoming the world." The closer we get to God, the greater is the power to overcome the attractions and the temptations of the world.

5. How Do We Respond to this Message Overall? First, we need to protect and stand guard over God's Word. Second, we need to receive it into our lives. We need to embrace it and let it become a part of our lives. Third, we need to live the Word. It's not just hearing the Word, it's obeying the Word that changes us. Fourth, we need to share the Word.

STATS, STORIES AND MORE

Notice that in this passage, Jesus prays in the presence of the disciples! There is something unique about praying this kind of prayer in front of whomever you pray for. It is unique for your kids to hear you pray in their presence; the same is true for spouses, and so on.

When I was growing up, my parents were pretty strict about family devotions. I think I rebelled somewhat against that. Before I went to school we read the Bible and got down on our knees and prayed. At a certain time every evening, I would leave soccer practice early because soccer practice was not as important as being home for family devotions. At this stage in my life, I think my parents probably had it right. Today, we put sports and extra-curricular activities for our kids far above anything spiritual. But I remember my dad praying for me, my mother praying for me. I remember specifically what they prayed, and I can tell you, at moments of decision in my life those prayers were stuck in my brain. There is something about praying for people in front of them and for them as Jesus did.

—Dr. Ed Dobson

APPROPRIATE HYMNS AND SONGS

Give Us Clean Hands, Charlie Hall, 1997 Generation Productions

The Lord's Prayer, Albert Hay Malotte, Arr. By Fred Bock, b. 1939, 1935 by G. Schirmer, Inc. This arrangement Copyright 1976 by G. Schirmer, Inc.

Be Still My Soul, Katharina Von Schlegal/Jane L. Borthwick/ Jean Sibelius, Public Domain

I Must Tell Jesus, Elisha A. Hoffman, Public Domain

Jesus, Draw Me Close, Rick Founds, 1990 Maranatha Praise Music, Inc.

Under the influence of William Farel, mentor of John Calvin, the city of Geneva, Switzerland, became Protestant on August 27, 1535. The city's Great Council of Two Hundred issued an edict of the Reformation. The next year, the Mass was abolished and the citizens pledged themselves to live according to the precepts of the gospel. ❀ Jacob Arminius, famous Dutch theologian, was ordained on August 27, 1588. ❀ On August 27, 1640, Henry Dunster, pastor and scholar, was elected as the first president of American's first college—Harvard. ❀ In 1722, Count Nicholas Ludwig von Zinzendorf, troubled by the suffering of Christian exiles from Bohemia and Moravia, allowed them to establish a community on his estate in Germany. The center became known as Herrnhut, meaning "Under the Lord's Watch." It grew quickly, and so did its appreciation for the power of prayer. On August 27, 1727, twenty-four men and twenty-four women covenanted to spend an hour each day in scheduled prayer, praying in sequence around the clock. Soon, others joined the prayer chain. Unceasing prayer rose to God twenty-four hours a day as someone—at least one—was engaged in intercessory prayer each hour of every day. This prayer meeting lasted over one hundred years and helped birth Protestant missions. ❀ On this day in 1826, George Müller preached his first sermon. He would later establish a famous orphanage in Bristol, England, and travel the globe as an evangelist. This is also the date of G. Campbell Morgan's first sermon, which he delivered at the age of thirteen in 1876. Morgan later became one of the most famous Bible preachers of his day.

WORSHIP HELPS

Call to Worship:
Shout joyfully to the Lord, all the earth; break forth in song, rejoice, and sing praises.
(Ps. 98:4)

Scripture Reading Medley:
Who can utter the mighty acts of the Lord? Who can declare all His praise?
The pillars of heaven tremble, and are astonished at His rebuke. He stirs up the sea with His power, and by His understanding He breaks up the storm. By His Spirit He adorned the heavens; His hand pierced the fleeing serpent. Indeed these are the mere edges of His ways, and how small a whisper we hear of Him!
Thus says the Lord, your Redeemer, and He who formed you from the womb: "I am the Lord, who makes all things, Who stretches out the heavens all alone, who spreads abroad the earth by Myself."
There is no other God besides Me, a just God and a Savior; there is none besides Me. Look to Me, and be saved, all you ends of the earth! For I am God, and there is no other.
(Ps. 106:2; Job 26:11–14; Is. 44:24; 45:21–22)

Pastoral Prayer:
Dear Lord, I pray that You would protect me from the world this week, that I would be one with the Father in my personal walk. I pray that You would make me holy through Your Word. I pray this for our congregation. Jesus could have prayed for many things, but this apparently is what mattered most. So I pray that You would protect us from the world and You would sanctify us through Your truth. I pray that we would guard Your Word and embrace Your Word and live Your Word and share Your Word. In the name of Christ our Lord we pray. Amen.

Additional Sermons and Lesson Ideas

Divine Resources for Life's Difficulties
By Dr. Denis Lyle

Date preached:

SCRIPTURE: 1 Thessalonians 2:13–20

INTRODUCTION: Do you view suffering for the Lord Jesus as a great privilege? He left the splendour of heaven to suffer and die for you and me! Not only that, but (as Paul lists in this passage) He gave us resources to deal with troubles that face us! Let's look at them together:

1. The Word of God Within Us (v. 13). The Thessalonians *appreciated, appropriated,* and *applied* the Word of God.
2. The People of God Around Us (vv. 14–16). Paul told the Thessalonians that *their experiences weren't new* (v. 14) and that *their enemies wouldn't escape* (v. 16).
3. The Glory of God Before Us (vv. 17–20). Paul, desiring to see the Thessalonians, was *hindered by Satan* (vv. 17–18), but there was *a day Paul kept in mind* (v. 19) and *a reward Paul had in store* (v. 19).

CONCLUSION: How do we make it through life's difficulties? Through His Word, His people, and in His glory!

Living with Leanness
By Dr. Melvin Worthington

Date preached:

SCRIPTURE: Numbers 11; Psalm 78:25–31; 106:13–16

INTRODUCTION: The Bible declares, "And he gave them their request; but sent leanness into their soul" (Ps. 106:15, KJV). What lessons can be learned from the Israelites' experience?

1. They Despised Manna. God had delivered the Israelites from the Egyptians. They walked through the Red Sea, but three days into the wildness they murmured for water. Six weeks later they were complaining, crying, and criticizing the provisions from God's hand.
2. They Demanded Meat. Not satisfied with God's provision, the Israelites clamored and called for the kind of food that would satisfy their sensual gratifications. They determined to have better food than the manna God continually provided.
3. They Discovered Misery. God gave them their request, but with the consequences they deserved. God's goodness cannot be measured by the degree to which He satisfies our cravings.

CONCLUSION: Praying according to God's will results in living with full souls. Selfish, stubborn praying according to our desires without considering the will of God may get us what we request, but we may also get undesired results through harsh consequences.

A Sunday Night Prayer

The British hymnist Frances Ridley Havergal was a radiant soloist and poet; she was much in demand in her day. Her winning personality and sizable talents were devoted totally to Christ, and we are still singing her great hymns in our churches. The day before she passed away at age forty-two, she had a talk with her sister about the miscellaneous poems and hymns she had been recently composing. Frances asked her sister Maria to collect and publish them after her death, if possible. "Shall the title be 'Under His Shadow'?" asked Maria. Frances replied, "Oh, yes; I am so glad you remembered it."

And so today, if you look hard enough in the used book markets, you can find a precious little book of poems, about the size of a deck of cards, entitled "Under His Shadow: The Last Poems of Frances Ridley Havergal." It was published in London by James Nisbet & Company in 1880.

Included among the poems is a prayer Frances wrote for her minister. It is simply titled "Sunday Night." Havergal, whose father was an Anglican pastor, knew that preachers and pastors sometimes have a hard time resting on Sunday nights. The stress and pressure of the Lord's Day sometimes leave our nerves taut and our thoughts racing. So she composed this prayer with its timeless appeal to God for His servants. I've found that with little effort I can convert phrases of this prayer as an intercession for myself. As I read this poem the first time, I wished I had been Miss Havergal's pastor so that I might have been the primary beneficiary of this wonderful petition. I'm not sure I have a member in my church who would really offer such a prayer for me. People just don't think of it. But I've found that with little effort, I can adopt this prayer for myself or for my friends in ministry. It is also a beautiful poem to quote should you ever been called on to conduct the funeral of a beloved pastor.

> Rest him, O Father! Thou didst send him forth
> With great and gracious messages of love;
> But Thy ambassador is weary now,
> Worn with the weight of his high embassy.
> Now care for him as Thou hast cared for us
> In sending him; and cause him to lie down

In Thy fresh pastures, by Thy streams of peace.
Let Thy left hand be now beneath his head,
And Thine upholding right encircle him,
And, underneath, the Everlasting arms
Be felt in full support. So let him rest,
Hushed like a little child, without one care;
And so give Thy beloved sleep tonight.

Rest him, dear Master! He hath poured for us
The wine of joy, and we have been refreshed.
Now fill *his* chalice, give him sweet new draughts
Of life and love, with Thine own hand; be Thou
His ministrant tonight; draw very near
In all Thy tenderness and all Thy power.
Oh speak to him! Thou knowest how to speak
A word in season to Thy weary ones,
And he is weary now. Thou lovest him—
Let Thy disciple lean upon Thy breast,
And, leaning, gain new strength to "rise and shine."

Rest Him, O loving Spirit! Let Thy calm
Fall on his soul tonight. O holy Dove,
Spread Thy bright wing above him, let him rest
Beneath its shadow; let him know afresh
The infinite truth and might of Thy dear name—
"Our Comforter!" As gentlest touch will stay
The strong vibrations of a jarring chord,
So lay Thy hand upon his heart, and still
Each overstraining throb, each pulsing pain.
Then, in the stillness, breathe upon the strings,
And let Thy holy music overflow
With soothing power his listening, resting soul.

SEPTEMBER 3, 2006

SUGGESTED SERMON

The State of Barrenness

Date preached:

By Dr. Stephen Olford

Scripture: Jeremiah 11:3; 17:5; 48:10, especially 11:3
... Cursed is the man who does not obey the words of this covenant.

Introduction: After twenty-one consecutive years in the pastorate in two metropolitan churches in London and New York, and having traveled vastly in religious circles, I'm aware that we can be in the most spiritual circumstances and yet know barrenness in our lives—a dryness and an aridness. God punctuates this amazing prophecy of Jeremiah with some of the most solemn warnings we'll find anywhere in Scripture. I have chosen three of them that have searched and researched my heart.

1. **Barrenness Is the Consequence of Disobedience to the Word of God (Jer. 11:3).** Contextually, this is an interesting verse. Undoubtedly it has reference to King Josiah in his eighteenth year after having rediscovered the Book of the Law. After reading it and searching his own heart, Josiah felt convicted and sought to bring about a renewal—a revival among his people. Josiah arranged to have the Scriptures read openly. If you read the story carefully, you'll discover that God's people didn't rise to the occasion. Because of their disobedience and refusal to bow to the authority of God's Word, the prophet Jeremiah came with this warning. A similar situation is found in 1 Samuel 15:10–23. It concerns King Saul who was commanded to smite the Amalakites. He chose his own terms of obedience and saved Agag the king and the best of the cattle. The prophet Samuel walked into that situation and heard the bleating of the sheep and the lowing of the cattle. Samuel promptly rebuked King Saul with these solemn words: "... you have rejected the word of the LORD, and the LORD has rejected you ..." (1 Sam. 15:26). There is no substitute for total obedience.

2. **Barrenness Is the Consequence of not Trusting the Power of God (Jer. 17:5).** Here are dramatic and devastating words addressed to God's people, who of all the nations of the earth had seen the mighty demonstra-

tions of God's power. Yet they had turned from Jehovah God and sought alliances with Egypt and Assyria. God's prophet had to come and say "Cursed be the man who trusts in man and makes flesh his strength" (Jer. 17:5). One illustration of this principle is Moses in his early days. Moses thought that "by his hand" he could deliver Israel (see Acts 7:25). He smote an Egyptian, ran into the desert, and for forty years God had to show him that he couldn't trust in his own hand. Only after those forty years of utter brokenness could God take a man who was afraid to even open his mouth and use him to deliver His people from slavery in Egypt. I want to remind every one of us that all power is inherent in God. All power ultimately belongs to Him.

3. **Barrenness Is the Consequence of Deceitfulness in Doing the Work of God (Jer. 48:10).** These are such vehement words that the higher critics and others have sought to remove it from the prophecy of Jeremiah and say that it's not part of Scripture, but that is completely unwarranted. We not only believe in the inerrancy of God's Word, but we also know that this teaching often occurs elsewhere in the Bible. One of these is in the New Testament: the case of Ananias and Sapphirah (Acts 5:1–11). There is nothing God hates more than deceitfulness in the work of the Lord. Ananias and Sapphirah were members of the Jerusalem church, and they had seen Barnabas come with all his wealth and lay it all at the apostles' feet. Ananias and Sapphirah decided that they too wanted to make a good impression on the leaders of the church, so they sold some land and gave part of the proceeds to the apostles while pretending to give it all. They conferred together to lie. They presented their gift to the apostles, but the discerning Peter by the power of the Holy Spirit saw right through the fraud and phoniness of it all and said, "Why has Satan filled your heart to lie to the Holy Spirit?" (Acts 5:3). Immediately, Ananias and then Sapphirah were smitten by the judgment of God. This illustrates the truth that God will not look with favor upon deceitfulness in the work of the Lord.

CONCLUSION: Let's bring our hearts into submission to God's Word; let's bring our lives into submission to God's Spirit; let's bring our entire actions into submission to God's work.

STATS, STORIES AND MORE

More from Dr. Olford:

My very dear friend, Dr. Alan Redpath, has a motto that has hung in every one of his studies during his pastoral years: "Beware of the Barrenness of a Busy Life." George Goodman, that great Brethren Bible teacher, used to say, "Beware lest service sap spirituality."

If you were to ask me what the single most important word in the Christian vocabulary is—from the moment of your commitment to Christ initially in salvation to that moment of final redemption when Jesus comes back again, from Genesis to Revelation—I would say *obedience*. There is no substitute for absolute obedience. I heard Dr. William Fitch once say at the Mid-America Keswick Conference in Chicago, "Any point of defective obedience constitutes *total* disobedience."

All across America today in evangelical circles among preachers, there's an attitude of "do it yourself theology." This means that your own brains will take you through, your own culture will take you through; your string of degrees will take you through, although God has condemned all these notions (Gal. 3:1–3)! That is no indictment upon hard work and hard study and hard application of truth, but our life is a miraculous life. I cannot by any means convert myself or by any means live by the power of an indwelling Christ in and of myself—since it's only Christ and Christ only who can do this in me. Having begun totally dependent on Christ, I must live my Christian life that way too.

APPROPRIATE HYMNS AND SONGS

I Surrender All, Judson Van De Venter/Winfield S. Weeden, Public Domain

Be Magnified, Lynn DeShazo, 1991 Integrity's Hosanna! Music (c/o Integrity Music, Inc.)

Cleanse Me, J. Edwin Orr, Public Domain

The Heart of Worship, Matt Redman, 1997 Kingsway's Thankyou Music (Admin. by EMI Christian Music Publishing)

My Jesus I Love Thee, William R. Featherston/Adoniram J. Gordon, Public Domain

FOR THE BULLETIN

Gregory the Great was consecrated pope on September 3, 590. Gregory did much good. Burdened for the evangelization of England, he sent Augustine to evangelize the British Isles. Gregory appointed competent men as church leaders and fought apostasy. He wrote evangelistic tracts to barbarian tribes and upheld biblical morality. He wrote liturgy and popularized the Gregorian chant. But Gregory also established the dogmas of purgatory and the Mass. He encouraged the worship of relics and popularized unlikely legends about the saints. He held tradition equal with Scripture. And he claimed universal jurisdiction over Christendom and assumed broad civil control of most of Italy. In short, Gregory became the father of the medieval papacy, with all the good and bad which that included. ✿ John Bunyan, author of *Pilgrim's Progress,* was buried on this day in 1688 in London's Bunhill Fields. ✿ Today is the birthday in 1708 of William Grimshaw, popular Anglican preacher. ✿ John Wesley had a conversation with his mother Susanna on September 3, 1739, in which she expressed her experience of finding assurance for forgiveness of sins while observing the Lord's Supper. On the same day two years later, September 3, 1741, he had a less fortunate conversation with Count Nicholaus von Zinzendorf. At a meeting at Gray's Inn Gardens, Zinzendorf and Wesley challenged each other's views on holiness. The two were unable to come to terms, and they departed to let Methodism and Moravianism go their separate ways. ✿ On September 3, 1939—the day Britain and France declared war on Germany after the latter had invaded Poland two days earlier—William Sangster began his ministry at Westminster Chapel in London. He became the city's "pastor" during the bombings of World War II.

WORSHIP HELPS

Call to Worship:
Awake my soul, and sing
Of Him who died for thee,
And hail Him as thy matchless King
Thro' all eternity.
—Matthew Bridges and Godfrey Thring, *Crown Him with Many Crowns*, 1852

Suggested Scripture Readings:
Exodus 17:1–7
Jeremiah 17:5–10
John 7:37–39

Pastoral Prayer:
Our heavenly Father, we bow in Your presence and in the name of the Lord Jesus and pray that You will bring us to the place of utter willingness to go all the way with You, cost what it will. Like the puritans of old, we ask for that humility to sit under the sentence of Your Word and behind the human vehicles to hear You saying to our hearts, "This do." And grant us not only obedience of heart, but lead us into the victory of which we've heard this morning. Write thy Word deeply upon each one of our hearts, dear Lord, and by the power of Your Holy Spirit, grant us the willingness, the broken-ness, the yieldedness to submit to whatever You, the Lord our God, demand of us. Implement everything You have said to us and lead us in victory. We ask it for Your dear Name's sake. Amen.

Benediction:
Beloved, if our heart does not condemn us, we have confidence toward God. And whatever we ask we receive from Him, because we keep His commandments and do those things that are pleasing in His sight (1 John 3:21, 22).

Additional Sermons and Lesson Ideas

Church

Date preached:

By Pastor J. David Hoke

SCRIPTURE: 1 Timothy 3:15

INTRODUCTION: Has anyone asked you, "What's church really all about anyway?" Paul gives two wonderful descriptions that capture the meaning and purpose of the Church.

1. Household of God. One of the most powerful images is that of the church as a family; this idea focuses on the essential ingredient of relationships. In families we are related to one another by blood. Do you see yourself as related to these people sitting all around you? Do you treat them as such?
2. Pillar of Truth. The church is a place where truth can be discovered and known. The church provides us with an environment where we can be challenged to live our lives on the basis of the truth we have come to know.

CONCLUSION: The church is composed of people redeemed by the *Son of God*, brought together by the *will of God* to live together as the *family of God*, in order to do the *work of God* in the power of the *Spirit of God*, all for *the glory of God*.

Kingdom Workers: Part Four

Date preached:

By Dr. Timothy Beougher

SCRIPTURE: 1 Corinthians 4:1–5

INTRODUCTION: In the previous verses Paul discussed our role as workers in God's kingdom; in this section he shares three significant insights about how we are to live and minister.

1. Our Privilege: We Are Servants of Christ (v. 1).
2. Our Responsibility: To Prove Faithful (v. 2).
3. Our Evaluation: Performed by God (vv. 3–5).

CONCLUSION: The Lord has privileged us to be His servants here on earth, so let's take very seriously our responsibility to be faithful to what He has called us, for God Himself will evaluate every one of us.

SEPTEMBER 10, 2006

SUGGESTED SERMON

The Majesty of the Unveiled Christ

Date preached:

By Dr. Denis Lyle

Scripture: Revelation 1:9–16, especially verse 13:
. . . in the midst of the seven lampstands [was] One like the Son of Man. . . .

Introduction: Have you ever faced a problem so big or a devastation so great that you began to question God? John lived in the midst of persecution so great that Christians were being tortured and killed daily, yet all His attention was refocused when He received a vision of the unveiled Christ. It had been over sixty years since John had seen the Lord Jesus, but he immediately recognized Him as "the Son of Man" (see Dan. 7:13, 14). Who did John see? Remember that while this is symbolic language, it still portrays actual and eternal truth.

1. **He Is the Commanding Christ (v. 13).** The clothing of Christ describes the Authority of the King! In ancient times, this was the recognized apparel of authority, dignity, and royalty. In Old Testament times, a long robe was the clothing of spiritual leaders of high rank, whether it be the high priest (Ex. 25:1), a king (1 Sam. 24:5), a prince, (Ezek. 26:16), or a judge (Ezek. 9:1). Jesus is all of these. Do you see how John saw Christ? If your life seems out of control, remember that Jesus is the King of kings, fully in charge of whatever is going on in your life.

2. **He Is the Consecrated Christ (v. 14).** The imagery of snow describes the purity of the King. Do you know what freshly fallen snow is like? Have you ever considered the fact that the Lord Jesus is the only Man who never had a guilty conscience? He is the only person who never had to confess a sin.

3. **He Is the Comprehending Christ (v. 14).** Christ's fiery eyes refer to the sagacity of the King. He has vision that penetrates. We would say today He has X-ray vision. Jesus cannot be deceived. He sees every minister, notes every member, observes every ministry, and views every motive with X-ray vision.

4. **He Is the Condemning Christ (v. 15).** From His fiery eyes John looks down to see Jesus' red-hot feet, glowing like burnished metal in a fiery furnace.

This refers to the severity of the King. His feet glowed to indicate the fire of the Final Judge. There will be no escape from the wrath of God when Christ's burning feet touch the earth. John now moves from sight to sound and he sees:

5. **The Communicating Christ (v. 15).** The voice sounding like many waters refers to the integrity of the King. This was the same voice that had calmed the storm, that taught His disciples, and that called everything into existence. Jesus' voice is still as powerful and loud as the roar heard at the base of a waterfall. At a time when so many voices are being raised against Christ, we can be assured that one day they will all be silenced. The coming Christ won't endure beatings and crucifixion again; He will come as the King of kings and Lord of lords to judge, rule, and reign.

6. **He Is the Controlling Christ (v. 16).** The seven stars He holds refers to the sovereignty of the King. The stars are the angels or messengers of the churches. The risen Lord holds in His very hand this moment His church, His people, and His servants. This church is not my church, your church, or our church; this church is His church.

7. **He Is the Conquering Christ (v. 16).** Christ holds a deadly two-edged sword; this refers to the ferocity of the King. One of these days the Lord Jesus is coming to do battle with the nations of the world; His weapon will be the Word of God (Eph. 6:17). When confronting great problems, what weapons are you using? Money, medication, manipulation, meanness, or memory? If Christ will use God's Word one day to conquer the world, why do you think it is insufficient for you today?

8. **He Is the Compelling Christ (v. 16).** Finally, John sees Christ's face shining with the glory of God; this refers to the glory of the King. Once that face was marred and spat upon, but here it shines in resplendent glory: unveiled, unmasked, and unadulterated!

Conclusion: John had become so preoccupied with Christ that although his circumstances had not changed, his despondency had lifted. What vision of Christ are you missing because you are so preoccupied with yourself, your problems, or your circumstances? In the midst of your despondency, turn around. Focus on Christ. Why? When you are preoccupied with the Savior, there is no time to fret over your problems.

STATS, STORIES AND MORE

More from Denis Lyle:

When trouble comes, we often focus on the hand of God and overlook the face of God; that is, we tend to question His works rather than reflect on His character. The apostle John received a fresh vision of God when the Emperor Domitian was on the throne in Rome; he was the cruelest of all Roman emperors, sentencing to death or torturing those who refused to worship him. In the midst of such suffering and stress, John was able to focus on Christ, for Christ unveiled Himself. The early believers did refuse to worship Domitian, and they were sentenced to death by the thousands. Some were thrown to the lions in the great coliseum; some were burned at the stake. Others were wrapped in the skins of wild animals and fed to the dogs or dipped in tar and lit as torches for the emperor's garden. Others were crucified—including mothers with babies draped around their necks.

What about you? Have you faced a devastating tragedy in your life? Has your life taken an unexpected turn? Is there any hope for your future? Does life seem too hard to bear when bad things happen to good people? when evil triumphs over good? when Satan seems to have the upper hand? when all hell breaks loose? when death still stings and the grave seems to have the victory? What problems are you facing that seem greater than you can bear? What situation in your life seems impossible? Amy Carmichael, the great missionary to India wrote, "When we are facing the impossible, we can count upon the God of the impossible."

APPROPRIATE HYMNS AND SONGS

O Worship the King, William Kethe/Johann Michael Haydn/Robert Grant/ William Gardiner, Public Domain

Great is the Lord, Michael W. Smith/Deborah D. Smith, 1982 Meadowgreen Music Company (Admin. by EMI Christian Music Publishing)

He is the King, Gary Sadler, 1993 Integrity's Hosanna! Music (c/o Integrity Music, Inc.)

I See the Lord, Mark McCoy/Andy Park, 1995 Mercy/Vineyard Publishing (Admin. by Music Services)

On September 10, A.D. 422, Celestine was elected Pope. He is best known for having sent Saint Patrick to Ireland as a missionary. ❁ The first Franciscans arrived in England on this day in 1224. ❁ Queen Elizabeth I was christened on September 10, 1533. ❁ New England Congregationalists, fearful that Harvard had become too liberal, established a new college called the Collegiate School at New Haven, Connecticut. On September 10, 1718, the name of the school was changed to Yale. ❁ In the late 1770s, John Wesley built his new chapel on City Road in London, then he built a manse next door. He moved in on September 10, 1779, writing in his journal, "This night I lodged in the new house in London. How many more nights have I to spend here?" The answer? Over eleven years, until his death in 1791. ❁ Today is the birthday in 1819 of Joseph Scriven, the author of "What a Friend We Have in Jesus." His life was marked by tragedy, including the drowning death of his fiancée on the night before their wedding. ❁ On September 10, 1846, Elias Howe patented the sewing machine. ❁ British born composer Henry Wellington Greatorex died on this day in 1858 of yellow fever in Charleston, South Carolina. His best known melody is the one traditionally sung to the "Gloria Patri." ❁ On September 10, 1952, two young missionaries, Walter Erickson and Edward R. Tritt, plunged into the remote Kebur and Karoon regions of Indonesia, seeking to advance the gospel to unreached tribes. Just over a month later, their mutilated bodies were found near the Ainim River.

WORSHIP HELPS

Call to Worship:
Oh, the depth of the riches both of the wisdom and knowledge of God! How unsearchable are His judgments and His ways past finding out! . . . For of Him and through Him and to Him are all things, to whom be the glory forever. Amen. (Rom. 11:33, 36)

Hymn Story: Turn Your Eyes Upon Jesus
  The beautiful hymn, "Turn Your Eyes Upon Jesus," was penned by Helen Howarth Lemmel, who was born in England in 1863. Her family immigrated to America when she was a child. Helen loved music, and her parents provided the best vocal teachers they could find. Eventually Helen returned to Europe to study vocal music in Germany. She eventually married a wealthy European, but he left her when she became blind. Helen struggled with multiple heartaches during midlife. At age fifty-five Helen heard a statement that deeply impressed her: "So then, turn your eyes upon Him, look full into His face and you will find that the things of earth will acquire a strange new dimness."
  "I stood still," Helen later said, "and singing in my soul and spirit was the chorus, with not one conscious moment of putting word to word to make rhyme, or note to note to make melody. The verses were written the same week, after the usual manner of composition, but nonetheless dictated by the Holy Spirit." Helen Lemmel, who wrote nearly five hundred hymns during her lifetime, died in Seattle in 1961, thirteen days before her ninety-eighth birthday.

Benediction:
And now may our hearts go forth blessing Him who said: "Do not be afraid; I am the First and the Last. I am He who lives, and was dead, and behold, I am alive forevermore. Amen."
Revelation 1:17, 18

Additional Sermons and Lesson Ideas

The Mastery of the Unveiled Christ
By Dr. Denis Lyle

Date preached:

SCRIPTURE: Revelation 1:17–19

INTRODUCTION: What is your reaction when you are faced with Christ's Glory? John was as we should be when we are faced with Christ:

1. Prostrate before Him in Sinfulness (v. 17). He lay before the resplendent Redeemer: undone, unmasked, and unraveled! The holiness of Christ exposed his own impurity just as it did to Isaiah (see Is. 6:5).
2. Prostrate before Him in Stillness (v. 17). John collapsed at Christ's feet as a dead man. We often express ourselves to God so much that we forget to be still in His presence (Ps. 46:10).
3. Prostrate before Him in Submissiveness (vv. 17–19). Have you ever surrendered your life to Christ so sincerely that you've fallen at the feet of the Savior as though dead? Once John saw the majesty of Christ and fell before Him, Christ called him into service (v. 19)—to help write the Word of God!

CONCLUSION: Do you long to do something of eternal significance? When have you fallen prostrate at the feet of the Lord Jesus? Does He have complete mastery over you?

The Ministry of the Unveiled Christ
By Dr. Denis Lyle

Date preached:

SCRIPTURE: Revelation 1:17–19

INTRODUCTION: As John lay prostrate before the feet of Christ, the Lord did something that was typical of Him. He reached down and touched John.

1. He Conveys His Sympathy (v. 17). Christ told John not to fear. As you read through the Gospels, Christ often touched people to heal and restore them. No wonder the risen Lord reaches out and touches John. Do you need to sense His touch or hear His voice saying, "Fear not"?
2. He Reveals His Identity (vv. 17–18). Christ said " I am," which reveals His deity (Ex. 3:14). "The first and the last" reveals His eternality. The words "I am He who lives" reveal His victory, so there's truly nothing to fear!
3. He Affirms His Authority (v. 18). The keys Christ possesses signify His sovereign authority to open and close the grave. Christ decides who dies and when.

CONCLUSION: Feel the hand of God comforting you despite your circumstances, and hear the voice of God affirming His authority over you. Fear not!

SEPTEMBER 17, 2006

SUGGESTED SERMON

The Message of Assurance

Date preached:

By Dr. Stuart Briscoe

Scripture: Haggai 2:20–23 and Zechariah 4:1–14, especially Zechariah 4:6b:
. . . "Not by might nor by power, but by My Spirit," says the LORD of hosts.

Introduction: The messages in the book of Haggai were given over a brief span of a few weeks in 520 B.C., in the city of Jerusalem to people who had returned to the devastated city after seventy years in exile. They returned to rebuild the city, restore the temple, and reestablish the worship of Jehovah. They had returned with great enthusiasm, but it had been quickly drained away. As a result, God sent the prophets Haggai and Zechariah to bring a series of messages. They were messages of assurance, and they were especially directed to a man named Zerubbabel, who was the leader of this remnant of Jews. Everyone today is searching for a word of assurance. The problem is that we often put our trust in things that eventually turn out to be untrustworthy. This is why we feel insecure in life. Both Haggai and Zechariah had a message of assurance for Zerubbabel—and for you and me.

1. **Assurance Number One: God Will Use You (Zech. 4:1–11).** In this vision the prophet Zechariah saw a big lampstand. Adjacent to it were two olive trees connected to the lampstand by channels or pipes through which flowed golden oil. In the Old Testament the lampstand represented the glory of the Lord, the brilliance of His presence. The key to this vision, however, is the two olive trees, for they represent two "well-oiled people"—the anointed ones (v. 14). What does anointed mean? It means that through the work of the Spirit of God, certain men and women are set apart by God and empowered. So these two olive trees represent two men who were anointed or set apart by God and empowered by His Spirit. These two men were Zerubbabel and his partner, Joshua, the high priest. So the message of this vision is this: One day the Lamp will shine brilliantly again, the temple will be restored, and the worship of Jehovah will thrive. This is going to happen because God has appointed these two anointed ones, who are like olive trees (see Ps. 52:8). They are promised

the golden oil of the Spirit flowing through them. Zechariah was saying, "You and your buddy, Joshua, have been set apart and empowered by the Spirit of God to be the resources through which this work will be completed for the glory of God." The key is verse 6. God says He would accomplish these things by His Spirit and not by human might or power. This is a word of encouragement to Zerubbabel, but it is also a word of assurance to the church of all ages. We have great challenges and inadequate resources, and very often we feel daunted by the task of serving Christ. But it isn't by our might or our power—it's by His Spirit. What we really need is a fresh dose of His anointing.

2. **Assurance Number Two: Jesus Will Come (Hag. 2:23).** As we read this verse, we get the feeling that it is referring to something bigger than Zerubbabel and his immediate concerns. It is, for it refers to the distant future, to things related to Christ Himself. The Old Testament is full of these kinds of hints and suggestions. For example, notice the statement that God would make Zerubbabel like His "signet ring" (Hag. 2:23). The signet ring was the symbol of authority given to the king. In Jeremiah 22:24–30 God warned that He was removing His signet ring (His royal authority) from the line of kings descending from King David, and soon everything came to an abrupt end. Jerusalem was destroyed. The temple was destroyed. The nation was taken into exile. But here God promised to restore the signet ring. And when you turn to Matthew 1:12, 13 and Luke 3:27, you find that Zerubbabel appears in both of the genealogies of Christ. The signet ring was restored to the line of David, to David's great Son and Zerubbabel's great descendant, to Jesus, the King of kings. If you want a word of assurance for the future, here it is: Jesus will come. I don't have time to get into Revelation 21 right now, but there is a day coming when God will say, "Enough is enough!" He will bring this tired world to an end, and He will make a new heaven and a new earth and a new Jerusalem. If you want a word of assurance, this is it: Jesus is Coming!

Conclusion: There's no assurance in the stock market, in world politics, and not even in our personal safety on the roadways as we go home. But there is assurance in the promises and the purposes of God! Make sure you align yourself with Him, and you'll have all the assurance you need.

STATS, STORIES AND MORE

More from Stuart Briscoe

I distinctly remember the time I was contemplating leaving the business world after investing eleven years in a burgeoning business career. I was thinking about leaving it simply to go out on a limb and do youth work. The big question I had in my mind was, "Well, am I sure that it's going to work out? Am I sure my family will be properly cared for? How can I be sure this is the wisest decision?" I talked to various people, and my immediate superior in the bank said to me, "Stuart, if you find you've made a mistake, I'll do my best to get you reinstated in the bank." My father-in-law came and said, "Stuart, I don't really know your God the way you know Him, but I think you're going to be all right; but if it doesn't work out, I'll do my best to make sure you're okay." And that was about as much assurance as I got, humanly speaking. After we'd taken the step and moved into that particular ministry, eleven years passed. Then it all happened again. We had to decide if we were going to leave that particular ministry, uproot our family, bring them across the Atlantic, and embark on a pastorate ministry. Would we be accepted? Would the children adjust? Nobody could give us any ironclad assurance, because nobody knows the future. But the one thing I discovered in both incidents is that God is in the business of working out His purposes. If we can align ourselves with His purposes as best we know how, we can be assured that God is at work, that He will continue to be at work, and that He will bring to completion what He has started. That's basically the message of Haggai.

APPROPRIATE HYMNS AND SONGS

Blessed Assurance, Fanny J. Crosby/Phoebe P. Knapp, Public Domain

A Broken Spirit, Don Harris/Martin J. Nystrom, 1993 Integrity's Hosanna! Music (c/o Integrity Music, Inc.)

It is Well with My Soul, Horatio G. Spafford/Philip P. Bliss, Public Domain

If the Lord Had Not Been On Our Side, Rob Mathes, 1996 Doulos Publishing (Maranatha! Music [Admin. by The Copyright Company])

O Love that Will Not Let Me Go, George Matheson/Albert Lister Peace, Public Domain

FOR THE BULLETIN

Johann Heinrich Bullinger, the Swiss reformer, passed away on this day in 1575. He became the successor to Zwingli. In 1549, along with Calvin and Farel, he wrote the "Consensus of Zurich," which brought together various Protestant groups in Switzerland. Several years later, he drew up a second confession that united Zwinglianism and Calvinism and firmly established the Evangelical Reformed Church. ✿ On September 17, 1656, a series of severe laws was passed against the Quakers in Massachusetts. Practicing Quakers were to be imprisoned at hard labor and then transported back to England. ✿ In 1725 John Wesley read *The Imitation of Christ* by Thomas A' Kempis, and he also read Jeremy Taylor's *Holy Living and Dying*. He said, "I began to alter the whole form of my conversation and to set out in earnest upon a new life." On September 17, 1725, Wesley took Holy Orders. ✿ On this day in 1776, a party of 247 Spanish colonists consecrated their California mission known as San Francisco. ✿ The United States Constitution was adopted by the Philadelphia convention on September 17, 1787. ✿ Today is the birthday in 1868 of Walter Gowans. Along with Rowland Bingham and Thomas Kent, Gowans founded the Sudan Interior Mission in Toronto, Canada. In 1982 the organization united with the Andes Evangelical Mission and changed its name to SIM International. ✿ Charles Filmore, pastor, evangelist, editor, and hymnist, died on this day in 1952. His most famous hymn was "Tell Mother I'll Be There." It was inspired by the telegram consisting of those words, sent by President William McKinley to his mother's nurses as she was dying. It became a much used invitation hymn, especially in the reclaiming of prodigal sons and daughters for the Lord.

WORSHIP HELPS

Call to Worship:
. . . This is the word of the Lord . . . "Not by might nor by power, but by My Spirit," says the LORD of hosts.
Zechariah 4:6

Responsive Reading from Isaiah 61:1–4, 7

Worship Leader:	The Spirit of the Lord GOD is upon Me, because the Lord has anointed Me to preach good tidings to the poor; He has sent Me to heal the broken hearted, to proclaim liberty to the captives, and the opening of the prison to those who are bound.
Congregation:	To proclaim the acceptable year of the LORD, and the day of vengeance of our God.
Worship Leader:	To comfort all who mourn, to console those who mourn in Zion, to give them beauty for ashes, the oil of joy for mourning,
Congregation:	The garment of praise for the spirit of heaviness; that they may be called trees of righteousness, the planting of the Lord, that He may be glorified.
Worship Leader:	And they shall rebuild the old ruins, they shall raise up the former desolations, and they shall repair the ruined cities, the desolations of many generations.
All:	Instead of your shame you shall have double honor, and instead of confusion they shall rejoice in their portion. Therefore in their land they shall posses double; everlasting joy shall be theirs.

Benediction:
Lord, may this assurance, may this calmness, may this inner sense of well-being so pervade our lives that it will become infectious and contagious, and in the realm of our influence we might begin to discover other people discovering blessed assurance. In Jesus' Name. Amen. (Stuart Briscoe)

Additional Sermons and Lesson Ideas

The Blessings of Living in a Non-Christian World   *Date preached:*
By Rev. Kevin Riggs

SCRIPTURE: Various, especially John 15:18–21

INTRODUCTION: Now, like no other time in our country's history, it is a great time to be a follower of Jesus Christ. With all the bad news in this fallen world, there is good news. Here are five blessings of living in a non-Christian world:

1. Our Lights Brighten (Matt. 5:14–16). Light shines best in total darkness; are you shining yours?
2. Our Hope Becomes Obvious (1 Pet. 3:15). In the context of so much despair in the world, are you ready to tell people about the hope you have in Christ?
3. Our Opportunities Become Limitless (Acts 2:41, 47). The more our culture rejects God, the more they will need Him. Are you helping people understand that God alone can meet their needs?
4. Our Christ Becomes Authentic (John 3:14; 12:32). As Mother Theresa said, "You will never know Jesus is all you need until Jesus is all you've got." Is Jesus all you have?
5. Our Faith Becomes Genuine (Matt. 24:13). As our world becomes darker, phony believers will disappear in the darkness. Are you staying in the light despite the darkness around you?

CONCLUSION: Praise the Lord for His blessings!

Generosity in Giving   *Date preached:*
By Dr. Melvin Worthington

SCRIPTURE: 2 Corinthians 8—9

INTRODUCTION: All material possessions come from God and He deserves a voice in directing the way we use them.

1. Generous Giving Is Practical. Giving provides funding for the local church, missions, and the overall advance of Christ's kingdom.
2. Generous Giving Is Plenteous. The Macedonian believes gave out of their poverty. Giving according to God's will and way has blessed results in an abundance of funds to meet the needs.
3. Generous Giving Is Pleasurable. God loves a cheerful giver.
4. Generous Giving Is Profitable. We are blessed, the work of God is supported, the gospel is proclaimed, and we are meeting our obligations as we seize the opportunity to give generously.
5. Generous Giving Is Purposeful. The love of Christ constrains us to give.

CONCLUSION: Generous giving is profitable to the Christian, the church, the community, and the country, and giving can extend to the ends of the earth.

SEPTEMBER 24, 2006

Are Your Knees Callused?

Date preached:

By Dr. Timothy Beougher

Scripture: Colossians 4:2–6, especially verse 2:
Continue earnestly in prayer, being vigilant in it with thanksgiving.

Introduction: Are your knees callused? The dictionary defines a callus as: "A localized thickening of the outer layer of the skin." Some of you work with your hands every day. Your hands are callused from extensive use. Today I want God to give us a fresh vision for prayer, a vision that will motivate us to spend time in prayer every day for God to be at work in our community and for lost people to be saved.

I. **Speak to God about People (vv. 2–4).** We tend to underestimate not only the power of prayer but also the importance of it. When we pray we are acknowledging to God that we are in a spiritual battle, and we need His power and wisdom if we are to achieve victory. Prayer is the key to evangelism.

   A. **How to Pray (v. 2).** First, we must pray *persistently*. The Greek for "continue earnestly" means to "adhere firmly to." It implies ongoing persistence that refuses to give up when you don't see immediate results. The beauty of prayer is that the more we pray, the more we become empowered to pray. Prayer is not like a cell-phone whose power runs down while you use it. Prayer is just the opposite. It increases in power the more it is used. Second, we must pray *alertly*. As we think about prayer being a weapon in the spiritual battle, consider the difference between two military scenarios: here in America, we have different levels of alert, but in several areas in the Middle East, they're on high alert 24/7. Because we're in an active spiritual battle, we need to stay on high alert at all times. Third, we must pray *thankfully*. As we pray with thanksgiving, we acknowledge God as the One who answers prayer. Gratitude is also a motivation for further praying. When we remember God's faithfulness to answer prayer, we will pray more.

B. **What to Pray (vv. 3–4).** First, we should pray for *opportunities to share* (v. 3). Paul did not see prayer primarily as a means to making life easier for himself, but as a means to spread the gospel. Most of us would have made it our top priority to pray for deliverance from prison; Paul's request for prayer was that others be delivered from the prison of sin. Second, we should pray for *clarity of speech* (vv. 3b–4), that we may proclaim "the mystery of Christ." Why is the gospel called a "mystery"? It's a mystery in that it is not self-evident. The gospel is not a mystery because it's confusing or obscure like a riddle, but because no one would have ever known it or imagined it unless God had made it plain to us. Who would imagine that the very God we sinned against, the very God we rebelled against, would provide the means for us to be forgiven (Rom. 5:8)!

2. **Speak to People about God (vv. 5–6).** Your life and words should be a reflection of your prayer life:

A. **Live Wisely (v. 5a).** Living wisely means we are careful not to say or do anything that would make it difficult to share the gospel. Whether we realize it or not, people are making decisions about the validity of Christianity based upon how we live.

B. **Make the Most of Opportunities to Share (v. 5b).** The phrase "redeeming the time" is a commercial term and means to "buy up." It's the picture of finding something on sale and buying all you can afford because the price is so good. That's what this verse is saying: when God gives you an opportunity to share, take it! Don't pass it up!

C. **Saturate Your Conversations with Grace (v. 6).** We must be kind, courteous, merciful, and compassionate (see Eph. 4:29).

D. **Season Your Conversations with Salt (v. 6).** Salty speech makes people thirsty for more. We should season our conversations with salt so that people's mouths water for the living water, Jesus Christ!

E. **Be Prepared to Answer Common Questions (v. 6).** When we are gracious and well informed, people will want to hear what we have to say. So we must be prepared!

Conclusion: Satan's strategy is to keep us off our knees, to keep our knees from becoming callused. If we fight the spiritual battle without spiritual weapons, we are powerless. I am asking God to give us a fresh vision for prayer and a fresh vision for outreach today.

STATS, STORIES AND MORE

Are Your Knees Callused?

James, the early leader of the church in Jerusalem, was nicknamed "camel knees". He spent so much time on his knees in prayer that his knees became callused and hardened just like those of camels who knelt in the hot desert sand. Eusebius, the historian of the early church, tells us that James was martyred for his faith by being pushed off the pinnacle of the temple. Eusebius says that the fall did not kill James, and that he managed to stumble to his knees to pray for his murderers before he died.

Quotes from Charles H. Spurgeon

It is the usual rule with God to make us pray before He gives the blessing.

There is a general kind of praying which fails for lack of precision. It is as if a regiment of soldiers should all fire off their guns anywhere. Possibly somebody would be killed, but the majority of the enemy would be missed.

The Gospel in Your Life

The Gospels of Matthew, Mark, Luke, and John
    Are read by more than a few,
But the one that is most read and commented on
    Is the gospel according to you.
You are writing a gospel, a chapter each day
    By the things that you do and the words that you say.
People read what you write, whether faithless or true.
    Say, what is the gospel according to you?
Do people read His truth and His love in your life,
    Or has yours been too full of malice and strife?
Does your life speak of evil, or does it ring true?
    Say, what is the gospel according to you?
—Unknown Author

FOR THE BULLETIN

Pepin the Short died on this day in A.D. 768, and was succeeded by his son Charles who is known to history as Charles the Great, or Charlemagne. ✱ On September 24, 787, the Second Nicene Council opened under Pope Hadrian I. The council condemned iconoclasm (the belief that the veneration of Christian images and relics was idolatry). ✱ On September 24, 1757, Jonathan Edwards was named the president of Princeton College, a role he filled until his death shortly thereafter. Edwards, often regarded as America's greatest theologian, is best known for his famous sermon, "Sinners in the Hands of an Angry God," which helped spark the Great Awakening. ✱ On September 24, 1770, New Englander Benjamin Randall heard George Whitefield preach and disdained his message. Later, hearing of Whitefield's death, Randall was converted and became the founder of the New England branch of the Freewill Baptist denomination. ✱ Welshman Thomas Coke became John Wesley's chief assistant in the new and quickly-growing Methodist movement. On September 24, 1785, he packed his bags and sailed for Nova Scotia where he wanted to establish the missionaries who accompanied him. But the voyage was ill-fated, taking three months rather than the expected one. Instead of landing in Nova Scotia, the damaged ship ended up in the Caribbean, limping into St. John's harbor on Antigua on Christmas Day. Coke and his associates abandoned any idea of going to Nova Scotia. Instead, they planted the missionary team on Antigua and on neighboring islands. By the time of Coke's death in 1814, there were over seventeen thousand believers in the Methodist churches there. ✱ On September 24, 1789, the United States Congress created the Post Office.

APPROPRIATE HYMNS AND SONGS

Better Is One Day, Matt Redman, 1995 Kingsway's Thankyou Music (Admin. by EMI Christian Music Publishing)

Close to Thee, Fanny J. Crosby/Silas J. Vail, Public Domain

A Heart Like Yours, John Barnett, 1998 Mercy/Vineyard Publishing (Admin. by Music Services)

Heart for the Nations, Martin J. Nystrom /Gary Sadler, 1994 Integrity's Hosanna! Music (c/o Integrity Music, Inc.)

Lord of the Harvest, John Chisum/Lynn DeShazo, 1995 Integrity's Hosanna! Music (c/o Integrity Music, Inc.)

WORSHIP HELPS

Call to Worship:
Sing to the LORD with the harp, with the harp and the sound of a psalm, with trumpets and the sound of a horn; shout joyfully before the LORD, the King. (Ps. 98:5, 6)

Pastoral Prayer:
Our Maker and Redeemer, we come to You with an attitude of persistence, with a mind of alertness, and with a heart full of thanksgiving. Help us to be persistent as we come to You day after day, hour after hour, to seek You and Your will. Help us to be alert as to the spiritual battle going on in our world, and to be standing guard, ready to pray like good soldiers. Make us sensitive to Your Spirit so we might pray any time You move our hearts to do so. We do thank You today, for You alone are our salvation and our hope. So we pray to You that You might grant us opportunities to share Your gospel with others. Give us clarity of speech that we may convey Your truths in an understandable and convincing manner. Work in us, Lord, that we might live wisely, making the most of every opportunity. We pray for Your wisdom in our conversations, that they might be saturated in grace and seasoned with salt. Prepare our minds and hearts to answer the curious, the skeptics, and anyone who is lost as they inquire about You. We pray in Jesus' Name. Amen.

Benediction:
Glory in His holy name; let the hearts of those rejoice who seek the LORD! Seek the LORD and His strength; seek His face evermore! (Ps. 105:3–4)

Additional Sermons and Lesson Ideas

Developing a Heart for Ministry
By Pastor J. David Hoke

Date preached:

SCRIPTURE: Romans 6:6–8; Acts 20:20

INTRODUCTION: After giving our lives to Christ, what comes next? Christian ministry and service is not an option; it's an imperative. Let's look at two essentials of our ministry:

1. Our Ministry Depends on Spiritual Gifts (Rom. 6:6–8). We are not called to attempt ministry *for* God, for Christ ministers *through* us, through our spiritual gifts. Spiritual gifts are those given individually to each believer; they function in the realm of the Spirit and are the means of bringing the blessing of God to others.
2. Our Ministry Depends on Small Groups (Acts 20:20). God has given us a pattern in His Word for the Church: celebrating together as a congregation, where we can receive sound teaching; and sharing our lives together in small groups, where we can encourage and strengthen each other.

CONCLUSION: Are you using your spiritual gifts for the benefit of the kingdom of God? Are you a part of a small group in your church? Whether it's discipleship meetings, prayer groups, Bible studies, or Sunday School, we need outlets for our spiritual gifts and input from others to strengthen us.

Meant for Good

Date preached:

SCRIPTURE: Genesis 50:19–21

INTRODUCTION Genesis 50:20 is the Old Testament counterpart to Romans 8:28. In the first book of the Bible, the Lord provides a case study on the overruling power of divine Providence.

1. The Pasture (Gen. 37:2–11). Here we see Joseph as a confident teenager, watching his father's flocks. Some periods of life are tranquil, and we cherish such times.
2. The Pit (Gen. 37:12–36). Without warning, Joseph's life was devastated by waves of stress and sorrow. His brothers recalled Joseph's reaction to what they did to him (Gen. 42:21). Life comes at us fast.
3. The Prison (Gen. 39—40). Things often get worse!
4. The Palace (Gen. 41—50). The unfolding story shows that God had purposes behind the mystery and misery of Joseph's troubles.

CONCLUSION: Life has periods of prolonged pain, and the devil may mean it for evil, but God intends it for good; all things work together for good to those who love the Lord!

OCTOBER 1, 2006

Spiritual Sacrifices

Date preached:

By Rev. Richard Sharpe

Scripture: Various, especially 1 Peter 2:5:
. . . you also, as living stones, are being built up a spiritual house, a holy priesthood, to offer up spiritual sacrifices acceptable to God through Jesus Christ.

Introduction: Once we accept Christ as our personal Savior, we are to work out our salvation with fear and trembling (Phil. 2:12). Part of working out our salvation is by offering spiritual sacrifices daily to the Lord. There are six sacrifices that we will discuss today that are necessary for our spiritual development in Christ.

1. **Offer the Spiritual Sacrifice of Your Body (Rom. 12:1-2).** The Greek word for "bodies" is *soma*, which indicates the whole person. Paul challenged believers to give all of themselves to the Lord. Each day when you get out of bed, you have a choice to make about whom you are going to serve. You can either be a carnal Christian and serve yourself, or you can be a spiritual Christian and serve the Lord.

2. **Offer the Spiritual Sacrifice of Love (Eph. 5:2).** We are commanded here to walk in love. The Greek word for love is *agape,* which refers to divine love or benevolence. We are to set our affection on God. Our first responsibility is to love God. As a result of our love for God, we are to love people as Christ loved them. We don't have to love some of their actions, but we can look beyond their actions and show them how much God loves them.

3. **Offer the Spiritual Sacrifice of Faith (Phil. 2:17).** Paul, writing to the Philippians from a Roman prison, spoke of the sacrifice of faith. The Greek word for faith is *pistis,* which refers to conviction, trust, and belief. Paul had the conviction that his imprisonment helped others grow in their conviction for the service of the Lord. He was willing to die, if necessary, so that their faith would grow. To help others grow in faith is a true sacrifice. God is in control of the results. Our responsibility is to be faithful to the Lord and faithful to teach those He allows to enter our lives.

4. **Offer the Spiritual Sacrifice of Gifts (Phil. 4:18).** Paul received a generous gift from the Philippians. Paul told them he was "full"; the Greek word is *pleroo*, which means that Paul was complete. Christ told his disciples that there are people who need a drink of water, who need something to eat, who were strangers and need help, who need clothes, who are sick and need someone to look after them, who are in prison and need a visitor (Matt. 25: 35, 36). We are to be the kind of people who meet the needs of such people. Some will say that they don't have anything to give, but that is never true.

5. **Offer the Spiritual Sacrifice of Praise (Heb. 13:15).** A great sacrifice is to praise God on a regular basis. The Greek word for praise is *ainesis,* which refers to speaking well about someone. When we say thank you to God for all that He has done for us, we are praising Him. This is an activity that should be done "continually." It seems that most Christians are grumblers rather than worshippers. Our responsibility each morning is to rise and praise the Lord for all His blessings to us. Did we get up this morning and praise His Name?

6. **Offer the Spiritual Sacrifice of Work (Heb. 13:16).** We are to do what is good. The Greek word for "good" is *eupoiia*, which refers to doing good deeds. The Greek word for "share" is *koinonia,* which means "partnership, communion, or fellowship." When we combine these two words, we find that God's people are to be partners in doing good for one another. God is well pleased when He sees His people working together doing His work. The world will stand up and take notice if Christians work together as the family of God.

Conclusion: As we have skimmed over the six sacrifices that are necessary for the church to move forward in our world, we have noticed that it requires great effort on our part. If we all offer these sacrifices, our world will wonder what is happening. In our world everyone seems to only be interested in his or her own little world, but we are interested in the next world. We need to take the challenge of starting each day with a review of what type of sacrifices we are to offer the Lord to advance His work in the world.

STATS, STORIES AND MORE

Offering Your Body as a Living Sacrifice

One Sunday in Copenhagen, Corrie ten Boom, age eighty at the time, spoke from Romans 12:1. After church two nurses invited her to their apartment for lunch, and Corrie went with them—only to discover they lived on the tenth floor, and there was no elevator.

She didn't think she could mount the stairs, but since the nurses were so eager for her visit she decided to try. By the fifth floor Corrie's heart was pounding. She collapsed in a chair on the landing. Looking upward, the stairs seemed to ascend to infinity, and Corrie wondered if she might die en route. But she bravely pressed on, one nurse in front of her and another following.

Finally reaching the apartment, Corrie found there the parents of one of the girls. She soon discovered that neither parent was a Christian, but both were eager to hear the gospel. Opening her Bible, Corrie carefully explained the plan of salvation. "I have traveled in more than sixty countries and have never found anyone who said they were sorry they had given their hearts to Jesus," she said. "You will not be sorry, either."

That day both prayed for Christ to enter their lives.

On her way down the steps, Corrie said, "Thank you, Lord, for making me walk up all these steps. And next time, Lord, help Corrie ten Boom listen to her own sermon about being willing to go anywhere you tell me to go—even up ten flights of stairs."[19]

APPROPRIATE HYMNS AND SONGS

Above All, Lenny LeBlanc/Paul Baloche, 1999 Integrity's Hosanna! Music (c/o Integrity Music, Inc.)/LenSongs Publishing Unaffiliated Catalog (UC)

A Debt of Love, Jane Ellen/Isaac Watts, 1997 Neil A Kjos Music Company (Admin. by Neil Kjos Music Company)

Here's My Heart, Julie Morrow, 1997 Blonde Strawberry Publishing

No Higher Calling, Lenny LeBlanc/Greg Gulley, 1989, 1999 Doulos Publishing (Maranatha! Music [Admin. by The Copyright Company])

I'll Live for Him, Ralph E. Hudson/C.R. Dunbar, Public Domain

FOR THE BULLETIN

On October 1, 1529, Martin Luther, Philip Melanchthon, Ulrich Zwingli, and Johannes Oecolampadius met at the Marburg Castle of Philip of Hesse to debate their theological differences. The discussions took place around a long table in the banquet hall. At the end of the three-day conference, the men had agreed on most things. But on the question of the Lord's Supper, they failed to reach agreement; and the Reformers were unable to join the German and Swiss factions. ❀ On October 1, 1543, King Henry VIII decreed that the English Bible would not be read by commoners. The nobility and the merchant classes were allowed to read the Scriptures to their families, but the common people were forbidden to do so under penalty of a month's imprisonment. ❀ Today is the birthday and the death day of John Peter Gabriel Muhlenberg, American patriot and Lutheran leader. He was born on October 1, 1746, and died on October 1, 1807. ❀ Several Christian organizations were begun on this day. On October 1, 1882, Pastor A. B. Simpson started a missionary training institute about twenty miles outside of New York City. It was the first Bible college and missionary training school in America. Today it is known as Nyack College. On October 1, 1921, the Latin American Mission was incorporated in Philadelphia by founders Harry and Susan Strachan. Columbia Bible College opened its doors in Columbia, South Carolina, on October 1, 1923. Jack McAlister founded the World Literature Crusade in Canada on October 1, 1946. In 1986 the name was changed to Every Home for Christ.

WORSHIP HELPS

Call to Worship:
O God, my heart is steadfast; I will sing and give praise, even with my glory. Awake, lute and harp! I will awaken the dawn. I will praise You, O LORD, among the peoples, and I will sing praises to You among the nations. For Your mercy is great above the heavens, and Your truth reaches to the clouds. (Ps. 108:1–4)

Scripture Reading Medley:
I beseech you therefore, brethren, by the mercies of God, that you present your bodies a living sacrifice, holy, acceptable to God, which is your reasonable service. And do not be conformed to this world, but be transformed by the renewing of your mind, that you may prove what is that good and acceptable and perfect will of God.

And walk in love, as Christ also has loved us and given Himself for us, an offering and a sacrifice to God for a sweet-smelling aroma.

Yes, and if I am being poured out as a drink offering on the sacrifice and service of your faith, I am glad and rejoice with you all.

Indeed I have all and abound. I am full, having received . . . from you, a sweet-smelling aroma, an acceptable sacrifice, well pleasing to God.

Therefore by Him let us continually offer the sacrifice of praise to God, that is, the fruit of our lips, giving thanks to His name. But do not forget to do good and to share, for with such sacrifices God is well pleased.

(Rom. 12:1, 2; Eph. 5:2; Phil. 2:17; 4:18; Heb. 13:15, 16)

Benediction:
Now may the God of peace who brought up our Lord Jesus from the dead, that great Shepherd of the sheep, through the blood of the everlasting covenant, make you complete in every good work to do His will, working in you what is well pleasing in His sight, through Jesus Christ, to whom be glory forever and ever. Amen. (Heb. 13:20, 21)

Additional Sermons and Lesson Ideas

Your Walk with God
By Dr. Denis Lyle

Date preached:

SCRITPURE: 1 Thessalonians 4:1–12

INTRODUCTION: How is your walk with the Lord? The Christian life can be compared to a walk (see Eph. 4:1, 17; 5:2, 8, 15; 2 Cor. 5:7; Heb. 6:1; 1 John 1:5). This study is both personal and practical in teaching us about the Christian walk.

1. Walk in Holiness (vv. 1–8). Holiness as described by Paul is:
   A. Attractive to the Eye of God (v. 1).
   B. Obedient to the Word of God (v. 2).
   C. Conducive to the Glory of God (vv. 3, 4).
   D. Evasive to the Discipline of God (vv. 5, 8).

2. Walk in Harmony (vv. 9, 10). Harmony both:
   A. Stems from Our New Nature (1 John 3:4).
   B. Shows in Our New Lives (vv. 9, 10).

3. Walk in Honesty (vv. 11, 12).
   A. Work Diligently (v. 11).
   B. Live Calmly (vv. 11, 12).

CONCLUSION: Are you walking with God in holiness, harmony, and honesty?

The Honor of the Christian
Adapted from the writings of Thomas Watson

Date preached:

SCRIPTURE: Psalm 16:6

INTRODUCTION: There are *common blessings* that are enjoyed by all humanity, but there are *crowning blessings* that are the special honor of the Christian. Three are especially joyful:

1. God's Name Written on Us (Rev. 3:12)
2. The Holy Spirit Dwelling in Us (2 Tim. 1:14)
3. The Guardian Angels Watching Over Us (Ps. 91:11)

CONCLUSION: There are two difficult tasks in ministry: to make the wicked sad, and to make the godly joyful. Our hearts should be filled with joy whenever we appropriate the honor and dignity of God's crowing blessings on our lives.

OCTOBER 8, 2006

SUGGESTED SERMON

Staying Steady in Life's Storms   *Date preached:*

By Dr. Timothy Beougher

Scripture: Luke 8:16–25, especially verse 24:
And they came to Him and awoke Him, saying, "Master, Master, we are perishing!"
   Then He arose and rebuked the wind and the raging of the water. And they ceased, and there was a calm.

Introduction: One of the top movies of 1996 was *Twister*, a movie about storm chasers who actually try to find violent storms and get in the middle of them. Spawned in part by the popularity of that movie, different "Storm Chaser" organizations have sprung up throughout the country, offering information on how to chase after storms. I don't know about you, but I have always thought it was better to try and avoid storms than to place myself in the middle of them. Most of us don't make it our goal in life to find storms, but when it comes to the storms of life, they have a way of finding us, don't they? Our Scripture today teaches us how to keep steady during life's storms.

1. **In the Storm of Confusion, Jesus Provides Truth (vv. 16–18).** In looking at verses 16–18, it is important to place them in context. Immediately preceding these verses, Jesus taught some important spiritual truths through what we know as "The Parable of the Sower" or the "Parable of the Soils." Jesus emphasized that our attitude toward the Word of God can be like seeds thrown on hard ground, shallow ground filled with weeds, or on good soil. The different types of soil represent different levels of receptivity to God's truth. In our society, each individual wants to make up his or her own "truth." However, God says that we need to make Him and His Word the basis for truth in our lives. In what direction are you headed today? Are you walking toward the truth or away from it? If you're walking away, remember that God allows U-turns!

2. **In the Storm of Loneliness, Jesus Provides a Family (vv. 19–21).** When we read these verses, on the surface it appears that Jesus is slighting his earthly family, but He is not doing that at all. Jesus always showed love and concern for His mother. When He was dying on the cross, He asked

John to take care of her. He was teaching about a larger spiritual family in which you and I can find a home. The blood of Jesus Christ provides a spiritual bond between believers that is even a greater bond than physical family ties—because it's eternal! When it comes to the storm of loneliness, this truth is most comforting. We live in a world plagued with loneliness. No matter what condition your biological family is in, you can find those who will love you and care for you in God's spiritual family. There's no such thing as a perfect church, but when we trust Jesus Christ as our Lord and Savior, we become part of "God's Forever Family." Whether or not God leads you to join this church, please join one somewhere!

3. **In the Storm of Adversity, Jesus Provides Peace (vv. 22–25).** This account takes place on the Sea of Galilee, where strong storms can come seemingly out of nowhere. This storm was so severe the disciples were convinced they were going to drown! This storm was a real storm on a sea with wind and waves, but it illustrates the different storms of adversity we face. Let me suggest five principles from these verses about "staying steady in life's storms". First, storms come into your life even when Jesus is with you. That shouldn't surprise us. Jesus has promised we will face storms in life (John 16:33). Second, we often wait until we come to the end of our resources before we cry out to God. The disciples were expert sailors, but they couldn't handle this storm. They finally went to Jesus for help, seemingly as a last resort. In a crisis our natural response is to cry out, "Calm the storm!" Jesus did calm this storm. Sometimes He does that, but, fourthly, sometimes He chooses to bring peace to *us* rather than to our circumstances. He may calm the outward storm of circumstance or the inward storm of our stress and emotions. Finally, with Jesus, we can always make it to the other side. When Jesus awakened and calmed the storm, He questioned the disciple's faith. He didn't expect them to calm the storm but to trust Him for their ultimate safety.

Conclusion: I know some of you are in storms right now—the storm of confusion, the storm of loneliness, or various storms of adversity. Trust Jesus to provide what you need.

STATS, STORIES AND MORE

We live in a world plagued with loneliness. The Beatles were exactly right when they sang, "Look at all the lonely people." Someone has defined a city as "a place where thousands of people can be lonely together."

Some television preachers say, "If you only have enough faith, your life would be filled with health and wealth. Your problems would be over." There's a word for that teaching: "Baloney!" I heard about a new Christian who had fallen prey to this teaching. He said to a pastor, "Now that I'm a Christian, I know this is the end of my problems!" The pastor responded, "Yes, the front end!" Having faith in Christ may lead to God's calming the storms of circumstance, but most often, faith leads to a calming of the inward storm of your emotions or stress. Corrie ten Boom has well said: "When your eyes are on the world, you are oppressed; when your eyes are on yourself, you are depressed; when your eyes are on Jesus, you are at rest."

An Old Hymn: "The Stranger of Galilee"

> I heard Him speak peace to the angry waves,
> Of that turbulent, raging sea;
> And lo! at His word are the waters stilled,
> This Stranger of Galilee;
> A peaceful, a quiet, and holy calm,
> Now and ever abides with me;
> He holdeth my life in His mighty hands,
> This Stranger of Galilee.
> —Leila N. Morris, 1893

APPROPRIATE HYMNS AND SONGS

The Solid Rock, Edward Mote/William B. Bradbury, Public Domain

Great Is Thy Faithfulness, Thomas O. Chisholm/William M. Runyan, 1923. Renewed 1951 Hope Publishing Company.

Let the Peace of God Reign, Darlene Zschech, 1995 Darlene Zschech (Hillsong) (Admin in U.S. & Canada by Integrity's Hosanna! Music)

O God Our Help in Ages Past, Isaac Watts/William Croft, Public Domain

His Strength is Perfect, Steven Curtis Chapman/Jerry Salley, 1988 Sparrow Song (a div. of EMI Christian Music Publishing)/Careers-BMG Music Publishing, Inc./Multisongs (a div. of Careers-BMG Music Publishing)/Greg Nelson

This is the anniversary of the 1871 Chicago fire. In his memoirs, Ira Sankey wrote of the evangelistic rally he and evangelist D. L. Moody were conducting that night:

Sunday evening, October 8, 1871, we were holding a meeting in Farwell Hall, which was crowded to the doors. At the close of his address Mr. Moody asked me to sing a solo, and standing by the great organ at the rear of the platform I began the old familiar hymn, 'Today the Savior Calls.' By the time I had reached the third verse . . . my voice was drowned by the loud noise of the fire engines rushing past the hall, and the tolling of bells, among which we could hear . . . the deep, sullen tones of the great city bell, in the steeple of the old courthouse, ringing out a general alarm. Tremendous confusion was heard in the streets.

The world's first rescue mission was opened in New York City by Jerry McAuley on October 8, 1872. ❀ Modecai Ham, starting an evangelistic campaign in Charlotte, North Carolina, grew discouraged by the opposition he faced at the meetings. On October 8, 1934, he sat down and wrote out a prayer on a piece of hotel stationary. It said, "Dear Father, Thou knowest the conduct of all in this town: how the antichrist has made his power felt; how the ministers have opposed. Father, please for Thy Name sake and Thy Son's sake, begin to deal with these. . . . O Dear Lord, come on Thy servant and make his messages a burning fire. Lord, give us a Pentecost. . . . O Lord, I need Your endorsement, and show this city that You are with me. . . . In His Name. . . . M. F. Ham." The Lord gloriously answered that prayer. During the meetings, Billy Graham, age sixteen, was won to Christ.

WORSHIP HELPS

Call to Worship:

I will sing of mercy and justice; to You, O LORD, I will sing praises. (Ps. 101:1)

Scripture Reading:

Truly God is good to Israel, to such as are pure in heart. But as for me, my feet had almost stumbled; my steps had nearly slipped. For I was envious of the boastful, when I saw the prosperity of the wicked. . . . Surely I have cleansed my heart in vain, and washed my hands in innocence. For all day long I have been plagued, and chastened every morning. If I had said, "I will speak thus," behold, I would have been untrue to the generation of Your children. When I thought how to understand this, it was too painful for me—Until I went into the sanctuary of God; Then I understood their end. . . . Whom have I in heaven but You? And there is none upon earth that I desire besides You. My flesh and my heart fail; but God is the strength of my heart and my portion forever. For indeed, those who are far from You shall perish; you have destroyed all those who desert You for harlotry. But it is good for me to draw near to God; I have put my trust in the Lord GOD, that I may declare all Your works.

(Ps. 73:1–3; 13–17; 25–28)

Invitation:

For many of you here, you feel as if the storms of life never cease. You have never felt the peace that comes with casting your cares and placing your faith in Jesus. I invite you to come to me or one of our church leaders here at this altar, or come to us after the service, and we will guide you and support you as you commit your life to Christ. God and His people are ready to receive you whatever your needs may be.

Additional Sermons and Lesson Ideas

Guidelines for Giving
By Dr. Melvin Worthington

Date preached:

SCRIPTURE: 2 Corinthians 8—9

INTRODUCTION: In this passage Paul gives us the Macedonians' model of giving:

1. Giving Is Personal. Scriptural giving begins with giving one's self to the Lord. Until we have given ourselves, our substance is not acceptable.
2. Giving Is Perceptive. It is impossible to give directly into the hand of God; we need a channel through which to give. Perceptive giving begins with giving tithes and offerings to one's local church.
3. Giving Is Progressive. Paul admonished the Corinthian believers to abound in giving just as they abounded in other graces.
4. Giving Follows a Pattern. God proved His love for us when He gave Christ, who gave Himself for us.
5. Giving Is Proportionate. Each Christian gives as God has prospered him. We are not required to give what we do not have but as God has provided.

CONCLUSION: Abounding in the grace of giving is a strong indication of one's spiritual growth.

Tragedy to Triumph
By Rev. Mark Hollis

Date preached:

SCRIPTURE: John 16:16–33

INTRODUCTION: Jesus was about to die. His disciples were about to experience profound grief. If we live long enough, all of us will face grief. If we follow Jesus, we find that He turns our tragedies into triumphs.

1. The Triumph of Joy over Grief (vv. 16–22).
   A. Jesus' Impending Death Would Bring Grief (vv. 16–20).
   B. Jesus' Resurrection Would Bring Joy (vv. 21, 22).
2. The Triumph of Intimacy over Distance (vv. 23–27).
   A. Jesus Promised a Relationship So Close We Can Tell God What We Need (vv. 23, 24).
   B. Jesus Promised a Relationship So Close God Wants to Help Us (vv. 25–27).
3. The Triumph of Peace over Trouble (vv. 28–33).
   A. In This World Our Faith Is Imperfect (vv. 28–32).
   B. Our Peace Is Found in Jesus' Victory Over This World (v. 33).

CONCLUSION: Our health fails. Our children disappoint. Tragedy strikes. God takes tragedy—even the deepest pain of our lives—and turns it into triumph.

Donald Cargill

About the time the Pilgrims sailed to America searching for religious liberty from the intolerance of established religion, one man decided to remain in the United Kingdom and preach with boldness. His name was Donald Cargill, and the nature of his life is reflected in the title of his biography: "Some Remarkable Passages in the Life and Death of that Singular, Exemplary, Holy-in-Life, Zealous, and Faithful-unto-the-Death, Mr. Donald Cargill."

Cargill always preached on the run. On one occasion soldiers pursued him to a raging river. To their astonishment, he dashed up a rocky ledge and took a flying leap over the torrent, safely landing on the other side. None of the troops dared follow him, and he escaped. The spot has ever since been known as "Cargill's Leap."

Eventually, the authorities' net tightened around him. His last sermon was from Isaiah 26. Patrick Walker, author of the prior-mentioned biography, wrote the following:

> I had the happiness to hear blest Cargill preach his last public sermon in Dunsyre Common where he preached upon that soul-refreshing text, Isaiah 26, the last two verses, "Come, my people, enter into your chambers. . . ."
>
> He insisted what kind of chambers these were of protection and safety, and exhorted us all earnestly to dwell in the clefts of the rock, to bind ourselves in the wounds of Christ, and to wrap ourselves in the believing application of the promises flowing therefrom, and to make our refuge under the shadow of His wings, until these sad calamities pass over, and the dove come back with the olive leaf in her mouth. These were the last words of his sermon.

Cargill was thereafter captured, imprisoned, and condemned. As he climbed the steps to the scaffold, he turned back and shouted, "The Lord knows I go up this ladder with less fear than ever I entered a pulpit to preach." Minutes later he was with the Lord.

Quotes for the Pastor's Wall

---

66 I find myself in the cleft of the rock and preach about it every Sunday. 99

—Andrew Bonar

OCTOBER 15, 2006

Preparing for the Task

Date preached:

By Rev. Charles McGowan

Scripture: Nehemiah 1:4—2:10, especially 2:5:
 And I said to the king, "If it pleases the king, and if your servant has found favor in your sight, I ask that you send me to Judah, to the city of my fathers' tombs, that I may rebuild it."

Introduction: The story of Nehemiah calls attention to the broken walls in our culture, our families, and our society. How does one become an instrument of God to rebuild a broken wall? The book of Nehemiah is the story of how God raised up one person to lead His people in the midst of a broken situation, to rebuild the wall around Jerusalem. In chapter 2, we uncover factors that are critical in preparing for the task of rebuilding.

1. **Pray (1:4—2a).**

   A. **Realize the Importance of Prayer.** The most important feature of the first two chapters of Nehemiah is prayer. In them we are impressed with the earnest fervor with which Nehemiah prayed. The burden produced tears and a commitment to fast as he cried out to God. The sad plight of the people in Jerusalem broke his heart. The ruins of the city meant to reflect the brilliance of the glory of God grieved him. The patience and persistence of his prayer is reflected in his continuing to pray for four months. Do you turn your energy to prayer when faced with broken situations?

   B. **Realize the Effectiveness of Prayer.** The day came when the heart of the king was turned. It wasn't too soon or too late. The timing was a part of God's perfect design. It was the pagan Persian king who posed the question as to what was the burden on Nehemiah's heart. What an encouragement! The Lord can use anyone to accomplish the work He's burdened us to do!

2. **Plan (2:2b–8).**

    A. **Plan in the Midst of Sorrow.** It was an ordinary day with Nehemiah going about his tasks as he usually did and doing them with excellence. The only thing different was his sad countenance, yet he was prepared to respond should the king inquire. When the day of inquiry came, Nehemiah responds with a clear and precise three-part answer: he wants to go to Jerusalem (v. 5), he needs a guarantee of safe passage (v. 7), and He will need supplies and materials (v. 8).

    B. **Plan in the Midst of Prayer.** It is clear that Nehemiah had been planning while he was praying. While on his knees before God, a plan began to form in his mind. There is no contradiction here. One indication that we pray believingly is to formulate a plan to move forward when God opens the door.

3. **Prepare to Encounter Resistance (2:9, 10).** For the first time in the story we meet those who would vigorously oppose the work God had ordained Nehemiah to lead. They knew Nehemiah's purpose was to come alongside his oppressed people and to organize and equip them to restore the glory of God by the rebuilding of the wall. He had no desire for personal gain or glory. But, because he was committed to God's purposes, he drew fire from the opposition. Don't forget that lots of God's people were in the area of Jerusalem. Some had never left. Some had already returned and had lived there for a long time. Yet there is no indication that there had been opposition from the enemy. It's only when one with a burden and a passion who says with God-given authority, "come and let us build" (2:17) that opposition begins. There is never spiritual warfare when one has no commitment to the purposes of God. Satan has no concern until a selfless, committed follower of Christ stands courageously and begins to move forward to repair broken walls for the glory of God.

Conclusion: Where are the broken walls that are a reproach to God and His people? The wall may be as broad as the culture in which we live or as near as our personal lives. In either case God is concerned for his glory and the welfare of his children. If we really care, God is apt to place a burden on our heart. If the burden is there, then pray, plan, and prepare for opposition. God will open the door and do amazing things to restore the broken wall and His glory.

Responding to God's Call

In his book, *Let Justice Roll Down,* John Perkins tells of how God led him back to his home state of Mississippi following his conversion as an adult in California. It wasn't easy since his experiences of growing up as an African-American in Mississippi were marked by injustice. He had vowed he would never return. Yet God's call on his life was irresistible. Racial prejudice and hatred had broken relational walls in his home state that only the gospel could repair. So, like Nehemiah, he returned to Mississippi and gave himself to the task.

The Power of Prayer

Sophia's husband, John Ironside, an ardent soul-winner, spent his short life preaching on the streets, in the parks, in halls and theaters, wherever he could. But at age twenty-seven he contracted typhoid and soon died, leaving Sophia with two small boys and no income. One of the boys, Harry (later a world-famous preacher), watched his mother closely. On one occasion the cupboard was bare. Sophia gathered her sons for breakfast, but their plates were empty and there was only water to drink. She shared with them a verse of Scripture that had become very meaningful to her, Isaiah 33:16: ". . . Bread will be given him, his water will be sure."

Bowing over the empty plates, she gave thanks and claimed that promise. As she finished praying, the doorbell rang. "Mrs. Ironside," said the neighbor, "I feel very bad. We have been owing you for months for that dress you made for my wife. We've had no money to pay you. But just now we're harvesting our potatoes, and we wondered if you would take a bushel or two on account of the old bill." In a few minutes, the potatoes were sizzling in the frying pan, and the boys had an answered prayer for breakfast.

FOR THE BULLETIN

Thomas Hastings, hymnist and composer, was born in Connecticut on October 15, 1784. He was an albino who suffered from very poor eyesight, but he took to music and by age eighteen was leading the choir in his local church. He became a powerful figure in the gospel music movement, and wrote the melodies to such hymns as "Majestic Sweetness Sits Enthroned" and "Rock of Ages." ❀ Little Charles Marriott was baptized on October 15, 1811. He would later become a leader in the Tractarianism movement. His father, John Marriott, wrote a hymn on this date, commemorating the event, and it became a well known baptismal hymn: "Grant to his child the inward grace, while we the outward sign impart; The cross we on his forehead trace, do Thou engrave upon his heart." ❀ Today is the birthday in 1844 of the German philosopher Friedrich Wilhelm Nietzsche. ❀ One of church history's longest building programs came to an end on this day in 1880, when the great cathedral of Cologne, German, was completed after 633 years of construction. ❀ Today is the birthday of William Temple, who was born on October 15, 1881. He became Archbishop of Canterbury in 1942, and died two years later. ❀ Charles Fox Parham opened the Bethel Bible Institute in Topeka, Kansas, on this day in 1900. Several months later, several students began speaking in tongues, giving rise to the modern Pentecostal movement. ❀ On October 15, 1932, a British maid named Gladys Aylward left from London's Liverpool Street Station for China. She became one of the most famous missionaries of the twentieth century. ❀ "I Love Lucy" premiered on television on October 15, 1951.

APPROPRIATE HYMNS AND SONGS

Be Bold, Be Strong, Morris Chapman, 1984 Word Music, Inc. (a div. of Word Music Group, Inc.)

In the Name of the Lord, Gloria Gaither/Sandi Patti Helvering /Phill McHugh, 1986 William J. Gaither, Inc. ARR UBP of Gaither Copyright Management/Sandi's Songs Music (Admin. by Gaither Copyright Management)/ River Oaks Music Company (a div. of EMI Christian Music Publishing)

I Need Thee Every Hour, Annie S. Hawks /Robert Lowry, Public Domain

Give Me a Clean Heart, Margaret Pleasant Douroux, 1970 Margaret Pleasant Douroux

Come All Christians Be Committed, Eva B. Lloyd/James H. Wood, 1958. Renewed 1986 Broadman Press ARR Distributed by Genevox Music Group

WORSHIP HELPS

Call to Worship:
... "Stand up and bless the LORD your God forever and ever! Blessed be Your glorious name, which is exalted above all blessing and praise! You alone are the Lord; You have made heaven, the heaven of heavens, with all their host, the earth and everything on it, the seas and all that is in them, and You preserve them all. The host of heaven worships You. (Neh. 9:5, 6)

A Word of Welcome:
As we study the story of Nehemiah today, we reflect on God's amazing ability to repair broken walls. I wonder if any of you came today with brokenness in your life. Maybe the walls of your relationships seem broken. Perhaps the worries of your life have almost caused you a nervous breakdown. Just as God rebuilt the broken wall of Jerusalem, He has built this church, Jesus said, "... on this rock I will build My church, and the gates of Hades shall not prevail against it" (Matt. 16:18). Jesus has brought us together to support you in rebuilding the brokenness in your life. Know that you are welcome here, and that we are here if you need us in any way.

Benediction:
The grace of our Lord Jesus Christ be with you all. Amen. (Rev. 22:21)

Additional Sermons and Lesson Ideas

Developing a Heart for Others
By Pastor J. David Hoke

Date preached:

SCRIPTURE: Various

INTRODUCTION: We must have loving relationships in the church without neglecting those outside the church.

1. Your Love Must Reach In (1 John 3:11, 14, 16, 18; John 13:34–35). Healthy, loving relationships must be built within the church. This is the proving ground for us as Christians. Those outside the church are watching what happens inside the church to see if we really are who we claim to be—followers of Jesus. All too often we fail at this point.
2. Your Love Must Reach Out (Matt. 28:18–20; Rom. 10:13–14; 2 Cor. 5:17–20). We will not share the love of Christ if we don't care about others' salvation. We must become people who care. We need to see with God's eyes and feel with His heart toward those who don't know Him.

CONCLUSION: A healthy spiritual life will be found in those who reach out with their words, time, and energy, in love both to one another and to those who are without Christ.

Courage When Fear Dominates
By Dr. David Jeremiah

Date preached:

SCRIPTURE: Psalm 34

INTRODUCTION: It is beginning to dawn on me more and more that for us to live in the world in which we live today, it takes courage. Psalm 34 was written against the backdrop of danger—when David was before Abimelech.

1. We Need Courage to Offer Up Our Praise (vv. 1–3)
2. We Need Courage to Own Our Problem (vv. 4–5)
3. We Need Courage to Overcome Through Prayer (v. 6)
4. We Need Courage to Obtain God's Provision (v. 7)
   A. God's provision involves deliverance (vv. 4, 6, 17–19)
   B. God's provision involves a Deliverer (v. 7)

CONCLUSION: When we are afraid, let us take courage and... offer up our praise, own our problem, overcome through prayer, and obtain the provision, not only of the deliverance, but also of the Deliverer. Hallelujah!

BAPTISM SERMON

Preparation For Ministry

By Pastor J. David Hoke   *Date preached:*

Scripture: Mark 1:9–11, especially verse 9:
Then a voice came from heaven, "You are My beloved Son, in whom I am well pleased."

Introduction: What prepares a person for effective ministry? How do you come from a place of accepting Christ as your Savior to being used by Him for His glory? What is it that can turn an ordinary, dull routine Christian walk into an extraordinary, exciting and adventurous Christian life? I suppose all of us want to be involved in living a life that counts. We all want to be involved in effective, fulfilling ministry. So what is it that gives ministry its power? What kind of preparation is necessary? Jesus Himself gave us a vivid example of that preparation in this passage in Mark 1. He shows us two points of preparation for ministry: obedience (vv. 9–11) and opposition (vv. 12–13). Today we will look at the first, obedience as displayed through baptism. There are four words I would like for you to consider in thinking of preparation for ministry:

1. **Obedience through Action.** In these verses we see the process of preparation through obedience. This was an essential step in the preparation of our Lord for His public ministry, and it is also an essential step in the preparation of every believer for ministry in His name. The first step in our preparation is the step of active obedience; this is what we see in the baptism of Jesus. We see His obedient submission to God. Jesus did not need to be baptized because He was repenting of His sins. He had no sins. By John's own admission, Jesus did not need to be baptized. But Christ came anyway. In coming, He said that it was necessary to fulfill all righteousness. But what did that mean "to fulfill all righteousness?" How could Jesus' coming to submit to a baptism He did not need fulfill all righteousness? In order to understand that, we must realize why He came. His motive was obedient submission to God. The baptism of John was ordained of God (Matt. 21:25). This is the real question for us: Is it of God? If something is of God, then we are called to obedience.

2. **Obedience through Identification.** Jesus identified with what God was doing. This was the underlying motive of His baptism. John's baptism was of God and Jesus identified with that which was of God. By His coming to submit to baptism, He said by His presence that He recognized God had ordained it. While we must be careful not to identify with the worldly ways of sinful men, we must also be careful to identify with all that is of God, including His people. It means we accept every blood-washed believer in Jesus as a full-fledged member of the body of Christ; we identify with them for what God is doing in their lives. It does not mean that we approve of all they do; indeed, there may be times when we can't associate with them in certain endeavors because of a conviction we hold. But in what is of God, we need to identify. We must always be willing to say "Amen" to what God is doing. We must be willing to identify with God's work.

3. **Obedience through Acceptance.** As we follow Jesus in obedient submission to and identification with God's work, there is acceptance and affirmation by God. Jesus heard the voice of God affirming His identity as God's Son and God's pleasure with Him. As Jesus heard the voice of acceptance, so we will sense God's acceptance of our obedience. We will hear the voice of the Spirit of God as He witnesses to our spirit that we are the children of God. There is nothing like being accepted. All of us long to be accepted for who we are. He receives us just as we are. Of course, He doesn't leave us that way. But He loved us while we were sinners. He loved us before we came to Him. And when we are obedient, he receives us with open arms. When we are obedient, God makes His approval known.

4. **Empowerment through Obedience.** When we are yielded to Him, God empowers us. Jesus was empowered for ministry. And we, like Jesus, are also empowered. Luke tells us that Jesus was praying as He came up out of the water. Verse 10 in our text tells us that in the midst of this act of obedience, the heavens opened up and the Spirit of God came upon Jesus. He was then anointed for His work. In Luke's Gospel, we read of Jesus after His baptism, that He was full of the Holy Spirit, led by the Spirit, and in the power of the Spirit. Then we are told how Jesus got up in the synagogue where He was raised and read that great passage from Isaiah 61:1, 2 which begins, "The Spirit of the Lord is upon Me . . ." (see Luke 4:18–19). Jesus was filled with the Holy Spirit; we can be also as we yield to Him.

We, like Jesus, can be empowered for ministry. We can receive that great baptism of the Holy Spirit, that great anointing of power. But we must be yielded in order to receive its full benefit.

Conclusion: The verses following these teach us that the Lord brings opposition to prepare us for ministry (Mark 1:12, 13), but how can we face opposition if we are not in the place of complete obedience to God? Do you need to take the step of obedience to be baptized? Perhaps many are here who have been living disobedient lives; the Lord is calling you to obey through your actions by accepting Him alone, by identifying with Him, and by allowing Him to empower you to do His work.

PRAYERS FOR THE PASTOR'S CLOSET

I Can Do It... If I'm Conduit

Lord, I am unworthy to stand in this place,
To read from this Book and to tell of this grace.
My heart is too dark with corruption and fear,
My tongue is too thick; and my thoughts are unclear.

It's not I, but it's Christ, in the pulpit today!
I'm a pipeline, a channel, a vessel of clay,
I am conduit through whom living currents are poured,
It's not I, but it's Christ, my Redeemer and Lord.

OCTOBER 22, 2006

SUGGESTED SERMON

Responding to Revelation

Date preached:

By Joshua D. Rowe

Scripture: Psalm 19:1–14, especially verse 1:
The heavens declare the glory of God; and the firmament shows His handiwork.

Introduction: I'm sure you've heard the saying, "A picture is worth a thousand words." If God would only paint us a picture, how much would it speak of who He is! Our Scripture today teaches us that He has done just that! God has given us His beautiful world as a picture of His glory. Not only this, He has given us Scripture, His written Word, as well. Let's look at Psalm 19 and how we can apply its truths.

1. **The Word of God through Nature (vv. 1–4).** God is the Creator. This fact is established in Genesis 1:1 and is echoed throughout all of Scripture and is evident in our world (v. 1). The general Hebrew word for God *(elohim)* is used in this section, and it is the same word used in the Genesis account of creation. *God has given us this general revelation of Himself to proclaim His glory.* The Word of God through Nature is:

   A. **Continual (v. 2).** The repetition of "day unto day" and "night unto night" emphasizes the unending nature of general revelation.

   B. **Universal (vv. 3, 4).** The Hebrew word translated "line" is often used for a family line or a measured area. Thus these verses convey that general revelation transcends all linguistic, cultural, and spatial barriers. Interpreting and applying the book of Psalms often depends on the preceding or following Psalm. In this case, at the end of Psalm 18, David told the Lord that he would give thanks to Him among the Gentiles and sing His praises (v. 49); he followed with Psalm 19, which is a cross-cultural proclamation of God's revelation! If we look down, we see God's wonderful creation, though what we see will differ depending on where we are in the world. But if we look up, we see the same sky, heavens, and sun as the rest of the world! This idea is echoed in Romans 1:20, 21—creation is the source of general revelation to people of all times, places, and cultures.

Application: The first application is simple: look up! We are so entertainment oriented that we often neglect praising God for His creation. These verses focus on the heavens, the sky, and the sun. How full of praise we would be if we would take time to look up. Secondly, general revelation should not only be means for praise, but a starting point for evangelism, for it's the common factor that binds all peoples, cultures, and languages. The created world we live in reflects the Creator!

2. **The Word of God through Scripture (vv. 4–11).** In a beautiful transition (vv. 4–6), the psalmist continued his use of nature to move us into his next section on Scripture, the Law of God. He compared it to the majestic sun, for no one can escape its heat, nor can we escape how God's Word searches our hearts. In verse 7 the special Hebrew name for God, Yahweh, is used in this section. Characteristics of His Word are reflected in the terms used in these verses: "perfect," "sure," "right," "pure," "clean," "true," and "righteous." His Word prompts action, as these verses describe: "converting," "making wise," "rejoicing," "enlightening," and "enduring." *God has given us this specific revelation to proclaim the character of God and their effect on us.*

Application: Scripture is not general but specific, and it is not revealed in nature, but through human language; we are responsible to share the Scriptures with others. Again, David's purpose in this Psalm was to praise God and to proclaim Him to the Gentiles; he shared the glory of God's Word with them! Perhaps you are gifted with language; consider missionary work as a Scripture translator! Maybe God is simply prompting your heart to donate to Wycliffe or another worthy translation ministry. Help get God's Word out!

3. **Our Response (vv. 11–14).** God has given us *senses to perceive His general and specific revelations and the will to respond to them.* David exemplifies the application of these verses clearly.

Application: First, we must fearfully obey (v. 11). God's Word keeps us from danger, so we must always obey it. Second, we must confess and repent (vv. 12, 13). We need to confess and ask forgiveness both for our character flaws and for our willful disobedience. David asked God to keep him from sins to help him be blameless. This is repentance and life through the Spirit. God works in us to change our character and keep us from sin! Finally, we must commit ourselves to God (v. 14). Let our response to God's Word be a commitment of our own words and hearts to Him.

STATS, STORIES AND MORE

Cross-Cultural Art and the Revelations of God

Do you remember being artistic as a child? Have you seen your own or others' children drawings? It's amazing how universal their pictures are. At a certain stage, when drawing people, there's usually a huge round circle for the head, two extra large eyes, and often little sticks for arms and legs. Did you know that's a universal phenomenon? That's how children around the world draw people when they're three to five years old. Life is perceived through certain senses on a universal level, for we all share the same senses. However, children also have a specific language through which they must learn specific lessons about life. They are then responsible to respond to what they see and hear as they learn and grow. This pattern is true of the revelation of God to man! He grants us natural revelation that everyone can see and perceive, but He also provides specific revelation through Scripture. Both aspects of God's revelation should cause us to praise Him and to respond with our very lives.

Appreciating Nature:

The last time I went to the beach, I noticed something tragic. The room had a wonderful view of the ocean. Seagulls and pelicans flew down the coast while majestic waves rhythmically crashed along the shore. I was there to do some work, so I naturally sat on the couch. I kept looking over my shoulder to see the ocean, but this became frustrating. I moved to every seat in the hotel room, but none had a direct view of the ocean. Why? They were all in a semi-circle aimed at the TV. What a sad indicator of our society's values. How should we respond to this tragedy in our culture? Let's rearrange things! I promptly moved the furniture to view the ocean and opened the balcony door to hear the crashing of the waves and chirping of the seagulls. How can you rearrange your everyday life? Take time to grill out on summer nights and eat outside with your family or friends. Schedule a walk or a day at the park each month to read the Psalms and have a time of praise. Pick a few clear nights per year to find a dark, comfortable place to look at the stars and remember God's promise to Abraham. Take time to allow God's Word through creation to resound in your heart.

—Joshua D. Rowe

FOR THE BULLETIN

The Dutch theologian, Jacob Arminius, 49, was buried on this day. He had died about noon on Monday, October 19, 1609, surrounded by family and friends. In his eulogy, it was said, "There lived in Holland a man whom they who did not know could not sufficiently esteem, whom they who did not esteem had never sufficiently known." He was buried on Thursday, October 22, beneath the paving slabs of his church. ❂ The author of the hymn, "Be Still My Soul," Katharina A. D. von Schlegel, was born on this day in 1697. Little is known about her life except that she was a German Lutheran. ❂ John and Charles Wesley sailed for Georgia on October 22, 1735. ❂ The College of New Jersey was founded by evangelical Presbyterians on October 22, 1746. Its name was changed in 1896 to Princeton University. ❂ William Miller of New York, by studying the prophecies of Daniel, concluded that Christ would return to earth on October 22, 1844. The financial panic of 1839 contributed to the belief that the end of the world was approaching. Enthusiasm for Christ's return became so great that prophetic charts were added alongside stock market listings and current events in the newspapers. As morning dawned on October 22, 1844, a foreboding fell over New England. People gathered on mountaintops and in churches. Normal activities ceased as everyone waited the sudden rending of the skies and the end of the world. When the day passed uneventfully, many Christians grew disillusioned, and the event became known as "The Great Disappointment." ❂ Charles "Pretty Boy" Floyd was shot and killed by FBI agents in Ohio on October 22, 1934.

APPROPRIATE HYMNS AND SONGS

All Creatures of Our God and King, St. Francis of Assisi /William H. Draper, Public Domain

Agnus Dei, Michael W. Smith, 1990 Milene Music, Inc. (Admin. by Opryland Music Group, Inc.)

Blessed Be the Lord God Almighty, Bob Fitts, 1984 Scripture in Song (a div. of Integrity Music, Inc.)

Come Christians Join to Sing, Christian Henry Bateman, Public Domain

Great is the Lord, Steve McEwan, 1985 Maranatha Praise, Inc.

WORSHIP HELPS

Call to Worship:
I will sing to the LORD as long as I live; I will sing praise to my God while I have my being. May my meditation be sweet to Him; I will be glad in the LORD. (Ps. 104:33, 34)

Scripture Reading:
Forever, O Lord, Your word is settled in heaven. Your faithfulness endures to all generations; You established the earth, and it abides. They continue this day according to Your ordinances, for all are Your servants. Unless Your law had been my delight, I would then have perished in my affliction. I will never forget Your precepts, for by them You have given me life. I am Yours, save me; for I have sought Your precepts. The wicked wait for me to destroy me, but I will consider Your testimonies. I have seen the consummation of all perfection, but Your commandment is exceedingly broad. (Ps. 119:89–96)

Pastoral Prayer:
The heavens declare Your glory, O God, and the skies proclaim the work of your hands. We praise you for the world You have created, for it reflects Your creativity, beauty, and majesty as Creator! Convict our hearts to notice your works and fall to our knees in praise to You. But Lord, it is so amazing that you didn't stop there! You didn't leave us creatures alone, but You gave us Your Word. We worship You for Your Word, and we ask for the motivation to share it with others. We truly serve an awesome God. Your world and Your Word speak volumes to us of your greatness, so Lord we ask that the words of our mouths and the meditations of our hearts be pleasing to You, our Rock and our Redeemer. Amen.

Suggested Scriptures:
Psalm 104; 111; 148
Isaiah 40:28
Romans 1:16–25

Additional Sermons and Lesson Ideas

How to be a Happier Person

Date preached:

SCRIPTURE: Psalm 119:1–8

INTRODUCTION: Psalm 119, the longest chapter in the Bible, is devoted to the theme of the wonders of God's Word. It is divided into twenty-two segments corresponding to the twenty-two letters of the Hebrew alphabet. In the first segment (vv. 1–8), we learn several things:

1. How Wonderful It Is to Obey Scripture (vv. 1–4). Blessed (that is, happy!) are those who read and heed God's Word. It promotes holiness and thus healthiness and thus happiness.
2. How Hard It Is to Obey Scripture (v. 5, 6). Like the Psalmist, we lament our shortcomings.
3. How Determined We Are to Obey Scripture (vv. 7, 8). Despite our shortcomings, we praise God and keep learning His Word, saying, "I *will* obey your decrees." As we do so, God will not forsake us; He will become our tutor.

CONCLUSION: Do you have a daily time set aside to get into Scripture? Are you determined to obey what you find there?

In His Image

Date preached:

By Dr. Melvin Worthington

SCRIPTURE: Romans 8:29

INTRODUCTION: God's goal in redemption is to conform every believer to the image of His Son. Being conformed to His image suggests that we are to become like (resemble) Jesus Christ.

1. We Were Created by the Sovereign (Gen. 1:1—2:7).
2. We Were Corrupted by the Serpent (Gen. 3; 1 Tim. 2:14).
3. We Were Converted by the Savior. God visited Adam and Eve in the Garden following their disobedience and provided a remedy for their sin (Gen. 3:15, 21).
4. We Are Conformed by the Spirit. The Spirit's work produces in us the character, compassion, concerns, and conduct of Christ (Rom. 8:29).

CONCLUSION: We are part of God's great design. We fell, but God picked us up. We shattered, but God remade us. We died because of sin, but God raised us to life. What a Savior!

OCTOBER 29, 2006

REFORMATION SUNDAY SUGGESTED SERMON

What Do You Want to Be Remembered For?

Date preached:

Scripture: 2 Timothy 3:10–12, especially verse 10:
But you have carefully followed my doctrine . . .

Introduction: Today is Reformation Sunday, the day commemorating the heroic stand of Martin Luther. On October 31, 1517, Luther posted his objections to the careless doctrine and lax morality in the Roman Catholic Church on the cathedral door in the little village of Wittenberg. He didn't realize what an impact that action would make. Few of us will be as famous as Luther; but we all underestimate the impact we'll make on this world. Your example, your words, your actions, your attitude about life, your spiritual formation—it all casts a wider shadow than you know. What do we want to be remembered for? The apostle Paul, awaiting execution, wrote his final letter to his protégé, Timothy, saying: "But you have carefully followed my. . . ." Paul knew his life had been a model for another. He wanted to be remembered for eight qualities.

1. **Our Doctrine.** *You have carefully followed my doctrine.* It's impossible to live correctly while believing incorrectly. Notice how Paul emphasized the subject of doctrine in his letters to Timothy (1 Tim. 1:3, 10; 4:1, 6, 13, 16; 5:17; 6:1, 3; 2 Tim. 3:10, 16; 4:3). The most important thing about us is the doctrines we hold, the truths we believe, and the Scriptures we embrace. In a world of political correctness, we hold to the authority of inspired Scripture, and nothing can pry that from our hands.

2. **Our Manner of Life.** We learn by watching others. That's why God put children in homes to observe godly parents. What one behavior of yours would you most like your children to emulate? What one behavior are you ashamed of more than any other? Which one do you not want your children to follow? How we answer these questions says a lot about us.

3. **Our Purpose.** We're happiest when we're fulfilling the purposes for which we are made. If I went to the hardware store and bought a mailbox, I could

use it to store bread in my kitchen or as an umbrella stand. We could pass it around the pews to collect the offering. But a mailbox is designed to send and receive information. Paul was made to receive and proclaim the message of God. You and I have a purpose, and we are happiest when we are doing that for which we are made.

4. **Our Faith.** Faith is the ability to trust God whatever the circumstances. Think of a pair of scales. On one side are painful perplexities. In Paul's case, there was a long series of weights. On the other side are God's promises. Take just one of those promises and drop it on the other side of the scales. Immediately the whole contraption reverses with a powerful thud. One little divine promise weighs more than all the problems, perils, and perplexities of life.

5. **Our Longsuffering.** This means putting up with imperfect circumstances without losing your temper and putting up with immature people without showing irritation.

6. **Our Love.** Look at 2 Timothy 1:7: "For God has not given us a spirit of fear, but of power and of love and of a sound mind."

7. **Our Perseverance.** A newspaper in Harvard, Massachusetts, sponsors an annual awards night for local athletes. Trophies are handed out. Organizers have created a new category they call Perseverance Awards, for students who were injured but didn't give up. Paul would have won the Perseverance Award. He never succumbed to discouragement—nor should we.

8. **Our Persecutions and Afflictions.** The apostle ended with a quality that doesn't spring from within but from without—persecution. Who could hate someone whose life was characterized by the first seven qualities? The answer is found in the preceding paragraph: ". . . in the last days perilous times will come: for men will be lovers of themselves, boasters, proud. . . ." Two groups of people serve as models for others. The first group is described in verses 1–9. The other groups is found in verses 10–12. Paul said to Timothy, "Don't follow that first group. Carefully emulate me."

Conclusion: Charles Spurgeon was walking up Norwood Hill with a friend. Some distance ahead was a lamplighter. Spurgeon watched until the old fellow had crossed over the top of the hill and was out of sight. Turning to his companion, he said, "I should like to think that when I've gone over the brow of the hill I shall leave lights shining behind me." May we live our lives and build our churches with ever-greater purpose and passion, so that when we have crossed over the brow of the hill, we shall leave a long, long row of lights shining behind us.

STATS, STORIES AND MORE

None of us may ever be famous, but there's a good chance that we'll influence someone who will influence someone who will influence someone who will do great things for the Lord. Dr. Paul Carlson, missionary physician in Congo, was slain for his faith. His death had a profound influence around the world. He was only 36 years old, but God greatly used the news of his murder to advance the cause of Christ in Africa. But wait! Who influenced Carlson? Clarence and Florence Johnson, overseers of the summer Bible camp that Carlson attended every year as a teenager, were highly influential during his formative years. No one may ever write a biography of Clarence and Florence Johnson. But they once had a high school student whose pathway crossed their own on a repeated basis; and whether they realized it or not, Paul Carlson mentored them; and just as young Timothy followed Paul's example, Carlson followed the Johnsons' example.

Think of the biographies you've read. Many of these books are about people who are household names in the world today; but in every biography, hidden away on page 27 or 34 or 74 is the name of some man or woman whose influence behind the scenes was invaluable and irreplaceable.

The Bible says that none of us lives to himself and none of us dies to himself. Like it or not, we leave our mark on other lives. We never know who is watching.

FOR THE BULLETIN

Maurice and Alice Abbott welcomed their son George into the world on October 29, 1562. After attending Oxford, George entered the ministry with strong Puritan leanings. When King James approved a new version of the Bible, George became a translator of the Gospels, Acts, and Revelation. In 1611, he became head of the Church of England, the only KJV translator to become Archbishop of Canterbury. He was also the only translator and the only Archbishop of Canterbury to kill a man. It happened when he joined friends in a hunting party. Abbott was stout, stodgy, and unfamiliar with bows. When a buck came into sight, he drew his arrow and let it fly. It flew right into Peter Harkins who quickly bled to death. ❂ Today is the birthday in 1869 of gospel musician E. O. Sellers. He worked with such evangelists as R. A. Torrey, Gipsy Smith, A. C. Dixon, and J. Wilbur Chapman. He is best known for his hymn, "Thy Word Have I Hid in my Heart." ❂ Missionary statesman A. B. Simpson passed away on this day in 1919. He had been frail for some time, and on Tuesday, October 28, while sitting on his front porch and engaging in a time of personal prayer, he suffered a seizure and was taken to bed. His family sat by his bed until morning when his labored breathing stopped. ❂ On the night of October 29, 1964, while her missionary compound in the Congo was under rebel occupation, medical missionary Dr. Helen Roseveare was overpowered by a soldier. "They found me, dragged me to my feet, struck me over the head and shoulders, flung me on the ground, kicked me, dragged me to my feet. . . ." Before the night was over, she had been sexually assaulted.

APPROPRIATE HYMNS AND SONGS

Praise to the Lord the Almighty, Joachim Neander /Catherine Winkworth, Public Domain

Let Everything That Has Breath, Matt Redman, 1997 Kingsway's Thankyou Music (Admin. by EMI Christian Music Publishing)

You're Worthy of My Praise, David Ruis, 1986 Maranatha Praise Music, Inc./ Shade Tree Music (Maranatha! Music [Admin. by The Copyright Company])

I Stand Amazed, Dennis Jernigan, 1991 Shepherd's Heart Music, Inc. (Admin. by Word Music, Group Inc.

My Saviour's Love, Charles H. Gabriel, Public Domain

WORSHIP HELPS

Pastoral Prayer:/Poem

Thanksgiving Day is still a month away, but it isn't too soon for us to thank God for the beauties of the autumn. Today is the birthday of an almost-forgotten Christian leader who wrote a beautiful hymn of thanksgiving. George Cotton was born on October 29, 1813, in England. He became an Anglican preacher, educator, and missionary who was appointed as Bishop of Calcutta. Arriving in India, he suffered an accident while disembarking from his ship and was drowned in the Ganges River. His hymn, however, lives on as a prayer of thanksgiving appropriate for us today:

We thank Thee, Lord, for this fair earth,
The glittering sky, the silver sea;
For all their beauty, all their worth,
Their light and glory, come from Thee.

Thine are the flowers that clothe the ground,
The trees that wave their arms above,
The hills that gird our dwellings round,
As Thou dost gird Thine own with love.

Yet teach us still how far more fair,
More glorious, Father, in Thy sight,
Is one pure deed, one holy prayer,
One heart that owns Thy Spirit's might.

So while we gaze with thoughtful eye
On all the gifts Thy love has given,
Help us in Thee to live and die,
By Thee to rise from earth to Heaven.

Additional Sermons and Lesson Ideas

When Millions Disappear
By Dr. Denis Lyle

Date preached:

SCRIPTURE: 1 Thessalonians 4:13–18

INTRODUCTION: Do you worry or wonder what will happen in the end? What about your Christian friends or family, will they be caught up in the rapture too? Paul gives us some truths to study about the coming of Christ:

1. The Rapture is a Positive Truth (vv. 13–16). It is *connected with the death of the believer* (vv. 14, 16), *confirmed by the resurrection of the Savior* (v. 14; the Greek word for "if" may be translated here as "since"), and *communicated by the revelation of the Lord* (v. 15).
2. The Rapture is a Precious Truth (vv. 16, 17). *The Lord will return* (v. 16), *the dead will rise* (v. 16), *the church will be raptured* (v. 17), and *believers will be reunited* (v. 17) to *reside with the Lord* (v. 17).
3. The Rapture is a Practical Truth (v. 18). Understanding the rapture is *comforting* (v. 18), *challenging* (1 Cor. 11:26; Titus 2:11–14; Heb. 10:26), and *cleansing* (1 John 3:2, 3).

CONCLUSION: Trust in the Lord and put your faith and hope in Him, for He is coming!

Taking Advantage of Living in a Non-Christian World
By Rev. Kevin Riggs

Date preached:

SCRIPTURE: Matthew 9:37–38

INTRODUCTION: As believers in the church, we need to take advantage of the awesome responsibilities that are before us.

1. Recognize the Time to Act Is Now (v. 37a). The harvest truly is plentiful, but we must pick the fruit before it goes bad. We need to stop complaining about the darkness and start lighting candles.
2. Realize the Work Will Be Hard (v. 37b). The reason there are few workers is not because people are unwilling to help but because the harvest is so great.
3. Rejoice that We Are not Responsible (v. 38). The fact we are to pray means that God is in charge. Our responsibility is to go and tell, but it is God's responsibility to convict and convert.
4. Respond by Getting Involved (v. 38). God has decided to reach people through people. If we want to make a difference, we must get involved; He calls us first to pray and then to go.

CONCLUSION: There are tremendous blessings and plenty of opportunities before us; won't you take advantage and obey His call?

NOVEMBER 5, 2006

SUGGESTED SERMON

Broken Commitments

Date preached:

By Rev. Peter Grainger

Scripture: Malachi 2:10–16, especially verse 10
Have we not all one Father? Has not one God created us? Why do we deal treacherously with one another by profaning the covenant of the fathers?

Introduction: Have you ever disobeyed God and immediately were faced with the damage it caused? We endanger ourselves and our relationships when we disobey God's Word, as was the case in Malachi's day. Look with me first at the two related problems that are addressed in these verses:

1. **Marrying the "Daughter of a Foreign God" (v. 11).** When the people of Israel were carried into exile, the Babylonians moved other conquered people into the land of Israel. This was a planned policy—not for ethnic cleansing—but for ethnic mixing. So when the Israelites were finally allowed to return home, they found a mixed population all around them of various races and cultures. Nothing is particularly wrong in that. What the prophet attacks, however, along with Ezra and Nehemiah, his contemporaries, is the practice of the Israelite men in marrying "daughters of a foreign god." The women they married did not worship Jehovah, the one true God.

   A. **Religious, not Racial Reasoning (Deut. 7:1–8).** There are good examples in the history of Israel of foreign women being welcomed into Israel; at least two (Ruth and Rahab) exist in the genealogy of Jesus Christ (Matt. 1:5). But Malachi speaks of a religious, not a racial problem. Inevitably, the Israelites' foreign wives would lead their husbands astray from following the true God—and their children may falter also. Within a couple of generations, the worship and witness of God's people, Israel, would disappear forever, merged into a multifaith mishmash.

   B. **Warning for Christians (v. 11; 2 Cor. 6:14–18).** This is not a reference to those who married as unbelievers and later one partner became a Christian. The New Testament addresses that situation with sympathy and understanding, along with helpful advice (see 1 Cor. 7:12–16; 1 Pet. 3:1–2). The reference here and in the New Testament is to someone who belongs to the Lord and then chooses to marry someone who does not.

2. **Divorcing the Wife of Your Youth (v. 14).** In poignant terms, the prophet describes how the men of Israel were throwing aside the wives who had stood by them since youth in favor of a "newer foreign model." It is possible that verse 13 refers to the floods of tears of these discarded wives who were crying out to God for justice and help. Thus when their husbands came to worship in that same temple, it's no wonder the Lord did not hear them; their prayers were drowned out by the wailing of their abandoned wives. Lifelong marriage was God's original intention, but the Law of Moses allowed for divorce in certain limited circumstances (Deut. 24: 1–4). Jesus spoke about divorce and went back to its ordinance at creation (Matt. 19: 3–9), stating that the only legitimate grounds for divorce is marital unfaithfulness. This was not the case in Malachi's day. Rather, the men were getting easy divorces for their own convenience and in direct disobedience to God.

3. **Damage Caused by Disobedience:**

A. **Damage in Our Relationship with God (v. 14).** This is the greatest damage we do. When we go against God's will and against his Word, our relationship with Him is damaged (see Ps. 66:18).

B. **Damage to God's People (v. 10).** The Lord is the Father of the nation of Israel. He is the one who created Israel as a people for Himself. So our relationship with God as our Father is not just an individual one but also a corporate one (Rom. 12:5). When we sin, we break faith with God's people, like a person who dishonors a family's name by his or her actions.

C. **Damage to Our Families (vv. 13, 15).** We have already spoken of the anguish and hardship caused to the wives of these Israelite men. The break-up of relationships causes enormous and immense damage to those involved. This affects not only wives and husbands but children also.

D. **Damage to Ourselves (vv. 11, 15).** Sin is always self-defeating. Of course, it looks attractive at first and appears to offer much. But like a parasite, it eats away at us and will in the end destroy us.

Conclusion: We will fill our hearts with something or someone. If God is not our fulfillment then we will seek it elsewhere. Perhaps God is warning someone here who is about to fall off the cliff. Perhaps God is speaking to someone whose conscience has become deadened and is in great danger. Certainly God is speaking to each of us here to be on guard (Eph. 6:10–11). His warnings are always warnings of love to His people. Let us hear and obey them.

STATS, STORIES AND MORE

I'll never forget a series of meetings I conducted many years ago. We'd had a wonderful week, and as the custom was during that particular period, they had a testimony meeting on that Friday night. A number got up to share what God had said to them and done in them that week. The period was almost over and I was about to gather up the thoughts and bring the closing message when a man, very distinctive, a little older than the rest, stood to his feet and said, "May I have a word?" His immaculate English, his perfect diction, marked him out right away as a well-educated man.

He said, "I have to say something; I can't go home without opening my mouth. I was saved as a boy; I did well in school, won a scholarship to Cambridge. While I was at university I was the leader of a Christian union there. Many a time I stood on the little pulpit we had and preached the gospel of Jesus. I went down from Cambridge to do my internship in London. In one of the great hospitals there, I became involved in a friendship. The moment that friendship started in my life, I knew, I KNEW, it was wrong. I tried to rationalize it. The Word of God spoke to me and rebuked me, but I silenced the voice of the Spirit. I seared my own conscience. I closed the Book and I continued the friendship; it was an unequal yoke. And for thirty-six years to this very day, I have lived in misery and defeat and utter uselessness. But this week God has brought me back to the point of departure, the point where I disobeyed my God, and I confess it publicly."

His wife was sitting right at his side. She was still an unconverted woman, and she looked up with tears in her eyes and said, "Darling why didn't you tell me before? I've longed to know reality in my life. You've never shared it with me." Miracle of miracles, that woman was converted on the spot. As they embraced each other and all wept, preachers as well as people, with tears of penitence and joy, we saw a mighty miracle and a mighty reunion take place. With all that joy there was deep, deep pain in my heart. Do you know why?

Thirty-six years wasted through disobedience! Barrenness is the consequence of disobedience to the Word of God.

—Dr. Stephen Olford

FOR THE BULLETIN

The Council of Constance convened on November 5, 1414. It was the largest church council in history and the most important since the Council of Nicaea in 325. Lasting four years, it ended one of the worst scandals in Christian history, the Great Schism, by deposing three rival popes. It also condemned the Reformers John Hus and Jerome of Prague. ✿ On November 5, 1605, King James I was set to open his first Parliament. An anonymous letter warned him not to attend due to a planned assassination attempt. A search of the House of Lords found twenty barrels of gunpowder hidden under piles of coal. Guy Fawkes was arrested on November 5 and taken to the Tower of London where he was presumably tortured until he named all his co-conspirators, all of whom were hanged. ✿ On November 5, 1872, Susan B. Anthony was fined one hundred dollars for trying to vote for Ulysses S Grant. ✿ Nikolai Odintsov, one of the best-known Baptist preachers in the Soviet Union and a Christian leader in Russia, was arrested on the night of November 5, 1929. He was sentenced to three years in Yaroslav Prison and then exiled to Siberia. His wife was finally able to visit him in Siberia, and found him physically weak but spiritually strong. The following year he was placed in a secret prison where he presumably died for his faith. ✿ The Cooperative General Association of Free Will Baptists and the General Conference of Free Will Baptists merged in Nashville, Tennessee, to form the National Association of Free Will Baptists, on November 5, 1935.

APPROPRIATE HYMNS AND SONGS

O the Deep Deep Love of Jesus, Samuel Trevor Francis /Thomas J. Williams, Public Domain

Grace, Pamela Furr \Raymond Charles Davis \Wayne Haun, 1996 Christian Taylor Music/Yes Mamm Music/Songs for Darshan/Magnasong Music Publishing/Richland Publishing Company (a div. of Daywind Music Publishing)/ (Admin. by Gaither Copyright Management)/ (Admin. by Curb Magnatone Music Publishing Limited Partnership)

More of You, Steve Merkel, 1997 Integrity's Hosanna! Music (c/o Integrity Music, Inc.)

Amazing Grace, John Newton /Edwin Excell /John P. Rees, Public Domain

I Love You Lord, Laurie Klein, 1978, 1980 House of Mercy Music (Maranatha! Music [Admin. by the Copyright Company])

WORSHIP HELPS

Call to Worship:

Oh, give thanks to the LORD! Call upon His name; Make known His deeds among the peoples! Sing to Him, sing psalms to Him; Talk of all His wondrous works! Glory in His holy name; Let the hearts of those rejoice who seek the LORD! (Ps. 105:1–3)

Offertory Comments:

As we study today about broken commitments, I'm afraid many of us here can relate. It's been eleven months since our New Year's resolutions. Thanksgiving and Christmas are now creeping up, and I'll bet a lot of our time and money have been spent lately on things of this world. Part of our commitment as God's church is to give back to God out of the abundance He has given to us. As a body of believers, I wonder if this is one of our broken commitments. May the Lord work in our hearts today to renew our commitment to Him, to give faithfully for the advancement of His kingdom!

Benediction:

Sweet Savior, bless us ere we go;
Thy Word into our minds instill,
And make our lukewarm hearts to glow
With lowly love and fervent will.
—Fredrick W. Faber, 1849

Additional Sermons and Lesson Ideas

Obedient Offspring

Date preached:

By Dr. Melvin Worthington

SCRIPTURE: Ephesians 5; Exodus 20; Colossians 3

INTRODUCTION: Scripture gives wonderful guidance for children and parents.

1. The Representatives. Obedient children recognize that parents are God's representatives. God is to the adult what parents are to the child—lawgiver, lover, provider, and controller.
2. The Relationships. Obedient children are careful to maintain good family relationships. Love given to children by parents is mysterious and probably the most perfect analogy of the love of God.
3. The Requirements. Children must obey their parents in adolescence and give them honor during adulthood. Jesus set the example when He was subject to His parents (Luke 2:51).
4. The Reward. Honoring and obeying one's parents help the child learn self-control, obedience to law, submission to authority, and respect for rules of health.

CONCLUSION: Jonathan Edwards was correct when he stated, "I now plainly perceive what great obligations I am under to love and honor my parents. I have great reason to believe that their counsel and education have been my making; notwithstanding in the time of it, it seemed to do me so little good."

Dealing with Open Sin in the Church

Date preached:

By Dr. Timothy Beougher

SCRIPTURE: 1 Corinthians 5:1–13

INTRODUCTION: Discipline and sin are words that we often avoid in attempting to maintain a positive atmosphere, but the Bible deals with this subject and so should we.

1. The Need for Discipline (v. 1). Sexual immorality is one that must be disciplined by the church according to Scripture.
2. The Failure to Discipline (v. 2). Paul rebuked the believers because they had failed in their responsibility to discipline a sexually immoral member.
3. The Procedure in Discipline (vv. 3–5; Matt. 18:15–17). First is *personal rebuke* (Matt. 18:15), then *plural rebuke* (Matt. 18:16), then *public rebuke* (Matt. 18:17a), and finally *probationary rebuke* (Matt. 18:17b).
4. The Reasons for Discipline (vv. 5–13). Discipline is for the good of the offender (v. 5), the church (vv. 6–8), and ultimately the world (vv. 9–13).

CONCLUSION: We should recommit ourselves to the Bible as God's Word and follow its model for discipline. We should pray for the health of this church and recommit ourselves to holiness, thus avoiding God's discipline.

NOVEMBER 12, 2006

Persecuted for Jesus' Sake

Date preached:

By Dr. Ed Dobson

Scripture: Various, especially 1 Peter 1:6, 7

In this you greatly rejoice, though now for a little while, if need be, you have been grieved by various trials, that the genuineness of your faith, being much more precious than gold that perishes, though it is tested by fire, may be found to praise, honor, and glory at the revelation of Jesus Christ.

Introduction: Today, we remember, reflect, and pray for brothers and sisters around the world who are facing persecution. When peace is consistent, often we become complacent. Scripture reminds us of the realities of persecution.

1. **Persecution Comes in Many Shapes and Forms.**

    A. **Persecution Is Personal (Matt. 5:10–12).** Notice the reason for that persecution in verse 10. It says "for righteousness' sake," because of your right living. Then in verse 11, your enemies "say all kinds of evil against you falsely for my sake." Some Christians are insulted, misrepresented, and mistreated because they're obnoxious. Jesus says the source of persecution ought to be because of your righteous living, and secondly, because of Him. Simply declaring yourself as a follower of Jesus Christ often results in persecution. Jesus says when you're persecuted because of Him, you're blessed! The Greek word for "persecuted" literally means to run after, to pursue someone with the intent to harm. It's sort of like a hunting term. You don't go out in the woods with a gun just to sit in the woods with a gun. No, you go out with a gun to kill a deer or something else. This means that Christians are in season and unbelievers hound them, go after them, intend to harm them, and falsely say all kinds of evil against them. They make up lies about you, misrepresent you, malign you, and accuse you. Now when this happens, if you get insulted for Christ, if you are persecuted for Christ, if people speak falsely against you for Christ, don't have a sour attitude about it, saying, "I can't believe this is happening to me. What's going on?" Jesus said in effect, "They hated Me, and they'll hate you. They persecuted Me, and they'll persecute you" (see John 15:20).

B. **Persecution Is Familial (Luke 12:51–53).** Jesus explained that the nature of having a relationship with Him can be divisive, even to the point of separating close family members from one another. Jesus said that following Him may cost you family relationships. What if that's the choice that you have—Jesus or your own children? Jesus, or your own family? Jesus or your own parents? Millions of Christians are making that choice every single day.

C. **Political and Religious Persecution (Acts 8:1–3).** Saul sought to destroy the church before His conversion; it's here described as a time of "great persecution". All over the world today there are religious groups and political groups and governments whose objective and driving passion is to finish what Saul started—destroying the church, dragging men and women off to prison, having them beaten, confiscating their property. They do so because they hate Christ most of all.

2. **Persecution Advances the Purposes and Plan of God (Acts 8:4).** Saul started out to destroy the church, to hinder the church, to frustrate the church, to limit the church, so he caused a great persecution to break out against the church. People were scattered since they could no longer stay in Jerusalem. And what happened? Everywhere they went they preached the gospel. You cannot destroy the church of God. Why? Because it's God's church! Even those who seek to harass and to imprison and to frustrate the church ultimately advance its cause.

Conclusion: "Remember the prisoners as if chained with them—those who are mistreated—since you yourselves are in the body also" (Heb. 13:3). "Remember" indicates not just recollection but a response. Persecution affects us all. Whether we grieve with others who are persecuted around the world, whether we are personally insulted or injured, whether our family disowns or disrespects us, whether our government or culture rejects or even kills us, persecution is very real in our world. Praise God that even persecution advances His kingdom. The applications for us today are twofold. First, are you willing to suffer persecution in whatever form it may come? Second, will you stand with, suffer with, pray for, minister to, or give aid to those brothers and sisters who are being persecuted? We must also remember Peter's words about persecution. First, it only lasts "a little while"; and second, it demonstrates "the genuineness of your faith," which ultimately brings "praise, honor, and glory" to God at Christ's return (1 Pet. 1:6, 7).

STATS, STORIES AND MORE

It was a Sunday morning I shall never forget. I was sitting on the platform of the Second Baptist Church in Oradea, Romania. It was the weekend of the first free elections in that country. I was sitting next to Josef Tson. Josef is an Oxford educated pastor, and for many years was pastor of the Second Baptist Church in Oradea, Romania. He had lived under the oppression of the communist reign. He had been imprisoned, interrogated, harassed, and finally banished from the country. He moved to the United States. Another pastor was chosen, a physician, Dr. Nick, and the church continued to flourish and multiply in spite of the harassment, in spite of the imprisonment, in spite of what was going on. Josef was back in the church for the first time since his exile. He had not been there, had not seen those people, and now he had returned. So I'm sitting on this crowded platform next to Josef who is about to preach. The place is packed with people. At that point in Romania, all of the women sat on one side of the auditorium and all of the men sat on the other. The aisles were full of young people who stood through the whole service. It was an electrifying moment, for the patron who had been in prison and had been banished from the country was now back in the church for the first time! Josef got up to preach and read 1 Peter 1:6. As I looked into the faces of that congregation and saw people weeping, I realized I was looking into the faces of people who had been imprisoned, who had lost jobs, who had lost families, who were denied education, denied advancement, denied housing for one reason—they were followers of Jesus Christ. I cried through most of the sermon.
—Dr. Ed Dobson

APPROPRIATE HYMNS AND SONGS

A Mighty Fortress is Our God, Martin Luther, Public Domain

I Was Glad, John Chisum /George T. Searcy, 1990 Ariose Music (Admin. by EMI Christian Publishing)/Tourmaline Music, Inc.

He Giveth More Grace, Annie Johnston Flint/ Hubert Mitchell, 1941. Renewed 1969 Lillenas Publishing Company (Admin. by The Copyright Company)

Hide Me in the Cleft of the Rock, Dennis Jernigan, 1987 Shepherd's Heart Music, Inc. (Admin. by Word Music Group, Inc.)

Rock of Ages, Augustus M. Toplady/Thomas Hastings, Public Domain

FOR THE BULLETIN

November 12, 1615 is the birthday of Richard Baxter, English Puritan and the author of *The Saints' Everlasting Rest.* ❋ John Bunyan, mender of pots and pans in Bedford, England, received a note inviting him to preach at a farmhouse on Sunday morning, November 12, 1660. Early that morning, he kissed his wife goodbye and reached the farmhouse about ten o'clock. A warrant had been issued for his arrest for unauthorized preaching, but Bunyan would not call off the meeting. As Bunyan read his Scripture and was preparing to preach, a knock sounded at the door. He was arrested and spent the next twelve years in Bedford Jail, using the time to write books, including the bestseller *The Pilgrim's Progress.* ❋ Today is the birthday in 1808 of Ray Palmer. When Palmer was twenty-four, he had worked himself to exhaustion trying to prepare for the ministry. His friend Lowell Mason asked him to write something for a projected hymnbook. Palmer gave Mason a copy of a poem he had written entitled "My Faith Looks Up to Thee." Palmer went on to become an outstanding hymnist, but he is still most remembered for his first poem, written out of exhaustion and prayer. ❋ On November 12, 1882, Arthur Polhill-Turner was converted while listening to D. L. Moody preach from Isaiah 12:2, and he later became a powerful missionary to China. On the same day seven years later, Moody began his last evangelistic campaign in Kansas City, Missouri. Becoming ill during the last service, he abruptly returned home and died a few days later, on December 22, 1899.

WORSHIP HELPS

Call to Worship:
Blessed *be* the LORD God of Israel from everlasting to everlasting!
And let all the people say, "Amen!" Praise the LORD! (Ps. 106:48)

Scripture Reading Medley:
Blessed are you when they revile and persecute you, and say all
kinds of evil against you falsely for My sake. Rejoice and be exceedingly glad, for great is your reward in heaven, for so they persecuted
the prophets who were before you.
If the world hates you, you know that it hated Me before it hated
you. If you were of the world, the world would love its own. Yet
because you are not of the world, but I chose you out of the world,
therefore the world hates you. Remember the word that I said to
you, 'A servant is not greater than his master.' If they persecuted
Me, they will also persecute you. If they kept My word, they will
keep yours also. But all these things they will do to you for My
name's sake, because they do not know Him who sent Me.
In this you greatly rejoice, though now for a little while, if need be,
you have been grieved by various trials, that the genuineness of
your faith, being much more precious than gold that perishes,
though it is tested by fire, may be found to praise, honor, and glory
at the revelation of Jesus Christ.
Matthew 5:11, 12; John 15:18–21; 1 Peter 1:6, 7

Benediction:
Grace to you and peace from God our Father and the Lord Jesus
Christ. (Phil. 1:2)

Additional Sermons and Lesson Ideas

The Marks of The Day

Date preached:

By Rev. Denis Lyle

SCRIPTURE: 1 Thessalonians 5:2, 3

INTRODUCTION: We often wonder what the judgment of God will be like—what will happen when He finally punishes all the evil that exists in the world. Paul, here in his section on "The Day of the Lord," teaches about that future "day" or period of time in which Christ judges the world and punishes the nations.

1. There Will Be a "Peace" in the World (v. 3). The world, basking in the false peace provided by the Antichrist, will be saying, "Peace and safety," but we will be saying, "Jesus is coming, and judgment is coming."
2. There Will Be Punishment on the World (vv. 2, 3). The judgment and punishment of God will come swiftly, like labor pains, from which the world will not be able to escape.

CONCLUSION: Have you heard the warnings from Scripture, perhaps in this very church, that judgment is coming if you have not given your life to Jesus? Are you trusting in a false peace?

Developing a Heart for God

Date preached:

By Pastor J. David Hoke

SCRIPTURE: Mark 12:30; John 4:24

INTRODUCTION: When you go to the doctor for a checkup, you will find that there are characteristics or indicators of health in the human body. This morning we need a "spiritual checkup" to find those same types of indicators in the spiritual body. The key examination is of our hearts: do we have hearts for God? If so . . .

1. We Should Love God Passionately (Mark 12:30). Loving the Lord involves the heart, mind, soul, and strength. To truly love God, we must love Him in all we do.
2. We Should Worship God Enthusiastically (John 4:24). Did you know our English word *enthusiasm* comes from the Greek words for "in" and "God"? The only way to truly worship God is to be filled with His Spirit.

CONCLUSION: As Christians our lives should be marked by a passionate love for God, and our gatherings should be marked by enthusiastic worship from a heart full of Christ's presence and grace. These are marks of a healthy Christian life.

Solomon Ginsburg

Solomon Ginsburg was one of the most colorful and effective missionaries of his day. His adventures are the stuff of movies. Solomon was born in Poland in 1867 to a Jewish rabbi who named him after the most glorious of all the kings of Israel. Rabbi Ginsburg wanted his boy growing up in his footsteps, a spiritual leader for the Jews of Eastern Europe.

One day Solomon and his father were celebrating the Feast of the Tabernacles by staying overnight in a small tent near their home. The boy picked up a copy of the Prophets and turned haphazardly to Isaiah 53. As he read the opening verses, his curiosity was stirred. "To whom does the prophet refer in this chapter?" he asked. When his father answered with "profound silence," Solomon repeated the question. This time his father snatched the book from his hand and slapped him across the face.

Years later Solomon traveled to London. Passing down Whitechapel Street, he met a Jewish friend who invited him to Mildmay Mission. "I am going to speak on the 53rd chapter of Isaiah," said the friend. "Won't you come?" Solomon attended, curious "to see if he had a better explanation than the one my father had given."

As he listened, he grew troubled. Christ seemed to have perfectly fulfilled Isaiah's prophecies in chapter 53. Solomon purchased a copy of the New Testament and was soon convinced that Jesus was the Messiah, and for three months a terrible war raged within him. What would his father think? his uncles? his family?

At last he heard Rev. John Wilkinson preach a powerful sermon on the text, "He who loves father or mother more than Me is not worthy of Me . . ." (Matt. 10:37). Returning home, Solomon paced the floor till midnight, finally surrendering his life to Christ in the early hours of the morning.

He was abandoned by his family, and his conversion brought him intense persecution. On one occasion he was beaten unmercifully, kicked till unconscious, and left for dead in a garbage container—bones broken and clothes soaked with blood. "Oh, but those were glorious times," he later said.

Solomon became a flaming evangelist across both Europe and South America. In 1911, needing rest, he decided to head to America on furlough.

His route took him to Lisbon where he planned to cross the Bay of Biscay to London, then on to the States.

Arriving in Lisbon, Ginsburg found the bulletin boards plastered with weather telegrams warning of terrific storms raging on the Bay of Biscay. It was dangerous sailing, and he was advised to delay his trip a week. His ticket allowed him to do that, and he prayed about it earnestly.

But as he prayed, he turned to his W.M.U. prayer calendar and found the text for that day was Deuteronomy 2:7—"For the Lord your God has blessed you in all the work of your hand. He knows your trudging through this great wilderness. These forty years the Lord your God has been with you; you have lacked nothing." The Lord seemed to assure him that his long, worldwide travels were under divine protection. Ginsburg boarded ship at once, crossed without incident, and caught the *Majestic* in London. His transatlantic voyage was smooth and restful.

Only after arriving in the United States did Solomon learn that had he delayed his trip in Lisbon, he would have arrived in London just in time . . .

. . . just in time to board the Titanic.

NOVEMBER 19, 2006

SUGGESTED SERMON

Unity: The Essential Requirement *Date preached:*

By Dr. David Jackman

Scripture: Philippians 1:27—2:4, especially 2:2:
. . . fulfill my joy by being like-minded, having the same love, *being* of one accord, of one mind.

Introduction: The principal that unity is strength is one that many of us have grown up with since childhood. The American slogan, "One nation, under God," is one that tries to emphasize unity. When John Donne said, "No man is an island," he meant that we all need one another and that we must work together if we are going to try to achieve our goals as a society. Despite all the analogies of how we're really strong, when we're working together life is actually full of disunities and differences that cause all sorts of weaknesses. It's this danger that Paul addressed to the Philippian church, for unity was just as essential in his day as it is in ours. Let's look at his teaching and how it applies to us:

1. **Gospel Partnership is Threatened by Suffering (1:27–30).** The opening verse teaches us the foundational truth that the gospel of Christ dictates the behavior of gospel Christians; this gospel actually creates the unity we must express as the church of Jesus Christ. Paul referred to our salvation as being united with Christ. It's a special type of unity because it's eternal! The Greek verb for "conduct yourselves" refers to being a good citizen. The Philippians lived in a city proud of its citizenship in the Roman Empire. While being a Greek city, they were a Roman colony with Roman citizens' rights. Paul used this idea here and in 3:20. Instead of living as Roman citizens and conducting themselves in a way that brings glory to Rome, they should live as citizens of a heavenly kingdom to bring glory to Jesus Christ. Verse 28 adds depth to the idea of unity. Paul was very conscious of an external threat to the unity of the Philippians. He told them not to be frightened; the Greek word used here carries the idea of a horse that has been frightened and shies away. Opposition leads to suffering, which threatens the gospel witness. Paul explained that the gospel demands willingness to not only share in salvation

in the life to come, but also in suffering here on earth for living the gospel lifestyle. This is a double privilege; we believe in Christ, and we are thankful for the salvation He provides. However, the Jesus on whom we believe suffered for us, so part of the privilege of believing in Him for salvation is suffering for Him. That, said Paul, is normal Christianity. Believers in the gospel are called to suffer for the gospel. Suffering for Jesus is a sign of your salvation (v. 28).

2. **Gospel Partnership is Threatened by Selfishness (2:1–4).** Here the focus is on dangers within the church, which are equally dangerous. In fact, many times external pressures lead to internal problems. In verse 1 Paul strongly exhorted the Philippians to remember the gospel principle that if suffering is a normal part of our Christian existence, then the resources listed in verse 1 are a normal part of the provision of God: "consolation," "comfort," "love," "fellowship," "affection," and "mercy." The Greek word for "encouragement" carries the idea of a child learning to write letters; the parent guides the hand of the child to empower him to learn. That's what comes from unity with Christ; He gives His life to us to strengthen us to live for Him. Similarly, there is a deep fellowship of the Spirit that deepens our unity, making us shareholders in the family's business. We share in the gifts and we know the deep love and affection of our father. Verses 2–4 show us what that sort of gospel partnership looks like. The gospel is all about self-giving love; look at the Cross! When the gospel is truly the center of our lives, we will all share this selflessness. What better to stop the work of the gospel than selfishness? Verses 3–4 highlight how this might happen. "Selfish ambition" and "conceit" are the sources of selfishness and disunity. No human can work for his own glory and the glory of God at the same time. When we've really grasped the gospel principle, we've sounded a resounding, "No" to selfishness, but an equally resounding "Yes" to the humility and suffering required in a life submitted to the gospel.

Conclusion: Our church can face the threats of external opposition and internal division when our selflessness makes us ready to live for Christ and never to allow a wedge to separate us from the love Jesus supplies us.

STATS, STORIES AND MORE

The Reality of Opposition

Our Christian faith is constantly downgraded, ridiculed, opposed, and somewhat suppressed by our culture. Are you going to declare that Jesus is Lord, or will you become more and more a secretive Christian until you eventually fade away? Suppose the police were listing every person here today to criminally prosecute later; would you come back next week? We only can continue in gospel practice if we're fully convinced of the gospel principle.
—Dr. David Jackman

A Little Kindness

Once when William Kellogg, of Kellogg's cereal fame, was motoring across the country, his roadster became stuck in the mud. This was in 1915 when travel was unbelievably inconvenient. A farm boy tried to help, but the problem was too much for him and his team of horses. The boy's father showed up with another team, and they pulled the car to safety. "What do I owe you?" asked Kellogg. The farmer just looked at him, and William finally asked the boy, "Doesn't you father hear well?"

"Oh, I hear all right," said the farmer, "but I was trying to recall where I've seen you before. About twenty-five years ago, my wife was very ill and our local doctor advised me to take her to the Battle Creek sanatorium. She was there quite a while, and I began to run out of money. In desperation, I went up to your office, and you assured me that my wife would not lack for treatment simply because I had run out of money. That's why, Mr. Kellogg of Battle Creek, you don't owe me a penny."[20]

APPROPRIATE HYMNS AND SONGS

Come, Now is the Time to Worship, Brian Doerksen, 1998 Vineyard Songs (UK/Eire) (Admin. by Mercy/Vineyard Publishing)

Called By Christ to Love Each Other, Jane Parker Huber/Dimitri Bortniansky, 1980 Jane Parker Huber (Admin. by Westminster John Knox Press)

Make Us One, Carol Cymbala, 1991 Word Music, Inc. (a div. of Word Music Group, Inc.)/Carol Joy Music (Admin. by Integrated Copyright Group, Inc.)

Savior Like a Shepherd Lead Us, Dorothy A. Thrupp/William B. Bradbury, Public Domain

We Stand Together, Chris Christensen, 1987 Integrity's Hosanna! Music (c/o Integrity Music, Inc.)

FOR THE BULLETIN

On November 19, 1600, King Charles I of England was executed by an order of Parliament. ❀ The seventeenth-century Puritan Richard Baxter was one of England's greatest preachers. Yet for ten of his best years, Baxter's voice was stilled, his sermons silenced, and his pulpit empty. King Charles II ejected Baxter and two thousand other Puritan preachers from their pulpits, and Baxter endured several imprisonments and suffered from various illnesses. While Baxter was away from his pulpit, he wrote some of the most powerful books ever written, including *The Saints' Everlasting Rest*, *The Reformed Pastor*—and 138 others! His diary reads on November 19, 1672: "The 19th of November was the first day, after ten years' silence, that I preached in a tolerated public assembly, though not yet tolerated in any consecrated church, but only, against law, in my own house." ❀ November 19, 1834 is the birthday of Samuel Trevor Francis, author of the hymn, "O the Deep, Deep Love of Jesus." ❀ Evangelist Billy Sunday was born on November 19, 1862, in Ames, Iowa. His father had died in the Civil War, and Sunday grew up in orphanages. From 1883 to 1891 he was a professional baseball player for Chicago, Pittsburgh, and Philadelphia. In 1886 he was converted through the ministry of Harry Monroe and the Pacific Garden Mission. After working with the YMCA and evangelist J. Wilbur Chapman, he became a sensational and dramatic evangelistic preacher, winning an estimated three hundred thousand converts. ❀ On November 19, 1863, Abraham Lincoln delivered the Gettysburg Address. ❀ On November 19, 1944, Dr. W. A. Criswell began his ministry at the First Baptist Church of Dallas, Texas.

WORSHIP HELPS

Call to Worship:
Come, let us, who in Christ believe, our common Savior praise,
To Him with joyful voices give the glory of His grace.
—Charles Wesley, 1741

Pastoral Prayer:
Our gracious God, we confess we are often double minded; we often have false motives and selfish ambitions. We ask You to continue to strengthen and equip us in every way, so that whatever it costs to do the gospel work in our day and generation, we may be guided by Your Spirit and truth, empowered by Your love, and strengthened by our union with You. Show us more and more how to live for Christ and His Kingdom in the details of our everyday lives. In Jesus' Name, Amen.

Offertory Scripture
Command those who are rich in this present age not to be haughty, nor to trust in uncertain riches but in the living God, who gives us richly all things to enjoy. Let them do good, that they be rich in good works, ready to give, willing to share, storing up for themselves a good foundation for the time to come, that they may lay hold on eternal life.
(2 Tim. 6:17–19)

Kids Talk

If you don't use the story about William Kellogg (see Stats, Stories, and More), tell it to the children. You can take a couple of Kellogg's cereal boxes to show the kids and talk about their favorite breakfast, then launch into the story, illustrating an act of kindness. A couple of extra details: Mr. Kellogg was traveling to San Francisco, accompanied by his chauffeur, Henry Johnson. This was when roads were poor, signs were nonexistent, and filling stations were few and far between. Kellogg's Franklin roadster got stuck just west of Omaha, Nebraska.

Additional Sermons and Lesson Ideas

Multiply the Membership

By Dr. Melvin Worthington

Date preached:

SCRIPTURE: Various passages in the book of Acts

INTRODUCTION: The rapid growth of the early church surges through the pages of Acts. From Jerusalem to Rome converts herald the gospel. Growth changed the church in Acts. Growth still changes churches. When the church grows, it exerts powerful influences on communities and nations.

1. The Dimensions of Growth. One type of growth recorded in Acts is statistical growth (Acts 2:41; 4:4; 5:14; 6:7; 9:31). Another type of growth is spiritual growth. Peter urged his readers to grow in grace and knowledge (2 Pet. 1:8; 3:18). Still another type of growth is stewardship growth (2 Cor. 8—9).
2. The Dangers in Growth. The dangers that accompany growth include motivation, methodology, manufacturing, and merchandizing.
3. The Dynamics of Growth. The dynamics of growth include the Spirit, the saints, the Scriptures, and the setting.

CONCLUSION: The credit for growth goes to God—not the pastor, the Christian worker, or the soul winner. God always causes the increase. Exalt the Sovereign rather than the servants.

House Rules

By Rev. Kevin Riggs

Date preached:

SCRIPTURE: Colossians 3:18–21

INTRODUCTION: Following the rules of the family as outlined by God will result in a healthier, happier home.

1. Wives, Respect (v. 18). By respecting your husband, God is asking you to voluntarily place yourself under his leadership for the sake of family unity.
2. Husbands, Love (v. 19). By loving your wife, God is asking you to serve her and to sacrifice for her, treating her as something priceless and valuable.
3. Children, Obey (v. 20). Learning to obey parents is how children learn to obey God.
4. Parents, Train (v. 21). It is the parents' responsibility to teach and discipline their children. God will hold parents responsible and accountable for such teaching and training.

CONCLUSION: In order for the family to be what God intended it to be, each person must fill his or her proper place.

THANKSGIVING SERMON

For Granted or Gratitude

By Pastor J. David Hoke   *Date preached:*

Scripture: 2 Corinthians 9:15
Thanks be to God for His indescribable gift!

Introduction: It is so easy to take things for granted. We live in a wonderful, free country. Most are well fed. Most have shelter and money. We might not be as well off as some, but compared to most of the world we are rich. We are not only blessed materially, we are blessed with friends, family, and a future. In spite of all this, we are sometimes slow to acknowledge our blessings. Because we have grown so accustomed to them, we take them for granted. Occasionally, we need to be reminded of just what we have been taking for granted and what we have to be thankful for. At special times like Thanksgiving, we should focus our attention on the things that really count. This American holiday of Thanksgiving is a special time of the year. It is a time when we look back on the blessings God has given us, and a time when we look forward to the blessings we will enjoy in eternity. Additionally, we can focus in on the present and celebrate the greatest gift of all, the gift of God's Son, Jesus Christ.

1. **The Basis.** What is the basis for true thanksgiving? For someone to be thankful, he or she must be grateful for something and to someone. The early Pilgrims had many difficult days in settling this new land. Governor Bradford of Massachusetts is believed to have made this first Thanksgiving proclamation three years after the Pilgrims settled at Plymouth:

Inasmuch as the Great Father has given us this year an abundant harvest of Indian corn, wheat, peas, beans, squashes, and garden vegetables, and has made the forest to abound with game and the sea with fish and clams, and inasmuch as He has protected us from the ravages of the savages, has spared us from pestilence and disease, has granted us freedom to worship God according to the dictates of our own conscience. Now I, your magistrate, do proclaim that all ye Pilgrims, with your wives and ye little ones, do gather at ye meeting house, on ye hill, between the hours of nine and twelve in the daytime, on Thursday, November 29th, in the year of our Lord One Thousand

Six Hundred and Twenty-Three, and the third year since ye Pilgrims landed on ye Pilgrim Rock, there to listen to ye pastor and render thanksgiving to ye Almighty God for all His blessings.

Those early Pilgrims recognized that the provisions they had experienced came from God. They were thankful, and they did not hide the fact that they were thankful to Almighty God.

But the greatest gift ever given, by the greatest Person, was God's Son, Jesus Christ. He's the real basis for all thanksgiving. Our key text says, "Thanks be to God for His indescribable gift!" (2 Cor. 9:15). The greatest gift that anyone has ever given to humankind is God's gift of eternal life through Jesus Christ. God sent Jesus because He loved us and so He could do the greatest work for us that anyone has ever done. That work was dying on the Cross for our sins so that we could be set free. Jesus paid the penalty for all your sins. He died so that you would not have to die. He suffered so that the bondage of sin could be broken. He took your place on the Cross. He died for you. And He did it all because He loves you. God responded to the greatest need, our sins, by giving the greatest Person, Jesus Christ, to make the greatest sacrifice, His death, so He could give us the greatest gift, eternal life. God gave Jesus. Thanks be to God for His indescribable gift!

2. **The Benefits.** There are over 550 references to thankfulness in the Bible. With such an emphasis on thanksgiving, there must be great benefits as well. Consider the benefits of cultivating this attitude of gratitude. Perhaps the greatest is that thanksgiving has a powerful effect on our lives. Thanksgiving makes us different. Look around you. Daily you will see people who are bitter. It's been said that "some people are bitter, not because they do not have anything, but because they do not have everything." We have been well taught to be greedy and ungrateful. We are bombarded by commercials that remind us of what we do not have. Christmas becomes a depressing time for many. We are led to believe that if we do not have things we will not experience happiness. Most unhappy people are unthankful people. At first glance, you may think them unthankful because they are unhappy. The opposite is true: they are unhappy because they are unthankful.

Thanksgiving has the power to transform us into different people. We will not only be different from the people around us, but we will also be different from the way we used to be. We will be transformed. We will be transformed in our thinking and in our temperament. As we seek to cultivate this attitude of gratitude, our thinking will be transformed. The way of the world is to concentrate on the negative, but the way of Christ is to emphasize the positive. We are to look for the good in everything. Philippians 4:8 tells us, "Finally, brethren, whatever things are true, whatever things are noble, whatever things are just, whatever things are pure, whatever things are lovely, whatever things are of good report, if there is any virtue and if there is anything praiseworthy—meditate on these things."

Conclusion: Thanksgiving is something unique that we can give to God. When you think of it, all the material things we give to God were given to us by Him, but our thanksgiving is ours—a personal gift and an offering of praise to God. We should learn how to express our thanksgiving well, not only to God, but to one another. We're sometimes too much like a little boy I heard about. On his return from a birthday party, his mother asked, "Bobby, did you thank the lady for the party?" Bobby replied, "Well, I was going to. But a girl ahead of me said, 'Thank you,' and the lady told her not to mention it. So I didn't." What kinds of attitudes characterize you? You can either take things for granted or take them with gratitude. Let's remember to "give thanks with a grateful heart." And let's remember Paul's prayer, "Thanks be to God for His indescribable gift!"

PRAYERS FOR THE PASTOR'S CLOSET

Almighty God, help Thy servants to do the work which will bear witness of Thee; help them to work while it is called day, so that at eventide they may have peaceful and grateful recollections. May we be jealous about our purity; may our life be a sacrifice; may our speech be a call to heaven. May our Christian name be a Christian reality, and our hope in Thee a light that shall make our whole life glorious!

—Joseph Parker

NOVEMBER 26, 2006

SUGGESTED SERMON

The Marks of Revival
Date preached:

By Rev. Charles McGowan

Scripture: Nehemiah 9:1–5, especially verse 3
And they stood up in their place and read from the Book of the Law of the LORD their God for one-fourth of the day; and for another fourth they confessed and worshiped the LORD their God.

Introduction: When you hear the word "revival," what comes to mind? Perhaps a tent with aluminum chairs set up and a dynamic preacher. Maybe you think of a service that occurs about once a year or a random outpouring of God's Spirit. Scripture displays true revival on several occasions. One of the best biblical pictures of revival is found in Nehemiah 8—10. The completion of the massive wall-building project created great encouragement and excitement, but God had a greater blessing in store. He chose to pour out great revival among the Jews in the area of Jerusalem.

1. **Brokenness (9:1, 2).** Contrast the opening verses of chapter 9 with 8:12. The great crowd gathered to listen to the Word of God celebrated with feasting in chapter 8. In chapter 9 the people began to fast. There is a close relationship between feasting and fasting. Feasting is related to thanksgiving and fellowship. Fasting is an expression of humiliation and brokenness. They always go together. A broken and contrite heart God will not despise (Ps. 51:17). It's the proud and self-righteous who are far from God. To avoid a daily attitude of brokenness before God is to develop a hard and indifferent heart. God desires that His children remain tender through repentance and brokenness.

2. **Reflection on God's Goodness (9:6–15).**

   A. **Prayer.** Most of chapter 9 is devoted to prayer. It's marked by acknowledgment of failure again and again, but also by praise for the character of God—for His covenant with His people; for delivering His people from bondage; for His tender, faithful guidance throughout Israel's history. God's forgiveness and provision are acknowledged as an outpouring of His grace. Is this not the story of all of God's children? Sin and rebellion are followed by God's patience. Our failure is followed by God's goodness. He pours out His forgiving grace on those who seek Him.

B. **Meditation.** The people lingered in the presence of God. For three hours the Word was read. For three more hours the people engaged in prayer and praise. What would happen if God's people today laid aside their self-interests and pleasures to pursue Him as these people did after the completion of the wall?

3. **Confession of Sin (9:2, 33).** The people's confession is reported in Nehemiah 9:2. The actual prayer recorded later in the chapter is worthy of careful study. The Israelites were quick to confess that God had always been faithful, but that they had been wrong (v. 33). They confessed the sin of their fathers, indicating that their sin was the same as that of their fathers. This is so unlike what our human nature is inclined to do. We may acknowledge our failure but hesitate to call it sin. The key to revival, whether it is personal or corporate, is the recognition of sin, the willingness to admit it without making excuses, and repenting of it in a spirit of contrition.

4. **Commitment to Obedience (chap. 10).** Revival is not merely an emotional stirring to the core of our being. It moves one to a renewal of his covenant relationship with God. Nehemiah 10 is a detailed account of what revival produced among the people. Revival touched the leaders of the people, including the governor (10:1) and the Levites (10:9–27). The leaders and the people made the same renewal vows. They committed to live as God's people, to separate themselves from pagan lifestyles (10:28–29), and to obey the commands and the decrees of God (10:29), specifically to keep the Sabbath (10:31) and to tithe (10:32). Now, in joyful praise and thanksgiving—accompanied by true repentance—they renewed their covenant relationship and experienced the deep satisfaction of having been forgiven and restored. That's revival.

Conclusion: It isn't necessary for us to view revival as something that comes only when our sovereign God chooses to give it. It is not a miraculous intervention from heaven for which we have prayed and waited. Revival is a gift from God at a time when we earnestly and humbly seek it. Revival is given as we come into His presence with praise and thanksgiving, but also with broken and contrite hearts that show we have repented of our sins. Revival becomes evident as we build patterns of spiritual devotion matched by a lifestyle of humble obedience to the God who redeemed us by the atoning death of his Son.

STATS, STORIES AND MORE

The Welch Revival

Evan Roberts was a coal miner—tall, blue-eyed, young, and thin. At age twenty-five, having just begun studying for the ministry, he asked his pastor for permission to hold some evening meetings. Only a few people came at first, but within days village shops were closing early for the services. People left work to secure seats at church. Services often lasted till 4:30 a.m. Sins were confessed, sinners converted, homes restored. All across Wales, theaters closed, jails emptied, churches filled, and soccer matches were canceled to avoid conflicting with the revival.

On March 29, 1905, Evan Roberts opened a series of meetings at Shaw Street Chapel in Liverpool. Thousands thronged around the church, and people poured in from all parts of England, Scotland, Ireland, mainland Europe, and America. Multitudes were converted or found new joy in Christ. Often Roberts didn't even preach. The very sight of him sent rivers of emotion flowing through the crowds. When he did speak, his message was quiet and simple: "Obedience to Jesus, complete consecration to his service, receiving the Holy Spirit and allowing ourselves to be ruled by him."

The Liverpool meetings left Roberts exhausted, needing weeks to recover. On his next preaching tour, a whirlwind of revival again swirled around him; but yet again, the young man returned home drained and exhausted. Roberts spoke four times more, then he retired to a friend's home for a week's recovery. He stayed seventeen years, and he never preached again. He spent his remaining forty-five years in secluded ministry and prayer, here and there, with friends. He died in 1951. His public ministry had lasted only months, but it had shaken Wales and England to their foundations.

APPROPRIATE HYMNS AND SONGS

Joyful Joyful We Adore Thee, Henry Van Dyke/Ludwig van Beethoven, Public Domain

Shout to the Lord, Darlene Zschech, 1993 Darlene Zschech (Hillsong) (Admin. in U.S. & Canada by Integrity's Hosanna! Music)

I'm Forever Grateful, Mark Altrogge, 1985 People of Destiny International (Admin. by PDI Ministries)

What the Lord Has Done in Me, Reuben Morgan, 1998 Reuben Morgan (Hillsong) (Admin. in U.S. & Canada by Integrity's Hosanna Music)

This is My Father's World, Maltbie D. Babcock/Franklin Sheppard, Public Domain

November 26, 1095, was the date of one the most effective sermons ever preached by pope, preacher, or prince. It was Pope Urban II's sermon in Clermont, France, launching the Crusades. He spoke in an open field to both clerics and the general public, describing how the Turks, an "accursed race," had devastated the kingdom of God by fire, pillage, and sword. Jerusalem was laid waste, and the Holy Land was in the hands of barbarians. The crowd, whipped into a frenzy, began chanting, "God wills it! God wills it!" A new era in European history began as the crusading passion, inspired by its pope, took hold of its people. ❈ The melancholy poet William Cowper was born on November 26, 1731. Teaming up with John Newton, Cowper produced some of the finest hymns in the English language, including "There is a Fountain Filled with Blood" and "God Moves in a Mysterious Way." ❈ The American Navy began using chaplains on November 26, 1775. ❈ George Washington proclaimed this day as Thanksgiving Day in 1789. It was not until Abraham Lincoln's presidency, however, that it became an annual event. ❈ In the early morning of November 26, 1800, a carpenter in India went down to the Ganges River to bathe. He slipped on the steps, and the resulting fall dislocated his shoulder. In pain, he sent his children for Dr. John Thomas who treated the man's shoulder while sharing the gospel of Christ with him. The carpenter, Krishna Pal, listened; and the next day he received a visit from missionary William Carey. Within a month, Krishna Pal gave his life to Christ, becoming Carey's first convert and the first native Indian whom he baptized after seven long years of labor. Pal was baptized in the Ganges River.

WORSHIP HELPS

Call to Worship:

"Blessing and honor and glory and power be to Him who sits on the throne, and to the Lamb, forever and ever!" (Rev. 5:13b)

Welcome:

On this Sunday after Thanksgiving, it's a good time to remind ourselves that there is no such day. *Every* day is Thanksgiving for the Christian. John Oxenham, in his delightful little book of verses, *Bees in Amber,* published in 1913, wrote a poem that expresses our gratitude to the Lord today for sustaining our hearts even when times are tough:

We thank Thee, Lord,
That of Thy tender grace,
In our distress
Thou hast not left us wholly comfortless.

We thank Thee, Lord,
That of Thy wondrous might,
Into our night
Thou hast sent down the glory of the Light.

We thank Thee, Lord,
That all Thy wondrous ways,
Through all our days,
Are Wisdom, Right, and Ceaseless Tenderness.

Kids Talk

If your church enjoys hymns, this would be a good day to introduce the children to the old classic, "Take Time to Be Holy." It's the birthday of the author, William D. Longstaff, who was born on November 26, 1822. Most children can understand the concepts in the first verse with just a little explanation.

Additional Sermons and Lesson Ideas

Thanks Giving

Date preached:

By Dr. Timothy Beougher

SCRIPTURE: 1 Corinthians 1:4–9

INTRODUCTION: We come to God so often with our complaints or requests that we tend to neglect giving thanks to Him. Let's look at some things we should be thankful for:

1. God's People (v. 4a).
2. God's Grace (v. 4b).
3. God's Spiritual Blessings (v. 5).
4. God's Gospel (v. 6).
5. God's Enabling (v. 7).
6. God's Preserving Power (v. 8).
7. God's Fellowship (v. 9).
8. God's Faithfulness (v. 9).

CONCLUSION: All believers have received these eight blessings; let's give Him thanks!

Practical Applications for the Lord's Coming

Date preached:

By Dr. Denis Lyle

SCRIPTURE: 1 Thessalonians 5:6–11

INTRODUCTION: Did you know that there is a difference between being ready to go to heaven and being ready to meet the Lord? Paul gives us practical applications to live in the light of His coming.

1. Wake Up (v. 6). The word "watch" used here implies alertness. Are you alert, doing the Lord's work in light of His coming?
2. Clean Up (v. 6). The word "sober" used here is the antithesis of being intoxicated (v. 7). Are you intoxicated by what the world has to offer, or focused on Christ?
3. Dress Up (v. 8). The day of the Lord should prompt us to love, faith, and hope.
4. Speak Up (v. 9–11). We are to comfort and edify one another concerning the Day of the Lord.

CONCLUSION: Others will be attracted to the gospel and more likely to heed the warnings of coming judgment if they see a practical difference in the lives of those of us who believe!

DECEMBER 3, 2006

Facing the Giant of Loneliness   *Date preached:*

Dr. David Jeremiah

Scripture: Ecclesiastes 4:9–12, especially verse 10b
Woe to him who is alone when he falls, for he has no one to help him up.

Introduction: As we begin the Advent Season, we're excited about celebrating the birth of Christ. But Christmas is lonely for some. Millions, in fact, struggle with loneliness year round. Someone has suggested that loneliness is a long period of stress that wears you down until you're defeated. It's a longing for completeness. Scripture warns us about being alone to face life's problems on our own (Eccl. 4:10b), and we need to realize that God has given us remedies for loneliness.

I. **Experiences of Loneliness.** Loneliness is something we all deal with at one time or another, but some are especially vulnerable.

   A. **The Lonely Single.** Every single knows the anguish of going home to cook a meal for one, then watching television alone at night.

   B. **The Lonely Spouse.** The institution God created to provide intimacy often becomes a place of loneliness. One woman wrote me: "I try not to dwell on it—the loneliness in marriage, but the truth is I am lonely. My husband and I are both Christians. We live relatively well. We're educated, and my husband is a good man. But my emotional needs are rarely met because he works all the time. It's the case of two people living parallel lives but never really meeting at all. I'm not going to nag, but the hurt is deep."

   C. **The Lonely Survivor.** These are people who live on after a loved one has died. They experience a kind of pain that is so intense there's nothing like it. Often divorce can be equally bad or worse.

   D. **The Lonely Senior Citizen.** Our population is graying, and some who once held a position of authority and respect now wonder if anybody needs them.

E. **The Lonely Sufferer.** One man wrote: "It's when the lights go out and the room is plunged into darkness that the awful awareness comes. The traffic of the hospital goes on like an uncontrolled fever outside my door. But inside, it's so still."

F. **The Lonely Servant of God.** See Numbers 11:14.

2. Examples of Loneliness in the Bible

A. **David the King.** We don't have to read much of David's story to know why he felt lonely (see Ps. 102:6, 7; 142:4).

B. **Jeremiah the Prophet.** Both Jeremiah and Lamentations contain vivid expressions of anguish (see Jer. 9:2; Lam. 1:16).

C. **Paul the Apostle.** "Demas has forsaken me . . . Crescens [has left for] Galatia, Titus for Dalmatia. . . . At my first defense no one stood with me, but all forsook me." (2 Tim. 4:10, 16) Ever feel like that? It isn't a sin to be alone. It becomes a sin when we start to indulge it, when we neglect the provisions God gives us to dispel loneliness.

3. The Escape from Loneliness. Let me suggest some things.

A. **Acknowledge the reality of your loneliness.** A. W. Tozer wrote: "Some say brightly, 'Oh, I am never lonely. Christ said, "I will never leave you nor forsake you," and, "Lo, I am with you always," so how can I ever be lonely when Jesus is with me?' " But Tozer added, "I do not want to reflect on the sincerity of any Christian soul, but this stock testimony is too neat to be real."[21] All of us know something about loneliness, so don't deny it. It's a part of human experience.

B. **Accept God's provision for your loneliness.** God created us with an emptiness that can only be filled by a relationship with God. Jesus cried, "My God, my God, why hast Thou forsaken me?" He was bearing our sins and pain, bearing our loneliness so that the love of God can fill our hearts.

C. **Allow God's Word to fill your mind.** There are so many passages of Scripture which apply here that I wish I could scroll them on a giant screen for you. You can search them out for yourself, but you might start with Psalm 27:10 and Hebrews 13:5, 6.

    D. Activate your network of Christian friends. I want to make a statement I hope won't be offensive. Loneliness is a choice. Moments of being alone may not be a choice, but lingering in the house of loneliness is. God has given us His Son, His Word, and His people—all of which are antidotes for loneliness. "But Pastor Jeremiah," you might say, "I don't know anybody." Well, the Bible says he who has friends must show himself friendly. You say, "Well, it's not my responsibility to take the initiative." Then, my friend, whose responsibility is it? If you sit around just waiting for someone to notice you and reach out to you, that could be dangerous. There are Sunday school classes, small groups, ministry teams, and Bible studies just waiting for you.

Conclusion: My recommendation is for you to remember that Jesus Christ has come to give you life everlasting. He's just waiting for you to make the decision to accept His free gift. Find Him. Find His Word. Find His people. And find His abundant life.

STATS, STORIES AND MORE

More from David Jeremiah

In Anne Frank's diary, along with the descriptions of dangers and despair, she recorded the feelings she had in her heart. Somehow despite all the suffering she experienced, Anne found joy. In fact, in 1944 when she was a young girl, she wrote these words: "Nearly every evening I go up to the attic, and from my favorite spot on the floor, I look up at the blue sky. As long as this exists, I think, and I may be able to live to see it, as long as I can see this sunshine and the cloudless skies, while this lasts, I cannot be unhappy. Riches can all be lost, but that happiness in your heart can only be veiled."[22]

I want to say with authority today that we have something far better than blue sky and clouds. We have Jesus Christ living in us. Though the world may crumble around us, He is the blue sky, He is the light from on high that thrills and encourages our hearts. I can look beyond my circumstances into the face of the One who loves me more than I know, and the One who would never allow anything to happen to me that was not for my own good, and I know with certainty that He cares and that if I will trust Him He will help me through the experience of life. He will never leave me alone.

FOR THE BULLETIN

Thomas Becket, Archbishop of Canterbury, returned to England on December 3, 1170, after six years exile in France. He would be slain on December 29. ❂ Felix Mantz, Anabaptist leader in Zurich, was arrested on December 3, 1527. As a result of his preaching, he was sentenced to death by drowning, becoming the first in a long list of Anabaptist martyrs. ❂ The Roman Catholic missionary, Francis Xavier, died on this day in 1552. ❂ Oberlin College in Ohio opened on December 3, 1833. Charles Finney later served as its president. ❂ Today is the birthday in 1841 of Clara H. Scott, author of the hymn "Open My Eyes, That I May See." Also born on this day in 1902 was Mitsuo Fuchida, the Japanese pilot who flew the lead plane in the attack on Pearl Harbor. He later became a Christian through the ministry of the Pocket Testament League. ❂ Paul Harvey began his national radio broadcast on December 3, 1950. He entered radio work as an outgrowth of evangelistic campaigns he conducted with the family of John W. Peterson. ❂ Hussein Soodman was an Assembly of God pastor in his mid-forties in Mashad, Iran. When his church was closed by the government in 1988, he conducted private services and then moved to a church in the city of Gorgan north of Tehran. Soodman was arrested by the Gorgan police, blindfolded, and ordered to return to Mashad. There he was again arrested and condemned. His blind wife was allowed to visit him twice. On December 3, 1988, he was hanged and buried in an isolated grave. His wife suffered a nervous breakdown and fellow Christians took in the couple's four children, ages ten to fifteen.

APPROPRIATE HYMNS AND SONGS

Amen, Ken Bible/Tom Fettke, 1997 Pilot Point Music (Lillenas [Admin. by The Copyright Company])

Beautiful Star of Bethlehem, Adger M. Pace/R. Fisher Boyce, 1967 James D. Vaughan Music Publisher a div. of SpiritSound Music Group

O Little Town of Bethlehem, Phillips Brooks/Lewis H. Redner, Public Domain

The Love of God, Frederick M. Lehman, Public Domain

He is Here, Kirk Talley, 1990 Kirk Talley Music (Admin. by Integrated Copyright Group, Inc.)

WORSHIP HELPS

Call to Worship:

Therefore, having been justified by faith, we have peace with God through our Lord Jesus Christ, through whom also we have access by faith into this grace in which we stand, and rejoice in hope of the glory of God. (Rom. 5:1, 2)

Pastoral Prayer:

Lord of Love, You have promised to never leave us or forsake us. You are here; You are near; You are a friend who sticks closer than a brother. Teach us to practice Your presence, to visualize Your nearness, to hear Your Word in our ears, and to feel Your fellowship in our hearts. When the days are dreary and the long nights weary, remind us that You care for us and You abide with us. You have not left us as orphans in the vast darkness of this universe; You have made us sons and daughters of light whose lives are to radiate cheer, joy, gladness, and victory. May the sunbeams of Your grace reflect from us onto the walls of other lives; and may we both know You and make You known. We ask in Jesus' Name. Amen.

Reading for the Advent Candle

There shall come forth a Rod from the stem of Jesse, and a Branch shall grow out of his roots. The Spirit of the LORD shall rest upon Him, the Spirit of wisdom and understanding, the Spirit of counsel and might, the Spirit of knowledge and of the fear of the LORD. His delight is in the fear of the LORD. . . . Righteousness shall be the belt of His loins, and faithfulness the belt of His waist. (Is. 11:1–3a, 5)

Additional Sermons and Lesson Ideas

No Other Name

Date preached:

By Dr. Melvin Worthington

SCRIPTURE: Acts 4:12

INTRODUCTION: The Bible presents Christ as the Son of God and the Son of Man. The heart of Christianity is the Person and work of Jesus Christ. No man can come to God except through Him.

1. The History Recorded. The birth of Jesus Christ in Bethlehem was no accident. It was the fulfillment of God's divine promise. He was promised in truth, portrayed in type, and presented in time.
2. The Hymns Reviewed. Hymns extolling the name of Jesus include the following: "His Name is Wonderful," "What a Lovely Name," "Praise the Name of Jesus," and many others. Such hymns emphasize the views of songwriters regarding the Person and work of Christ.
3. The Hope Reaffirmed. There is no other name through which pardon comes. There is no salvation apart from Him.

CONCLUSION: There is no other name in which we can trust. We have the history, the hymns, and the hope (see John 1:12).

Welcome Advent

Date preached:

SCRIPTURE: Matthew 1:18–25

INTRODUCTION: As we approach this Christmas season, let me offer some suggestions for making it a more relaxed, more worshipful season for your family.

1. Make a budget and keep it. We need to learn to enjoy giving and receiving less, that we might give and receive more.
2. Make a prayer list and remember it. This Christmas, remember that there are some lonely people around you. As we make our shopping lists, let's make a special list just for this season and pray for a handful of souls who need our intercession.
3. Make a commitment and honor it. Determine to invite two people (or more, if you'd like) to one of our Christmas productions or services as a means of reaching out with the gospel.
4. Make a date and enjoy it. Find a special person in your life and make a special date to be with that one whom you're often too busy to see.
5. Make a gift and dedicate it to Christ. How odd that we often give so much to others that we have nothing left for the Birthday Child Himself.

CONCLUSION: This can be our best Christmas ever. Let's make it more a time of excitement and less a time of exhaustion. Just a little planning will go a long way.

The Pastor's Humor / Bob Stromberg:

Pastors deal with heartaches in life, but they need laughter too. What role does laughter have in the life of a pastor?

To laugh is an important thing. We need to laugh. That's part of our emotional health. I'm not made the same as you, so you might not need to laugh as much as I do, or you might need to laugh more. But we all need to laugh. It is an emotion God has given us.

What role does laughter have in the life of a church?

A function of laughter and humor in the church is to break down walls that people put up. People come from outside the church, and many of them don't know Jesus. Laughter's major function is to break down those walls. I think laughter is one of the best tools God gives us to break down barriers so people can breath again. I once had an interviewer who came to see my play, *Triple Espresso.* He was a critic. His comment was, "Well, *Triple Espresso* will make you laugh till you're silly, but don't expect to be moved emotionally." Well, I say, "Isn't laughter an emotion?" When people come to church, the last thing they're thinking about doing is laughing. It's a treat to be able to guffaw, or laugh out loud, or laugh until you're weeping like I did last night as I listened to several Christian comedians.

Is it easier to make people cry than it is to get them to laugh?

It's easier to manipulate them into crying. But I don't know how you manipulate people into laughing. It's a very honest emotion. It's a hard one. People don't fake it very well.

Is there a role for humor in the pulpit in the Sunday sermon?

There certainly is. I would emphasize that people have to be who they are. Pastors are not usually professional comedians, and if they try to become a comedian it may lessen their impact. But they *can* be people with a good sense of humor.

Can pastors learn to be better humorists in the pulpit?

Well, certainly they can develop their ability to tell a joke. But frankly, the pastor's job is difficult as it is. I would never want to discourage somebody from developing what God has given them in humor; but frankly, I think this is an area in which the time would be better spent preparing your sermon and working on your communication and your study skills. Perhaps God has gifted others who can impart the gift of laughter. More and more churches are inviting Christian comedians for various functions in their church just to make people laugh.

I've noticed there's a whole new generation of Christian comedians now. What's their role in the church?

This has just boomed in the last couple of years. In fact, there's a Christian Comedians Association now that has over two hundred members. Not all of them are working all the time, but they are all people who are interested in developing the use of comedy. Their function, I believe, is to break down walls between people, to make the church a place people want to attend. On Palm Sunday morning I'm going to be in a church in California. I asked them what they wanted me to do. They said, "We want you to be really funny, and then point the way toward Easter." I can do that.

There isn't a verse that says "Laughter is the best medicine," but Psalm 126:2 refers to our mouths being filled with laughter.

People don't laugh much now. They go through weeks and months without truly laughing. They might say, "Oh, I laughed at that show last night," but they actually didn't; they just chuckled or gave a little giggle. They thought they laughed, but they didn't laugh from the gut or from the heart. They didn't experience what could just be a blessing of laughing that way. So for someone to come into the church and say, "I went to the church and I experienced a powerful emotion—I laughed," that's great. I pray for that everywhere I go. And for *Triple Espresso,* which is a "secular play," I pray that God will surround our theater or church or wherever we are with the blood of Christ and fill it with the Holy Spirit and touch people with the joy of the Lord. I also pray that He will use the laughter he's allowed me to help people enjoy and to minister to people in any unique way that He understands. He knows what people need and he can use the laughter, like he can use music, dance, drama, He can use comedy and laughter to minister to people in wonderful ways.

DECEMBER 10, 2006

SUGGESTED SERMON

Why Those Dirty Shepherds?   *Date preached:*

Scripture Reading: Luke 2:8–20, especially verse 8
Now there were in the came country shepherds living out in the fields, keeping watch over their flock by night.

Introduction: Why those dirty shepherds? Why didn't the angels appear to . . . well, rabbis or priests? Why not to fisherman, potters, or princes of Israel? Why to shepherds? Well, here are six possibilities:

1. **God Does the Unexpected.** He seldom works as we expect, and this actually attests to the authenticity of the story. If you had been a Jewish writer wanting to make up a story about the entrance of the Messiah—the Savior of the World—into human history after two thousand years of prophecy, would you have invented a tale in which He was born in a stable and laid in a feed bin? Would you have made the announcement to a bunch of shepherds? One Jewish scholar wrote: "[The circumstances Luke records] afford the strongest indirect evidence of the truth of this narrative. For if it were the outcome of Jewish imagination, where is the basis for it in contemporary expectation? Would Jewish legend have ever presented its Messiah as born in a stable, to which chance circumstances had consigned his mother. The whole current of Jewish opinion would run in the contrary direction."

2. **Jesus was the Son of a Shepherd-King.** There is great emphasis in the Gospels on the fact that Jesus had descended, as to His earthly nature, from the line of David, the shepherd-king who had once kept flocks in those very fields. A thousand years before, the boy David was among flocks in those same rugged pastures. Now another Shepherd-King—the Son of David—had been born. It was to a new generation of shepherds, to the vocational descendants of David, that the announcement was made of the Great Shepherd who was coming into the world.

3. **The Angelic Choir Needed an Outdoor Audience.** This might seem a trite and inconsequential point, but as I visualize the scene in my mind it seems like a practical consideration. No house, temple, chapel, or cathe-

dral could have contained the angelic numbers that night. Highest heaven was evidently emptied as the blackened sky was filled with ten thousand times ten thousand angels. Only a group under the open skies could have received the message.

4. **Jesus Came to the Poor and Humble.** He came to redeem common, ordinary people like us. The appearance to the shepherds is the perfect compliment to His being born in a stable and laid in a manger. It symbolized His poverty. He left the ivory palaces of heaven to enter a world of woe. He who had been rich became poor that we through His poverty might become rich (2 Cor. 8:9; see Is. 61:1–3). It is helpful to balance this point by remembering Matthew's account in which the star appeared to the wise men, who were the exact opposite of shepherds. They were cultured, respected, wealthy, Gentiles. Jesus came for all.

5. **A Lamb Was Born that Night.** Perhaps most importantly, this message was given to shepherds because of the nature of the message itself. The Lamb of God had come into the world. The picture of a Lamb is the Bible's most consistent picture of Christ. Who would be a more appropriate audience for the Good News about the birth of the Lamb than an audience of shepherds? But there's more. The Hebrew scholar Alfred Edersheim tells us that the flocks near Bethlehem were no ordinary sheep, but were those being raised for sacrificial uses in the temple. "How right the angels should appear to them that night."

6. **These Shepherds Were Spiritually-Minded Men.** I think we can read between the lines and assume that here was a handful of men devoted to the Lord. As Jesus later put it, God hides His secrets from the "wise and prudent" and reveals them to babes (Matt. 11:24). It's possible for shepherds to have great depth. Consider David. It was while keeping his father's sheep that he developed his spiritual muscles. And notice in this passage how quickly the shepherds believed and obeyed the angelic message.

Conclusion: 1 Corinthians 1:26, 27 tells us that ". . . not many wise according to the flesh, not many mighty, not many noble are called. But God has chosen the foolish things of the world. . . ." You may not be a great scholar or a powerful leader, but God can reveal Himself to you and use you for His glory in ways greater than you can ever imagine. Let Him have His way with you this Christmas season.

STATS, STORIES AND MORE

The Lamb of God

When Adam and Eve sinned, they became self-conscious and tried by their own efforts to cover themselves up and hide their guilt. It was impossible, so God introduced us to an immutable spiritual law built He into the spiritual world—we can only be redeemed by the shedding of the blood of an innocent sacrifice, a lamb. God clothed them with the skin of an animal. What kind of animal? We don't know, but in the next chapter, Abel brings to the Lord a lamb, the best of his flock, as a sacrifice. In Exodus, the Passover lamb was slain and its blood painted across the doorposts of the Israelites' homes. The Lord said, "When I see the blood I will pass over you" (Ex. 12:13). In Leviticus, the Israelites were told to offer the best of their flocks as a sacrifice for sin (Lev. 23:12). Isaiah, in predicting the coming of Messiah, said, "He was led as a lamb to the slaughter. . . ." (Is. 53:7). When John the Baptist introduced Christ to the masses, he said: "Behold! The Lamb of God who takes away the sin of the world!" (John 1:29). Peter added, "Knowing that you were not redeemed with corruptible things, like silver or gold, from your aimless conduct . . . but with the precious blood of Christ, as of a lamb without blemish and without spot." Down to the last book of the Bible, we see the importance of the Lamb. Innumerable angels sing, "Worthy is the Lamb who was slain to receive power and riches and wisdom, and strength and honor and glory and blessing!" (Rev. 5:12). In the last chapter of the Bible, we read: "There shall be no more curse, but the throne of God and of the Lamb shall be in it, and His servants shall serve Him" (Rev. 22:3).

APPROPRIATE HYMNS AND SONGS

Angels We Have Heard on High, James Chadwick/Edward Shippen Barnes, Public Domain

Angels from the Realms of Glory, James Montgomery/Henry T. Smart, Public Domain

Good Christian Men Rejoice, John Mason Neale, Public Domain

It Came Upon a Midnight Clear, Edmund H. Sears/Richard S. Willis, Public Domain

Wise Men Still Seek Him, Chris Machen, 1997 Pilot Point Music (Lillenas [Admin. by The Copyright Company])

FOR THE BULLETIN

On December 10, 1518, Ulrich Zwingli was elected pastor in Zurich. He began his ministry there on January 1, 1519, by introducing expository preaching to the pulpit after an absence of hundreds of years. ✱ On this day in 1520, Martin Luther took the papal bull Exsurge, Domine (the document threatening him with excommunication) to the upper end of Wittenberg, Germany, and burned it. ✱ On December 10, 1524, the Dutch Lutheran, Henry van Zutphen, was burned to death. Escaping from the monastery at Antwerp in 1523, Zutphen had preached the gospel for two years before his enemies sought him out one night, surrounded the house where he slept, pulled him from bed, beat him with clubs, dragged him over snow and ice, and finally threw him on a slow fire to burn to death. ✱ Another Reformation hero, Nicholas Cop, preached a blistering sermon at the University of Paris, sparking riots that forced him to flee the city. On December 10, 1533, King Francis I issued orders for his arrest. Cop made it successfully to Switzerland. ✱ A young ruffian named Robert Robinson attended an open-air service conducted by evangelist George Whitefield, who preached from Matthew 3:7: "Brood of vipers, who warned you to flee from the wrath to come?" The message pierced Robinson's heart, for he felt Whitefield was speaking directly to him. Two years and seven months later, on December 10, 1755, Robert Robinson, age twenty, gave his life to the Lord Jesus. He later went on to write the hymn, "Come Thou Fount of Every Blessing!"

Call to Worship:
"Where is He who has been born King of the Jews? For we have seen His star in the East and have come to worship Him." (Matt. 2:2)

Reading for the Advent Candle
Who has believed our report? And to whom has the arm of the LORD been revealed? For He shall grow up before Him as a tender plant, and as a root out of dry ground. He has no form or comeliness; and when we see Him, there is no beauty that we should desire Him. He is despised and rejected by men, a Man of sorrows and acquainted with grief. And we hid, as it were, our faces from Him. . . . Surely He has borne our griefs and carried our sorrows. . . . He was wounded for our transgressions, He was bruised for our iniquities; the chastisement for our peace was upon Him, and by His stripes we are healed.
(Is. 53:1–5)

Benediction:
All glory for this blessed morn
To God the Father ever be;
All praise to Thee, O virgin born,
All praise, O Holy Ghost, to Thee.
—Caelius Sedulius, Fifth Century

Additional Sermons and Lesson Ideas

The Personality of the Holy Spirit
Based on an outline by Rev. R.A. Torrey

Date preached:

Scripture: Various

INTRODUCTION: If you know the Holy Spirit, you will soon come to understand His work. If you do not know Him, and you try to understand His work, you are almost certain to fall into error and fanaticism.

1. The Pronoun. Scripture repeatedly uses not the pronoun "it" but "Him," in reference to the Holy Spirit, which implies a true personality (see John 14:26; 16:7, 8, 13, 14).
2. The Characteristics Ascribed to Him. All the distinctive characteristics of personality are ascribed to the Holy Spirit in the Bible (see Gen. 1:26; Neh. 9:20; Rom. 8:26, 27; 14:30; 1 Cor. 2:10; 12:11; Eph. 4:20).
3. The Personal Acts of the Holy Spirit (Is. 63:10; John 14:16, 7, 26; 16:7; Acts 5:3; 13:2; 16:6–7; 20:28; Rom. 8:26; Heb. 10:29; 1 John 2:1).

CONCLUSION: The Holy Spirit is a Person, the third Person of the Trinity. But—to put it in a more personal and practical way—is He a Person in your thoughts of Him and in your attitudes towards Him?

The Wonder of God's Ways
By Dr. Timothy Beougher

Date preached:

SCRIPTURE: 1 Corinthians 1:26–31

INTRODUCTION: Have you ever questioned why God does things as He does sometimes? Would you not agree that sometimes God's ways seem mysterious to us? Today we're looking at a passage that gives insight into the wonder of God's ways.

1. Man's Worldly Perspective (vv. 26, 27). Paul lists some human standards of success: noble birth, worldly possessions, wisdom, and influence.
2. God's Heavenly Perspective (vv. 27–29). God uses people and situations we would never consider in our human thinking. He can use you and me!
3. Believers' Transformed Perspective (vv. 30, 31). God has transformed us so that every aspect of who we are is for the glory of God.

CONCLUSION: When we look at God and His ways through the lenses of Scripture we realize His ways are truly wonderful!

DECEMBER 17, 2006

SUGGESTED SERMON

A Root out of Dry Ground
Date preached:

By Rev. Charles McGowan

Scripture: Isaiah 53:1–6, especially verse 2:
For He shall grow up before Him as a tender plant, and as a root out of dry ground. . . .

Introduction: One of the amazing facts related to Christmas is that Jesus survived the efforts of Herod to kill him. More amazing yet is the impact of his life, death, and Resurrection. Isaiah spoke prophetically of this with these words: "For He shall grow up before Him as a tender plant, and as a root out of dry ground." The "dry ground" of which Isaiah spoke consisted of the humble circumstances of his birth, his growth and development, his nationality, the politics of his day, and the disciples whom he trained. Yet, the "root" sprang up and continues to spring up and thrive in the hardest and driest of soil. Reflect on the "hard soil" in which Jesus takes root and thrives.

1. **The Human Heart.** The Lord Jesus never finds the human heart to be fertile soil. It is characterized by darkness, greed, envy, and pride. In the human heart he finds not sickness, but death. This has been illustrated through the ages by the dramatic conversion of people such as Augustine, whose heart was consumed with hedonism and hardened indifference to the faith of his praying mother. Or think of Saul of Tarsus, the great persecutor of the early church whose hard and callous heart became the seedbed of the gospel. What an encouragement to someone who feels his heart is too deeply stained for God to accept him! And what an encouragement to someone whose current place in life might be characterized as dry and barren!

2. **Our Culture.** Evidence surrounds us that our culture is barren and dry. One only needs to survey the world of entertainment. Examine the ugly side of the Internet or the content of much of our culture's music. Whether it be television or the curriculum of a typical secular university, you find much barren and dry soil. The living Christ, however, takes root and thrives in the dry soil of an ungodly culture. This has always been true. Against the backdrop of the barren Middle Ages, the Reformation

was born. As the Reformers planted the rediscovered gospel of grace, the living Christ sprang up as a vibrant plant. Or think of David Wilkerson proclaiming the gospel in the barren territory of New York City gangs— only to see lives changed by the living Christ who sprang up in the most unlikely places. So we should not lose heart. The seed is planted and watered even in the hardest and driest of soils. Then, in his own time, Christ springs up and grows, changing lives and cultures.

3. **Your Place of Ministry and Service.** There are certain areas of the world where the soil is unusually hard and dry. The resistance to the gospel is strong and sometimes met with hostility. There are places where the messenger is in grave danger as he seeks to plant the seed. But, in God's time, the seed sprouts. Think of China enslaved for decades by oppressive Marxism during the twentieth century. Yet as doors began to open late in the century, it became obvious that the living Christ had taken root and flourished there. Or think of the drift of the modern church in some parts of the world toward ministries devoid of the historic gospel message. Those who remain faithful are inclined to develop an Elijah complex, assuming that all hope is lost. Yet the history of the church is replete with stories of the living Christ springing up in the midst of the sleepy, drifting church. Or think of families that appear hopeless: the husband totally consumed in patterns destructive to his marriage and family; marriages that are in disarray and on the verge of dissolution; children in rebellion. Only the eyes of faith could see the living Christ taking root in places such as these. Yet testimonies abound of the gospel doing what trained counselors could never do as the living Christ is embraced.

Conclusion: This is the message of Christmas: no circumstance, no matter how hopeless, is beyond the reach of the One who takes root in the most barren and driest places imaginable. Offer Him the soil of your barren, broken, and hopeless circumstances. Expect him to do what he has done through the ages—grow up as a tender plant and overshadow your life and circumstance with His grace.

STATS, STORIES AND MORE

This story has been told in a variety of ways, but this is the researched version that appeared in newspapers nationwide on December 25, 1994 from the Associated Press.

Eighty years ago, on the first Christmas Day of World War I, British and German troops put down their guns and celebrated peacefully together in the no-man's land between the trenches.

The war, briefly, came to a halt.

In some places, festivities began when German troops lit candles on Christmas trees on their parapets so the British sentries a few hundred yards away could see them.

Elsewhere, the British acted first, starting bonfires and letting off rockets.

Pvt. Oswald Tilley of the London Rifle Brigade wrote to his parents: "Just you think that while you were eating your turkey etc. I was out talking and shaking hands with the very men I had been trying to kill a few hours before!! It was astounding."

Both armies had received lots of comforts from home and felt generous and well disposed toward their enemies in the first winter of the war, before the vast battles of attrition began in 1915, eventually claiming 10 million lives.

All along the line that Christmas Day, soldiers found their enemies were much like them and began asking why they should be trying to kill each other.

The generals were shocked. High Command diaries and statements express anxiety that if that sort of thing spread it could sap the troops' will to fight.

The soldiers in khaki and gray sang carols to each other, exchanged gifts of tobacco, jam, sausage, chocolate and liquor, traded names and addresses and played soccer between the shell holes and barbed wire. They even paid mutual trench visits.

This day is called "the most famous truce in military history" by the British television producer.

FOR THE BULLETIN

On this day in 1770, the German composer Ludwig van Beethoven was baptized. His compositions have been used for several hymns, including Henry Van Dykes "Joyful, Joyful, We Adore Thee." ❁ British preacher and hymnist John Rippon died on December 17, 1836. He served over sixty years at London's Carter Lane Baptist Church, but is best known today for editing and publishing several hymnbooks and bringing to popularity the hymn "How Firm a Foundation." ❁ This is an important day in the life of another London pastor. On this day in 1853, Charles Spurgeon arrived in the city to preach the next day at New Park Street Chapel with a view toward accepting the pastorate of that congregation. Arriving by train on a cold day, he felt despondent and alone. At a boarding house, he was put in a small room over the street where he slept little. "Pitiless was the grind of the cabs in the street . . ." he recalled, "dark and pitiless even the gas lamps which seemed to wink at me as they flickered amid the December darkness. I had no friend at all in that city full of human beings." ❁ On the same day, December 17, 1853, Lutheran missionary Eduard Raimund Baierlein arrived at Madras, India, to begin his ministry there. ❁ Evangelist Rodney (Gipsy) married "Miss Pennock, daughter of Captain Pennock, of the mercantile marine" on December 17, 1879. He later said, "I do not think I shall ever know in this world how much of my success is due to my wife, her beautiful Christian life, and the unselfish readiness with which she has given me up to leave her and the children for the work to which my Master has called me."

APPROPRIATE HYMNS AND SONGS

Come Thou Long Expected Jesus, Charles Wesley/Rowland H. Prichard, Public Domain

O Come O Come Emmanuel, John M. Neale/Henry S. Coffin/Thomas Helmore, Public Domain

How Great Our Joy, Theodore Baker, Public Domain

Thou Didst Leave Thy Throne, Emily E.S. Elliot/Timothy Richard Matthews, Public Domain

Infant Holy Infant Lowly, Edith M.G. Reed/A.E. Rusbridge, Public Domain

WORSHIP HELPS

Call to Worship:
Glory to God on high!
And heav'nly peace on earth;
Goodwill to men, to angels joy,
At the Redeemer's birth!
—Isaac Watts, 1707

Hymn Story: "Joy to the World"
Until Isaac Watts came along, most of the singing in British churches was from the Psalms of David. As a young man in Southampton, Isaac had become dissatisfied with the quality of music, so he invented the English hymn. He did not, however, neglect the Psalms. In 1719 he published a unique hymnal—one in which he had translated, interpreted, and paraphrased the Old Testament Psalms through the eyes of New Testament faith. He called it simply, *The Psalms of David Imitated in the Language of the New Testament.* Taking various psalms, he studied them from the perspective of Jesus and the New Testament, then formed them into verses for singing. "Joy to the World" is Isaac Watt's interpretation of Psalm 98:4, which says: "Shout joyfully to the Lord, all the earth."

Reading for the Advent Candle:
"The Spirit of the LORD God is upon Me, because the LORD has anointed Me to preach good tiding to the poor; He has sent Me to heal the brokenhearted, to proclaim liberty to the captives, and the opening of the prison to those who are bound; to proclaim the acceptable year of the Lord, and the day of vengeance of our God. To comfort all who mourn. To console those who mourn in Zion, to give them beauty for ashes, the oil of joy for mourning, the garment of praise for the spirit of heaviness; that they may be called trees of righteousness, the planting of the LORD, that He may be glorified." (Is. 61:1–3)

Additional Sermons and Lesson Ideas

It's Incredible!
By Dr. Melvin Worthington

Date preached:

SCRIPTURE: John 1

INTRODUCTION: Millions observe the annual celebration of Christmas commemorating the birth of the Lord Jesus Christ. We must see more than a Babe in Bethlehem. John 1 teaches us the following truths regarding the incarnation.

1. The Foretelling. Genesis 3:15 contains the first proclamation of the Incarnation. The Incarnation was not an afterthought with God; it was foreknown and foreordained in God's plan and purpose.
2. The Fulfillment. John 1:1–5, 14–16, 30 provides the basic information about the Incarnation. John established the fact of Christ's Preexistence (vv. 1, 2), Christ's Person (v. 1), Christ's Power (v. 30), and Christ's Presence (v. 14).
3. The Focus. The incarnate Christ Reveals the Sovereign, Reflects the Standard, Redeems the Sinner, Resides in the Saint, and Responds to our Supplication.

CONCLUSION: During this special season, let's take time to pause, ponder, and proclaim the thrilling, timely truth that the birth of the Babe in Bethlehem was incredible, for He was Immanuel, God with us, the incarnate Christ, the Messiah.

Reasons to Live a Holy Life
By Rev. Kevin Riggs

Date preached:

SCRIPTURE: 1 John 3:1–10

INTRODUCTION: As true believers, we must demonstrate our love for Christ by the conduct of our lives. We are to strive to live a holy life. In this passage, John gives us three reasons to live a holy life.

1. God Loves Us (1 John 3:1–3). Love is a far greater motivator than guilt. Thus, it is my love for God that should cause me to do what is right.
2. Jesus Died for Us (1 John 3:4–8). How you live your life tells people whom you belong to. Our motivation for living right is love.
3. The Holy Spirit lives in us (1 John 3:9, 10). Our ability to live a holy life comes from the Holy Spirit who lives within us. Through the Spirit we are the children of God.

CONCLUSION: As true believers, let's demonstrate our love for Christ by the conduct of our lives.

DECEMBER 24, 2006

Come, Your Hearts and Voices Raising

Date preached:

Scripture: Luke 1—2, especially 1:46
. . . "My soul magnifies the Lord"

Introduction: Most people miss Christmas. They're so caught up in the retail rush that they're exhausted and perhaps depressed by the holiday pressures. We know depression rates and suicide numbers increase during this season. But as we read through the Christmas story as Luke presented it in the first two chapters of his Gospel, we find seven distinct people or groups who celebrated that first Christmas. They all had exactly the same response to the stupendous events of that day.

1. **Elizabeth's Response (Luke 1:39–42).** Luke's Gospel begins, not with the birth of Christ, but with the birth of the forerunner, John the Baptist. Zacharias and Elizabeth, an older couple, were given the promise of a child. When Mary came to visit to share her own news, Elizabeth was "filled with the Holy Spirit" and "spoke out with a loud voice" (Luke 1:41, 42). I imagine Mary and Elizabeth might have given each other some little gifts as tokens of their love; they may have crowded into the kitchen and cooked a feast. But the giving of gifts and the eating of food wasn't their main concern. They were full of praise and thanksgiving at what God was doing in their lives in sending these two babies into the world.

2. **Mary's Response (Luke 1:46).** Then it was Mary's turn to be full of praise and thanksgiving: "And Mary said, 'My soul magnifies the Lord, and my spirit has rejoiced in God my Savior.'" And here we have this wonderful hymn of praise, the Magnificat. When you magnify something, you don't really make it larger—but you do make it larger in your own eyes.

3. **Zacharias' Response (Luke 1:67, 68).** After Mary returned home, Elizabeth gave birth to John. At that time Zacharias' mouth was opened to say: "Blessed is the Lord God of Israel, for He has visited and redeemed His people . . ." (v. 67).

4. **The Angels' Response (Luke 2:13, 14).** The first verses of Luke 2 describe the birth of Christ, then the scene shifts to shepherds' field. It says about the angels: "And suddenly there was with the angel a multitude of the heavenly host praising God and saying: 'Glory to God in the highest, and on earth peace, goodwill toward men!' "

5. **The Shepherds' Response (Luke 2:20).** "Then the shepherds returned, glorifying and praising God for all the things that they had heard and seen, as it was told them."

6. **Simeon's Response (Luke 2:25–29).** Forty days later, Mary and Joseph took Jesus to the temple to present Him to the Lord. There the old man Simeon ". . . took Him up in his arms and blessed God and said: 'Lord, now You are letting Your servant depart in peace, according to Your word.' "

7. Anna's Response (Luke 2:36–38). Anna also gave thanks to God and spoke of Him.

Conclusion: Seven times people were exposed to Christmas in Luke's Gospel, and seven times they worshipped. Seven times their hearts were filled with praise and thanksgiving. Seven times they blessed the God of Israel and magnified the Lord. What should our response be to Christmas?

A. **Worship Him personally with whole-life praise.** The worship that came from all these people did so because their whole lives were given to God. For example, see the description of Zecharias and Elizabeth in Luke 1:6, of Simeon in 2:25, and of Anna in 2:37. Their entire lives were doxologies of praise.

B. **Worship Him publicly with whole-church praise.** Mary could have worshipped in private, but she needed someone with whom to share her joy, so she sought the one special person with whom she could share the news—her relative Elizabeth—and they praised the Lord together. The news of Christmas is too great to enjoy alone. The angels worshipped in a great masses of celestial multitudes, and the shepherds praised the Lord in a joyful little assemblage of their own. We need to worship with our fellow believers.

C. **Worship Him privately with whole-hearted praise.** Luke 2:19 says: "But Mary kept all these things and pondered them in her heart." Sometimes we need to take time to ponder these things in our hearts, as Mary did.

During this Christmas season, I've enjoyed sitting at my desk in the soft glow of a single lamp, reading through the Christmas story morning after morning, or contemplating and praising and worshipping God.

CONCLUSION: I encourage you to do the same. As hymnist Paul Gerhardt put it long ago:

> Come, your hearts and voices raising,
> Christ the Lord with gladness praising,
> Loudly sing His love amazing,
> Worthy folk of Christendom.

STATS, STORIES AND MORE

I Would Praise More

The Duke of Wellington wasn't an easy man to serve. He was demanding, not one to shower subordinates with compliments. Yet he realized his methods left something to be desired. In his old age someone asked him what he would do differently if he could. Thinking a moment, he replied. "I'd give more praise." He was speaking of praising his men; but a lot of us could say the same thing about our relationship with the Lord.

Church Attendance

In a little village in the Alps, a little church was built without any interior lighting. In every pew, a place was provided for the attenders to place their lamps. When the church was full, the church was all aglow with warm and light. When one person or another was absent, their spot was dark. And when the crowd was very low, the church was dim.

Pondering in our Hearts

In his autobiography, Dwight Eisenhower tells of planning the D-Day Invasion of Europe. It was during intense moments of preparation that word came of the death of his father. It was impossible for Eisenhower to leave his command. He couldn't possibly return home, nor was it possible for him to take time off. But, as he wrote in his book, it was also not possible to go ahead with business as usual. Sending everyone out of his office, he set aside thirty minutes to think about his dad, to write out his thoughts in a diary. That's all he could do. But if General Eisenhower, in the midst of planning the invasion of Europe, could shut the door and spend a half hour thinking about his earthly father, should we not find a way of shutting the door, opening our Bibles, and thinking about the birth of our earthly Savior during this holy season?

FOR THE BULLETIN

On December 24, 1223, Francis of Assisi assembled animals in a cave near Greccio, Italy. He built a crib, arranged some hay, and crowds gathered to see history's first recorded nativity scene. There on Christmas Eve, Francis preached the wonder of God made man. ✿ Several Christmas carols were written or published on this day. On December 24, 1534, Martin Luther wrote "From Heaven Above to Earth I Come." Journalist James Montgomery published his "Angels from the Realms of Glory" on Christmas Eve, 1816. Two years later, Joseph Mohr of Oberndorf, Austria wrote "Silent Night, Holy Night." And on December 24, 1865, Phillip Brooks penned "O Little Town of Bethlehem." ✿ On December 24, 1784, a conference convened in Baltimore to form the Methodist Episcopal Church in America. Francis Asbury was appointed America's first Methodist Bishop. ✿ Moody Memorial Church (originally Northside Tabernacle) was dedicated by Dwight L. Moody on this day in 1871. ✿ Southern Baptist missionary Lottie Moon, age seventy-two, died aboard ship in the harbor at Kobe, Japan, on December 24, 1912. ✿ American manufacturer and hymnist William H. Doane passed away on December 24, 1915. He composed the tunes to many of Fanny Crosby's most enduring songs, including "I Am Thine, O Lord," "More Love to Thee," "Near the Cross," "Rescue the Perishing," "Take the Name of Jesus with You," and "Pass Me Not, O Gentle Savior." ✿ William C. Poole, author of the hymn "Just When I Need Him Most," died on this day in 1949. ✿ On December 24, 1968, the Apollo 8 astronauts orbited the moon and broadcast back a reading of the creation story of Genesis 1.

APPROPRIATE HYMNS AND SONGS

Go Tell It on the Mountain, John W. Work, Jr., Public Domain

Joy to the World, Isaac Watts/ George Frederick Handel, Public Domain

Hark the Herald Angels Sing, Charles Wesley/ Felix Mendelssohn, Public Domain

The First Noel, Public Domain

Silent Night Holy Night, Joseph Mohr/Franz Gruber/John Freeman Young, Public Domain

WORSHIP HELPS

Call to Worship:
". . . behold, I bring you good tidings of great joy which will be to all people. For there is born to you this day in the city of David a Savior, who is Christ the Lord."
Luke 2:10, 11

Pastoral Prayer:
Oh Lord, what a day this is! A day of tender thoughts, of sweet songs, of a blessed Baby. We thank you for the animals, the boards and straw and stone walls for the stable. We thank you for the lowly shepherds, the glorious angels, even for the innkeeper. All the elements of this age-worn story are just as dear and precious to us as they've been to every generation for two thousand years. Most of all, our Lord, we thank you for Jesus. For Him who was born King of the Jews, for Him who is named King of our hearts. Our heart calls out above the cacophony of the world, and we say, "Happy Birthday, Lord!" For unto us was born that day a Savior, who is Christ the Lord; and we have come to adore Him.

Reading for the Advent Candle
For unto us a Child is born, unto us a Son is given; and the government will be upon His shoulder. And His name will be called Wonderful, Counselor, Mighty God, Everlasting Father, Prince of Peace. Of the increase of His government and peace there will be no end, upon the throne of David and over His kingdom, to order it and establish it with judgment and justice from that time forward, even forever. The zeal of the LORD of hosts will perform this.
(Is. 9:6–7)

Additional Sermons and Lesson Ideas

Good Cheer for Christmas
Adapted from a sermon by Charles Haddon Spurgeon

Date preached:

SCRIPTURE: Isaiah 25:6

INTRODUCTION: We have arrived at the great merry-making season of the year. Isaiah 25:6 describes the provisions of the gospel in terms of a joyous celebration.

1. The Feast. God provides a feast of good things.
   A. The Food: 1) Justification; 2) Adoption; 3) Eternal Love; 4) Union with Christ; 5) Resurrection and Everlasting Life
   B. The Wine: 1) Perfect Peace; 2) Deepest Joy; 3) Steadfast Hope
2. The Banquet Hall: "In this mountain" refers to three things: 1) Calvary; 2) The Church; 3) Heaven
3. The Host: The Lord makes the feast, and He will not even permit guests to bring their own wedding garments; they must stop at the door and put on the robe He provides.
4. The Guests: It is "for all people." No one is excluded. This phrase "for all people" permits missionary enterprises in every land.

CONCLUSION: ". . . the one who comes to Me I will by no means cast out" (John 6:37). Some very odd people have come to Him, some wicked people, some hardened people, but the door was never closed in anyone's face. If you believe in Christ, all these things are yours. Come, poor trembler, the silver trumpet sounds, and this is the note it rings: "Come and welcome, come and welcome, come and welcome."

The Little-Known Christmas Names of Christ
Date preached:

SCRIPTURE: Luke 1—2

INTRODUCTION: We know Him as Jesus, Christ, the Babe in the manger, and the Son of God. But hidden away in the Christmas story are some other wonderful names of our wonderful Lord.

1. The Son of the Highest (Luke 1:32)
2. The Horn of Salvation (Luke 1:69)
3. The Dayspring from on High (Luke 1:78)
4. The Consolation of Israel (Luke 2:23)
5. The Glory of Israel (Luke 2:32)

CONCLUSION: Which of these wonderful names means the most to you today?

DECEMBER 31, 2006

Overcoming Impatience

Date preached:

By Rev. Todd M. Kinde

Scripture: James 5:7–12, especially verse 8:
You also be patient. Establish your hearts, for the coming of the Lord is at hand.

Introduction: As we approach this New Year of 2007, I wonder what your New Year's resolutions will be. Let me suggest that in this "get it now" day and age, all of us need to commit to be more patient. James gives us practical advice to learn patience and suffering, which are marks of a true follower of Christ. Chapter 5 begins by admonishing those who treat others unjustly to repent. Specifically, the wealthy landowners were not paying fair wages to the laborers. Now those who are being treated unjustly are addressed and called "brothers." True disciples are to be patient in suffering until the Lord's coming.

1. **The Patience of the Farmer (vv. 7, 8).** James used an illustration from nature, which says that we are to have the patience of a farmer until Jesus returns. The farmer waits patiently for the land to yield its valuable crops and the rains to water the land. You are to be patient as you await the coming of Christ to dispense justice. Do not take matters into your own hands. Followers of Christ do not try to get even for a wrong that has been done to them. Patience is the attitude of the person who is willing to wait for God to act and intervene with His own judgment. In the meanwhile God is patient with you, desiring everyone to come to repentance (2 Pet. 3:9).

2. **The Punishment by the Judge (vv. 9, 12).** The Lord's coming is near (v. 8). In fact, the Judge is standing at the door (v. 9). The Greek word for "coming" used in verses 7, 8 is *parousia* and was used to refer to the royal entrance of a king into a city in his realm. Jesus is depicted as a royal King who will come with justice and mercy (Is. 9:7). Since the Judge is standing at the door, we will not grumble against one another. Grumbling is a very serious sin. The nation of Israel was judged and condemned to wilderness wandering in part because of their grumbling (Ex. 16; Num. 14:27–30). You may be one who whines out loud or you may be one who rolls the eyes; either way, it's a sin that will be judged (Jude 14–16). Jesus

taught against swearing just as James did here in verse 12 (see Matt. 5:33–37). This is not the forbidding of making oaths altogether. God has made an oath (Ps. 110:4), and Paul calls God as his witness (2 Cor. 1.21; Gal. 1:20). What is forbidden is an exaggerated defense of yourself to convince others that you are right. The pattern of Christian speech is unconditional truthfulness with sincerity and simplicity, avoiding all exaggeration. You will be judged for every word that comes from your mouth (Matt. 12:36–37).

3. **The Perseverance of the Saints (vv. 10–11).** We are given some examples of saints who have patiently persevered. The prophets of God were persecuted and suffered because they spoke the Word of the Lord to selfish people. Elijah was hounded and hated (1 Kings 18:10, 17). Jeremiah was thrown into a cistern and nearly starved to death (Jer. 38:1–13). Amos was falsely accused of conspiracy and was told to leave (Amos 7:10–13). Just before his own martyrdom, Stephen spoke of the persecution of the prophets and of Jesus Christ (Acts 7:51–53). The prophets are an example for every true follower of Christ relating to patience and perseverance. Similarly, Job is an example of all who persevere. Job suffered the loss of his wealth, possessions, health, and family. Yet through the testing of his faith, he remained loyal. At the end of the test he was restored to even greater blessing (Job 42:12–17).

Conclusion: "The Lord is very compassionate and merciful" (v. 11). This is our hope: suffering produces perseverance; perseverance, character; and character hope (Rom. 5:1–5). Christ's first coming was to endure suffering to give us hope. When Christ returns, He will come in glory and the fulfillment of hope.

STATS, STORIES AND MORE

Patience in Palestine

In Palestine the early rains come in October and November soon after the seed is planted, and the latter rains come in April and May as the grain is nearing maturity. The farmer waits patiently for both. Perhaps there is some allusion to the first and second coming of Christ in this illustration. The prophets who waited patiently for the coming of Messiah may be a reference to the first coming of Christ (5:10), while our own patient waiting is a reference to His second coming.

Never Give UP

"Never give in! Never give in! Never, Never, Never, Never!" Winston Churchill

"With the help of God, I never gave up." President Herbert Hoover, when asked by Norman Vincent Peale the secret of his success in life as a Christian statesman

"Don't give up at halftime. Concentrate on winning the second half." Alabama Coach Bear Bryant

"If you run into a wall, don't turn around and give up. Figure out how to climb it, go through it, or work around it." Michael Jordan

"If I had to cram all my tournament experience into one sentence, I would say, 'Don't give up and don't let up!' " Golfer Tony Lema

"When you get into a tight place and everything goes against you, till it seems as though you could not hang on a minute longer, never give up then, for that is just the place and time that the tide will turn." Harriet Beecher Stowe

"My mother, a very poor woman in Columbus, Ohio, taught her kids to pray, to read the Bible, to follow Jesus Christ and never to give up." Captain Eddie Rickenbacker

"I . . . recollect that he was, from a boy . . . always resolutely determined never to give up any point or particle of anything on which his mind was set." Thomas Carey, about his brother William, the "father" of modern missions

FOR THE BULLETIN

John Wycliffe, a brilliant professor at Oxford, became England's leading theologian. Long before Luther, Wycliffe took the Bible as the only source of truth and proclaimed the gospel of justification by grace through faith. For that reason, he's called "the Morning Star of the Reformation." He died on December 31, 1384. Forty-one years later, his bones were exhumed, burned, and thrown into the river. As an ancient biographer wrote, "They burnt his bones to ashes and cast them into the Swift, a neighboring brook running hard by. Thus the brook conveyed his ashes into the Avon, the Avon into the Severn, the Severn into the narrow seas and they into the main ocean. And so the ashes of Wycliffe are symbolic of his doctrine, which is now spread throughout the world." ❀ Today is the birthday of two famous Moravians. Christian David was born in 1690, and Peter Bohler was born in 1712. Bohler was instrumental in the conversion of John Wesley. ❀ The first known New Year's Eve Watch Night service was held on December 31, 1770, at Saint George's Methodist Church in Philadelphia. ❀ The ball dropped for the first time in Times Square at midnight on December 31, 1907, signaling the start of a new year. ❀ John R. Mott, Methodist layman, YMCA leader, and the founder of the Christian Student Movement, died on this day in 1955. He tirelessly promoted the missionary cause among students and was considered by many the leading missionary statesman of his day. ❀ Missionary Helen Roseveare was rescued from rebels in Congo on December 31, 1964, after months of terror and abuse.

APPROPRIATE HYMNS AND SONGS

All the Power You Need, Russell Fragar, 1995 Russell Fragar (Hillsong) (Admin. in U.S. & Canada by Integrity's Hosanna! Music)

Leaning on the Everlasting Arms, Elisha A. Hoffman/Anthony J. Showalter, Public Domain

May the Mind of Christ My Savior, Kate B. Wilkinson, Public Domain

Have Thine Own Way, Adelaide A. Pollard/George C. Stebbins, Public Domain

Near the Cross, Fanny J. Crosby/William H. Doane, Public Domain

WORSHIP HELPS

Call to Worship:
Dear Shepherd of Thy chosen few,
Thy former mercies here renew;
Here, to our waiting hearts, proclaim
The sweetness of Thy saving Name.
—William Cowper, *Jesus Where'er Thy People Meet*, 1769

Invitation:
As 2006 draws to a close, I'd like to ask all of you here a question. What is the most important New Year's resolution you need to make? Maybe you've never truly admitted you're a sinner in need of Jesus' forgiveness and saving grace. Perhaps, although you have made that choice, you have fallen far from an obedient life. You could be a visitor or someone who doesn't have a church home, and you need to truly commit and join this church. The Lord allows for beautiful new beginnings. Let the front of this, our meeting place, be the altar upon which you dedicate or rededicate your life to Christ. As the years pass, God never changes. Come to Him.

Suggested Scripture Reading:
Job 23:1—24:1
Psalm 86
Hebrews 11:1—12:3

Kids Talk

Gather the children around and talk to them about new beginnings, about new promises for the coming year, and about the opportunity we have once a year to make some decisions (resolutions) to improve certain areas of our lives. Share any of your resolutions with them that would be appropriate and then, using the microphone, ask them if they have any resolutions they'd like to share. Pray with them for a great coming year.

Additional Sermons and Lesson Ideas

Focus on the Family
By Rev. Denis Lyle

Date preached:

SCRIPTURE: 1 Thessalonians 5:12–28

INTRODUCTION: Just as a child needs a family to protect and provide for him, so a believer needs the church family if he is to grow, develop his gifts, and serve the Lord. In this section Paul focused on the family of the local church:

1. The Leadership of the Church (vv. 12, 13). These leaders are to be *recognized, responsible, and respected*; the result will be peace in the church.
2. The Members of the Church (vv. 14, 15). Church members should be *practical, patient, and placid.*
3. The Worship of the Church (vv. 16–28). *The spirit of praise must be evident, the Word of God must be central, the lives of believers must be pure,* and *the fellowship of the saints must be sincere.*

CONCLUSION: Have you neglected your family here? Let's strive to maintain a functioning body with leaders, members, and worship services fully functioning according to the Word of God.

As Time Goes By

Date preached:

SCRIPTURE: Psalm 90

INTRODUCTION: Here at the hinge of the old and the new years, we need the perspective of Moses, the man of God, who wrote this grand Psalm 90. He saw time in three dimensions.

1. From Everlasting to Everlasting (vv. 1, 2). This is an appropriate description of our infinite God.
2. From Year to Year (vv. 3–12). Our time on earth is temporary, and we should value each year as an opportunity to serve God and present Him with a heart of wisdom.
3. From Day to Day (vv. 13–17). Life is broken down from eternity into years, and from years into days. We should rejoice and be glad all our days as the Lord establishes the work of our hands.

CONCLUSION: "Another year is dawning, dear Father let it be, on earth or else in heaven, another year for Thee." —Havergal

Drinking Preachers:
The Underappreciated Role of Water in Caring for the Preaching Voice

Jesus Christ walked on a body of water, but the rest of us are walking bodies of water. The human body is approximately two-thirds water; and if you don't believe it, just consider this odd little fact. The ashes of the average cremated person—who is totally dehydrated, of course—weigh nine pounds, about the same as when he or she was born. Or, to employ another bit of useless trivia, the average person produces twenty-five thousand quarts of spit in a lifetime. That's enough to fill two large swimming pools.

We drink approximately sixteen thousand gallons of water during the course of a lifetime, and water is involved in virtually every function of the body. It transports nutrients and waste products into and out of cells. It is instrumental in the digestive, absorption, circulatory, and excretory functions. It is at the heart of the body's "climate control" system, layering the body with a coat of sweat when it's in danger of overheating.

Nutritionists tell us, in fact, that it is almost impossible to drink too much water.

Preachers need to drink a little more that most people. Here's why. Water lubricates the lungs, larynx, esophagus, throat, mouth, tongue, and lips—all the bodily parts involved in generating and projecting speech. Our vocal cords are surrounded by a mucous membrane that needs to stay wet and fluid if our voices are going to work properly.

It's just like oil in your car's engine. You wouldn't want to drive your vehicle if your oil was low; neither do you want to speak if your body is dehydrated. It's exactly the same.

Don't think, however, that you can solve the problem by chugging a bottle of water just before preaching. Remember that there are two tubes descending into your body from your mouth. One sends food into your stomach, and the other sends air into your lungs. That's why we sometimes choke on a drink and spew it across the table; it goes down the wrong pipe. To benefit your voice, the water has to go into your stomach, work its way through your digestive system, and have enough time to make the return trip to properly hydrate your voice.

That's why on Sunday mornings, preachers should drink a glass of water the moment they get up. It takes approximately four hours for the water we drink to return to our vocal cords in the form of lubricating phlegm.

Professional musicians know that the two most important things they can give their singing voices are sleep and water. Without proper rest, a singer's voice becomes cranky and uncooperative. Without water, it becomes stiff and raspy.

If you're like me, you take your water in the form of coffee—which is counterproductive. Dark beverages take longer for the body to process, and the caffeine serves as a diuretic that actually exacerbates the hydration problem.

The answer is to figure out ways of getting more pure water into your system. So go ahead and buy those cases of drinking water at the grocery store. I hate paying for something I can get for free out of my tap, but I'll have to admit I drink more water when I have a bottle of it sitting on my desk. And your desk is a good place for it; not the refrigerator. Experts recommend drinking water at room temperature, since cold water tends to make the vocal cords tense up. Just think how your body feels when you jump into a pool of cold water.

One of the best ideas I've come up with is to start drinking water (without lemon) when I eat at restaurants. This habit saves me enough money to pay for all my bottled water! Here are some other ideas:

Drink a glass of water after brushing your teeth three times a day.

Never pass a drinking fountain without stopping for a few slurps.

Except for your wake-up coffee in the morning, switch to decaffeinated drinks. I'm even having my afternoon cup of Earl Gray in decaffeinated form, and it doesn't bother me a bit.

Buy sports beverages when they're on sale, and take one with you to the gym each day. Exercise is important, but it's also a significant drainer of the body's water reserves.

Now lay down this book and go have yourself a good drink of water.

WEDDING SERMON

A Proverbial Wedding

Dear friends, we have gathered here to join our two friends in marriage, _____ (groom's name), and _____ (bride's name). We love these two, and it is our joy to share our time with them today and extend to them our prayers and support. Marriage is a wonderful relationship, but sometimes it is wonderfully challenging; and today I would like to give us some advice about the marital union that comes from heaven itself. In the middle of the Bible is a unique book of wisdom and insight called Proverbs. It's made up of short epigrams of wisdom, little sayings that someone once called "heavenly rules for earthly living." Quite a few of them apply to marriage; and I've chosen three of them as a special message especially for this couple, though they apply equally well to every husband and wife present today. Weddings, after all, are timely reminders to all of us about the sanctity and sweetness of marriage.

The first verse I want to share is Proverbs 10:12: "Hatred stirs up strife, but love covers all sins." On a day like this when dreams are being made and longings are being fulfilled, it's hard to realize that there may come difficult moments in a marriage. But every friendship has its challenges, for we are all imperfect people. As time goes by, we get on each other's nerves, we grow disillusioned with each other's ways, and we sometimes have moments when we think that, given the right circumstances, we could almost grow to dislike the person whom we love so much. At such moments, a marriage will take one of two directions. Some people succumb to anger and hatred, and the relationship sours. But others choose to love the other person despite his or her faults and failures, and that love heals and restores the relationship. Love is a choice. Love is choosing to tap into the love of God Himself, for He loves us despite all our sins with an everlasting love. God's love covers over a multitude of sins, and it alone can keep a marriage strong and sweet and steadfast through the undulating days of our lives.

I also commend to you Proverbs 14:26, which says, "In the fear of the Lord there is strong confidence, and his children will have a place of refuge." When the Bible talks about the fear of the Lord, it refers to a reverent respect for God in all that we say and do. It means that we never lose the wonder of His awesome presence around us. It means that we worship Him with all our hearts. When we fear the Lord, we restrain ourselves from evil, for we recognize He is holy. We read His word, for we recognize He is wise. We attend church, for we know He is worthy of our worship. We guard our words, for we know He is always present. According to Proverbs 14:26, there is something about that kind of living that makes us confident people and that gives our children a sense of security and a place of refuge.

So we need the love of God and the fear of God. But there's another verse I'd like to recommend to you—Proverbs 17:1: "Better is a dry morsel with quietness than a house full of feasting with strife." So many families in the United States strive to become more and more affluent, to live in better and better houses, and to accumulate an estate full of gadgets, electronics, stocks, bonds, cars, trucks, and assorted possessions. Yet they are increasingly unhappy, and their homes are growing more troubled every day. The Bible recommends a quiet home and a quiet heart. Sometimes we need to turn off all the noise and just be together—talking, reading, sitting by the fire, enjoying life's simple pleasures together. I encourage you, _____ and _____, to cultivate a friendship and to cherish the quiet moments. It's possible to gain the whole world but to lose your own home. Remember: A couple is rich not because they have all they want, but because they have learned to enjoy all they have.

May the Holy Spirit, then, grant you the love of God that covers all sins, the fear of God that brings reverence to our lives, and the quietness of God that graces our marriages with the blessings of contentment and companionship.

If then, _____ (groom) and _____ (bride), you are ready to enter into this kind of relationship. I ask you to join hands for the offering of your vows one to the other.

_____ (groom), do you promise before God to take this woman as your beloved wife, to honor and cherish her in the bonds of marriage, to remain faithful to her in body, soul, and spirit, and to care for her with the love of Jesus Christ as long as you both shall live?

(Groom answers "I do.")

_____ (bride), do you promise before God to take this man as your beloved husband, to honor and cherish him in the bonds of marriage, to remain faithful to him in body, soul, and spirit, and to care for him with the love of Jesus Christ as long as you both shall live?

(Bride answers "I do.")

Then you are each given to the other as husband and wife, to have and to hold, to honor and to cherish, from this day forward till death do you part.

The wedding ring is a symbol of this marriage, for it shows all the world that you belong to one another, and its unending circle represents the perpetual nature of your vows. As you place the rings on each other's fingers, repeat after me: "With this ring, I join you in the circle of marriage through the grace of the Father, Son, and Holy Spirit."

WEDDING SERMON

The Marriage Covenant

By Pastor J. David Hoke

Address to the Attendees:

We welcome you today to the marriage of _____ and _____. We are met together in the presence of God to join this man and this woman in holy matrimony. This is indeed a joyful time, in which we witness the love of these two people expressed in the joining of their lives together for life. So we invite you to join with us, as participants in this service, not only to witness this union, but to renew your own commitment to your husband or wife.

Ladies and Gentlemen, marriage is of God. It is ordained in heaven. It is the first and holiest institution among men. God Himself gave the first bride away. God Himself performed the first wedding ceremony. In the Garden of Eden, God Himself hallowed and sanctified the first home. And so, as we gather here today, we recognize that marriage is an act of God and not of man.

Therefore, this covenant is not to be entered into unadvisedly or lightly, but reverently, discreetly, advisedly, and soberly, in the fear of God. Into this covenant _____ and _____ come now to be joined.

Address to the Couple

1. Marriage Is a Covenant of Faith and Trust. This requires openness of life and thought, freedom from doubt and suspicion, and commitment to speak the truth in love to one another.

2. Marriage Is a Covenant of Hope. The marriage covenant endures all things. Both husband and wife must commit themselves to interpret each other's behavior with understanding and compassion, and to never give up trying to communicate with each other.

3. Marriage Is a Covenant of Love. Both husband and wife must empty themselves of their own concerns, and take upon themselves the concerns of each other as they love and care for each other.

Do you both come freely, and without reservation, desiring to commit yourselves to one another in this covenant of marriage?

(To the groom): _____, will you have _____ to be your wedded wife, to live together in the covenant of marriage? Will you love her, comfort her, honor her, and keep her, in sickness and in health, and forsaking all others, be faithful to her as long as you both shall live?

(To the bride): _____, will you have _____ to be your wedded husband, to live together in the covenant of marriage? Will you love him, comfort him, honor him, and keep him, in sickness and in health, and forsaking all others, be faithful to him as long as you both shall live?

(To the father or person giving away the bride): Who gives _____ (bride) to be married to _____ (groom)?

Real love is something beyond the warmth and glow, the excitement and romance of being deeply in love. It is caring as much about the welfare and happiness of your marriage partner as you are about yourself. But real love is not total absorption in each other; it is looking outward in the same direction—together. Love makes burdens lighter, because you divide them. It makes joys more intense, because you share them. It makes you stronger, so you can reach out and become involved with life in ways you dared not risk alone.

Marriage and home are built upon the foundation of the most sublime dedication known to the human heart—that of unselfish love and heavenly affection. Even though speaking to her mother-in-law, with many tears and deep searching of heart, giving up her native home and country and people, Ruth spoke of that dedication in these immortal words: "Entreat me not to leave thee, or to return from following after thee: for whither thou goest, I will go; and where thou lodgest I will lodge; thy people shall be my people, and thy God my God. Where thou diest, will I die, and there will I be buried: the Lord do so to me, and more also, if ought but death part thee and me" (Ruth 1:16–17, KJV). This can also be your commitment to one another this day.

Personal Vows:

(Groom): I, _____ , take you, _____ , to be my wife, to have and to hold from this day forward, for better for worse, for richer for poorer, in sickness and in health, to love and to cherish, until we are parted by death. This is my solemn vow.

(Bride): I, _____ , take you, _____ , to be my husband, to have and to hold from this day forward, for better for worse, for richer for poorer, in sickness and in health, to love and to cherish, until we are parted by death. This is my solemn vow.

Ring Service:

(To the groom): _____, do you possess a token of your love and affection to give to your bride, a seal of this holy covenant? (Groom: "I do.") What is it? (Groom: "A ring.")

In all ages and among all peoples, the ring has been a symbol of that which is measureless; and thus, in this holy hour, a symbol of your measureless, boundless devotion. It is a circle; it has neither beginning nor ending; so your commitment should also be unending. It is gold; which is precious; so also is your commitment precious. And the sign and seal of this commitment will be this ring. As a ceaseless reminder of this sacred committal, place this ring on the wedding finger of your bride and repeat after me:

As a symbol of my vow, with this ring, I thee wed, with loyal love, I thee endow, all my worldly goods, with thee I share, and with them I give you myself.

(To the bride) _____, do you possess a token of your love and affection to give to your husband, a seal of this holy covenant? (Bride: "I do.") What is it? (Bride: "A ring.")

Invested with the same significance as the ring you have just received, so this ring is a circle of precious gold indicating the longevity of your love and the pricelessness of your devotion. Place this ring on the wedding finger of your husband and repeat after me:

As a symbol of my vow, with this ring, I thee wed, with loyal love, I thee endow, all my worldly goods, with thee I share, and with them I give you myself

Pronouncement:

For as much as _____ and _____ have consented together in holy wedlock, and have witnessed the same before God and this assembly, and have committed themselves completely to each other in the covenant of marriage, I do pronounce that they are now husband and wife according to the law of God. What God has joined together, no man may put asunder. You may kiss the bride.

WEDDING SERMON

A Traditional Wedding

Dearly beloved, we have gathered together here in the sight of God and his angels, and in the gathering of this church, to join together in holy matrimony these two people, this man, _____ (groom's name), and this woman, _____ (bride's name), that henceforth they may be one, serving God as one, living life as one, traveling onward, upward, heavenward as one in the grace of God, in the blessings of Christ and in the communion of the Holy Spirit.

_____ (groom) do you promise before God that you will take this woman as your wedded wife and will serve her in the faith of God as your own self, in health, infirmity, and all other circumstances, as a Christian should serve his wife, and will keep faith and fidelity with her, so long as you both shall live? (The groom will answer "I do.")

_____ (bride) do you promise before God that you will take this man as your wedded husband and will serve him in the faith of God as your own self, in health, infirmity, and all other circumstances, as a Christian should serve her husband, and will keep faith and fidelity with him, so long as you both shall live? (The bride will answer "I do.")

Who, then, gives this woman to be married to this man?

Simon Peter, in his first epistle, exhorted husbands and wives to be pure and innocent, and to diminish the importance of jewelry, clothing. Peter tells us to emphasize matters of the heart, of the attitude, and of the soul, what he calls "the incorruptible beauty of a gentle and quiet spirit, which is very precious in the sight of God." He tells husbands and wives to dwell with one another with understanding, giving honor to one other; for, as he says, "you are heirs together of the grace of life." Those rare and remarkable couples who foster the inner glow of a growing friendship, who are patient with one another, and who learn to enjoy one another beyond all other human companionship, will bring to fruition a happy home of holiness and hallelujahs.

They will bear with one another's faults, help each other overcome weaknesses, enhance each other's strengths, encourage each other's pursuits, and forgive each other's sins. They will endure to the end while enjoying the undulating journey of married life and entrusting their burdens to Him who dwells in the highest heavens and in the humblest homes of His people.

Will you then, _____ (groom) and _____ (bride) in token of your willingness to be united this day in the bonds of marriage, join hands and repeat after me:

I, _____ (groom), take you _____ (bride) as my wife, to have and to hold from this day forward, for better, for worse, for richer, for poorer, in sickness, in health, and all other circumstances, as long as we both shall live.

I, _____ (bride), take you _____ (groom) as my husband, to have and to hold from this day forward, for better, for worse, for richer, for poorer, in sickness, in health, and all other circumstances, as long as we both shall live.

The words "ring" and "crown" both come from a Latin term indicating a curved piece of metal of great significance. In placing the ring on the other's finger, you are both in effect placing a crown on the head of the other, acknowledging a willingness to be mutually submissive one the other and to reign in life together through the One, Christ Jesus. The man who has found a godly wife is more blessed than a king, and the wife with a godly husband is richer by far than a queen. The two of you must crown one another's hearts with love and laughter. Your home is your castle, and your lifelong romance is a reflection of the royal love bestowed by the King of kings. The wedding band, then, is a small-sized crown, placed on the finger instead of the brow, perpetually worn, which bespeaks of your exclusive relationship to each other.

_____ (groom), will you repeat after me: With is ring, I thee wed in the name of the Father, Son, and Holy Spirit.

_____ (bride), will you repeat after me: With is ring, I thee wed in the name of the Father, Son, and Holy Spirit.
You are now each given to the other as husband and wife from this day forward; and by the authority vested in me as a minister of the gospel of Jesus Christ, it is my privilege to pronounce you husband and wife.

FUNERAL SERMON

Suitable For a Non-Christian

Today we have come in honor and memory of _____.

Personal Comments:

Scripture: Psalm 145:8–9 and 1 Corinthians 15:3–4

Introduction: All of us face the sadness and tragedy of death, and just as our friend has passed away, so will all of us also one day meet with the same appointment. At such times, we need the reassurance of eternal life. In our friend's case, we know little of his spiritual condition, but we know much of our Lord's character. Psalm 145 says that He is gracious and full of compassion, slow to anger and great in mercy. The Lord is good to all, and His tender mercies are over all His works. None of us knows the heart of another person, but we do know the heart of our God, and so we entrust our friend into the gracious hands of the God of mercy who does all things well. It is possible, however, to be sure of our own spiritual condition, and today gives us the opportunity to check our own souls and to make sure we're ready for the moment of death. Someone once said, "You're not ready to live until you're ready to die." Because of this, I would like to share with you three facts about the greatest Person in human history, the Lord Jesus Christ.

1. Jesus Died for our Sins (1 Cor. 15:3). In sharing the message of the gospel with people, I often encounter various questions and objections. The one aspect of the message that is almost universally accepted is that we are all sinners in need of help. The Bible says, "There is none righteous, no, not one," and "for all have sinned and fall short of the glory of God" (Rom. 3:10, 23). Because of that, none of us can gain heaven or eternal life on the basis of our own merits. Suppose that I had lumber and a hammer and nails here on the platform today, and suppose I was hard at work building something. If you asked me about it, I would say, "I'm building a ladder. It's going to be tall enough to climb to the moon." Such an idea is preposterous, but no more so than thinking that we can climb to heaven on

the ladder of good works or righteous living. That's why God Himself (who is perfect) became a man—Jesus Christ—who shed His blood to make atonement for our sins. He died in our place. He died to justify us before God. Romans 5:8 says, "But God demonstrates His own love toward us, in that while we were still sinners, Christ died for us."

2. Jesus Was Buried (1 Cor. 15:4). According to the Scripture, Christ died about three o'clock in the afternoon after hanging on the cross for six hours. His body was removed in the late afternoon, hastily cleaned, wrapped in a shroud, and buried in a tomb provided by a wealthy Jewish leader named Joseph of Arimathea, who had become a disciple of Jesus (Matt. 27:57). A heavy stone was rolled across the mouth of the tomb, and there was no way out of it. The tomb was sealed, and a military guard was stationed to keep away looters. There the corpse of Jesus lay in the darkness for three days. Jesus' physical death was real, and so was His burial.

3. Jesus Rose Again (1 Cor. 15:4). On Sunday as the sun rose over Jerusalem's eastern hills, the greatest miracle in recorded history occurred. The crucified body of Jesus rose from the stone slab of the tomb, rising out of the burial clothes and passing through the solid wall of the burial cave. He rose from the dead, and His physical body was transformed and glorified for eternity. He appeared repeatedly for forty days before ascending to heaven to resume His place at the right hand of the throne of God. The resurrection of Jesus Christ reversed the tragedy of death and provides eternal hope for all of us. He once said, "Because I live, you will live also" (John 14:19).

Conclusion: Through His death, burial, and resurrection, Jesus Christ offers us the free gift of everlasting life, and it is a gift we receive by faith. The Bible says, "Believe on the Lord Jesus Christ, and you will be saved" (Acts 16:31). We cannot know the eternal condition of another's heart, but we can be sure of the eternal condition of our own. And if you haven't yet received forgiveness for your sins and everlasting life, I invite you to come to Christ Jesus today. As John 3:16 says: "For God so loved the world that He gave His only begotten Son, that whoever believes in Him should not perish but have everlasting life."

FUNERAL SERMON

For General Use

Today we have come to celebrate the life and home-going of _____.

Personal comments:

Scripture: John 14

Introduction: At times like this, death intrudes upon our thoughts and we must confront the unwelcome reality of our mortal passing. Throughout His earthly ministry, Jesus continually thought about death and dying, for He came specifically to confront this enemy of our soul. His own death was very much on His mind in the Upper Room, as He met with His disciples for the final time before going to the cross. It was a tense meeting, and a sense of foreboding filled the air. The disciples sensed impending trouble, and their hearts were troubled. In John 14, Jesus spoke words of calm and reassurance. He told them, "Let not your hearts be troubled . . ." (v. 1). Today He would say the same to us. We're in a room that is filled with the air of sorrow and with the atmosphere of grief. Our hearts are heavy and our minds are distressed. Hear the voice of Jesus. Listen to Him just as if He were here present, speaking these words to us audibly: "Let not your hearts be troubled." That is the opening sentence of the fourteenth chapter of John's Gospel, and in the remainder of the chapter Jesus gives us eight reasons to obey Him. In this passage Jesus is basically saying to us, "Despite the sorrow you are facing right now, there are eight great comforts for your soul."

1. We can trust Him (v. 1). At a time like this, we can either collapse in the fog of grief or we can rest in our faith in Christ. He pleads with us here to simply trust Him.

2. We have a home that Jesus prepared for us (v. 2). There's an old song that says, "I've got a mansion just over the hilltop." That's a biblical reality, described for us in greater detail in Revelation 21–22.

3. We have a Savior coming for us (v. 3). The return of Christ is quickly approaching, and wise Christians keep their eyes glued to the Eastern sky, awaiting the first glimpse of His coming.

4. We know the way, the truth, and the life (vv. 4–6). Jesus didn't just come to show us the way. He said, "I *am* the way." He didn't come to preach the truth. He said, "I *am* the truth." He didn't come just to give us life. He said, "I *am* the life." All we need is in Him.

5. We have the Father Himself revealed to us in Christ (vv. 7–11). When we see Jesus, we are seeing the very image of God the Father. He is the manifestation of God for us (see also Col. 1:9; Heb. 1:3).

6. We have the privilege and power of prayer (vv. 13–14). Jesus reassures His disciples that though He may not be physically present, they have access to God the Father in His Name through prayer.

7. We have the Holy Spirit to help us (vv. 15–26). He is called "the Helper," the One who comes alongside to help us.

8. We have the very peace of Christ Himself to sustain us (v. 27–31). This is our Lord's version of Isaiah 26:3, which promises "perfect peace" to those whose minds are fixed on God.

Conclusion: Our hearts are troubled, today; but Jesus gently admonishes us to let His perspective overcome our own. Today He says to us, "Let not your hearts be troubled; you believe in God; believe also in Me."

FUNERAL SERMON

For A Christian

Today we have come in honor and memory of _____.

Personal Comments:

Scripture: 1 Thessalonians 4:13–18

Introduction: When we gather like this in memory of our loved one, it is not for the sake of the person lying before us. It is for us, that we may be strengthened by each other's love, and that together we might find the strength of the Lord. The Lord imparts strength through the truth of His Word, so I'd like to devote the remaining time to reminding us of the Bible's great teaching in the last paragraph of 1 Thessalonians 4. Let's look at this passage verse by verse:

1. We Must Not Be Ignorant of God's Truth. "But I do not want you to be ignorant, brethren, concerning those who have fallen asleep . . ." (1 Thess. 4:13). For our hearts to be strengthened, our minds must grasp God's truth. Ignorance can lead to needless levels of distress. To use a graphic example, suppose you had a son serving in a war zone, and one day you received a message that they were missing in action. The message turned out to be mistaken because of confusion on the front lines; and so another message was sent telling you that your loved one was safe. In fact, your son was being furloughed home and would be arriving shortly. If you had only received the first message without the second one arriving, you would be in a state of anxious distress. Ignorance would result in needless, hopeless grief. Today we are coping with bad news—our loved one has died. But the Lord wants us to know the rest of the story. He does not want us to be ignorant about what has happened to our loved ones.

2. We Must Not Sorrow as Those Who Have No Hope. ". . . lest you sorrow as others who have no hope" (1 Thess. 4:13). The Bible states this so wisely. It does not forbid grief, and it does not tell us to avoid sorrow. Many godly men and women grieved in the Bible when their loved ones died (see John

11:35; Acts 8:2; Acts 9:39). But we are not to grieve like unbelievers who have no hope. The Bible warns us against excessive sorrow, for that kind of despair betrays our lack of faith in God and His Word.

3. We Must Remember that Christ Died and Rose Again. "For if we believe that Jesus died and rose again . . ." (1 Thess. 4:14). That's the Christian's sustaining secret. When Jesus died, He provided a basis for our living *a forgiven life.* When He rose again, He provided a basis for our living *a forever life.* His victory over death turns every funeral inside out for those who love Him.

4. We Must View Death as a Phase and not a Finality. ". . . even so God will bring with Him those who sleep in Jesus" (1 Thess. 4:14). Jesus Himself initiated this terminology for death in John 11 when He told His disciples that Lazarus, who had died, was merely sleeping. Death is a phase, not a finality. It's temporary, not terminal. All three Synoptic Gospels tell of a ruler named Jairus who came to Jesus in great urgency, begging Him to come and touch his twelve-year-old daughter who was dying; but before Jesus arrived, the little girl passed away. Going to the house, Jesus saw the commotion as people were crying and wailing loudly. He said to them, ". . . The child is not dead, but sleeping." But they laughed at Him (Mark 5:35–40). In Acts 7, we have the account of the first person to be martyred for his faith in Christian history, Stephen, who was stoned to death by a Jewish mob because of his preaching. The writer of Acts said simply that he fell asleep (Acts 7:60). The Bible does not teach that the soul goes to sleep. In fact, the Bible teaches that when we die, our soul goes to be with Jesus and enjoy being in His presence. Jesus said to the dying thief on the cross next to Him, ". . . today you will be with me in Paradise" (Luke 23:43). The soul doesn't fall asleep, but the body does. What is the significance of that term sleep? There are two wonderful implications here. The first is rest. When someone falls asleep, he or she is resting (see Rev. 6:11; 14:13). The second is rising. Sleep is a temporary state. We fall asleep only to awaken in the morning. We die only to rise again. This same body will be reconstituted and resurrected at the last trumpet, and all believers will rise again.

5. We Must Look Forward to a Day When We Shall All Be With the Lord. This passage promises a day when Jesus Christ will return to earth and catch us all up to be with Him, reuniting our souls with our bodies, reuniting us all

with one another, and reuniting us all with Himself (1 Thess. 4:15–17). The end of verse 17 says, "And thus we shall always be with the Lord." We'll never be away from Christ's presence again!

Conclusion: Paul concludes with this statement: "Therefore comfort one another with these words" (1 Thess. 4:18). And so as best as I can, I want to dispense the comfort of Christ into our hearts, telling you—even as I remind myself—that: We must not be ignorant of God's truth, we must not sorrow as those who have no hope, we must remember that Christ died and rose again, we must view death as a phase and not a finality, and we must look forward to that day when we shall all be with the Lord.

> *When we all get to heaven,*
> *What a day of rejoicing that will be;*
> *When we all see Jesus,*
> *We'll sing and shout the victory.*

FUNERAL SERMON

Suitable For the Funeral of a Young Person

Today we have come in honor and memory of _____.

Personal Comments:

_____

Scripture: Isaiah 57:1, 2; 2 Kings 4:26; 2 Samuel 12:23

_____

Introduction: It's hard enough to lose a loved one who was like Abraham, old and full of years when he died. It's much harder for us to bear the death of someone in childhood or in the prime of life. We instinctively ask "Why?" and that is a valid question. Many of the heroes in the Bible asked "Why?" at one point or another in their lives, and sometimes the Lord gives us answers. I don't have a complete set of answers today, but I do have three verses from the Old Testament that may help answer that question to a degree. I'd like to share them with a prayer that God will use them to comfort our hearts. Here's what the Bible tells us about the death of a young person:

1. It is Best. Isaiah 57:1, 2 is an incredible and frequently overlooked explanation of this truth. It says in the *New Living Translation:* "The righteous pass away; the godly often die before their time. And no one seems to care or wonder why. No one seems to understand that God is protecting him or her from the evil to come. For the godly who die will rest in peace." According to Isaiah, God sometimes gives us a divine detour to heaven because, being omniscient, He knows what lies ahead and wants to spare that person from impending trouble or tribulation. Who knows what tragedies or temptations may have faced our friend, but God in His goodness said, "I will save my child from this sin or sorrow or suffering." Going to heaven is never a bad thing, and it is infinitely better than a lifetime of hardship. Sometimes it is God's mercy to remove us from earthly service at a young age.

2. It is Well. The second verse I'd like to show you is 2 Kings 4:26, which is one of the most comforting verses in the Bible regarding the death of a child. In this passage the prophet Elisha had a rewarding friendship with

a Shunammite couple whose little son had died. The woman saddled her donkey and rode off to find Elisha. Seeing her coming, the great prophet knew something was wrong. He asked, "Is it well with the child?" And she replied, "It is well." The child had passed away, but the woman spoke truthfully. It was well with the child, for he was in the arms of his heavenly father. Today we can say, despite our tears and pain, it is well with the child.

3. It is Brief. Our separation, though sad, is brief. This was David's consolation upon the death of his son in 2 Samuel 12:23, when he told his servants, "I shall go to him, but he shall not return to me." Soon and very soon we'll be reunited; that is the promise of God. We're only here for a twinkling of an eye, but our eternal home will be a place of endless fellowship through the unlimited ages of eternity. In his book on heaven, evangelist D. L. Moody quoted another pastor as saying the following:

> When I was a boy, I thought of heaven as a great, shining city, with vast walls and domes and spires, and with nobody in it except white-robed angels, who were strangers to me. By and by my little brother died; and I thought of a great city with walls and domes and spires, and one little fellow that I was acquainted with. He was the only one I knew at that time. Then another brother died; and there were two that I knew. Then my acquaintances began to die; and the flock continually grew. But it was not till I had sent one of my little children to his Heavenly Parent—God—that I began to think I had a real, vested interest in heaven myself. A second went, a third went; a fourth went; and by that time I had so many acquaintances in heaven, that I did not see any more walls and domes and spires. I began to think of the residents of the celestial city as my friends. And now so many of my acquaintances have gone there, that it sometimes seems to me that I know more people in heaven than I do on earth."[i]

Conclusion: Our hearts are heavy, and we cannot help asking "Why?" We don't know all the answers, but we know this about our sadness and separation today. It is best. It is well. It is brief. And it will be worth it all when we see Jesus.

Special Services Registry

The forms on the following pages are designed to be duplicated and used repeatedly as neeeded. Most copy machines will allow you to enlarge them to fill a full page if desired. Since they also are included in the CD-ROM in the back of the book, you may use that digital file to customize the forms to fit your specific needs.

Sermons Preached

Date	Text	Title/Subject

Sermons Preached

Date	Text	Title/Subject

Marriages Log

Date	Bride	Groom

Funerals Log

Date	Name of Deceased	Scripture Used

Baptisms / Confirmations

Date	Name	Notes

Baby Dedication Registration

Infant's Name: _____

Significance of Given Names: _____

Date of Birth: _____

Parents' Names: _____

_____

Siblings: _____

_____

_____

_____

Maternal Grandparents: _____

Paternal Grandparents: _____

Life Verse:_____

Date of Dedication: _____

Wedding Registration

Date of Wedding: _____

Location of Wedding: _____

Bride: _____

     Religious Affiliation: _____

     Bride's Parents: _____

Groom: _____

     Religious Affiliation: _____

     Groom's Parents: _____

Ceremony to be Planned by Minister: _____ by Couple: _____

Other Minister(s) Assisting: _____

Maid/Matron of Honor: _____

Best Man: _____

Wedding Planner: _____

Date of Rehearsal: _____

Reception Open to All Wedding Guests: _____ By Invitation Only: _____

Location of Reception: _____

Wedding Photos to be Taken:_____ During Ceremony

                    _____ After Ceremony

Other _____

Date of Counseling: _____

Date of Registration: _____

Funeral Registration

Name of Deceased: _____

Age: _____

Religious Affiliation: _____

Survivors:

   Spouse: _____

   Parents: _____

   Children: _____

   Siblings: _____

   Grandchildren: _____

Date of Death: _____

Time and Place of Visitation: _____

Date of Funeral or Memorial Service: _____

Funeral Home Responsible:_____

Location of Funeral or Memorial Service: _____

Scripture Used: _____Hymns Used: _____

Eulogy by: _____

Other Minister(s) Assisting: _____

Pallbearers: _____

Date of Interment: _____Place of Interment: _____

Graveside Service: _____Yes   No _____

Subject Index

Scripture Index

SOFTWARE LICENSE AGREEMENT

CAREFULLY READ THE FOLLOWING TERMS AND CONDITIONS BEFORE USING THIS SOFTWARE. USING THIS SOFTWARE INDICATES YOUR ACCEPTANCE OF THESE TERMS AND CONDITIONS. IF YOU ARE NOT IN AGREEMENT, PROMPTLY RETURN THE SOFTWARE PACKAGE UNUSED WITH YOUR RECEIPT AND YOUR MONEY WILL BE REFUNDED.

LICENSE

The SOFTWARE may be used on a single machine at a time. This is a copyrighted software program and may not be copied, duplicated, or distributed except for the purpose of backup by the licensed owner.

The SOFTWARE may be copied into any machine-readable or printed form for backup, modification, or normal usage in support of the SOFTWARE on the single machine.

You may transfer the SOFTWARE and license to another party if the other party agrees to accept the terms and conditions of this Agreement. If you transfer the SOFTWARE, you must either transfer all copies, whether in printed or machine-readable form, to the same party or destroy any copies not transferred; this includes all modifications and portions of the SOFTWARE contained or merged into other software and/or software programs.

YOU MAY NOT USE, COPY, ALTER, OR OTHERWISE MODIFY OR TRANSFER THE SOFTWARE OR DATABASE(S) OR ANY ADD-ON PRODUCT'S TEXT EXCEPT AS EXPRESSLY PROVIDED FOR IN THIS LICENSE.

IF YOU TRANSFER POSSESSION OF ANY COPY OR MODIFICATIONS OF THE SOFTWARE TO ANOTHER PARTY, EXCEPT AS EXPRESSLY PROVIDED FOR IN THIS LICENSE, YOUR LICENSE THEREUPON IS AUTOMATICALLY TERMINATED.

LIMITED SOFTWARE WARRANTY

LIMITED WARRANTY. *Nelson Electronic Publishing* warrants that, for ninety (90) days from the date of receipt, the computer programs contained in the SOFTWARE will perform substantially in accordance with the *User's Guide*. Any implied warranties on the SOFTWARE are limited to ninety (90) days. Some jurisdictions do not allow limitations on the duration of an implied warranty, so the above limitation may not apply to you.

CUSTOMER REMEDIES. *Nelson Electronic Publishing's* entire liability and your exclusive remedy shall be, at our option, either (a) return of the price paid or (b) repair or replacement of SOFTWARE that does not meet *Nelson Electronic Publishing's* Limited Warranty and that is returned to us with a copy of your receipt. This Limited Warranty is void if failure of the SOFTWARE has resulted from accident, abuse, or misapplication. Any replacement SOFTWARE will be warranted for the remainder of the original warranty period or thirty (30) days, whichever is longer. Outside the United States, neither these remedies nor any product support services are available without proof of purchase from an authorized non-U.S. source.

NO OTHER WARRANTIES. To the maximum extent permitted by applicable law, *Nelson Electronic Publishing* and its suppliers disclaim all other warranties, either expressed or implied, including, but not limited to, implied warranties of merchantability and fitness for a particular purpose, with regard to the SOFTWARE and the accompanying written materials. This Limited Warranty gives you specific legal rights. You may have others, which vary from state to state.

NO LIABILITY FOR CONSEQUENTIAL DAMAGES. TO THE MAXIMUM EXTENT PERMITTED BY APPLICABLE LAW, IN NO EVENT SHALL *NELSON ELECTRONIC PUBLISHING* OR ITS SUPPLIERS BY LIABLE FOR ANY DAMAGES WHATSOEVER (INCLUDING WITHOUT LIMITATIONS, DAMAGES FOR LOSS OF BUSINESS PROFITS, BUSINESS INTERRUPTION, LOSS OF BUSINESS INFORMATION, OR ANY OTHER PECUNIARY LOSS) ARISING OUT OF THE USE OF OR INABILITY TO USE THIS PRODUCT, EVEN IF *NELSON ELECTRONIC PUBLISHING* HAS BEEN ADVISED OF THE POSSIBILITY OF SUCH DAMAGES. BECAUSE SOME STATES DO NOT ALLOW THE EXCLUSION OF LIABILITY FOR CONSEQUENTIAL OR ACCIDENTAL DAMAGES, THE ABOVE LIMITATION MAY NOT APPLY TO YOU.

Should you have any questions concerning this Agreement, please contact:

Nelson Electronic Publishing
Thomas Nelson, Inc.
501 Nelson Place
Nashville, TN 37214-1000
615/889-9000